D0537399

A2-Level
Sociology

The Revision Guide

301.076 HAL

Editors:
Gemma Hallam, Katherine Reed

Contributors:
Ellen Bowness, Anna Hazeldine, Sean Purcell, Kate Redmond, Neil Renton, Frances Rippin,
Rachel Selway, Emma Singleton, Andrew Walker

Proofreaders:
Sarah Acford-Palmer, Kate Houghton, Linda Parkins, Carol Potter, Edward Robinson, Jennifer Underwood

Published by Coordination Group Publications Ltd.

This book is suitable for:

AQA and OCR.

There are notes at the tops of double pages to tell you if
there's a bit you can ignore for your syllabus.

ISBN: 978 1 84146 368 1

Groovy website: www.cgpbooks.co.uk
Jolly bits of clipart from CorelDRAW®
Printed by Elanders Hindson Ltd, Newcastle upon Tyne.

Text, design, layout and original illustrations © Coordination Group Publications Ltd. 2005
All rights reserved.

Contents

We deliberately haven't put answers in this book — because there are lots of valid ways to answer essay questions. Instead, we've put in a section about how to do well in your exam — which includes some sample exam answers.

The Nature and Distribution of Power

*Welcome to Sociology. This first page plunges you straight into the hot topic of Power. As with any topic in Sociology, you have to understand the different views and interpretations theorists have about it. These two pages are for **AQA**.*

Power *is about the ability to* Control *and* Influence

The pluralist **RA Dahl (1961)** gives this **definition** of power:
"**A** has **power** over **B** to the extent that s/he can **get B** to **do something** s/he **wouldn't otherwise have done**".

This is a **useful starting point** for understanding power. From this definition of power, you can see that power relationships can involve processes such as **coercion (force)**, **manipulation**, **bargaining** or **persuasion**. You also need to think about this definition in terms of **society as a whole** and the way that **some social groups** and **institutions** have **power over others**.

Authority *is Legitimate Power*

Most sociologists agree that there's a **difference** between **power** and **authority**. **Authority** suggests a sort of power relationship which is **accepted** by the people who are ruled over — they give their **consent**. It's useful to remember the phrase "**authority is legitimate power**".

For example, most people obey **traffic lights** when they drive. This isn't because anyone **coerces** us to do it — there's no one standing over us with a gun. It's because we know the **law** says we must stop at a red light, and we recognise the authority of the law, so we obey the law. We give our **consent** to the government that makes laws governing the rules of the road.

Max Weber *said there are* Three Types *of* Authority

Weber (1864-1920) was one of the "founding fathers" of sociology.

1)	**Charismatic**	People give their **consent** to a **charismatic leader** because of the leader's **exceptional qualities**. The leader inspires great **loyalty** and **devotion**. **Religious** leaders are often charismatic. Examples of charismatic leaders might include: Napoleon, Gandhi, Moses and Fidel Castro.
2)	**Traditional**	People give their **consent** because they **always have**. Established customs and practices are seen as "right" because they've always been that way. For instance, a traditional society might accept their elders as rulers because the elders have always been the rulers of the society.
3)	**Rational legal**	People give their **consent** to an **impersonal legal framework** (a set of rules). The rules are **rational** because they **make sense** and have a particular and **obvious aim.** A modern example would be stopping at a red light to avoid vehicle crashes.

These types are **ideals** — pure theoretical ideas. Weber suggested that in **real life**, authority could be a **mixture** of the "ideal" types defined above. So in our traffic light example, Jim Random might obey traffic lights because it's part of a **legal system** of understandable rules (rational legal), and because we've **always** obeyed traffic lights (traditional) and partly because he **loves** the Prime Minister (charismatic).

Stephen Lukes *has a* Radical *view — he says there are* Three Faces *of* Power

1)	**Decision-making**	The power to **make** and **implement decisions** which **affect other people**.
2)	**Non decision-making**	The power to **set agendas** — i.e. **limit** what's being **discussed**. If a topic isn't even discussed, **no decision** can be made about it.
3)	**Shaping desires**	The power to manipulate what people **think they want** — powerful groups can make people think they **want** or **consent** to something which actually **harms their interests**.

Lukes suggests that the **third face of power** (shaping desires) is the strongest, because it's never questioned. He suggests that power is exercised **invisibly** by controlling what people **want**. This is related to the ideas of **Habermas** and **Gramsci**. **Habermas** argued that capitalism creates **false needs** — things that people **don't really need**, but **think** they do. **Gramsci** argued that capitalism has a **dominant ideology** which tells people that society is **fair** and capitalism is **best** for everyone.

Karl Marx *said only* One Group *holds power in society — the* Bourgeoisie

1)   **Karl Marx (1818-1883)** believed that power in society is **finite** (in other words there's only so much of it), and that it can only be held by **one person** or **group** at a time. This view of power is called the **Zero Sum Model**.

2)   Marx saw society in terms of social classes **competing** for power. Under capitalism, the **capitalist** class (**bourgeoisie**) hold **all the power** and use it to their advantage and to the detriment of the **working class (proletariat)**.

3)   Marxists tend to reject the idea of authority as legitimate power, suggesting that the working class are **falsely persuaded** to consent to the rule of the capitalist class. He saw authority as just **disguised power**.

4)   Marxist sociologist **Miliband (1969)** suggests that **political power** is held by the same class who hold **economic power**.

The Nature and Distribution of Power

Elite Theorists *see society as ruled by a small, powerful* **Elite**

1) **Classical elite theorists** like **Vilfredo Pareto (1848-1923)** and **Gaetano Mosca (1858-1941)** saw society as divided between the rulers (**the elite**) and the ruled. The **elite** take all the **important decisions** in society and these decisions are almost always in their **own interest**. So far, they agreed with the Marxist viewpoint.

2) The big difference between elite theorists and Marxists is that the elite theorists thought **elite domination** was **desirable**, **inevitable** and **natural**. They said the elite become the elite because they are **better** than the rest of us. They saw the **rest of society** as a disorganised and apathetic **rabble**. This is **very different to Marxists** who thought that elite domination was unfair and exploitative.

C. Wright Mills *introduced the idea of the* **Power Elite**

1) In a more **modern** and **radical** study of the power of elites, **C. Wright Mills (1959)** studied three important institutions in American society — the **business community**, the **military** and the **government**.

2) Mills claimed that the elite in all three institutions formed a **single ruling elite**, which he called the **Power Elite**. Military, industrial and political power were all intertwined in the power elite.

3) He concluded that **unelected elites** sharing the same **social background** dominate American society and run economic and foreign policy in their own interests. Mills argued that the power elite **weren't accountable** to the people. He saw **little difference** between American political parties, so no chance to vote for **alternative** policies.

Statistics show the **majority** of British **MPs**, high ranking **civil servants** and **business leaders** come from the same **social** and **educational** background — this phenomenon has been referred to as the **"Establishment"**.

In a study of top decision makers, **Lupton and Wilson (1973)** found that connections between them were strengthened by close **marital** and **kinship ties**. Strong internal ties within the elite group make it harder for outsiders to break in.

Functionalists *and* Pluralists *see power as* **Dispersed** *through society*

1) **Pluralist RA Dahl (1961)** found that instead of one elite group dominating society and hogging all the power, there were actually **"multiple centres of power"** — lots of small groups competing for power. Pluralists believe that all sorts of political parties and interest groups can have **power** over political **decision-making**.

2) **Functionalists** believe that the amount of power in society can **increase** or **decrease** depending on how many people see it as legitimate. This is the **Variable Sum Model**. Pluralists mostly believe the amount of power is **constant**.

3) Pluralists are **criticised** for focusing on only the **first** of Lukes' **faces of power** — the power to make decisions.

Some Postmodernists *claim that* **Power** *and* **Politics** *have* **Changed**

Jean Baudrillard (1983) says that politicians and political parties have **no power** to change the world. All they do is maintain the **illusion** that politics goes on as **normal**. Baudrillard suggests that there's **no real difference** between political parties or politicians and **no real power** — he sees politics as having turned into a **media-driven** system of **signs** with **no hard reality** behind it.

Lyotard (1984) sees postmodernist politics as being about a **loss of faith** in **big political ideologies** that say what society should be like (see p.10 for more). Lyotard sees power as belonging to whoever has the most **useful knowledge** — individuals, corporations, governments, etc.

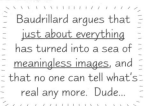

Baudrillard argues that *just about everything* has turned into a sea of *meaningless images*, and that no one can tell what's real any more. Dude...

Practice Questions

Q1 What is the difference between power and authority?

Q2 List the three types of authority itemised by Max Weber.

Q3 What are Stephen Lukes' "three faces of power"?

Q4 Explain what is meant by the Zero Sum Model and Variable Sum Model views of power.

Exam Question

Q1 "Authority is legitimate power." Evaluate this view. (40 marks)

Three faces of power, and five mighty morphin power rangers...

... who don't seem to be on the syllabus this year for some reason. Before you can get anywhere with politics and protest, you've got to have an idea of what power is, and who has power in society. Of course, different sociological schools of thought have very different ideas about power. Learn a few names so that you can drop them in your essays — but make sure you keep it relevant.

The Modern State

*These pages have definitions and theories about the modern State. For **AQA** and **OCR**.*

Most sociologists **Agree** with **Weber's Definition** of the **Modern State**

According to Weber, the modern State is "a **human commodity** that successfully claims the **monopoly** of the **legitimate use** of **physical force** within a **given territory**".

In other words: ⟹

1) The State is **created by people**.
2) The State can **use force legitimately** — **other** violence in society is **illegitimate**.
3) The State **rules** over a **clear geographical area** — in our case the UK.

The **State** is traditionally made up of **Four Main Institutions**

1) The **government**, who **make laws**.

2) The **Civil Service**, who **implement laws**.

THE STATE

3) The **police**, who **enforce laws**.

4) The **Armed Forces**, who **protect** the **territory** from threats from outside.

Government is often divided into **three branches** — the legislature, the executive and the judiciary.

1) The **legislature passes laws**. In the UK, **Parliament** (House of Commons and House of Lords) is the legislature.
2) The **executive** suggests new laws, and **runs the country**. The executive is often called "the **government**". Confusing.
3) The **judiciary interprets laws**. The **courts** are the judiciary.

In modern times, the State has extended its role into **health care**, **education**, and **nationalised** (state-run) **industries**.

Pluralists see the **Modern State** as a **Neutral Arena** for debate

1) Pluralists see the power of the modern democratic State as **legitimate** and acting in the interests of society in general. Pluralists see the State as a **neutral arena** where competing interest and pressure groups lobby for **influence**. They say the State **arbitrates** (settles arguments) between competing interest groups, but is neutral itself.

2) Pluralists say the modern State is democratic because of the **multi-party system**, and because of the participation of **interest groups** and **pressure groups**. **Dahl (1961)** looked at the role of interest groups in local politics in the USA, and found that **several groups** had influence. An important study by **Hewitt (1974)** shows the **crucial role** of interest groups and pressure groups in **influencing Parliament**. Hewitt said that no one group got its own way all the time.

3) A study by **Grant and Marsh (1977)** showed that business interests in the form of the CBI (Confederation of British Industry) didn't have massive influence over British government policy. A **plurality** of **other interest groups** influenced policy away from what the CBI wanted.

Critics of pluralism claim that **some interest groups** have **more influence** than others. **Marsh and Locksley (1983)** found that the CBI were successful in getting their own way in key decisions (completely the opposite of what Marsh had found in his earlier study with Grant — Sociology is a funny old thing).

Marxists say the **State Supports** the interests of the **Bourgeoisie**

> Engels was Marx's friend and worked with Marx on the Communist Manifesto.

Marx said: "The State is but a committee for managing the affairs of the bourgeoisie."
Marx and **Engels** asserted that the State only became necessary when society became **divided** on grounds of **class**. They said that in primitive society there were no classes and therefore no need for a State.

Marxists claim that the role of the modern State is to **maintain**, **preserve** and **perpetuate** the rule of the **capitalist class** over the **workers**. This is achieved in the following ways:

1) **Coercive force** — the **police** are used to contain or suppress **demonstrations** and **riots**.

2) The **illusion of democracy** — universal voting makes it **look** as though everyone has a say and that society is **fair**. This creates the **false consciousness** that the current system is legitimate. However, political parties only represent the interests of **capitalism**, so there's **no real choice**.

3) **Ideology** — a set of ideas by which the State gains approval and consent by persuading people to accept ruling class values. The neo-Marxist **Gramsci (1891-1937)** called this kind of domination **hegemony**. Gramsci, Althusser and Poulantzas all extend the definition of the State to other institutions which pass on values e.g. **churches**, **mass media**, the **family**.

> Althusser called the army, police and courts the <u>Repressive State Apparatus</u>, and the church, family, education and media the <u>Ideological State Apparatus</u>.

Critics say it's **hard to prove** Marxist theory. Concepts like **ideology**, **hegemony** and **false consciousness**, which are key to the Marxist viewpoint, are **difficult to define** and even more **difficult to research**.

The Modern State

Some theorists Criticise the Modern State as being Patriarchal and Racist

1) **Patriarchy** means a social system in which **men have more status and power** than women. Radical feminists view the **State** as a **patriarchal institution** which legitimises and maintains patriarchy.

2) Evidence for this view is that women are **under-represented** at the **top levels of the State** in the UK, e.g. in 2003, only 18% of MPs and 16% of the House of Lords were women, and less than 10% of company directors were women.

3) On the other hand, British society is **much less sexist** than it was 50 years ago, and women now have a **legal right** to **equal pay and opportunities** in the workplace. The feminist **Sylvia Walby (1990)** admits that there have been huge improvements in state policy towards women, but she argues that the State hasn't succeeded in enforcing equal opportunities laws. Walby claims that the State doesn't do enough to **protect** women from patriarchy.

Some people see agencies of the State as **institutionally racist** (see p.47). There's little evidence for blatant racism on the part of the State in the UK. However, State policies and attitudes can sometimes **unintentionally disadvantage** ethnic minorities.

Neo-liberals are Opposed to State Intervention in the Economy

1) Neo-liberals argue that the keys to lasting economic prosperity are **individual economic enterprise** and a **market** (economy) which is **free** from **state intervention**. Neo-liberal theorists, like **Hayek (1944)**, argue that state intervention in the economy can **stifle capitalism** and make the economy **less efficient**.

2) Neo-liberals therefore believe that **state interference** in the economy such as high taxes, state ownership (nationalisation), or generous welfare benefits should be **rolled back** (i.e. reduced).

3) The influence of neo-liberal thinking can be seen in the **Conservative governments** of Mrs Thatcher (1979-1990) which **privatised** state industries, **lowered taxation** and **reduced universal benefits**.

4) The **traditional challenge** to the neo-liberal view is the **reformist socialist view** (see p.7). The reformist socialist view is that the State **should intervene** in the economy in order to improve **social welfare** and **equality**. The reformist socialist view is associated with Old Labour, e.g. the post-war Labour government which created the Welfare State.

Third Way theorists want a State with Social Welfare and Capitalist Economics

1) The "**Third Way**" was an idea put forward by the sociologist **Anthony Giddens (1998)** and later adopted by Tony Blair's **New Labour Party**. Giddens has described it as "the modernising left."

2) Third Way theorists argue that the **world is changing**, for example through globalisation, and that **political ideologies** need to **change** and **adapt** as well if they are to remain relevant. The Third Way therefore includes **elements** of **both** traditional **left-wing** (socialist) and **right-wing** (neo-liberal capitalist) approaches.

3) Third Way theory suggests that the **traditional Welfare State** should be **reformed** because it **encourages dependency** (a neo-liberal idea). However, it also argues that the State should reform and manage the **global economy** to such an extent that it is able to **intervene** to **invest in its citizens**, e.g. through **education** and **social policy**. They argue this will **empower the population** to lead more prosperous, healthy and fulfilling lives.

Globalisation has changed the role of the State

1) As part of the process of globalisation (see glossary) **transnational corporations** (**TNCs**) have developed and become very powerful economically. **Sklair (1995)** claims that there's a **transnational capital class** who have gained power at the expense of nation states — he claims the State just isn't as important any more.

2) There's a trend towards **internationalisation** of politics, which has reduced the influence of nation states. For example, some important decisions are taken by the **European Union** rather than by its **member states**.

Practice Questions

Q1 Traditionally, what four things make up the State?
Q2 Briefly summarise the Marxist view on the role of the State.
Q3 Briefly summarise the Pluralist view on the role of the State.

Exam Question

Q1 Evaluate the view that the people in positions of most power in society have not been directly elected. (40 marks)

No need to get in a State about it...

There are a lot of strong opinions on these two pages. You need to be able to evaluate these different views fairly and objectively, whatever your own personal opinion. And I bet you do have a personal opinion. If you find yourself taking sides and thinking "stupid liberal do-gooders" or "blimmin' Tories" then take some deep breaths and start again.

Political Participation

*There are a range of types of government in the modern world — monarchies, democracies, dictatorships, oligarchies and totalitarian systems. Some encourage political activity, some don't. People can participate in political action in different ways. For **OCR** and **AQA** — the different types of government on p.8 are OCR only, though you might find them useful for AQA.*

Direct Democracy was the First type of democracy

1) **Direct democracy** means **every citizen** has a **direct influence** on every decision.

2) **Direct democracy** was the **first kind** of democracy — it goes right back to the **Ancient Greeks**. In the 5th century BC, **Athens** had a system of direct democracy. All 40 000 Athenian citizens had the right to **speak** and **vote** at the **assembly**, which met about 40 times a year. Decisions were taken on the basis of a **majority vote**.

3) Since the Ancient Greeks, there have been few attempts at direct democracy, simply because it tends to be rather **time-consuming**. However, the use of **referenda** by governments can be seen as an experiment in direct democracy.

Monarchy means rule by a King or a Queen

1) Monarchies can be **limited**, **constitutional** or **absolute**.

2) A **limited monarchy** is one in which the King or Queen has only **ceremonial** powers e.g. the British monarchy. Whilst on paper the Queen appears to have considerable powers (patronage, royal assent etc.), in reality the UK is a democratic state with a ceremonial monarchy.

3) A **constitutional monarchy** is one in which the monarch has some powers which are clearly defined by a written constitution. A good example is **Sweden** where the King has a number of defined powers, e.g. chairing the committee for foreign affairs.

4) An **absolute monarchy** is one in which the monarch is really "sovereign" — he or she rules on their own and has absolute power. The powers of an absolute monarch aren't limited by a constitution. A good historical example is the "divine right" monarchies of Europe in the Middle Ages — kings believed they had a "divine right" (i.e. had been chosen by God) to rule. A more **modern** example is the **Saudi royal family** in Saudi Arabia.

Sovereignty means the power to make the laws or to rule. In the past in Britain, the monarch was called "Sovereign" because they made the laws. They sometimes get called this today, but it's Parliament who makes the law — Parliament has "sovereignty".

Dictatorships, Oligarchies and Totalitarian systems Don't value participation

1) A **dictatorship** is rule by **one absolute ruler** whose word is law. They're similar to absolute monarchies — the difference is that monarchs **inherit** their power whereas dictators tend to **seize** it by **military force** or **conquest**. Opposition **political activity** is outlawed in a dictatorship. A recent example would be **Saddam Hussein** in Iraq.

2) An **oligarchy** is rule by a **minority** portion of the population, e.g. in **apartheid-era South Africa** when the 25% of the population who were white monopolised **all power** and **wealth** in the country.

3) A **totalitarian** system is a government where total control is in the hands of a ruling **political party** who follow an official ideology. There's **total control** of all aspects of life. Elections are held but there's only ever **one party** to vote for, and all opposition is crushed. An example is communist rule in the former **Soviet Union** and its satellite states.

The more Modern form of democracy is called Representative Democracy

1) It would be very difficult and time consuming to consult every citizen of a modern state on every issue that faced the country, so a system of **representative democracy** has evolved.

2) In a representative democracy, the people vote to **elect representatives** to make decisions on their **behalf**. These representatives (**MPs** in the UK) are accountable to the voters at the next election — they can get voted out.

3) **Joseph Schumpeter (1942)** defined democracy as a system where there is a "competitive struggle for the people's vote". For a government to be a democracy, there must be **more than one candidate** or party standing in an election.

4) Modern ideas of democracy are also associated with certain **liberal values**, e.g. belief in **civil liberties** and **freedom of expression**, belief in the **rule of law**, belief in the right to **trial by jury** etc.

5) All **modern representative democracies** also favour **capitalism**, though it's conceivable that a socialist party could win an election on a platform of ditching capitalism in favour of full-on socialism. Some political thinkers see a **correlation** between the belief in a **free competition** for the **people's vote** and **free market economics**.

Political Participation

Citizens of a **Representative Democracy** participate through **Political Parties**

1) **Politics** in modern representative democracies like the UK is where **belief systems** (represented by political parties, e.g. the Liberal Democrats, Labour, the Conservatives) **compete for power**. People **vote** to decide who has power.

See p.6-7 for ideology and political parties.

2) Citizens can participate by **supporting** and **voting** for a particular political party that they share beliefs with. They can also **join** that political party — and help out with election campaigns, or become an **activist** (someone who attempts to influence the party's policies).

Voting Patterns have Changed

Crewe (1983) found that in the 1964 election, 64% of manual workers voted Labour, and 62% of non-manual workers voted Conservative.

1) In the **1960s**, people mainly voted according to their **social class**. The minority of middle class voters who voted Labour, or working class voters who voted Conservative were called **deviant voters**.

2) **Crewe (1983)** identified several reasons why working class people switched from Labour to Conservative in the 1980s.
   - **Manual workers** in heavy industry traditionally voted Labour. These industries were in **decline**.
   - There was a "**new working class**" living in the South and working in the service industry and high tech industry. They were mainly owner-occupiers, and no longer identified with **Labour**.
   - **Party image** was increasingly important, and Labour leaders **Foot** and **Kinnock** had **poor public image**.

3) **Marshall (1988)** criticises Crewe, saying that there's **not enough evidence** for the "new working class".

4) **Butler and Kavanagh (1985)** point out that the **Falklands War** was a big factor in **Mrs Thatcher's** popularity.

People also **Participate** in **Politics** by getting involved with a **Pressure Group**

Pressure groups can be either **protective** (also called **sectional**) or **promotional**. **Protective**, or **sectional**, groups seek to protect the interests of a particular group, e.g. trade unions protect groups of workers, the CBI protects the interests of business, and the British Medical Association looks out for doctors. **Promotional** groups promote causes, e.g. Greenpeace and Friends of the Earth promote environmental causes.

Pluralists argue that pressure group activity is an essential feature of modern democracy.

1) Pressure groups give **valuable input** to government policy, and provide expert opinion.

2) Pressure groups provide a vehicle for many **views** to be **represented**.

3) **Pluralists** say pressure groups have **equal access** to government. The state is seen by pluralists as a **neutral arbiter** between different **pressure groups** with different opinions.

Marxists suggest that pressure group activity doesn't enhance democracy at all.

1) Pressure groups tend **not** to be **democratic**. Members have little say in the running of the group.

2) Pressure groups are **not equal** — some have more resources and therefore much more influence than others. Marxists claim that the most powerful groups are always pro-capitalist ones.

3) Marxists think pressure groups shouldn't be powerful as they aren't **accountable** to the people.

4) Marxists think the state **isn't neutral**, and can't be a neutral arbiter between pressure groups.

Practice Questions

Q1 Take a piece of A4 paper. On the left-hand side list the different types of government mentioned on p.8, and on the right-hand side explain what opportunities for political action each system allows.

Q2 What's the difference between direct and representative democracy?

Q3 Who are the "new working class" and how do they vote, according to Crewe?

Q4 Outline the arguments for and against the idea that pressure group activity makes society more democratic.

Exam Question

Q1 Examine the view that voting behaviour in the UK is no longer class based. (12 marks)

I vote we stop learning about this and go and watch telly...

No no no that was a joke. Keep learning. Learn I say! Learn! There's a lot to get through on these two pages — OCR people can be asked about systems of government, and what kind of political activity people are allowed in each system. AQA people need to know about participation — that means voting and pressure group activity. So learn faster. Faster I say!

New Social Movements

These two pages look at the emergence of new social movements, and global social movements.
*These pages are for **OCR**, but might be useful for **AQA**.*

The **Young** tend to participate in politics through **New Social Movements (NSMs)**

Hallsworth (1994) defines NSMs as movements which **challenge** the **established political** and **cultural order** in capitalist societies. This includes feminism, environmentalism, the civil rights movement and anti-racist movements.

NSMs can either be **defensive** or **offensive** — which has nothing to do with whether they offend people, by the way.

- **Defensive** movements are concerned with **protecting** the environment or people from things they see as a threat, e.g. **nuclear power**, **genetically modified crops**, **global capitalism**, etc.
- **Offensive** movements want to **promote** and widen the **rights** of the groups they represent. Examples of offensive movements are **gay rights groups**, **human rights groups** and **anti-racist groups**.

1) Hallsworth claims that most members of NSMs tend to be **young** (mainly between 16 and 30) and **middle class**, particularly from the **public sector middle class** (teachers, social workers, etc). *This includes young people whose parents are teachers, social workers etc.*

2) NSMs are informally organised, and non-bureaucratic.

3) NSMs tend to operate outside of traditional politics. Unlike pressure groups and political parties, NSMs tend to favour **direct action**, such as demonstrations, civil disobedience and sit-ins (see p.14-15).

Sociologists apply different **Theories** to the phenomenon of **NSMs**

1) **Marcuse (1969)** argues that young people form and join NSMs because they are **alienated** by **capitalism**.

2) Marcuse is a **Marxist** who says that capitalism produces a **shallow**, **superficial** mass **consumer culture**. He says that NSMs reject the **shallowness** and **emptiness** of consumer culture.

3) **Marcuse** sees NSMs as having the potential to **liberate** people.

1) **Habermas (1987)** argues that people form and join NSMs as a response to the **intrusion of the state** into private life, and the **failure of the state** to solve problems or control industrial capitalism.

2) He says that NSMs are deliberately non-bureaucratic.

Giddens (1973) argues that an increase in **risk** has motivated people to start NSMs. Late 20th century peace movements responded to the increased risk of war, especially nuclear war. Environmentalist movements have responded to the increased risk of environmental disasters.

Melucci (1989) says that people join NSMs to give them a sense of **collective identity**. *There's more about identity and protest on p.16.*

Some sociologists link NSMs with **Postmodernism**

1) **Crook, Pakulski and Waters (1992)** argue that **postmodernisation** is causing a shift from **old politics** to **new politics**. They define **old politics** as based on **political parties** and **class**, and belonging to a specialised **political sphere**. They define **new politics** as based on **NSMs** and moral issues, and belonging to people's wider lifestyle.

2) Crook, Pakulski and Waters say that a **decline** in the importance of **class** is partly responsible. They claim that class-based party politics is becoming less relevant.

3) The rise in importance of the **media** is another factor. They say that the media **dramatises** potential scenarios such as global warming and nuclear war, which makes people feel that they have to do something about them.

1) **Nancy Fraser (1995)** suggests that what constitutes the "**public sphere**" (where politics goes on) has changed.

2) She argues that it has **fragmented** into **several** public spheres where **special interest groups** can argue issues before trying to get their views onto the **mainstream agenda**.

3) She also claims that the public sphere has **widened**, and that the **personal** and **private** have **become political** — for example, sexual harassment was once seen as private flirting, but feminists have made it political.

1) Postmodernist **Jean-François Lyotard (1984)** claims that in the postmodern era people have lost faith in what he calls "**metanarratives**" — the big sweeping political ideologies of the modern era that say what society should be like.

2) He suggests that politics has become more **localised** and **limited** in scope, and more concerned with **single issues**.

New Social Movements

New Social Movements are becoming more Globalised

Globalisation is the trend of national boundaries becoming less important

1) Because of improvements in communications, consumers are able to purchase goods from all over the world. This has changed a system of national economies into a **global economy**.
2) **Transnational corporations** such as Nike, McDonald's, and Coca-Cola have tremendous power.
3) Global corporations with their brands, logos and associations with **lifestyles** are shaping a global culture.
4) The effects of **global economic activity** such as **pollution** don't respect national boundaries.
5) A highly mobile global population means that **diseases** such as **HIV** are global problems.

An environmentalist slogan says "Think Global. Act Local"

According to **Cohen and Rai (2000)**, global social movements are simply new social movements which are concerned with **global issues** rather than issues within individual countries. They highlight the **human rights movement** and the **women's movement** as examples of successful global social movements. Environmentalism is another example. Many environmentalist NSMs have a global membership, e.g. **Greenpeace** and **Friends of the Earth**.

The Global Anti-Capitalism movement developed at the end of the 1990s

The two most quoted examples of anti-capitalist political action are the **World Trade Organisation demonstrations** in **Seattle 1999** and the **G8 Summit demonstrations** in **2001**. At both there was serious disorder and some rioting. **Reasons** for the development of a **global anti-capitalist movement** include:

1) **International organisations** seem to be running the world — e.g. the G8, the EU, the UN.
2) Improvements in **communications** (especially the **Internet**) have allowed activists to **organise** and **network** effectively.
3) The **financial crisis** in East Asia 1998 rocked many people's faith in the **sustainability** of global capitalism.
4) The politics of liberal democracies tend not to offer **alternatives** to capitalism.

1) Marxist **Callinicos (2003)** suggests that the apparently **diverse** interests of global social movements are linked by the **common source** of their **concerns** — what else but global capitalism (he is a Marxist after all).
2) For instance, he says it's **global capitalism** that causes pollution and therefore creates **environmental protestors**, and it's **global capitalism** which keeps LEDCs (Less Economically Developed Countries) in poverty and therefore creates protesters against **Third World Debt**.
3) It's worth remembering that global social movements cover a **huge political spectrum**. Callinicos may well be **exaggerating** their **revolutionary potential** as an anti-capitalist force.

1) **Naomi Klein (2001)** argues that young people involved in global social movements are fed up with the global branding of **youth** and **youth culture**.
2) In *No Logo*, Klein argues that people involved in global social movements believe that political parties and "old politics" are powerless to challenge the **dominance** of **global corporations**.
3) **Global branding** gives protesters a **target** for their protests, e.g. producing a spoof advertisement or logo with an anti-capitalist message. This is called **culture jamming**.
4) The **McLibel case** shows the effects of culture jamming. Protesters produced anti-McDonald's leaflets and McDonald's sued for libel. The court case gave the protesters massive **publicity**. The judge agreed with some of their claims.

Practice Questions

Q1 What are the differences between NSMs and more traditional ways of participating in politics and power?
Q2 Give five reasons why global social movements have emerged.
Q3 What does Marcuse say about NSMs?
Q4 What is "culture jamming" and why is it done?

Exam Questions

Q1 Outline and assess the view that new social movements form because people no longer have faith in politics. (60 marks)

Q2 Outline and assess the extent to which global social movements can be seen as anti-capitalist in nature. (60 marks)

Culture jam — that must be the kind with mould growing on it...

The basics of these pages are reasonably straightforward — all you need to learn are the ways that new social movements differ from old social movements, and a few examples of new social movements and global social movements. If you actually want half-decent marks, you'll need to learn the names and dates of a few theorists, and there are plenty of those here. As usual.

Influences on the Political Process

*These pages examine the influence of political parties and the mass media on the political process. They're for **AQA**.*

The **Influence** of **Political Parties** on the **Political Process** is in **Decline**

1) For many years the UK was seen as the classic model of the **Two Party System** — i.e. a system where two **big**, **powerful** and **distinct** political parties compete for power. Other parties exist in a two party system but they don't have a **realistic chance** of winning an election and forming a government.

2) Sociologists have been writing about the decline of the influence of the main political parties since the 1960s. In this view, the fact that political parties have **fewer members** and **fewer activists** shows that they're **less likely** to **inspire** people to go and **vote**.

There's some powerful evidence that the influence of political parties is in decline:

1) **Party membership** and **activism** is declining among Britain's three major parties. For instance, **Labour Party** membership is currently less than **300 000**, having fallen from a peak of **400 000+** in **1997**. **Conservative Party** membership has fallen from over **1 million** during the time of Mrs Thatcher to fewer than **325 000** today.

2) Young people especially are turning to **New Social Movements** to participate in Politics (see p.10).

3) The differences between political parties appear to be **less pronounced** resulting in voter "apathy" e.g. only **61.3%** of the electorate **bothered to vote** in the 2005 **general election**.

However, **Reiter (1989)** is **sceptical** of the claim that political parties are in decline. He says there isn't enough evidence across different countries, and over a long enough period of time.

Neo-Marxist **Martin Jacques (1997)** suggests that because of the decline in political parties, British politics should move away from the "Westminster model", which focuses exclusively on the mainstream parties. Jacques suggests a greater appreciation of new forms of political participation.

Ideologically, British **Political Parties** appear to be becoming **Less Distinct**

1) **"New Labour"** under Tony Blair has dropped many of the **traditional**, **left-wing** policies and commitments of the Labour Party, e.g. **democratic socialism**, **nationalisation** and **redistribution of wealth**.

2) New Labour now competes in elections as a party who could **manage the capitalist economy** better than its traditional managers, the Conservative party (political ideology and the political parties are discussed on p.6-7).

3) Policies on **taxation**, **foreign affairs** and **economic management** have become very **similar** in the **Conservative Party** and the **Labour Party**. This gives voters less choice, which may make them less bothered to go and vote in elections.

Ketchup.

HP sauce.

The candidates debated the only issue they didn't agree on.

"Voter Apathy" is when people **Don't Bother** to vote

Voter apathy is particularly marked amongst the **young** and amongst **ethnic minority** groups. Several measures have been proposed to tackle this apathy. Some have already been adopted.

Already adopted:

1) Making voting **easier** by making it easier to apply for a **postal vote**. ⟵

2) Making it easier to **register** to vote — you can register online in some areas.

3) **Educating the voters**, e.g. **Citizenship** is a **National Curriculum** subject in schools.

The postal vote system in the UK has been criticised as <u>open to fraud</u>. Researchers and journalists have shown it's possible to register a postal vote in <u>someone else's name</u>. This accusation has <u>damaged trust</u> in the electoral system.

Not yet adopted:

1) Making **voting** easier by using **new technology** e.g. Internet voting and text message voting. If it's good enough for Pop Idol, it's good enough for choosing our government...

2) Extending polling day to several days.

3) **Redesigning ballot papers** to make them easier to understand.

4) Giving people the option to register a positive abstention — i.e. a box to tick that says "none of the above" or "abstain".

All of the measures appear to focus on the **voters** as the problem rather than the **decline** and **ideological convergence** of the political parties themselves.

Some countries, e.g. Australia have tried to tackle the problem of voter apathy by making **voting compulsory** by law. This has not yet been proposed in Britain.

Influences on the Political Process

The **UK Mass Media** were **Pro-Conservative** until the **late 1990s**

1) Up until 1997 the only paper that ever expressed consistent support for the Labour Party was the **Daily Mirror**. The rest tended to support the Conservatives.

2) In the late 1990s "New Labour" made it a **priority** to win the support of **big media owners**, particularly **Rupert Murdoch**. Murdoch's News International controls the **Times**, the **Sun** and **Sky television**.

3) The results can be illustrated by the contrasting ways in which Sun headline writers treated two Labour leaders — Neil Kinnock in 1992 and Tony Blair in 1997. The Sun's 1992 election day headline was "**If Kinnock wins today, will the last person to leave Britain turn off the lights**" (Neil Kinnock was the Labour party leader in 1992, and would have become Prime Minister if Labour had won the 1992 election). The Sun's 1997 election day headline was "**THE SUN BACKS BLAIR — give change a chance**".

4) The support of significant sections of the **mass media** has been cited as a crucial factor in the **continued electoral success** of New Labour. "**Spin doctors**" are party PR officers whose job it is to **manipulate** the media and make sure that the party is presented in a sympathetic light, and that the party's opponents are presented negatively.

Marxists suggest that **Media Ownership** makes the media **Pro-Capitalist**

1) Traditional Marxism claims that the media **directly** presents news stories which serve the **interests** of the ruling class, because the media is itself **owned** by the **ruling class**.

2) **Miliband (1969)** said that the mass media was the "new opium of the people" — it keeps the proletariat subdued by showing them nice mindless entertainment. **Marcuse (1964)** said that the media gives people "false needs" which keep them consuming the goods that capitalism produces.

3) Neo-Marxists suggest that the world view of the capitalist class is broadcast and reinforced by the mass media through an **indirect approval process**. Editors are from middle class backgrounds, so they tend to select material which reflects their own ideas.

4) **Gramsci**'s idea of **ideological hegemony** (see p.4) really applies here. Ruling class values are portrayed through the mass media as natural and common sense. Ideas that question capitalism are ridiculed as crazy.

5) A recent **example** of this was an attack on the policies of the Liberal Democrats by The Sun in which they superimposed Lib Dem leader **Charles Kennedy's face** on the label of a **bottle of whisky** to illustrate an article about the Lib Dems. The headline was "Red Kennedy", suggesting that the Liberal Democrats were **socialists** (red is the colour of socialism), and the subheading was "**Loony left policies of Lib Dems' boozy chief**".

The work of the **GUMG** suggests that **News** is **Politically Weighted**

The GUMG studied news reports of industrial disputes in the 70s and 80s

Method:	The Glasgow University Media Group studied television news over a long time span to look for evidence of bias. They performed detailed content analysis on television news bulletins.
Finding:	The selection of news was biased in favour of dominant class values. Voice-over scripts were biased in favour of dominant class values. Management had more access to the media than union leaders. Filming and editing were biased in favour of the police.

Practice Questions

Q1 Explain what is meant by the Two Party System?

Q2 Give three pieces of evidence which suggest that the influence of political parties is in decline.

Q3 Give three ways in which Marxists say the media promotes the interests of the ruling class.

Exam Question

Q1 Assess the view that the differences between political parties have diminished. (40 marks)

Do you know who Gramsci is? Well do you?

Gramsci (1891-1937) was a Marxist who founded the Italian Communist Party in 1921. He was chucked into prison by the Italian Fascists, who came to power under Mussolini. And while he was in prison, he did an awful lot of writing. There are some nice letters to his sister, and quite a bit of writing about ideology. Anyway, I digress... onwards to p.14.

Direct Action

*These pages examine forms of direct action engaged in by New Social Movements. They're for **OCR** and **AQA**.*

Direct action happens **Outside** normal **Political Processes**

Direct action is political activity which happens outside the normal political processes. It includes **peaceful demonstrations**, **sit-ins** and **boycotts**, as well as violent action such as **riots**, **vandalism** and **terrorism**.

Some direct action is **large-scale** and **public**, e.g. **demonstrations** and **marches**.
Some is **targeted**, e.g. letter and leaflet campaigns, vandalism and boycotts.

1) **New Social Movements** are far more likely to engage in **direct action** than traditional political activity. They don't have a **strong voice** in party political debate. Members of NSMs often feel they **have to take direct action** in order to get their views on the **mainstream agenda**. Getting noticed by the **media** often plays a big part in this.

2) Some say NSMs have **redefined** what is meant by **political action** — taking the political to new areas like the private sphere, e.g. by targeting the issue of domestic violence.

3) The political activity of NSMs is **deliberately** different from that of old social movements.

Direct Action is often **Against The Law**

1) Most illegal direct action is **peaceful**. **Civil disobedience** means direct action which breaks laws. For instance **mass trespass** is a common form of civil disobedience practised by **anti-motorway protestors** who put themselves physically **in the way** of developers in an attempt to protect woodlands etc. The **Reclaim the Streets** movement causes traffic congestion by organising **street parties** in the middle of busy roads, blocking the road off for the day.

2) Some **direct action** is **violent and criminal** and has been characterised as **terrorism**. Terrorist direct action has been taken against the **USA** and its allies by anti-American Islamist groups, e.g. Al Qaeda. Some Palestinian nationalist groups use terrorist actions, such as **suicide bombs**, against Israel.

3) Terrorism also happens on a smaller scale. For example, the direct action of some **animal rights groups** includes sending **letter bombs** to scientists involved in testing with animals, **threatening** the **families** of scientists involved in animal testing, putting **bricks through windows**, and **fire bombing** of shops selling fur goods.

Riots are a **Common** form of **Direct Action**

1) Riots are outbreaks of **serious urban disorder** on a large scale. They're often violent, and that violence can be directed against both property and people.

2) Often riots are understood as the **desperate actions** of people not represented in any other way. In this view, social groups not represented by "Old Politics" (parties and pressure groups) resort to riots to get their **voices heard**. This view **ignores** other kinds of direct action that can be used to attract attention.

3) Riots are not a modern phenomenon, despite the fact that most sociological research has focused on the inner city riots of the **1980s** (Brixton, Toxteth, Tottenham). Throughout the **18th** and **19th centuries** there were frequent riots in the UK in response to problems that came with **industrialisation**.

4) **Peaceful demonstrations** and marches can get **violent** and turn into **riots**.

According to **Benyon (1987)** there are **Four Types** of **Explanation** for **Riots**

1) Conservative	Conservatives see rioting as a primarily **criminal** and **unjustifiable** activity. Rioters are seen as selfish, greedy, envious and lacking moral fibre. New Right sociologists like **Murray** suggest the **subculture** of the **underclass** which **embraces criminality** is to blame for rioting. The solution from this perspective is to break the **"dependency culture"** which breeds such **deviant** values.
2) Liberal	Liberals identify factors like **unemployment**, **poverty**, **poor housing** and **limited opportunities** as the main causes of riots. When added to **discrimination** (e.g. black youths discriminated against by the police using "stop and search" in Brixton), riots are likely to take place.
3) Radical	Radicals like Marxists suggest riots are **conscious legitimate political acts** by groups with **no other way** of expressing their grievances. Marxists see rioting as a reaction by the working class to the injustices and exploitation of the capitalist system. The involvement of black working class people in riots has been seen by Marxists as an expression of **anger** at the way white society has **discriminated** against black people.
4) Feminist	**Feminists** have suggested that rioting by **young working class males** is an attempt to **assert masculinity** at a time when **traditional male roles** and male jobs are in **decline**.

Remember also that in large **demonstrations** that have developed into riots, **anti-capitalist NSMs** have played a part in organising and coordinating activity on the Internet, e.g. in Genoa at the 2001 G8 Summit.

Direct Action

Recent riots in Oldham and Bradford have been linked to Ethnic Tension

1) A series of riots occurred in the northern, mostly working class towns of **Oldham**, **Leeds** and **Bradford** in **2001**. The riots all involved serious clashes between **young Asians** and the police.

2) These riots differed from the inner city riots of the 1980s, because they took place in a context of a rapid increase in political activity of **far right organisations** like the **British National Party** (BNP) and the **National Front** (NF). Both the BNP and NF have concentrated in recent years on northern towns, especially **Oldham**, to recruit members and mobilise public opinion.

The bits in quotes are from the BNP's mission statement and published stance on immigration.

3) The **BNP** is a political party which "exists to secure a future for the **indigenous** peoples of these islands". They want to **end immigration**, and to offer immigrants money "to return to their lands of **ethnic origin**". Some people believe the BNP are **racist**, although the BNP **deny** this.

4) Also, **socio-economic deprivation** among both white and Asian groups, housing segregation (the council estates were mainly white), and resulting **educational segregation** have all been put forward as explanations of the riots.

Strikes are a form of Direct Action taken by Trade Unions

1) Strikes are where workers deliberately **withdraw their labour**, under the direction of trade union leaders.

2) Strikes are **direct action** by **workers** against their **employer**. Large scale strikes can also be used to influence governments.

3) There were **frequent strikes** in the **1970s**. Trade union law was changed by the Conservative government in the 1980s to make it more difficult for workers to go out on strike, and since then strikes have become much rarer.

Strikes are heavily class-based. The working class (i.e. the workers) are protesting against either their boss, or the state.

Trade Unions are a pressure group, rather than a New Social Movement. Still, strikes count as a form of direct action.

Direct Action involves issues of Class, Gender, Ethnicity, Disability, etc.

Direct action has been taken by many different groups for many different reasons.

1) Women have participated in "**Reclaim the Night**" rallies against male sexual violence.

2) Disabled people have chained themselves to Downing Street railings in protest against government social policy.

3) Muslim groups have organised **demonstrations** against the Iraq war. **Moderate** groups also engaged with the normal political process by **voting** for MPs who opposed the war. **Radical** groups **rejected** the normal political process.

4) **Peaceful direct action** such as **sit-ins** and **marches** characterised Civil Rights protests in 1960s America. Racist groups sometimes responded with violence. The **Civil Rights** movement started with **civil disobedience** and a **boycott**.

In **1955**, a **black** woman from Montgomery, Alabama, **refused to give up her seat** on the bus to a **white** person. At that time, black passengers were supposed to sit at the back of the bus and give up their seats to white passengers if the bus was full. She was **arrested**. Local church minister Dr Martin Luther King called for a **boycott** of the bus company by all black people in Montgomery, which lasted until the **bus segregation laws** were **removed**.

Practice Questions

Q1 Give five examples of types of direct action.

Q2 Give two reasons why NSMs use direct action.

Q3 Give four types of explanation for why riots break out.

Exam Questions

Q1 Outline and assess the view that riots are caused by economic and social deprivation. (60 marks)

Hmm, perhaps someone will fire bomb J-Lo...

I'm not suggesting that that would in any way be a good thing, you understand. She may be annoying and a wearer of bunny rabbits, but fire bombing is not the answer. Perhaps instead we could hold a sit-in outside her house, and refuse to move until J-Lo promises to stop making irritating rom-coms and singing lies about being just plain ol' Jenny from the block. Or perhaps not.

Protest and Identity

*Protest and direct action can be part of the process which constructs a person's identity. This is just for **OCR**.*

An individual may create their own **Identity** through **Protest** and **Political Action**

1) Identity is the sense a person has of who they are. A person's identity can have many sources, including their class, gender, sexuality or ethnicity.

2) **Personal identity** is how a person sees themselves, and **social identity** is how an individual is perceived by others. **Personal** identity and **social** identity are not always the **same**.

3) Identities can be influenced by **politics and protest**. Belonging to a political movement based on class is likely to heighten the part of your identity that's based on class. The same goes for **gender**, or **sexuality**, or **ethnicity**.

There are several different kinds of feminism within the broader feminist movement. Liberal feminism aims for equality of opportunity for women, and works towards changing the law to make things equal for men and women. Radical feminism stresses women's identity as women. They blame men , rather than socialisation, for women's disadvantaged position.

Ken Plummer (1995) has written about new social movements based on sexuality, e.g. the lesbian and gay rights movement. He's also written about queer theory, which says that gender and sexual identities are very fluid, and can keep changing. Queer theory disapproves of the division of the world into strict categories of gay and straight.
Stephen Whittle (2000) has written about transgender identities, and transgender rights.

There are NSMs based on ethnicity. The Black Power movement in 1960s America aimed to find a distinctive identity as Black Americans and emphasised the common experience of oppression. The Civil Rights movement aimed to get black people equal opportunities in society.

Identity Politics is politics that comes from a Shared Experience of Injustice

1) Identity politics is based on **differences** between people. Identity politics is the politics of movements which represent the interests and identity of a particular **oppressed group** within a society, rather than society as a whole. Members of the group unite around a **shared identity**. Feminism, Disability Rights, Black Power, and Gay Pride are all varieties of identity politics.

2) Individuals who feel they are **oppressed** or **discriminated** against may create a positive sense of **personal identity** through **protest** and **political activity**. This sense of **positive personal identity** helps to counteract the **negative social identity** that they feel society has given them. In other words, **society** may see an individual as **inferior**, but **protest** and **politics** can give them the sense of being **just as good** as anyone else.

3) For example, LGBT (lesbian, gay, bisexual and transgender) people who feel oppressed by **homophobia** may gain a positive sense of identity by joining a **Gay Pride** group. **Black Power** creates a positive personal identity for black people who have felt oppressed by **racism**.

Some critics **question** the idea of shared experience. Not all women are the **same**, for example — a black woman may have a very different experience of society to a white woman, and a working class woman may have a different experience to a middle class woman. Commenting on **Betty Friedan's (1963)** statement that women should get out of the house and into the workplace, black feminist **bell hooks (1981)** pointed out that the **experience** of being a **stay-at-home housewife and mother** was pretty much limited to **white middle class women**. Black and working class women had been doing paid jobs for years.

It can be argued that identity politics **excludes** people who aren't part of the group, e.g. a lesbian activist group would exclude men. Identity politics can also **marginalise** groups — i.e. keep them **away** from **mainstream politics**.

Postmodernists say Identity Politics is more important than Party Politics

1) Postmodernists like **Lyotard (1984)** argue that people have lost faith in "metanarratives" (see p.141) and party politics.

2) Postmodernists such as **Nancy Fraser (1989)** say that political life has become de-centred — this means people's political goals reflect their personal and social identity, instead of an ideology that applies to all of society.

3) This process has been amplified by **globalisation** and **world travel**. People can consider themselves part of a global social group of say, women, or deaf people, or gay men, or Muslims.

1) **Stuart Hall (1992)** claims that identity is **fragmented**. According to Hall, people no longer have a **single identity** linked to a class or ideology. Instead they possess a **number** of sometimes **contradictory** identities, which he calls "**fragmented identity**".

2) Hall suggests that the increase in number of **New Social Movements** concerned with a huge number of **identities** and **issues** (e.g. feminism, ethnic minority issues, national liberation, environmental concerns, sexuality) have helped to **fragment** people's identity. An individual could be a **Green**, **Welsh Nationalist**, **lesbian feminist** and sometimes identify as **Welsh Nationalist**, other times as **Green**, etc.

Protest and Identity

Globalisation has been a factor in the growth of Identity Politics

Improved communications and world travel have given people a much broader base to draw on for the construction of their identity. **Stuart Hall (1992) suggests** that this has had an impact on **national identity** in the postmodern era. He argues that it's now more difficult for nations to create **unity** amongst their citizens using the idea of national identity.

Hall identified **three ways** in which people had responded to these trends:

Reaffirming	Some have seen globalisation as a **threat to national identity** and have aggressively **reaffirmed** the old identity. This can be seen in **far right** reactions to **immigration** and **asylum** in the UK.
Defending	**Ethnic minorities** have also felt threatened by globalisation and have constructed **counter defensive** identities based on their **cultures of origin** — e.g. Rastafarianism.
Constructing	Some groups have reacted to globalisation by constructing new **hybrid identities** — e.g. the construction of **Black British** and **British Asian** identities for Black and Asian communities in the UK.

Hall concludes that people increasingly no longer define themselves by either nation or class — hence the growth in "new politics" and decline in "old politics".

Globalisation has resulted in **uncertainty** and **diversity**. A side effect has been the attempt to achieve a more **stable identity** by placing greater emphasis on **ethnicity**. Hall gives examples of **ethnic conflict** in the **former Yugoslavia** as an example of this trend — different groups **demanded statehood** on the grounds of **ethnicity**, and sought to maintain **ethnic homogeneity** within their territories.

Class based "Old Politics" may Not be Quite Dead Yet

So, not the last resting place of party politics after all...

1) Despite massive interest in the growth of **New Social Movements** (NSMs), **protest**, and **Identity Politics** in the last thirty years, it would be **inaccurate** to suggest that the **old politics** represented by the political parties and pressure groups is **dead and buried**.

2) It's true that some rather high profile NSMs have been able to exert significant pressure on governments, e.g. **environmentalism**, but many NSMs have had limited success.

3) It would also be easy to exaggerate the importance and growth of NSMs. Whilst **most** people **know about NSMs**, very **few** are active **participants** in them. NSMs have recruited well amongst the educated young middle class but they haven't shown evidence of a more broad-based appeal.

4) People may grumble about party politics, but most people still go out and vote.

Some social movements try to get particular social groups to participate in mainstream politics.

1) The **women's suffrage** movement campaigned to get women the vote in the early 20th century.

2) The **Civil Rights** movement in America fought for black people's rights, and actively encouraged black people to register to vote.

3) There are campaigns to increase the number of **women in Parliament**. **Emily's List** was launched in 1993 to raise money to help **women in the Labour Party** stand as MPs. The Labour Party has enforced **all women shortlists** of candidates for some constituencies to make sure their candidate will be a woman. Some feminists find this **patronising**.

These groups aren't about identity, they're about equality.

Practice Questions

Q1 What's the difference between personal and social identity?

Q2 Describe three ways people may create their identity through protest and political activity.

Q3 What is Identity Politics?

Q4 What contribution has globalisation played in the development of identity politics?

Exam Question

Q1 Outline and assess the view that falling voter turnout in elections is evidence of the decline of class based politics and the emergence of identity politics.

(60 marks)

She's the only Green Welsh Nationalist Lesbian Feminist in the village...

This identity stuff's a bit complicated. I guess you could sum it up by saying that some people define themselves by what they're protesting about, and the group they protest with. Some criticise identity politics and say it creates inward-looking groups who exclude outsiders. Supporters of identity politics say it gives people a sense of power. I say just learn it.

Theories of Religion

*Sociologists disagree about religion. Some think it's great and stops society descending into chaos, others think it's just there to oppress people. God doesn't seem to have much to do with it. This section is for **AQA**. OCR folks have covered it at AS.*

Marx said Religion helps to Oppress Workers and Inhibits Social Change

1) Karl Marx said that in **capitalist** society there was a **conflict of interests** between the **ruling class** and the **working class** because the ruling class **exploit** the working class to get the most profit out of them.

2) But — there's **something stopping** the working class from **uniting** and **overthrowing** the ruling class. Marx says the working class are in a state of **false consciousness**. This means they're **not aware** of **how unfair** society is.

3) This is where **religion** comes in. Marx is **very critical** of religion. He says it **keeps** the working class in a state of **false consciousness**. He said, "**Religion is the opium of the people**". This means that it **dulls the pain** of oppression like **opium** — a **drug** which kills pain. It doesn't take the oppression away, though.

> ### Marx said that religion justifies social inequality
>
> 1) People have **the afterlife** to **look forward** to if they're **good**, so they **don't break the rules** and don't challenge the capitalist system.
>
> 2) Religion **consoles** people with the **promise of life after death** and so they **put up** with their **suffering** here **on Earth** more easily.
>
> 3) Religion often tells people that their **position is decided by God**. This encourages false consciousness by blaming God instead of **blaming capitalism**.
>
> 4) If **God is all powerful** he could **do something** about the suffering **if he wanted to**. He **doesn't** do anything — so people think this must be **how society is meant to be**.

Marxism says that religion **passes on beliefs** that **oppress the working class**. It argues that religion is a **conservative** force which prevents revolution — it keeps things the same. The **rich stay rich** and the **poor** keep on working. It's a **neat social control**.

But... there are problems with applying this Marxist view to today's society. **Fewer people go to a place of worship** than in the past — if people **don't go to worship**, it's **hard** for them to be duped by formal religious ideology. Also, religion can bring about **change**, but Marxists tend to ignore this.

Functionalists see religion as Maintaining Harmony and Social Cohesion

Functionalists also see religion as something that **inhibits change** and helps **keep society as it is**. But they think this is a positive role, which creates **social order** based on **value consensus**.

1) **Durkheim** studied **Aboriginal** society and found that the **sacred worship of totems** was equivalent to **worshipping society itself**. Durkheim said that sacred religious worship encourages shared values.

2) **Malinowski (1954)** looked at how religion deals with situations of **emotional stress** that **threaten social order**. Unpredictable or stressful events like births and deaths create **disruption**. Religion **manages these tensions** and recreates stability.

Religions have ceremonies for dealing with birth and death.

3) **Parsons** wrote in the 1930s and 1940s that religion provides **guidelines** for human action in terms of "**core values**". Religion helps to **integrate** people into a value consensus and allows them to **make sense of their lives**.

4) Functionalist **Bellah (1967)** suggested the idea of **Civil Religion**, which is when secular (non-religious) symbols and rituals create **social cohesion** in a similar way to religion. **Flags**, famous **political figures** and even **royal deaths** bring about some kind of **collective feeling** that generates **order** and **stability**.

> Functionalism ignores **dysfunctional** aspects of religion. There are **religious conflicts** all over the world. Religion can be a source of **oppression**. Religion can also bring about **change**, and Functionalism ignores that as well.

But in some cases Religion can Encourage Social Change

1) Marx's good pal **Engels** reckoned that in **some circumstances** religion could actually be a **revolutionary** force. Sometimes **religion** is the **only means of change** because all other routes have been blocked.

2) **Early Christian sects** opposed Roman rule and brought about change. **Jesus** himself encouraged social change.

3) In the 1960s and 1970s, **Catholic priests** in **Latin America** criticised the bourgeoisie and preached **liberation theology** — using religion to free people from oppression. This led to **resistance** and **social change** — in 1979, revolutionaries threw out the oppressive government in **Nicaragua**. Neo-Marxist **Otto Maduro (1982)** studied liberation theology. He said religion is "often one of the main available channels to bring about a social revolution".

4) Reverend **Martin Luther King** and the **Southern Baptist Church** resisted oppression and segregation, bringing about **political** and **social rights** for black people in **1960s America**.

5) In Iran, **Islamic fundamentalism** encouraged **social change**. In 1979, there was a **revolution** against the Shah, led by followers of the Shia ayatollah **Ruhollah Khomeini**. Khomeini set up a **religious government** that followed Sharia law.

Theories of Religion

Weber said that Religion can Create a Capitalist Work Ethic

Weber's book *The Protestant Work Ethic and Spirit of Capitalism* looked at how the **religious** ideas of **Calvinism** brought about social change. Weber spotted **two important things** in Calvinism:

1) **Predestination**: This is the idea that your **life** and whether you're going to heaven are **predetermined** by **God**. Calvinists believed only a **few** were **chosen** for heaven. This created **anxiety** — no one knew if they were chosen.

2) **Ascetic Ideal**: **Working hard** in your job was a **solution** to this anxiety. Success might be a sign that you were chosen for heaven. Early Calvinists lived a **strict** and **disciplined** life of hard work and simple pleasures.

Weber claimed that the ascetic ideal helped create an ethic of **disciplined hard work**. This is the **spirit of capitalism**. Not only was there a build-up of **capital**, there was the right **work ethic** for capitalism. Religion **indirectly** brought about change.

However — **Eisenstadt (1967)** contradicts Weber's theory by claiming that capitalism occurred in **Catholic** countries like Italy **before** the **Protestant Reformation happened** and before the ideas of **Calvin ever came out**.

Feminists point out the Sexism in Religion

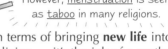
However, menstruation is seen as taboo in many religions.

1) Women's capacity to **have babies** gives women an **important role** within religion, in terms of bringing **new life** into the world. Women's role as **primary caregiver** is seen as **important** by traditional religion — it's the job of a mother to raise her children to **believe in God** and worship God. Feminists say this **traps** women in **traditional** roles.

2) Because women are **sexually attractive** to men they're perceived to be **distractions** from worship. Many religions believe in giving worship to God through a denial of sexuality (e.g. priests in the Roman Catholic Church have to be **celibate**). Religions have historically seen women as "**temptresses**" of men — think of Eve and the apple.

3) Women are **excluded from power** in many religious organisations.

4) Feminists argue that religious texts **transmit messages** to readers through stories that reflect and uphold a **patriarchal** society. This patriarchal ideology says that women are part of the profane and imperfect, and maintains **conformity** and the **submission** of women.

   profane = opposite of sacred or holy

5) **Simone de Beauvoir (1953)** saw religion as **exploitative** and **oppressive** towards women. She thought that religion promotes the idea that if women **suffer** in their present lives, then they'll receive **equality in heaven**, which allows women to **put up with** being treated as **inferior** to men in the hope of gaining in the afterlife. Spot the **similarity** to **Marx's** ideas on religion — just swap "women" for "working class" and you're there.

There are Problems with Feminist Anti-Religious Views

1) Women are not necessarily **passive victims** of religious oppression. Women may **actively resist** oppression — e.g. in **Afghanistan** under the Taliban it was forbidden for girls to go to school, so women educated girls in secret.

2) Religion **isn't necessarily patriarchal**. For example, **veiling** can have **positive functions** for Muslim women. The veil can **affirm Muslim identity** and **protect** women from sexual harassment in public.

3) Patriarchy within a society may be transmitted by other social and cultural activities, not by religion.

For Postmodernists there's No Universality in religion

Lyotard (1984) discarded all **metanarratives** (stories about how the world is and should be) **including religion**.

Postmodernists **reject universal truths**, and the postmodernist view of religion favours a **pick and mix** approach to belief.

Practice Questions

Q1 In what ways does Marx say religion justifies social inequality?

Q2 What is the role of religion, according to Functionalists?

Q3 What two aspects of Calvinism favoured a strong work ethic, according to Weber?

Q4 Give three examples of feminist views of sexism in religion.

Exam Question

Q1 Evaluate the view that there is sexism in religion. (40 marks)

The function of religion is to give you someone to pray to before exams...

There's an awful lot to learn here, I'll be honest. To make it easy on yourself, take each kind of theory individually. Once you've read it through, what Marxists and Functionalists think about religion ought to be no big surprise. The next step is to learn the key names and studies. Cover up each subsection and work on it until you can remember the names and ideas.

Religious Organisations

Religious groups organise themselves into different forms. They differ in leadership, relationship to the state and politics, how they worship and who they appeal to. Sociologists have put forward different classifications of religious organisations.

A *Church* is a *Well Established Religious Organisation*

Social historian **Ernst Troeltsch (1912)** distinguished between different kinds of religious organisation, and used the word **church** to mean a **large religious organisation**. He said churches usually have four main features:

1) A church claims **monopoly over the truth** — it says its claims are **absolutely true** and others are **false**.
2) Churches have a **complex rigid hierarchy** and a **bureaucratic structure** with lots of **rules and regulations**.
3) Churches often have a **close relationship** to the **State**. Some nations have an official national religion — Weber used the term "**ecclesia**" for this.
4) Churches are closely integrated into **mainstream society**. Churches act as a **conservative** force, resisting change. This is why the **upper classes** are more likely to join — even though churches are **universal** and **inclusive in principle**.

Examples of churches include the **Roman Catholic Church**, the **Church of England** or the **Episcopalian Church**.

Troeltsch studied churches in **16th century** Europe. **Steve Bruce (1995)** says that Troeltsch's points don't always apply to churches any more because there's **religious pluralism** these days. The Church of England doesn't claim a monopoly over the truth and it isn't always conservative.

Religious pluralism = lots of different types of religious groups.

Sects *are* Small, Radical Religious Movements

Troeltsch defined sects as being almost the **opposite of churches**. Few religious groups fall into the category of sect.

People who are **dissatisfied** with mainstream religion can be attracted to a sect. Sects are often formed by people **splitting off from a church** because they **disagree** with the church's **practices** or **theology**.

1) Sects claim a **monopoly over the truth** and are intolerant towards other religious organisations.
2) Sects have **no complex hierarchy**. They often have a **charismatic leader** who **persuades** members to **follow his / her teaching**.
3) Sects are **small**. Their members follow with **total commitment**, and they can be **manipulated** by the sect's leader.
4) Sects are separate from the state — they're in **opposition** to mainstream society. Sects can sometimes offer an alternative way of life for **deprived** and **marginal** groups.

Examples of sects include **early Methodists** and **Calvinists** (although over time these have become more mainstream). This category also includes **extremist** groups like the **People's Temple** in America who were led to mass suicide by Jim Jones, or the **Branch Davidians** led by David Koresh.

These extremist groups are generally called cults in everyday language.
Watch out though — in sociology, cult means something else (see below).

Denominations *are* Subsets of *Churches*

Troeltsch **originally classified** religious organisations into **churches** and **sects**.
The term "**denomination**" was added later.

1) Denominations don't usually claim **a monopoly over the truth**. They see themselves as a **possible route to the truth**. They are **tolerant** towards other religious organisations.
2) Like a church, they have a **hierarchy** and **bureaucratic structure** but it isn't as complex.
3) They have a reasonably **large membership**, but not as large as an established church.
4) Members of denominations are usually **not as loyal** as members of churches.
5) Denominations **aren't closely connected to the State** but they do get involved in society and **comment** on **current events**.

Examples of denominations are **modern Methodists** and **Baptists**.

This is only one definition — cults are sometimes defined as movements offering a 'new path to salvation'.

Cults *are* Mystic Movements

Bruce (1995) defined cults as movements without a fixed set of beliefs. They emphasise the **inner power** of the **individual** and **mysticism.** Cults are usually loosely knit and don't have a hierarchy.

Religious Organisations

New Religious Movements can be Affirming, Rejecting or Accommodating

The term **new religious movement** (or NRM for short) includes a **huge range of movements** from diverse sources. They've increased significantly since the 1960s. They don't always fit the old church-sect-denomination-cult divisions. Sociologist **Roy Wallis (1984)** identified three types of new religious movement:

World-rejecting movements cut themselves off from society — similar to sects

1) World-rejecting movements are very **critical** of wider society and are often in conflict with the State.
2) **The Unification Church**, better known as the 'Moonies', is one example of a world-rejecting movement.
3) World-rejecting movements require **total commitment**. They demand **significant lifestyle changes**. Members often turn away from family and friends — world-rejecting movements have developed a reputation for **"brainwashing"** members. It's often hard to leave a world-rejecting movement.

World-affirming movements are tolerant of other beliefs — similar to cults

1) They're similar to **self-help** and therapy groups — they try to **"unlock spiritual power"**. **Transcendental Meditation** is an example of a world-affirming movement.
2) World affirming movements seek **wide membership**.
3) World-affirming movements **don't require** especially high levels of **commitment**.

World-accommodating movements are traditionally religious — similar to denominations

1) World-accommodating movements often come from **traditional** religions.
2) They try to rediscover **spiritual purity** lost in traditional religions. **Pentecostalism** is a movement within Christianity that aims to bring the Holy Spirit back into worship.
3) World-accommodating movements allow people to carry on with their **existing lifestyle**.

These terms tend to be used differently by different people — they aren't clear-cut definitions.

New Age Movements are a type of New Religious Movement

1) **New Age Movements** are close to cults and world affirming movements. New Age ideas often aren't linked to an organisation, but spread through a culture. Examples include **dowsing**, **feng shui**, **crystals, neo-paganism** and **Reiki**.
2) **Heelas (1996)** claims that New Age beliefs are dedicated to **"self-spirituality"** and the development of the self.
3) **Bruce (1995)** highlights **three themes** to New Age Movements: **New Science** rejects many claims of traditional science, **New Ecology** is concerned for the environment and **New Psychology** sees the self as sacred.
4) New Age appeals to **women** more than men and **middle class** more than working class.

Millenarian Movements believe in Salvation through a Cataclysmic Event

Millenarian movements claim that members will achieve **salvation** through a **cataclysmic** event — a major disaster. Millenarianism is connected to **apocalypticism** which believes that **divine forces** will **overthrow** the existing social order.

Millenarian movements are associated with **deprived groups** or areas where there has been **radical social change**.

Practice Questions

Q1 Give two characteristics of a church.
Q2 Give two characteristics of a sect.
Q3 Name the three kinds of NRM identified by Wallis, and give an example of each.
Q4 What are the three New Age themes identified by Bruce?

Exam Question

Q1 Identify and explain three differences between churches and sects. (8 marks)

Not just a building with a steeple, then...

Classifying religious organisations is really hard. Some religious groups don't fit easily into these categories — or they might fit into more than one category. Another thing to watch out for is that Sociologists sometimes disagree about how to define terms, especially "cult" and "NRM". Learn the definitions on these pages — but remember that you might come across alternatives.

Religious Organisations

People join religious organisations for different reasons. Lots of them probably believe in God, but they do so in different ways.

The **Growth** of **New Religious Movements** isn't easy to explain

The **interactionist** (also known as **interpretivist**) idea is that **new religious movements (NRMs)** provide **certainty** in times of **uncertainty**. When there's uncertainty, new religious movements have **greater appeal** and **grow** in numbers. **Weber** set out three kinds of **uncertainties** that cause people to turn to religion:

1) **Marginality** — inequality, immigration and racism may **marginalise** some groups. So, some new religious movements may help marginalised people **make sense** of their situation, and may promise a better life after death as **compensation**. Theologians call this the "**theodicy of disprivilege**".

2) **Relative deprivation** — the concept of marginality doesn't explain why **white, middle class groups** join new religious movements. According to **Glock and Stark (1965)**, some middle class people may see themselves as **deprived in comparison to their peers**, though they aren't absolutely deprived.

3) **Social change** — transformation of society can result in **uncertainty** and **anomie** (a state of moral confusion in society caused by an absence of shared norms and values). The breakdown of **community**, the process of **secularisation** (see p.26), **cultural diversity** and bad news such as **terrorist attacks** may generate uncertainty.

Modernity and postmodernity create uncertainty. Some sociologists believe industrialisation causes **alienation**, increased bureaucracy and disillusion with work, which creates **uncertainty**. Postmodernity and the choice people have in constructing their identity may create **uncertainty** and a **crisis of identity**.

Melton (1993) didn't agree that NRMs emerged in periods of uncertainty. He looked at the founding dates of non-conventional religious organisations in the US. **Rapid growth** took place in the **1950s** — in a period of **stability** and **certainty**. Why do these sociologists never agree...

Wallis (1984) Explains the **Appeal** of the **Three Kinds** of **NRM**

1) **World-rejecting movements** grew in numbers in the 1960s. There was a lot of **freedom** for people, but also **uncertainty**. It was a period of **radicalism** with lots of alternative world views — often called the "sixties counter-culture". Wallis argues that some people got **disillusioned** with this counter-culture and wanted more **concrete** beliefs.

2) Wallis claimed that **world-affirming movements** develop as a means of coping with a **crisis of identity** in more successful groups (e.g. the middle class). They try to unlock **human potential** and help people solve their problems. **Bruce (1995)** claims that they're a response to the **rationalisation** of the modern world where it's hard to find satisfaction from work.

3) **World-accommodating movements** appeal to those who are dissatisfied with existing religion, but still maintain similar beliefs and disciplines.

Some people find uniformity strangely comforting...

New Age Movements appeal to people already **Examining** their ~~Navels~~ Identity

1) New Age beliefs appeal to people who have **turned away from traditional religion**. New Age beliefs say that people can find salvation, peace or perfection **inside themselves**. They often appeal to **middle class** people working in "**expressive professions**" — actors, writers, social workers, counsellors, therapists etc.

2) New Age Movements help some people cope with the **uncertainties** of modernity. In the modern world, people have a lot of **different roles**. New Age beliefs can help people find a sense of **identity**.

3) New Age movements may also reflect a **cultural change** in mainstream society. People are surrounded by non-conventional religious ideas like horoscopes, feng shui and self-help books. **Mass communication** gives us an awareness of different movements. In a **postmodern** society of **choice** and **diversity**, people can **pick and mix** from all kinds of New Age philosophies to help them construct their own identity.

Some Religious Movements attract people who **Desire Social Change**

1) Sects and denominations often attract people who want **social change**. People **turn away** from the **established church** because they feel it isn't acting in their **interests**.

2) This doesn't always have the intended aim. **Halevy (1927)** claimed that **Methodism** prevented revolution in the 19th Century. Dissatisfied workers turned away from the established state church to find enlightenment with the Methodists. Although they **changed religion**, they **kept on working**.

Religious Organisations

Niebuhr believed Sects were Shortlived

Niebuhr (1929) argued that sects wouldn't survive beyond one generation.
They'd either mellow into denominations, or disappear completely.

1) Sects rely on a **charismatic leader**. If the leader **dies**, the group can often no longer hold itself together.

2) A problem arises when the **second generation** are born into a new sect. They didn't decide to join the sect so they sometimes don't follow with the same religious fervour.

3) Some people join only in times of crisis and leave when the crisis is over. If a sect **demands change** in society and the change actually comes about, the sect **isn't needed any more**.

4) It's difficult to **maintain extreme teachings** and **totally reject society**. A sect can survive if its ideologies become **less rejecting** and **more accommodating**. Sects can eventually become **denominations.**

> The Methodists are a good example of this. As the Methodist movement became **upwardly mobile** in the **19th century**, its members **modified their beliefs** in order to make them more **socially acceptable**. The strict **disciplines** of the sect were **relaxed**, and it gradually became a **denomination**.

Some sects **deliberately destroy themselves** — e.g. Jim Jones' People's Temple, and the Heaven's Gate sect.

Others are **destroyed by society** and law-enforcement agencies — e.g. David Koresh's Branch Davidian sect.

Modern culture is fast-changing anyway — sects aren't immune from the tendency to be easy-come, easy-go.

Wilson argued that Some Sects could survive as Sects

1) **Wilson (1970)** argued that **conversionist** sects (e.g. evangelical sects) are the most likely to **develop into denominations**. They can still convert people and "save souls" whether they're a sect or denomination.

2) Wilson classified **Introversionist** sects as separate from the world, and claimed they therefore can't become denominations. The Amish, Shakers and Mennonites are Christian introversionist sects. Amish and Mennonites have a fairly high degree of second generation retention. Shakers, on the other hand, are celibate, so need to attract new believers or risk dying out as Niebuhr predicted.

3) **Adventist** sects are classified by Wilson as waiting for the **end of the world**, or the **second coming of Christ**. The whole point of adventist sects is to separate from the world in preparation for the end, so becoming a denomination is not an option.

> **Wallis (1984)** thought that a **world-affirming sect** could survive by changing its emphasis, in order to **maximise** its **appeal**. For example, the **Transcendental Meditation** (TM) sect started out as very **spiritual**, then identified with **1960s counterculture** (the Beatles were visitors to the TM ashram in India). In the 1970s, TM aimed to sell itself to new believers on the strength of **material gains** that it claimed could be had via meditation.
>
> World-affirming movements like TM can change quite easily. They can also develop a small **core** of **committed** believers, almost like world-rejecting movements.

Practice Questions

Q1 Give three sources of uncertainty which cause people to turn to religion.

Q2 Which kind of NRM appeals to successful people undergoing a crisis of identity?

Q3 Give three reasons that Niebuhr suggests for sects disappearing after one generation.

Q4 Which kind of sects are most likely to turn into a denomination, according to Wilson?

Exam Question

Q1   Assess the view that sects and cults are short-lived.   (40 marks)

Lots of religions don't condone sects before marriage...

Different religious movements are always going to appeal to different people. I mean, a middle aged Protestant looking for a more exciting church is probably going to go for something different than a tofu-eating reflexologist looking for something to bring out their inner goddess. Sects and cults tend to market themselves, and even change their beliefs to appeal to more "customers".

Religion and Social Groups

Gender, age and ethnicity are all factors affecting religious participation levels. You're least likely to participate if you're a young, white, working class male, and most likely if you're an elderly, Asian, middle class female. But it's really up to you.

Religious Participation varies by Age

Age affects how religious people are.

1) People **under 15** and **over 65** are more likely to be involved in religious activity. However, participation by those under 15 usually takes the form of **Sunday school** and **religious playgroups**.

2) The **over 65** group is the **most religious** in terms of **belief**. They aren't necessarily the most likely to practice their religion by going to church, because of difficulty with mobility.

3) However, some recent studies claim that the **elderly** are **increasingly losing faith** in God.

4) **Middle aged** groups are more likely to get involved in **world-affirming movements**.

5) **Sects** and **cults** are more likely to be populated with **young adults**.

- **Sects** often appeal to young adults by messages of **friendship** and **companionship** — this can be attractive to those who are experiencing forms of **anomie** (lack of social/moral standards) and **detachment** from the world, and those who have few responsibilities (e.g. marriage).

- **Cults** appeal to the **inner thoughts** and **feelings** of young adults who are often alienated from the primary cultures of society. **Cults** are attractive to individuals who are often already engaging in **counter culture** activity.

6) Young adults may be less religious than older people because of the way that society is changing. An increase in **rationalisation** means there's less **need** for religion to explain things.

This is linked to secularisation — see p.26-27

Religious Participation varies by Gender

1) **Women** are **more likely to attend church**, and more likely to say they belong to a religion (British Social Attitudes Survey, 1991). This has traditionally been explained by women's traditional role as **primary caregiver**. Going to **church** and **raising children** to be **religious** is traditionally seen as an **extension** of that role.

2) **Differential socialisation** is also a factor. The argument goes that girls are socialised to be **passive** and to **conform** — which fits in with the behaviour of more **traditional** and **conservative** religious groups.

3) Another argument is that **women** simply **live longer**. More women are on their **own** as they get older, and they may **turn to religion** for a sense of community. **Older** people are **more religious anyway**.

4) More **men** than **women** have **turned away** from organised religion in the 20th century.

Remember **de Beauvoir's ideas** about a **theodicy of disprivilege** that applies to **women** — women suffer in the here and now, and believe they'll get their **reward in heaven**. This can be used to explain women being more religious than men.

Women often have Significant roles in New Religious Movements (NRMs)

1) Women generally **participate** in **sects** more than men.

2) Also, many sects and NRMS were **established** by **women**, e.g. the Seventh Day Adventists were founded by Ellen White, and the Christian Science movement was founded by Mary Barker Eddy.

3) **Glock and Stark (1965)** have argued that the gender difference in membership of NRMs is because **deprivation** (social, physical and mental) is **disproportionately** experienced by **women**.

4) **Bruce (1995)** suggests that men are interested in NRMs that advocate **esoteric knowledge**, whereas women are interested in subjects that can be classified as **New Science**, **New Ecology** and **New Spirituality**.

5) Some sociologists claim that New Age movements appeal to women, because they emphasise "feminine" characteristics such as healing, caring and cooperation.

The Nation of Islam is a religious and political organisation founded in the USA in the 1930s.

Remember, some NRMs have **narrow beliefs** about **women's role** in society, and therefore may **not appeal** to women. Some new evangelical right wing Christian movements believe that women should not work outside the home. This view is shared by the Nation of Islam.

Religion and Social Groups

Religious Participation Varies by Ethnicity

The 1994 PSI Fourth Survey of Ethnic minorities (**Tariq Modood et al,** published **1997**) found that, in England and Wales, **ethnic minority groups** are **more religious** and participate more in religion than white groups.

1) Religion maintains a sense of **community** and **cultural identity** within ethnic minority groups.

2) **Johal (1998)** claims that in a multi-faith society such as the UK, **religious identity** has become of key importance to members of ethnic minorities.

3) **Davie (1994)** argued that identification with a **religious organisation** was important to Indians, Pakistanis and Bangladeshis in the UK because it gave a sense of cultural identity and a feeling of **belonging**.

- **Modood** found that Pakistani and Bangladeshi Muslims in the UK identified themselves primarily as **Muslim**.
  i.e. rather than British, Pakistani, or Bangladeshi
- Many young Muslims have a deeper **knowledge of Islam** than their **parents** do.
- Many Muslim girls feel more **liberated** by wearing headscarfs and dressing modestly because they are not subjected to the same **stereotypes** and values as non-Muslim girls.

4) Afro-Caribbean identity is largely based on **ethnicity** rather than religion. However, the Rastafarian movement is a religious and political movement in which black identity is key — it's based around resistance to racism.

1) **Afro-Caribbeans**, who are mainly Christian, attempted to incorporate themselves into the established churches of the UK but found **racism** within many congregations. One way to tackle this was to develop their own churches and ways of worshipping — e.g. Pentecostal churches.

2) **South Asians**, however, had to establish their faith in a country with **radically different** systems of belief. Religion acted as a **support mechanism** for new immigrants, allowing them to share their culture. South Asians **quickly established** religious organisations — mosques, Sikh gurdwaras, etc. **Bruce (2002)** calls this **Cultural Transition**.

Modood (1994) and **Saeed (1999)** found some evidence for a decline in religious practice among Asians in the UK.

Religious Participation Varies by Class

1) The **middle class** is disproportionately **Anglican** and **Quaker** compared with a more **Roman Catholic** or **Methodist** working class (this can be partly explained due to their popularity in Victorian industrial areas). These results can be seen across many countries such as the U.S. and this would seem to back up Marx and Weber's opinions on Protestantism and capitalism.

2) Religious participation is greater in the **middle classes**, partly because religious affiliation is seen as a **desirable** social characteristic. Church is an opportunity for **social networking**.

3) Some argue that participation in **denominations** and **sects** is based on **class position**, claiming that there are middle class denominations and working class denominations.

4) **Bruce (1995)** found that cults are primarily middle class — in his opinion because they fulfil spiritual needs for people who have little financial pressure.

Practice Questions

Q1 Why do young adults participate more in sects and cults?
Q2 What role does religion play in upholding patriarchy according to feminists?
Q3 Why do middle class people participate more in cults?

Exam Questions

Q1 What are the arguments for and against the view that women are oppressed by religion? (12 marks)

Q2 Critically evaluate the argument that religion continues to have an important role in the lives of ethnic minorities in the UK today. (40 marks)

"Ah no, this is the women's church. Men's church is next door"...

Well, obviously it's not quite like that. The examiners will expect you to know how religion relates to age, gender, ethnicity and class, and also how religious participation relates to those things. You should mention a few studies too — no, don't kid yourself that you can remember them all — what did Glock and Stark argue? What was Johal's study about? Davie's? Saeed's? Ha!

Secularisation

There's an argument among sociologists about whether the world (and the UK) is getting less religious, or not.

Secularisation is when Religion Loses Its Influence over society

Bryan Wilson (1966) defined secularisation as a **"process whereby religion loses its influence over the various spheres of social life"**. Secularisation is said to be a result of the social changes brought about by **modern, urban, industrial society**.

1) **August Comte** claimed that **science** was the **final stage** in the **development of human thought**.
He said modern society would be dominated by **science** and not religion.

2) **Max Weber** believed that **modern society** would be the age of **technology**, **rationality** and **bureaucracy**.
He said rationality and efficiency **sweeps away magic**, **myth** and **tradition**.

Church Attendance and Membership is in Decline

Source: UK Christian Handbook:
Religious Trends 1988/99

Counting bums on pews gives **supporting evidence for secularisation**:

1) **UK church membership** and **attendance** has gone down —
attendance has fallen by almost 1 million in the last 20 years.

2) Attendance at ceremonies such as **baptisms** and **marriages** has
also dropped. **27%** of babies in the UK were baptised in 1993
compared to **65%** in 1900.

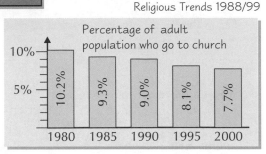

Measuring secularisation by counting **bums on pews** has **limitations**:

1) People may **attend church** but **not believe in God**. They might
attend a service, baptism or wedding out of friendship for the
people involved, for respectability or because of family duty. Or even to get their kids into a certain school.

2) **Davie (1994)** pointed out that people may **not attend church** because of their **lifestyle** but they do still believe in
God. The 2001 Census found that 72% of the population identified themselves as Christians. **Davie** claims that
belonging to a church and **believing** in religion have become increasingly **separated**.

3) To make comparisons with the past you have to use **old statistics**, which may not be reliable.

Pluralism gives people Choice

Religious pluralism is about **diversity** in types of religious organisations and beliefs in society.
As a result the **established, national church loses its influence** in integrating people into **shared values**.
Multi-cultural societies are more likely to have religious pluralism.

Some sociologists use pluralism as evidence against secularisation

1) The increase in **New Age movements** since the 1980s can be seen as evidence that
the **sacred** is becoming **important** again — this is called **resacrilisation**, by the way.

2) **Glock and Bellah (1976)** argue that pluralism is evidence of religion being **transformed**.
It shows a trend towards **individuation** — people being free to sample different belief
systems to find their **own religious meanings** (this is often called **"spiritual shopping"**).

Wilson and Bruce use pluralism as supporting evidence for secularisation

1) Pluralism gives people **choice**. People might feel freer to choose to **reject religion altogether**.

2) Although some people in modern society have joined **new religious movements**, they are still a **small
proportion** of the population. Some sociologists claim the **growth** in NRMs has been **overestimated**.

Desacrilisation is where Religion or Spirituality is Less of a Force in Society

1) Weber thought that magic and myth become less important in modern society. Similarly, **Bruce (1995)** sees **science**
and rationality as **undermining religion**. We demand pills when we're ill and use science to explain natural disasters.

2) **Berger and Luckman (1971)** claim that the supernatural or religion used to be necessary to **explain our problems**, but
we now see **science** as **more plausible**.

3) However, the **death** of a loved one, **injustice**, **natural disasters** and **terrorist atrocities** still sometimes lead people
to prayer and faith in the supernatural. Modern science **can't explain everything** to everyone's satisfaction.

4) **Postmodernists** claim that we've moved **beyond scientific** rationality and we now **mistrust science**.

5) Belief in **astrology** and **lucky charms** and **fanatical interest** in magical fantasy like **Harry Potter** and
Lord of the Rings demonstrates that people still have an interest in **magic**, **myth** and the **irrational**.

Secularisation

Some *Religious Institutions* have become *Secularised*

1) **Secularisation** of **religious institutions** is when the church becomes **less religious** in its beliefs to **fit in** with the rest of **society**. For example, many churches will now allow divorced people to marry.

2) American sociologist **Herberg (1956)** thinks church attendance shows **commitment to community** and not religion — people go to church to **meet up with friends** and feel like **part of something**.

3) Remember that **not all religious institutions** have become more **secular**. There is a trend towards **fundamentalism**. The **New Christian Right** in the USA are against divorce, homosexuality and pre-marital sex.

The *Church* may have *Lost Some Functions* and become *Disengaged*

Differentiation is where society becomes more specialised so each institution in society has fewer functions than in the past. For example, the church used to have an important educational function. But since the 19th century, more separate institutions have developed for this role and state involvement has increased.

According to **Bruce (1995)**, religion becomes **less important** in society as some of its previous functions are taken over. **Wilson** says that religion has little influence, and is only involved in symbolic "**hatching, matching and dispatching**" rites.

Disengagement is when the church is separated from the State.

1) According to Bruce, religion has **less influence** as a result.

2) **Parsons (1974)** claims that although the church may have lost its functions and become disengaged from the state and politics, religion can still be **significant in everyday life** and encourage **shared values** in society.

3) Religion is still closely linked to **politics** in the **Middle East** and **Northern Ireland**.

Secularisation is very *Difficult* to *Measure*

There's more about sociological research methods in Section 11.

1) There are lots of different **measures of secularisation**. Some are more valid and reliable than others. **Surveys** show **high levels of religiosity**, but **quantitative measurements** of **church attendance** are low. **Different religious groups** measure membership in **different ways**, anyhow.

2) The term **secularisation** is a general term that's sometimes applied just to Christianity. It's important to know **what's being measured** — the decline of **religion in general** or the decline in **Christianity** in particular.

3) It's difficult to measure and make comparisons because sociologists use **different definitions of religion**. Some sociologists use **substantive definitions** which say **what religion is** — e.g. "religion is belief in the sacred". Some sociologists use **functional definitions** saying **what religion is for** — e.g. "religion is for creating value consensus".

4) Functional, inclusive definitions of religion include a lot more institutions than the traditional religions. **Luckmann (1967)** claims that **Marxism** is a religion, because it's a human attempt to make sense of our place in the universe.

5) To measure whether society has become **more secular** you have to compare it to **the past**. Some sociologists argue that we tend to see the past as a **golden age** of religion where **everyone** believed — which is **far too simplified**.

6) Research into secularisation can also be rather **ethnocentric** — focusing on **Christianity** and what the **predominantly white British mainstream** does. Islam, Hinduism and Sikhism are also changing and developing in different ways.

Practice Questions

Q1 How did Bryan Wilson define secularisation?

Q2 How does religious pluralism support secularisation?

Q3 What is meant by desacrilisation?

Q4 Define the term disengagement.

Q5 Give one reason why it can be difficult to measure the importance of religion.

Exam Question

Q1 "The UK is now a secular society." Evaluate this view in the light of sociological argument and evidence. (40 marks)

So, science is the new God, and religion is just *so* last season...

Or maybe not. The sociologists just can't seem to agree. Fewer people are going to church, but that might not necessarily mean that they've stopped believing in God. And pluralism and NRMs — some sociologists use these as evidence in favour of secularisation, while others use them as evidence against. I think they all need to stop squabbling, apologise and shake hands.

Development and Underdevelopment

*This whole section is for **AQA**. Ignore it if you're studying OCR. There are different ways of defining and measuring development and underdevelopment, and tons of theories to explain why some countries are more developed than others.*

Development is **Defined** in **Different Ways**

1) Development is usually used to mean economic growth, industrialisation, and high living standards, e.g. high life expectancy and universal education. Countries which have achieved this are called **MEDCs** (More Economically Developed Countries). Countries which haven't are called **LEDCs** (Less Economically Developed Countries).

2) This definition is **ethnocentric**. It defines development in terms of "Western" ideals — which may not be 100% valid.

3) **Undeveloped** countries aren't developed **yet**. **Underdeveloped** countries haven't developed as much as other countries with the same resources.

> GNP = economic value of goods and services produced by a country over a year.

Development is **Measured** in **Different Ways**

1) Capitalists argue that **economic indicators** such as **Gross National Product** (**GNP**) are the only effective ways of defining a country's potential for developing (along capitalist lines).

2) However, GNP doesn't tell you how wealth is **distributed**. In a country with a high GNP per capita (per person) there may be a **minority** living in **deprivation**.

3) Economic indicators also ignore **externalities** caused by economic progress — e.g. pollution.

4) Some claim development is better measured by **social factors**. They measure development using **lists** of **basic human needs** — e.g. the Human Development Index (HDI), Human Poverty Index (HPI) and Personal Quality of Life Index (PQLI). Unlike economic indicators, these can show that there is deprivation even in "developed" countries.

All **Development Theories** have their foundations in **Marx**, **Durkheim** and **Weber**

1) **Marx** said that capitalism and industrialisation were about obtaining the **maximum** amount of **profit**. Capitalists in developed countries **exploit** underdeveloped countries to get **raw materials**, and to get a wide **market** for the goods produced by capitalism. Marx thought that capitalism would give way to **communism**.

2) **Durkheim** argued that societies would **progress** through **industrialisation** and that the most developed nations were those which had industrialised first. Durkheim saw the West as the most advanced society, and thought underdeveloped countries could improve their progression by taking on the **characteristics** of Western countries.

3) **Weber** argued that society was becoming more **rational** and **bureaucratic** — people needed to make more choices and come up with new, scientific ideas to solve social problems like deprivation. Less developed societies would need to copy Western **attitudes** in order to allow progress and economic development.

Modernisation Theory says countries **Progress** towards **Liberal Capitalism**

Modernisation theory says that **all countries** move **towards liberal capitalism**. **Undeveloped** countries are seen as **inferior** to **developed** countries that have achieved a higher rate of **production**, **consumption** and **wealth**.

Rostow (1971) suggested that all countries go through a five stage process of development:

1) Basic, **agricultural** society.

2) **Transition**, or preparing for "take off" — farmers produce a surplus and make money from selling cash crops. Small towns develop, and there's some industry on a very small scale.

3) **Industrialisation** or "take off" — rapid growth of manufacturing. People move from rural to urban areas.

4) **Drive to Maturity** — lots of investment, and the right social conditions for growth. Large cities develop.

5) **Mass consumption**, or "developed economy" — wealth spreads, people buy more and the service sector grows.

The explanation for poverty and underdevelopment is insufficient agricultural surplus to fund investment, insufficient investment in technology, and not enough hard working business people to create opportunities.

Kerr (1962) focused on **cultural factors** — he believed that countries need Western style politics and social values in order to develop, and they should replace traditional culture with Western values.

Neo-liberalism believes in using **Free Trade** to help countries **Develop**

1) Neo-liberalism says that government intervention **distorts** the natural economic processes of the **free market**.

2) Neo-liberals such as **Friedman (1962)** believe in using **free market trade** to help the development of countries. Neo-liberalism is favoured and pushed by the International Monetary Fund and the World Bank.

3) They point to **Newly Industrialised Countries** (NICs) such as the "**Tiger Economies**" to prove that removing tariffs (charges for importing and exporting) and encouraging free trade can lead to development. "Tiger Economies" are South East Asian Countries such as Singapore and Hong Kong that have experienced a period of growth over the last 20 years.

Development and Underdevelopment

Modernisation Theory and Neo-liberalism are both criticised

Both are criticised for being **ethnocentric** (arguing for the superiority of Western culture and industrialisation), and critics say this leads them to distort the true history of Western involvement in developing countries.

Neo-liberals and modernisation theorists also argue that Western methods of development are easily imitated and likely to succeed — which isn't necessarily true. In fact, the Tiger Economies got into serious economic trouble in 1997 after attempting to **extend too far** and **too fast**.

Dependency Theory says Developed countries Exploit Underdeveloped ones

1) **Dependency theory** was a reaction **against modernisation theory**. The key dependency theorist is **Frank (1967)**.

2) Dependency theory says that developed countries **exploited** underdeveloped nations during colonial times (esp. the 19th C.) when they controlled them as part of an **empire** (see p.30-31), and prevented them from industrialising.

3) When the underdeveloped nations got political independence, they were often still **economically dependent** upon their former imperial rulers. The poor nation's main trading partner is often its former colonial ruler.

4) The theory says richer developed nations organise trading relationships in their favour. They set the price for goods.

5) **Dependency theory** is Marxist — it argues that **workers** in the poorest nations are **exploited** by the **ruling class**. They're paid very low wages, so the profits from the goods they make and grow go to the ruling class. Developed nations pay a low market price for the goods, and sell the goods in the developed nation for a profit.

6) The theory goes on to say that profits pass from **workers** in **satellite areas** (less developed agricultural areas), to the **ruling class** in the **metropolis** (big cities — former outposts of colonial power), and out to the **developed nations**.

The theory doesn't fully define what development is or give realistic suggestions for how it can be resolved. It also doesn't explain why **socialism also exploited** and created dependency — e.g. the Eastern European satellite states depended on Russia. Dependency theory is criticised for being **deterministic** — it assumes that **everyone in LEDCs** will be **exploited**, and it doesn't accept that some LEDCs might **choose** capitalism, instead of being pushed into it.

World Systems theory says there's one global economy

1) **Wallerstein (1974)** suggested World Systems theory, which treats the entire world as one economy, rather than looking at development country by country. World Systems theory divides the world into **core** (developed countries), **semi-periphery** (e.g. South Africa, Mexico) and **periphery** (e.g. Ethiopia).

2) According to the theory, **core** countries make **full use** of the global economy, and can affect any other country — in other words, they have a global "**reach**". Core countries are the ones which get the most out of capitalism. The core takes up all the surplus profits generated by the whole world — periphery and semi-periphery countries.

3) World Systems theory says the **semi-periphery** countries are **exploited** by the core countries, but they also **exploit** the **periphery** countries. In the theory, because they exploit as well as being exploited, they aren't fully "on the same side" as the periphery countries — no unity amongst the exploited means no united action to change the system.

This theory is also criticised for being too **deterministic**. It doesn't allow for **individual countries' characteristics**, and it still holds up the **core countries** as the model for perfect development.

Practice Questions

Q1 What are the five stages of development according to Rostow?

Q2 What is the central idea of dependency theory?

Q3 What is World systems theory?

Exam Questions

Q1 Compare and contrast dependency theory and World systems theory as explanations of underdevelopment. (40 marks)

Q2 "Modernisation theory is the only accurate way of defining development".
Assess arguments for and against this view. (40 marks)

Singapore and Hong Kong have stripy economies that go 'RAAAR'...

And they go stalking through the jungle, swishing their tails... or they would, if they weren't just boring old economies. Quick point — don't use the terms "first world", "second world" and "third world" — the second world doesn't exist any more after the fall of Communism. Pages 30-31 will help with all this — they give some of the historical background to colonialism, and its effects on trade.

Relationships Between Societies

This fine pair of pages is about colonialism, international trade, and globalisation. Globalisation has economic, political and cultural aspects. No, don't switch off, this really isn't that boring. Honestly. Look, there's a photo of a burger and everything.

The **History** of **Colonialism** has shaped **International Trade Relations**

1) A colony is a territory that's **controlled** by a **foreign power**. Back in the 16th and 17th centuries, **European** countries began to **colonise Asian**, **African** and **American** territories. The height of colonialism was in the **19th century**.

2) European nations colonised foreign territories for three main reasons:

- Colonies were **economically important**. **Raw materials** and **food** were sourced in the colonies, and taken back to Western Europe to fuel **industrial-capitalist development**.
- Having **colonies** and building up an **empire** added to a nation's **power** and **influence** — the colonising country could put military bases and trading ports in the colony.
- Europeans also saw colonialism as a way of **"civilising"** native people. They saw traditional Asian, African and American cultures as **inferior**, and tried to **replace** them with Western values, including Christianity.

3) Colonialism strongly shaped **economic development** in the colonies. The colonisers set up plantations to grow **cash crops** such as coffee and cotton. They used slave labour and low-paid labour and sold the crops for high prices in the European market.

4) Former colonies are often **under-industrialised**, because they were used only for primary sector industries such as agriculture and mining. Former colonies didn't get the chance to develop **manufacturing** industry.

5) Former colonies which rely on **agricultural exports** are hit hard by **global recession** — when the **market price** of cash crops drops, their **national income drops**.

Globalisation has resulted in a **Global Economy** as well as **National Economies**

Giddens notes that **technological change** has transformed the way people live — global **communication** and **travel** are now easy. Goods can be **transported** across the world, and **information** can be transferred across the world **instantaneously**.

1) **Globalists** (sociologists who believe that society is becoming globalised) argue that **international trade** and investment have caused national economies to blend together into a **global economy**.

2) **Trans National Corporations** (**TNCs**) operate across national boundaries. They tend to have their headquarters in MEDCs and set up production in countries where there's **cheaper labour**, in order to maximise their profits.

3) **Fröbel et al (1980)** first referred to the **New International Division of Labour** — manufacturing tends to be done in developing countries, and knowledge-intensive work is done in MEDCs. **International division of labour** also means that **different stages of production** can be done in **different countries** — the car industry is a good example.

4) **TNCs** have a **positive** effect — they bring **jobs** and **investment** to developing countries, which can help with their national strategy for development. There's also a benefit for **international consumers** — cheap consumer goods.

5) However, some argue that this is a new form of **exploitation**. **Neo-Marxist** critics of globalisation say that the people of the developing world are turned into **"wage slaves"** for the capitalist system.

6) TNCs aim to create **global markets** for the goods they manufacture. They affect cultures throughout the world.

7) **TNCs** also have an effect on the **business culture** of host nations. TNCs can be categorised as three types — **ethnocentric** (headquarters in country of origin runs everything and sets corporate culture), **polycentric** (managed locally, according to guidelines set by headquarters) or **geocentric** (management is integrated across all countries).

Weberian sociologist Ritzer (1993) writes about global standardisation and "rationalisation".

1) He refers to a **"McDonaldisation"** of production across the world. He says products are made with the same values as a **fast food** outlet: the product is made in **assembly line** conditions, it must be **inexpensive** to make and must be **standardised** at all times, across all the countries where it's made and sold. A Big Mac is the same everywhere.

2) Ritzer picks out five themes within this McDonaldisation — **efficiency**, **calculability**, **predictability**, increased **control**, and the replacement of **human** workers by **machines**.

Sweet, juicy global standardisation.

There's also **Globalisation** in **Politics**

1) Politics is increasingly carried out on an **international** level, rather than a national level.

2) The United Nations is responsible for enforcing international law, and peacekeeping etc.

3) There's increased **international political cooperation** — e.g. the **European Union**.

4) **International** non-governmental organisations (**NGOs**) coordinate **aid** and **campaigning**.

Relationships Between Societies

Increased Communication spreads Cultural Goods across the world

1) The increase in **international media** communication in the last few decades has meant that cultures that were once local have become international and global. British and American pop music is everywhere. American and Indian films are seen internationally.

cultural goods = films, clothes, food, music, books etc.

2) Postmodernists argue that this allows people to consume a **plurality** of cultures. They think that globalisation leads to **hybridity** (a **pick and mix** of cultures) rather than one culture being imposed over another.

3) Critics point to the concentration of the **production** of cultural goods in the hands of a few large **TNCs** which have a lot of power in developing countries. They fear that TNCs will replace traditional culture with Western culture to try and **create new markets** for **Western cultural goods**. Critics refer to cultural globalisation as **cultural imperialism**.

4) Those who believe in the **positive** effects of cultural globalisation argue that it's a **two way process**. Western culture is transmitted to new societies, and other identities and cultures get passed on to societies in MEDCs. An example of this would be the increase in screenings of **Bollywood films** in Western mainstream cinemas.

Global Organisations are seen by some as More Powerful than Governments

1) TNCs operate in **many countries** — they have a global reach. Many are as powerful as nation states in economic terms, and some critics point to their perceived lack of respect for local cultures as a key feature of globalisation.

2) National governments often find it hard to **control** TNCs and are **reluctant** to act against the interest of the TNC. The host nation **risks losing large numbers of jobs** if the TNC decides to pack up and **move to another country**.

3) **International political agencies**, such as the **United Nations** and the **European Union (EU)**, have taken some power and decision-making away from national governments.

4) Critics claim that this means nation states lose the ability to **determine their own future**, as they must constantly **negotiate** with other governments and agencies to try and get the best policy for the nation.

Leslie Sklair (2000) sees globalisation as a form of **transnational capitalism** (capitalism which crosses national boundaries). He thinks it isn't worth analysing nation states — power is held by TNCs, bureaucrats and global media.

There's Evidence to say that the role of the Nation is still as Important as ever

1) **Realists** point out that **national interest** still determines **most policies** within a nation and in international negotiations. For example, the US refuses to sign up to the Kyoto Protocol (an international environmental strategy) **partly** because it's not in the interests of the US because of the potential effects on employment.

2) **Hall (1995)** argues that in a global world, **national identity** becomes very **important** to people as a way of ensuring there are still differences between the countries of the world. As a result, the nation state can be strengthened.

3) Increasing fears over the loss of power from national government to the EU has meant that many people in the UK are ever more determined to protect the **sovereignty** of the nation.

4) There's a trend towards **devolution** — i.e. giving power to local bodies, e.g. the Scottish Parliament and Welsh assembly. Nations **within** the UK have reasserted their identity and control over key issues and policies.

Practice Questions

Q1 Explain the three main reasons why European nations colonised foreign territories.

Q2 What is the New International Division of Labour?

Q3 What is "McDonaldisation"?

Q4 Why do critics of cultural globalisation refer to it as cultural imperialism?

Exam Questions

Q1 What are the arguments for and against the view that we live in a 'McWorld'? (12 marks)

Q2 Critically evaluate the argument that economic globalisation benefits less developed societies. (40 marks)

Q3 "Despite globalisation, identity, culture and power are held by local communities and nation states rather than international organisations and agencies." Explore the arguments for and against this statement. (40 marks)

So the world is turning into McDonald's? I reckon Ritzer was just hungry...

Hallucinations and bizarre fantasies are common during extreme hunger. But seriously, globalisation is a big thing in Sociology. Giddens is obsessed by it. It's a many armed beast, is globalisation. It's got cultural, technological, political and economic aspects. Pretty much everything we buy has some kind of global connection. Think of how much stuff has 'made in China' stamped on it.

Strategies for Development

There are different sociological perspectives on development strategies. And unfortunately, you have to know them all.

Aid can be given in Three Different Ways

1) **Bilateral Aid** is where a **government** (e.g. the UK) gives **direct financial support** to another **government** that needs help (e.g. Malawi).

2) **Multilateral Aid** is from **international bodies** such as UNESCO, the World Health Organisation, the International Monetary Fund (IMF) and the World Bank. Multilateral aid can be either **grants** or **loans**. The IMF and World Bank give **loans**, and charge **interest** on the loans.

3) **Non-Governmental Organisation** (NGO) give logistical support and direct financial donations. They get their money from the **public**. Examples of NGOs are Oxfam and Christian Aid.

The United Nations recommend rich countries should give 1% of their GDP in aid. In fact, very few developed countries meet the UN criteria. The UK gives around 0.4% of GDP.

Different Theories have Different Views of Aid

Modernisation theory says aid helps LEDCs "Westernise"

1) **Modernisation theory** believes that developed countries should give **aid** to countries that are prepared to accept Western styles of development, i.e. **industrial capitalism**.

2) Modernisation sees aid as having a **"trickle down effect"**. The argument is that aid goes to the elites of LEDCs, and the elite create wealth and prosperity. Associated factors such as **employment** and **increased standards of living** should **filter down** to **local economies** and **local people**.

3) Modernisation theorists were largely justified in the mid 20th century, as many poor countries (newly independent from colonialism) received aid and experienced **growth** and **success**. However, growth stalled later, and the poverty gap increased rather than decreased in some countries.

Neo-Marxist dependency theorists see aid as a tool to serve capitalism

1) Aid is often **tied** (given with conditions attached). A common condition is that local markets should be opened up to **free trade**, allowing foreign companies (including TNCs) to import and export goods without trade or customs levies. Neo-Marxists view this very **negatively**, believing that LEDCs are often exploited economically by TNCs.

2) **Bilateral aid** often requires the **recipient** nation to **buy goods** from the **donor** nation, or employ **technical experts** from the donor nation. These requirements help the **donor** nation.

3) Critics of Western aid such as **Teresa Hayter (1971, 1981, 1989)** see it as a tool for the richest countries to **politically influence** LEDCs. **Western** countries tended to give aid to countries with **right wing** governments rather than to countries with **socialist** or **communist** governments. This happened a lot during the Cold War.

4) To get a loan from the World Bank or IMF, LEDCs have often had to agree to make **political** and **economic changes** called **"Structural Adjustment Programmes"**. These are often **industrial-capitalist** in nature (e.g. privatisation of state run services). Evidence shows that some of these programmes **haven't succeeded** in developing poor nations.

New Right theory says that aid creates dependency

1) **New Right theorists** generally don't believe in giving anyone "something for nothing". They argue that aid teaches LEDCs to be **dependent** on MEDCs, rather than standing on their own two feet. They say that LEDCs start to see aid as a right, rather than as a safety net, or last resort.

2) **Neo-liberals** believe that aid mucks about with the proper operation of the **free market** — they think that the free market is the best way of encouraging development, through **enterprise** and **investment**.

International Trade and TNCs can help Development

A recent view is that **trade** is more productive in development strategies than **aid**. This view is influenced by the New Right.

Not all trade-based strategies are New Right theorists, though — e.g. the **fair trade movement** aims to **insulate** agricultural workers in developing countries from the **ups and downs** of the world market. Fair trade businesses pay farmers a fixed **"fair"** price for their crops, whatever the global market price is. Neo-liberals claim that fair trade is just **aid under another name**, and say that **subsidies** don't encourage producers to be efficient and enterprising. They'd rather leave it to the free market.

1) TNCs can have both **positive** and **negative** impacts on development in LEDCs and NICs. They **provide investment** to developing countries, which can help with their own national strategy for development. They also provide **jobs**, which increases the host nation's **wealth**. Workers in the host nation have increased **spending power**.

2) TNCs can cause **rapid economic growth** which can be **too fast** for a host nation's **infrastructure** to cope with.

3) Those who define development in quality of life terms are concerned about **working conditions** in TNC factories.

Strategies for Development

NGOs and Charities mainly provide Emergency Aid

1) **NGOs** and **charities** such as Oxfam, Save the Children and the Red Cross/Red Crescent mainly respond to **emergencies** — e.g. the 1984 **famine** in Ethiopia, the crisis in the Darfur region of Sudan and the 2004 **tsunami** in South East Asia.

2) **Disaster and emergency relief** is obviously a **short-term** thing. It's different from **long-term development strategies**. That being said, economic and social development **can't take place** where large numbers of people are starving or homeless. It's essential to **fix** the **immediate damage** before going on to **plan strategies** for the long term.

3) NGOs also participate in **development**. They develop **local communities** through education and village clinics and work with **governments** and **businesses** to co-ordinate national development.

Four stages of NGO and charity involvement

1) Relief and aid	**Food** programmes, **urgent** medical care
2) Community Development	Community **health centres**, community **education**
3) Systems Development	Working with **government** and **private business**
4) People's Movements	Encouraging **locally managed development**

Many LEDCs face a Debt Crisis — they spend more on Debt than Investment

Throughout the 20th century, **LEDCs** have had to **borrow money** from **richer nations** and **international organisations** both for survival and for development. The **World Bank** and **International Monetary Fund** (IMF) have lent large sums of money to LEDCs to fund development projects.

The World Bank and IMF are clubs which loan money to fund development projects in member countries. It's not just LEDCs who borrow money — the UK has taken out loans from both organisations.

1) If you ask for a **loan** from your **local bank**, it'll come with a set of conditions — you have to pay **interest**, you have to pay a certain amount **back** each month, and if you **don't** pay it back they'll take your house off you. If you don't pay enough off each month, the **interest** starts to **pile on**, and you can find yourself in **financial trouble**.

2) It's exactly the same with **nations**. Many poor countries spend **more** repaying **debts** and the interest that's built up on their debts than they spend on their own **infrastructures**. As **Hayter** points out, that's **not good** for **development**.

Dependency theory puts the crisis down to colonialism, corruption and greed.

1) Dependency theorists argue that many countries are poor because **colonialism** restricted their economic development. Countries that gained independence were forced to **borrow money** to invest in development.

2) Dependency theorists also argue that aid doesn't go to the right place — much of the aid given to countries is absorbed by **governments** who either **embezzle** the money (i.e. steal it for themselves) or invest in products that **don't help** a country to develop (e.g. **weapons**). There's an **investment gap** that has to be filled with **loans**.

3) In the 1980s and early 1990s, the **richest nations** and the **international lending organisations** significantly raised levels of **interest** paid on loans. Countries had to **borrow more** to meet **interest payments**. Dependency theorists think this rather suited the West as they saw an **increase** in the **debt owed** to them — they were suddenly looking at receiving a lot **more money** in debt repayments from the poorer nations.

There's an ongoing **campaign** to **reduce debt**, or **scrap** debts entirely. Many countries have had their **total debt** reduced, but this hasn't **yet** made a significant impact on the absolute poverty experienced by people within the poorest nations.

Practice Questions

Q1   What are the three types of aid that can be given to less developed countries?

Q2   Explain how the "trickle down effect" works, according to Modernisation theory.

Q3   What are the causes of debt according to dependency theorists?

Exam Question

Q1   "Aid is merely a tool for spreading capitalism across less developed countries".
Assess sociological views on this statement.   (40 marks)

Lend us twenty million euros, would you...

You've probably heard Bono banging on about debt in developing countries, unless you've been in a cave on the moon with cushions strapped to your ears. You might even have heard him there — being a rock star, his voice does carry a fair way. You probably haven't heard of all the theories and sociologists' names on these pages, though, so you'll need to learn them for later.

Urbanisation and the Environment

Some sociologists say that cities are a focus point for modernisation, investment and economic development. Others say that development in cities doesn't help the poor, and damages the environment too much. The rest just live in them and leave it at that. Those last ones are my favourite type of sociologist. There don't seem to be enough of them.

Urbanisation goes along with Industrialisation

Urbanisation means the increase in **urban populations**, compared to **rural populations**. During periods of industrialisation, people have **migrated** from rural areas to urban areas in search of **work**.

Industrialisation means the change from **agriculture** and small scale "cottage industry" to large scale manufacturing in factories. Factories are **centralised workplaces** — they require people to move to where the work is.

In Western Europe, there was a **rapid increase** in urban populations in the **19th century** as a result of **job opportunities** offered by the **Industrial Revolution**. In Mexico, industrialisation and urbanisation happened in the **20th century**.

Modernisation theory argues that Urbanisation is key to Development

1) In modernisation theory, the growth of cities symbolises the triumph of Western models of development and Western ideals. The city is seen as a place that rejects traditional goals and aspirations and replaces them with notions of **meritocracy**, **activism** and **individualism**.

2) **Hoselitz (1964)** argues that the **cities** encourage people to **work**, and contribute to the economy, because the system within **urban** areas is focused on **achieved status** (success based on achievement rather than social position) and **meritocracy** (allocation of people to positions in society based on **ability** rather than **family**).

3) Critics of this theory argue that it is **ethnocentric**, because it's ⟵ based on Western cities, Western capitalism and Western ideals.

4) Additionally, it's seen as rather **unclear** in places — it doesn't say how power, wealth and development move from urban areas into rural areas, it just **assumes** that they do.

Ethnocentrism refers to an idea that one set of cultural values are superior to another. It's normally used in the context of the West versus other cultures — to say a theory is ethnocentric usually means it sees everything from a Western point of view.

Some see Development as the move from Rural Lifestyles to Urban ones

1) Some sociologists, especially modernisation theorists, see development as the shift from the characteristics of **rural** life to **urban** life.

2) Taking this view means that it's **easy** to measure development — it's just a calculation of how **urbanised** society has become. This can be measured by counting the number of **cities** and urban townships, and the numbers of **people living, working** and **socialising** within them, and comparing it to the number of people who live, work and socialise in the countryside .

Dual Economy theory says that Rural and Urban economies are Separate

1) **Dual economy** theorists argue that urbanisation leads to two very **different** types of society within one country — **rural** society and **urban** society. They function as **two separate economies** with little connection between them.

2) The **rural** economy is **localised** and focused on **subsistence**. The **urban** economy is **national** and **international** and focused on **economic growth** and development.

3) The theory is based on the idea that **colonialism** pushed progression in **urban** areas at the expense of **rural** areas, which became marginalised.

See p.30 for more on colonialism.

4) It's a useful theory to explain the point that the needs and problems of **urban** areas are very **different** to **rural** areas.

5) However, **critics** point to the fact that dual economy theory still assumes that rural economies are "**backward**".

Dependency Theory — Poverty in LEDC cities is caused by Colonialism

1) Dependency theorists believe the cities described by modernisation theorists don't exist. They say cities in LEDCs aren't success stories of meritocracy and achieved status, where hard work always brings big rewards. They're actually polarised between the "**haves**" and the "**have nots**". They blame **colonialism** for this.

2) Dependency theory says that urbanisation doesn't bring solutions to the developing world, just more problems, e.g. inequality, urban poverty, bad public health. The developing world doesn't have the infrastructure to deal with them — there's poor health care, limited access to education, and little social security (if any at all).

3) According to the theory, only the parts of the city where **capitalist elites** live and work are anything like the modernisation theory model of a city. Those parts were **designed** under colonialism to house the **colonial elite**.

4) The theory says LEDC cities depend on trade with rich nations, and serve rich nations rather than their own people.

5) Dependency theory **ignores** countries where urbanisation actually **has** brought **economic benefits** for the people.

Urbanisation and the Environment

Development and industrialisation always has an Impact on the Environment

1) Industrialisation creates air, water and land **pollution**, and uses up **natural resources**.
2) Rapid urbanisation results in **overcrowding**. Urban **infrastructures** often **can't cope** with the influx of people. Rural-urban migrants settle in makeshift **squatter** settlements without proper **water supply** or **sanitation**.
3) Urban areas are polluted by **industry** and by **motor traffic**. This affects **public health**.
4) The new **international division of labour** means that polluting heavy industry is concentrated in LEDCs.
5) LEDCs don't have **equal access** to "clean" technology — e.g. equipment to reduce air pollution from power plants.

There are different Theoretical views on how to Manage the Environment

The Neo-liberal view — there's a trade-off between pollution and economic development

1) Countries need to calculate the **costs** and **benefits** of any development strategy. Economic development usually has environmental costs such as deforestation, drought and loss of productive land space.
2) If a country works out that this cost is too high compared to the benefits of a development strategy, then they won't pursue that strategy. This may have an impact on their **competitiveness** in the **international economy** — they'll be less economically competitive compared to countries that have decided to go ahead with the strategy.

The Structuralist view — the debt crisis needs to be solved first.

1) The desire by developing countries to share in the benefits of capitalism results in countries always favouring **economic** development over **environmental** concerns.
2) **Structuralist** theories make the assumption that the developing world would be able to do more about environmental issues if it were free from debt.

> Structuralist theories are ones which say the structure of society is responsible for social problems. Marxism is a structuralist theory.

Some sociologists argue that Sustainable Development is the solution

1) **Sustainable development** has been high on the development agenda over the last 20 years. It's a strategy that looks for **solutions** to development problems that don't have **negative consequences** on the environment.
2) Neo-Marxist **Redclift (1987)** points out that the idea of sustainable development is **only needed** because development is defined in **economic** terms and characterised by trading **natural resources** for **money**.
3) Redclift also says that some environmentalists who **claim** to be in favour of sustainable development don't give high enough priority to the needs of the **poor**. Redclift says sustainability must be about **policies** to **manage resources** in such a way that they continue to meet the **basic needs** of the **majority** of people — i.e. it requires **political effort**.

There are Conflicts between the Green Agenda and Brown Agenda

1) The **Green Agenda** is a global initiative to reduce the impact of human activity on the world's ecosystems.
2) The **Brown Agenda** is an initiative of the **World Bank** to improve **environmental health** in LEDC cities.
3) The Green agenda is about **long-term** impact on a **global** scale, while the Brown Agenda is about **short-term local** action. Action taken to fix urban environments on the Brown Agenda may go **against** the Green Agenda.

Practice Questions

Q1 What is urbanisation?
Q2 What is the dual economy theory?
Q3 What do neo-liberals say about the conflict between environment and development?
Q4 What is sustainable development?

Exam Questions

Q1 Assess the ways sociologists have explained the relationship between urbanisation and development. (40 marks)

Q2 Critically evaluate the argument that concerns for economic development must come before environmental issues. (40 marks)

Pop another environmentally friendly non-wood log on the fire...

When you look at interpretations of urbanisation, remember that modernisation theory and dependency theory are pretty much opposite. So, given that modernisation theory says that cities are wonderful and promote development, dependency theory must say they're awful. If modernisation theory says something is black, dependency theory says it's white. And so on.

Aspects of Development: Education

You might not be in the mood to believe this, but good education has been proven to improve standards of living, raise participation in civic activities and make for a happier, harder working populace. In the last fifty years, developing countries have spent more of their budgets on improving the education of their people — with mixed results.

Good Education improves the Living Standards of people in LEDCs

Education is necessary for **development**. In Rostow's model of development (see p.28), an educated workforce is necessary for industrial take-off. Many other sociologists think education is very important for development.

1) **Economic development** requires expert, technical knowledge on a local level. Not all expertise can be brought in from other countries. International organisations and MEDCs are generally keen to see LEDCs **train** their own people in the **specialist skills** required in the long term development of a country.

2) Education also gives people the **values** and **attitudes** required in the process of development. Literate, numerate people can fully understand what action is required for development and **participate** in deciding what action to take in their communities and their country.

3) Education can act as a **unifying force**. It can give people a common set of **values** and ideas about their country, which helps to overcome class, ethnic and religious **differences** in a country.

4) Many people in the developing world are keen to participate in education because they want to obtain **achieved status** — a qualification, improved employment opportunities, etc. Education acts as an **empowering** tool for groups in society that have traditionally been **excluded** from **social mobility**, e.g. women and the poor.

Universal Education is still Unavailable for many in the Developing World

1) **External aid** and increased **investment** in the developing world has led many countries to introduce **universal education** — but provision is often **patchy**.

2) Some countries have universal education for **primary school** age (up to about 11 years old), some have universal education up to 14 or 16 years old, and some still haven't introduced universal education.

3) Even in countries that have **universal education** as a policy, not every child **actually goes to school**. This is because of other **family commitments** and needs — e.g. children may be required to **work** on the **family farm**.

4) In many countries, parents still have to **pay school fees** to get their child into school. Also, **school supplies** aren't provided by the state like they are in the UK. Families have to **buy** books, pens, pencils, erasers, school uniform etc.

The Growth in Education doesn't mean Quality Education

Much of the **increase** in education has had to be supplied by education **systems** that were designed to meet the **basic needs** of a **few**. Basic education systems have been put under **strain**.

Lessons aren't always of **high quality**. Some education doesn't provide enough **useful knowledge**.

The Growth in Education has raised problems with Employment

1) While young people are in schools and colleges being educated, they're not out **working** and contributing to the **local** and **national economy**.

2) Because more people are studying and fewer people are working, governments get less revenue from income tax. Governments have less money coming in but have to **pay out more** to **provide education**.

3) Bright, educated people from rural areas tend to **migrate** to the **cities** to look for jobs. This contributes to **over-urbanisation** and urban **overcrowding**.

4) The more educated citizens **sometimes struggle** to find **employment** in their own country, or they can simply earn a lot more by moving away to countries that have **better job prospects** — this is called the "brain drain", by the way. The end result is that the country **fails to develop** because the educated have **left**, to use their education elsewhere.

Marxist Dependency Theorists see Education as Cultural Imperialism

Dependency theorists really frown on the idea that education **trains** people for **development**. They **strongly disapprove** of education that gives people the **values** and **attitudes** that are needed for "imperial-capitalist" (i.e. Western) development — they call this **cultural imperialism**.

Dependency theory sees **education** as a potential **tool** for keeping people **culturally** and **economically** dependent on the developed world — it trains them to get the kind of **jobs** that **benefit TNCs** and the **developed world**.

Aspects of Development: Health

At the start of the 21st century, health in the developing world is still poor compared to the developed world. Good health care provision is essential for the development and protection of people in the developing world.

Physical Quality of Life Index (PQLI) Measures Health and Education

1) **David Morris** developed the PQLI in **1979**. It measures **infant mortality**, **literacy** and **life expectancy**. It's useful for sociologists concerned with development as a social issue rather than an economic issue.

2) The PQLI also allows you to compare trends across countries. However, there are problems in collecting reliable data.

Education, Poverty and the role of MEDCs all impact on Health in LEDCs

1) Poverty forces people to suffer poor **public health** and a **bad diet**.

2) It also prevents them from gaining a good quality of **health care**. Universal free health care is **rare** in the developing world — people usually have to **pay** to see a doctor. There are also **not enough doctors** and **nurses** to go around.

3) The lack of good **health education** in the developing world means many people (particularly those in traditional, rural areas) do not know how to **prevent disease** and are not aware of **basic treatments**.

4) Drugs companies may sell drugs in the developing world that **can't be sold in the West** because of **safety** reasons. Or they may set the **price** of life-saving drugs so **high** that many in LEDCs can't afford them.

5) **Western products** may be used **inappropriately**. For example, **baby formula milk** is heavily advertised in LEDCs. Some mothers don't have access to **clean water** to make the milk with, so many babies die from **infections**. Also, poor mothers may **water down** the formula too much (to make it last longer), resulting in **malnutrition**.

6) Also, TNCs that have set up in the developing countries often pay little attention to the environment, or health and safety. For example, the Bhopal poison gas leak of 1984 happened because safety procedures were inadequate.

> **Example: HIV/AIDS in South Africa**
> - **Insufficient health education** in poor areas meant people **didn't know** how HIV was transmitted.
> - Clinics could be a **day's walk** away.
> - **Transnational drugs companies** refused to allow local drugs companies to make **cheap versions** of anti-HIV drugs. This was overturned by the courts in 2001.
> - In the 1990s, the **South African government** was **reluctant** to **distribute** anti-HIV drugs.

They doubted that HIV caused AIDS.

There are different Theoretical Views about Health Inequalities

Modernisation theorists believe **Western** medicine is **superior**, and that Western medicine and **health education** would **solve** the problems of **high infant mortality** and **low life expectancy**. **Rostow (1971)** said that **high tech medicine** used in the developed world should be **transferred** to developing nations so that **quality health care** can be provided.

Marxist **Navarro (1976)** believed that high tech Western health care is not the immediate priority for the developing world. Poor nations need to focus on **basic health procedures** to **save lives** and **improve quality of life**. Doctors from these nations need to be encouraged to stay and work in their own countries, not to migrate to MEDCs for better pay.

Dependency theory blames **colonialism** and **exploitation**. Colonialism introduced European diseases to Africa, America and Asia. Colonialism also replaced food crops with cash crops, resulting in malnutrition. Dependency theory also blames the developed world for **poverty** and **debt**.

Practice Questions

Q1 What are the advantages and disadvantages of universal education?
Q2 What is PQLI?
Q3 What do modernisation theorists argue is crucial for development in health?

Exam Questions

Q1 How can education be used as a tool for development in the developing world? (12 marks)

Q2 Critically evaluate the argument that the health concerns of the developing world have largely been caused by the policies of the developed world. (40 marks)

This subject is certainly draining my brain...

With every page it feels emptier and emptier, and soon there will be nothing left. Anyway, it's those dreaded words "cultural imperialism" again. It's really hard to think about development without slipping into some kind of "them and us" thinking — either assuming that the West knows best, or assuming that the West is all bad, and that poor countries should be left to get on with it.

Aspects of Development: Gender

Recently, sociologists (particularly feminists) have pointed out that women and men experience development and under-development in different ways. And you know what that means — more radical feminists. Should be interesting.

There's **Gender Inequality** in the **Developing World**

Evidence from studies into gender in the developing world shows that in many cases women get a worse deal than men.

- Women have **lower life expectancy** than men in **some countries** (usually women live longer than men).
- Women are **paid less** than men.
- Women get **less education** than men.
- Women's **health** is **poorer** than men's health, and women have less access to health care than men do.
- There's even a **greater chance of abortion** if a foetus is **female**.

The Gender Empowerment Measure (GEM) is a indicator of the progress made by women in a society

1) The GEM focuses on **social indicators** of gender equality — female and male participation in **decision making**, **economic participation**, and **economic power**.

2) In other words, it monitors whether women have the right to **vote**, how many women there are in **parliament**, how many women have **top management jobs**, and the **GDP per capita** of the **female population**.

3) This measure has continually shown that women haven't reached **social equality** with men.

The Gender-related Development Index (GDI) measures several development-related factors

1) The GDI measures **life expectancy**, **literacy**, years in **school**, number of **women in work** and **women's income**.

2) It has a more **positive** story to tell about women and development. Sure, men still generally have better income, literacy and so on, but women have **improved** in most categories for development.

3) **Women's literacy** and **numeracy** has improved, and the chances of death during or after **childbirth** has fallen.

Some say **Women** feel the **Negative Side Effects** of development **More** than **Men**

1) According to Marxist feminists, women experience a **dual burden** of **paid work** and **domestic responsibilities**.

2) When a country **industrialises**, men go from **one** form of work (agriculture) to **another** form of work (manufacturing industry), but women go from **one** form of work (housework and childcare) to **two** forms of work (housework and childcare plus a paid job outside the home).

3) Women in developing countries often work **longer hours** than **men**, in poor conditions.

This is quite simplified, and it's a broad generalisation anyway.

Technology can change **Women's Employment Patterns**

1) **Swasti Mitter (1995)** writes about the impact of **ICT** on **female** employment in **developing countries**. She says that computer technology can be a real **boon** to women — it allows them to work from home and work **flexible hours**.

2) Many ICT jobs which have been outsourced to NICs from MEDCs go to women — e.g. call centre jobs, data entry, medical transcription services.

3) Mitter points out that many women in developing countries like India, Malaysia and Brazil now work in **ICT**, but they're concentrated towards the bottom end of the work ladder.

Radical Feminists argue that **Development Benefits Patriarchy**

1) Radical feminists see development as a tool to make women more dependent upon men.

2) Radical feminists say TNCs actively seek to employ women as they are cheaper, more efficient, and docile.

3) If women do experience **improvement** in their position in society, e.g. **greater life expectancy** through better **health care** or **increased income**, it's because the **patriarchy** of the developed **world** allow it for **productivity** reasons.

Radical feminism can be **criticised** for failing to see the **exploitation** experienced by **men**.

Socialist Feminists believe **Socialism** can bring **Equality** to poorer countries

1) Socialist feminists argue that socialism can bring about a society that **isn't gendered** — i.e. that treats men and women **equally**. They push for **socialist revolution** that totally **changes** the way people see "men's jobs" and "women's jobs", as well as moving ownership of the means of production from capitalists to workers.

2) Socialist feminist **Mies (1986)** argues that traditional Marxism and capitalism both **undervalue** the work women do.

Aspects of Development: Demography

Demography is the study of population change. It's been a big thing in world Sociology since, well, forever.

High Population Growth can be a Problem

Malthus (1798) thought that population growth could cause problems — a population could grow faster than its capacity to feed itself. He pointed out that limited resources would cause death which would balance the birth/death equation.

Neo-Malthusian **Ehrlich (1968)** believed that the "population explosion" was putting too much stress on the resources of the world, leading the developing world, in particular, to experience problems such as famine and malnutrition. He believed over-population was damaging development and the environment.

1) The work of Malthus and Ehrlich has been used by **modernisation theorists** who argue that over-population in the developing world is one of the biggest obstacles to development. Any economic surplus has to be spent on feeding the population and building an infrastructure to cope with increased population, instead of on industry.

2) In addition, modernisation theorists criticise the **anti-contraception policies** of **religions** such as Roman Catholicism for fuelling the over-population problem.

3) Modernisation theorists argue that the solution is to persuade governments to **promote birth control**, and for **Western governments** and **international organisations** to **fund birth control** programmes. Modernisation theorists also suggest that money should be spent on **educating women**, because educated women tend to have fewer babies.

Modernisation Theory's approach to Demographics is Criticised

1) Modernisation theory is criticised for blaming the wrong people — it puts the blame for over-population at the feet of the governments of the developing world, religious organisations and the people themselves. Marxists would blame the global capitalist system instead.

2) The theory is based on **statistical data** from the time of writing — the facts may have **changed** since the study was written. When Ehrlich was writing, the rate of population growth was increasing. Evidence from **Carnell (2000)** shows that the **prediction** made by Ehrlich is wrong — annual population growth has actually slowed.

3) **Harrison (1990)** points out that **birth rate** isn't the problem. Population growth is caused by a **decline** in the **death rate**, especially the infant mortality rate. People are having the same number of babies, but **fewer** are **dying**. Harrison does agree with Ehrlich that population growth threatens the environment, though.

4) There's actually not a lot of evidence that **food resources** aren't coping. **Food production** has **increased**, and the world has the capacity to produce **more** food than it produces now. **Boserup (1965)** said that **population increase** determined **agricultural change**, so that agricultural production always kept up with the population.

The food supply looks fine to me...

5) **Dependency theorists** argue that the West continues to take the very best resources a developing nation has, leaving the inhabitants with little land of any quality. **Land reform** and **redistribution** to the poor would be a better solution rather than population control.

6) **Adamson (1986)** believes that **poverty** causes **high population**, rather than vice versa. Poverty forces people to see children as **economic assets** who will bring money into the household and support them in **old age**. People often have large families as a means of economic survival. Parents can't guarantee that their children will survive into adulthood, so they have more children to increase the chances of at least one surviving into adulthood.

Practice Questions

Q1 What are the findings of the GEM and the GDI? Why do they differ?

Q2 Why do Modernists believe over-population is an obstacle to development?

Q3 Why do sociologists argue that over-population is understandable?

Exam Questions

Q1 What are the causes and consequences of over-population in the developing world? [12 marks]

Q2 Assess the argument that women are disadvantaged in the developing world. [40 marks]

Sometimes it's hard to be a woman...

... Givin' all your looove to just — one maaan. Oops, the radical feminists wouldn't be impressed with that at all. I bet it's actually quite hard being a radical feminist. Blaming men for everything that's wrong with the world must use up a lot of energy. And soon it's going to be hard being anyone at all because the world will be full up and there won't be any room to lie down.

Social Class and Occupation

*This section is for **AQA** (though OCR people might find it useful background). This is a synoptic module which means you'll have to make links between this topic and other topics you have studied in Sociology.*

Societies are Stratified — divided into Layers

Stratification means the way societies are divided into **layers**. The **richest** and **most powerful** are at the **top**, the **poorest** and **most powerless** are at the **bottom**. In between are lots of **strata** (layers, like the layers in rock) organised in a **hierarchy**.

A **stratified** society can contain inequalities of **status**, **income**, **class**, **religion**, **ethnicity**, **gender** and **age**.

Social class is the main stratification system in **modern**, **Western capitalist societies** like the **UK**. Social class is partly based on **economic** factors — **jobs**, **income** and **wealth**. Social class also has elements of **power** and **prestige**.

Other stratification systems include the caste system as used in India, and the feudal system as used in medieval Britain.

Sociologists often talk about Four Social Classes in the UK

1) The **upper class** are **wealthy** and **powerful**. The original upper class was the **landowning aristocracy**. Their wealth is **passed on from generation to generation**. People who have made a lot of money from business or from the entertainment industry are also sometimes considered to be upper class.

2) The **middle class** earn their money from **non-manual work**. Teachers, doctors, managers and pretty much anyone who **earns their living sitting in an office** are middle class. The middle class is **getting bigger** because there are **more non-manual jobs** these days, and fewer manual jobs.

3) The **working class** make their money from **manual work**. Farm labourers and factory workers are working class. The working class have **poorer life chances** than the middle class.

4) The **underclass** get their money from **state benefits**. They include the long-term unemployed and the homeless. The underclass have **the poorest life chances**.

> Sociologists have most often focused on the division between the <u>middle class</u> and the <u>working class</u>.

> See p.44 for more on Marxist stratification.

Marx divided society into just Two Social Classes

1) The **proletariat** (workers) produce goods of economic value. According to Marx, they don't own the means of production — all they own and control is their own labour power.

2) The **bourgeoisie** (bosses) own the means of production. Marx said they exploit workers in order to generate profit.

3) There wasn't a clearly defined **middle class** at the time when Marx was writing his economic theories.

Relating Class to Occupation poses Problems

1) Occupation does bring **status** and **prestige** with it. People **judge** each other by the jobs they do.

2) Two individuals in the **same occupational class** can have very different **income** and **prestige** status — e.g. a highly paid consultant neurologist compared to a low paid junior doctor.

3) Basing class entirely on occupation misses out most of the **upper class** — a lot of them **don't have jobs** as such, but live off **rental income** from property, and income from **share ownership**.

A good social class scheme must **represent** what people in society **really think** about the **status** that goes with each occupational class — it must be **devised** and **tested** by **research**. There are far **too many occupations** for a research sample to say what they think of them **all**, so sociologists usually ask individuals about 20 or so **common** and **representative occupations**. They make inferences about the rest of the occupations in society — which is the tricky bit.

The Government used to use a scale of Five Classes called the RG scale

1) This scale is called the **Registrar General's Scale** (RG scale), and was used until 2000.

2) The **never employed** aren't included, and **unemployed** people are classified according to their **last job**.

3) The RG scale is based on the **head of household's** occupation (usually the man).

4) **Married women** were classified according to their **husband's job** — this was **sexist**.

	Class	Example
middle class	I) **Professional**	Lawyer, accountant, doctor
	II) **Intermediate**	Teacher, nurse, manager
	III) **skilled non-manual**	Office worker, sales assistant
working class	III) **skilled manual**	Electrician, plumber
	IV) **semi-skilled manual**	Postman
	V) **unskilled manual**	Labourer, refuse collector, cleaner

5) Also, because the RG scale only considered the head of household's job, it didn't matter what kind of job **other people in the home** had. For example, it **wouldn't distinguish** between a household made up of **two lawyers** and a household made up of a **lawyer** and a **cleaner**.

"Head of household" meant highest male earner, or if no male, highest female earner.

6) There can be **huge variations** in **income** and **life chances** between different occupations within a class.

Social Class and Occupation

The Government now uses a scale of Eight Classes called the NS-SEC

Since 2000, the **government** has used a new scale — the **National Statistics Socio-Economic Classification** (**NS-SEC**). The NS-SEC has **eight classes** based on type of **employment**, rather than **skill level**:

1) **higher managerial** and **professional**	Lawyer, doctor, company director
2) **lower managerial** and **professional**	Nurse, social worker, police officer
3) **intermediate**	Secretary, personal assistant, paramedic
4) **small employers** and **self-employed**	Owner of a restaurant, self employed plumber
5) **lower supervisory** and **technical**	Builder's foreman, sales floor supervisor in a shop
6) **semi-routine**	Postman, receptionist, sales assistant in a shop
7) **routine**	Waitress, van driver, farm labourer, cleaner
8) **never worked** and **long term unemployed**	last worked more than a year ago

Class 1 can be divided into a) large employers and managers, and b) higher professional.

The NS-SEC is derived from Goldthorpe's social class scheme — see below.

1) The NS-SEC is based on three areas:

   - **Employment relations** — whether someone is an **employer**, **self-employed** or **employed**, whether they're **salaried** or paid a **weekly wage**, and how large an organisation they work in. *This is Weberian — see p.45.*
   - **Labour market situation** — income, benefits and job security, promotion prospects.
   - **Work situation** — where the person is in the **workplace hierarchy**, and how much **control** they have at work.

2) The RG was replaced by the NS-SEC because of the recent changes in **employment patterns**. There were fewer **manual** workers and far more workers in **service industries**, so **skill level** was no longer a good way to classify workers.

3) The NS-SEC takes into account changes in social position of some occupations (e.g. shop assistants).

4) Each **individual worker** is classified, rather than classifying a whole **household** by one person's job.

5) The NS-SEC still doesn't account for the "idle rich" — wealthy **upper class** people who don't need jobs.

Goldthorpe's Scheme has Seven Classes

1) In the 1970s, Goldthorpe (a Weberian) based his social classification on **market situation** and **work situation**. He adapted it in the 1980s to include employment relations.

2) Goldthorpe used this scale in his Oxford Mobility study — there's more about it on p.50.

I)	**upper service class**	lawyer, doctor, large employer
II)	**lower service class**	teacher, nurse, manager
III)	**routine non-manual class**	secretary, personal assistant
IV)	**petty bourgeoisie**	self employed, small employers
V)	**lower technical, supervisors**	foreman, dental hygienist
VI)	**skilled manual class**	bricklayer, electrician (employed)
VII)	**unskilled manual class**	waitress, labourer, cleaner

Wright's Scheme combines Marxism with Bureaucracy

1) **Erik Olin Wright's** (1985, 1990, 1997) scheme has a traditional **Marxist** divide between **owners** and **employees**.

2) It also classifies employees in two dimensions — firstly, whether they're **managers**, **supervisors** or **workers**, and secondly whether they've got **skills and qualifications** or not.

Practice Questions

Q1 Give one problem of using occupation to measure class.

Q2 What class was missing from the Registrar General's scale?

Q3 Give an example of a semiroutine occupation from the NS-SEC scheme.

Q4 What class would a self-employed electrician be in the Goldthorpe scheme?

Exam Question

Q1 Assess the validity of judging social class solely on occupation. (40 marks)

Oh how I wish this was a classless society — there'd be less to learn...

What a lot of class schemes. For the bare basics, learn the NS-SEC, the RG, and the differences between them. If you want to look like you're really on the ball, you can mention that class/occupation schemes can be Marxist (based on economics and income) or Weberian (based on labour market position and employment relations). The NS-SEC is well Weberian. Innit.

Theories of Stratification

There's no dispute that power, status and economic assets aren't equally distributed within society. There is an awful lot of debate about why. A sociologist's answer depends on their fundamental beliefs about the nature of society. Off we go again...

Functionalists say the Class System helps society to Run Smoothly

1) Functionalism says that society is a meritocracy — the most able people rise to the top.
2) Fundamental to **Functionalism** (try saying that quickly...) is the **strong belief** that the class system enables each individual to find their **right place** and **role** in society.
3) Functionalists say that the **most important** positions in society must be filled by the brightest and most able people.
4) According to **Functionalism**, the people who do well in terms of the common values of society will be at the top of the stratification system. High **status**, **power** and high income are **rewards** for conforming to society's values.
5) Most people **don't object** to people in powerful positions getting **extra status** and **rewards**. According to functionalists, this shows that they support the values which underpin the system.

Talcott Parsons was an influential Functionalist

1) Parsons established the Functionalist position that stratification is **inevitable** and **useful** in all societies.
2) He argued that stratification systems **evaluate** individuals in terms of **common social values** — high status is a reward for **conforming** to society's values.
3) In Parsons' view, stratification **reinforces** the **collective goals** of society and establishes **order**.

I know my place — Me too. Comforting, isn't it.

I doubt Parsons was thinking about strata in rock...

Davis and Moore (1945) argue that without a stratification system, society would break down

1) According to Davis and Moore, stratification has the function of **role allocation**. It makes sure the most able and talented do the most important jobs.
2) **Inequality in reward** (pay) and **status** are essential to **motivate** the best individuals to take on the most important roles and jobs. These roles usually require long periods of training. High rewards compensate people for spending a long time in education and training.

This argument may sound familiar — it's often used to justify high rewards given to company directors and even famous sports stars.

Functionalists have been accused of Overlooking the "Uneven Playing Field"

1) **Tumin (1953)** is the **most important critic** of Davis and Moore. He pointed out that individuals with the same talent and ability don't have an equal chance to "reach the top". He says that this **inequality of opportunity** is **overlooked** by Davis and Moore.
2) **Tumin** also criticises the functionalist concept of some roles being more "functionally important" than others. It's not clear who can decide **which jobs** are **more important** than others. Some of the essential jobs in society such as nursing, teaching and childcare are paid considerably less than some less useful jobs such as advertising, PR and entertainment.
3) Also, Tumin said that Davis and Moore ignore the influence of **power** on rewards. **Pay inequality** may be to do with differences in **bargaining power**, rather than difference in usefulness.
4) Tumin wasn't having any truck with the idea that stratification **motivates** people, either. He thought that social stratification can be a barrier to motivation. The **lower** a person's social class, the **more likely** they are to **leave school** without good qualifications, and the **less likely** they are to be **motivated** to chase a **high status** position.
5) High status groups can put up **barriers to entry** — using their power to restrict access to the group. This allows them to set a high market price for their services.
6) Davis and Moore assume that the **number** of people who are **talented enough** to fill high status jobs is (curiously) **identical** to the number of high status jobs up for grabs. There's actually **no evidence** for this. The pool of talent could be much larger than Functionalists think it is.
7) Functionalists **ignore** the negative aspects of stratification. Stratification is a system of haves and have nots. People in the bottom strata can feel excluded from society. Stratification can actually divide society rather than integrating it.

Theories of Stratification

The New Right argue that the Social Stratification system is Unequal but Fair

New Right thinking became popular in the 1980s. It's based on **19th century liberalism**, which saw the **free market** as the **best** way of sorting out everything in society from boredom to backache. The New Right say **governments shouldn't intervene in the market** or promote equality as this takes away motivation for people to **pull themselves up by their bootstraps**.

New Right thinking is sometimes known as **neo-functionalism** (or political functionalism) because it pursues the same themes.

1) **Peter Saunders (1990)** is a key British New Right sociologist. **Saunders** argues that societies with stratification systems based on economic differences aren't inevitable (as Parsons thought) but they are a good idea.

2) Saunders says **stratification** is a good idea because **unequal rewards motivate** people to **work hard**. He says that in a society with equal rewards, some people wouldn't pull their weight. He sees physical force as the only alternative to unequal rewards — and obviously prefers unequal rewards.

3) Saunders says that **inequality** promotes **economic growth**. Individuals are motivated to **start businesses** so that they can make money, which **benefits society** by creating **jobs** and **wealth**. He points to the rise in small businesses and entrepreneurs in modern society to demonstrate how anyone can do well if they work hard enough.

4) New Right thinkers like Saunders believe in legal equality and equality of opportunity, rather than equality of outcome. Saunders says that it's more important for society to be a meritocracy than for society to be equal.

5) In a **free market**, market forces control who earns what, according to **supply of talent** and **demand for talent**. People whose skills are highly **demanded**, but in short **supply**, can earn a lot of money. A system based on the free market is **unequal** (some people earn a lot more than others) but it's **fair** according to New Right thinkers because every individual can try to be successful in the market place.

1) **Saunders (1996)** sees Britain as pretty **close** to being a **meritocracy**. He thinks that **economic rewards** match up with **merit** and **ability**.

2) He argues that what **looks** like **inequality of opportunity** between middle class and working class is actually caused by **inequality of ability** and **effort**. In other words, he thinks that middle class children **deserve** better jobs because they're more able, and they work harder.

Not surprisingly, this view is highly controversial...

Critics of Functionalism and New Right theory point out Social Problems

1) **Gordon Marshall** and **Adam Swift (1993)** say that capitalist societies are not as **meritocratic** as the New Right claim.

2) They argue the **free market** does not guarantee a **fair chance** for all. Opportunities vary according to which class you are born into — for example, inherited wealth plays a large part in starting small businesses. **Luck** can play a part in success, too.

3) Evidence also shows that people from **working class** backgrounds have **less chance** than upper class people of getting top jobs — even when they have the **same educational qualifications**. **Class** still plays a part even when people have **equal ability**.

4) They also criticise functionalists for largely ignoring **social problems** such as **poverty**, which result from the stratification system.

Practice Questions

Q1 In what way did Parsons say that stratification was useful for society?

Q2 Explain what Davis and Moore mean by role allocation.

Q3 Why does Saunders say stratification is a good idea?

Q4 Give one criticism of New Right thinking on stratification.

Exam Questions

Q1 Examine the view that social inequality is an inevitable product of a successful society. (12 marks)

Q2 "Modern Britain is a meritocratic society." Discuss with reference to one or more of the following topics: education; work and leisure; health; families and households. (40 marks)

New Wrong thinking had even more critics than usual...

There's a pattern to Sociology teaching at A-level: you study the main theories about each topic and then evaluate and compare them... It's a good approach because it teaches you to look at topics from different points of view. It can get a bit repetitive though. Functionalist, Marxist and Interactionist views come up over and over again. What about Zoroastrian views? Huh?

Theories of Stratification

Surprise — some more theories of stratification! Sorry, I should have warned you on the last page. That was a cruel trick.

Marxists see stratification as a Deliberately Divisive tool for Exploiting workers

1) For Marx, **class** was the key to understanding **absolutely everything** in society. And I mean e-v-e-r-y-t-h-i-n-g.

2) Class emerges in a society which can **produce more** than it **needs** to. Marx called this extra production "**surplus value**" and argued that it was the class who **controlled** this **surplus value** that controlled **society**.

3) Marx argued there are **only two classes** (strata) in society — the **proletariat** and the **bourgeoisie**. For Marx, a class is a **social group** who share the **same relationship** to the means of **production**.

Producers	Proletariat or subject class	Majority	Only own their labour	Poor
Non-producers	Bourgeoisie or ruling class	Minority	Own the means of production	Wealthy

The ruling class own the means of production

1) Those who own the means of production can control both the **price** at which they **sell** the goods produced, and the **wages** they pay those who produce the goods.

2) It's only by paying the workers **less** than they **sell** the goods for that they can make a **profit**. It is this profit which gives them the **wealth** and **power** to **control** the rest of society in their own interests.

The subject class are the producers

1) They **don't own** the means of production. They only own their **labour**. Because they only own their labour power they have **very little control** in society.

2) They're **completely dependent** on the **ruling class** for **wages** to live on.

1) Marx argued that all other forms of power come from **economic** power.

2) Marxism says the **education** system, **legal** system, **police** and **media** are all instruments of ruling class power. This is because those with **economic power** also have the power to **shape** and **control** the institutions in society. According to Marxism, all these institutions serve to keep the subject class in its place — powerless.

3) The ruling class also use **institutions** in society to **control ideas** and **values** in society — via the **dominant ideology**. For example, the notion that capitalist society is meritocratic and anyone can get to the top is a "false truth" according to Marxism. **Institutions** in society such as education spread this idea, and everyone's happy in the belief that society is fair. This is **useful to the ruling class** — it prevents workers from rising up and starting a revolution.

Marx thought that Workers should have a Revolution and bring in Communism

Marx thought society could be **equal** if the **means of production** were owned by **everyone**, so everyone benefited rather than a few. He was certain this would be the end result of capitalism — workers would eventually realise their power and strength, and overthrow the ruling class in a **revolution**, creating a new equal society which Marx called **communism**.

The 20th century saw the **start** and **end** of some large scale communist societies such as the USSR. The **failure** of these communist societies, and the high levels of both **corruption** and **inequality in communist societies** have caused many sociologists to say that Marx was wrong and **egalitarian societies aren't possible**. Modern Marxists argue that the USSR and China **weren't true communism**.

China is still officially communist, but it's adopted "capitalism with Chinese characteristics", a mixture of both ideologies.

Neo-Marxist theories of stratification try to explain the Middle Class

In traditional Marxism, there's **no middle class**. There clearly **is** a **middle class** in **modern society**, and modern Marxists have grappled with different ways of explaining it.

1) **Erik Olin Wright (1978, 1989)** developed a Marxist analysis of class which explained the middle class of salaried professionals which grew in the late 20th century. This group have some control over the means of production, and may own bits of it but they don't control large sections of labour power. This group is called the **petty bourgeoisie**.

2) Wright says these individuals may experience "**contradictory class locations**" — they have **things in common** with **both** classes at **different** times. For example, they may own shares (part-ownership of modern means of production) but may also lose their livelihood at the will of the ruling class (e.g. if they lose their job, or the share price falls).

3) Wright concludes that **class conflict** and **exploitation** are more **complicated** in the late 20th (and now 21st) century than Marx predicted but class is **still** the basis of power and wealth in society.

4) **Edgell (1993)** accuses Wright of leaving Marx behind and having more in common with **Weber**.

The **key message** from neo-Marxists is: **don't dismiss Marx's theory completely** just because he didn't mention a middle class.

Theories of Stratification

Weber argued Class is "Unequal Access to Material Resources"

Weber considered many of the same issues as Marx. Like Marx, he argued class and stratification come from an **economic** basis. Unlike Marx, he didn't go into any detailed predictions about the future, or analysis of the past.

Weber said that there are **three distinct areas** or forms of **stratification** in modern society.

Class power	Economic power to access **material goods** and **resources** in society.
Social power	Status and prestige, and being respected by others.
Party power	Political power and ability to **influence decision-making**.

These tend to be **interlinked** in real life — a person with **social power** is also likely to have **political** and **economic** power.

1) **Weber** concentrated on class power. He argued that an individual's **class power** and **class position** derives from their market position — i.e. their **economic chances**, and their ability to **control** their **wages** and **working conditions**.

2) An individual's **market position** varies partly depending on how in **demand** their skills and talents are — i.e. how much an employer is willing to pay for their services. Be careful though — market position isn't just an individual's ability to get a job. It also covers their **ownership** of **property** and **assets** (e.g. shares).

3) Stratification isn't a case of **two classes** opposed to each other (Marx) or a **competitive meritocracy** (Functionalism and New Right) but a **complex** hierarchy of layers, each with their own class or market position.

Neo-Weberian Theory influences modern Class Schemes

The big name in neo-Weberian theory of class is John **Goldthorpe**. Goldthorpe categorised **seven classes** based on occupation, with **three main classes** — service class ("white collar" professionals), intermediate class and working class.

An individual's **class position** is the **market position** he or she has in the **labour market**.
When the labour market **changes**, it may be necessary to **re-categorise** the classes.
Goldthorpe has been criticised for **neglecting** the particular position of **women** in the labour market — see **Arber**, **Dale** and **Gilbert (1986)**.

See p.41 for more on Goldthorpe's class scheme, and the NS-SEC classification which was developed from it.

Postmodern theory argues that Class is Dead

Postmodern theory says class is **no longer** of **central significance** in modern society. They **criticise** sociology for still focusing on **class** when other forms of **inequality** and **identity** are more relevant.

1) **Cultural differences** (values, lifestyles and beliefs) are what classify individuals to particular groups or strata in current society.

2) Postmodernists argue individuals are not governed by their economic position. Crucially, they say individuals can **place themselves** in groups or strata and move from one to another as their identity develops and changes.

3) **Pakulski and Waters (1996)** argue society has changed from an **economic class society** in 19th century, to a **hierarchical class society** in the first half of the 20th century, to a **status society** in the late 20th century.

In contrast, **Westergaard (1995)** criticises postmodern theory for ignoring the evidence that class still matters. He argues that as gaps between rich and poor are widening, class is **more** significant, not less, in the late 20th and 21st century.

Practice Questions

Q1   What are the two classes described by Marx?

Q2   What three types of power does Weber acknowledge?

Q3   What do postmodernists say about class?

Exam Questions

Q1   Assess the importance of class in British society from different sociological perspectives.   (40 marks)

Q2   Identify and explain two ways in which the concept of class can be related to one or more of the following topics: families and households; health; education; work and leisure.   (8 marks)

You should have guessed when there were no Marxists on the last page...

You knew deep inside it was too good to be true. Marx ignores the middle class, mainly because there wasn't really a middle class in the 1840s. Neo-Marxists acknowledge that society today is more complex. Weberians base everything on labour market position. And postmodernists pop up to say that class doesn't exist in a postmodern world, and that identities are all self-built anyway.

Differences in Opportunity

An individual's chance of experiencing good and bad sides of life are greatly influenced by the social groups they're born into. You'll see this referred to as life-chances. From a sociologist's perspective, the evidence shows we're not born equal.

The **Higher** an individual's **Social Class**, the **Better Chances** they have in life

This is almost **common knowledge** — but in sociology you have to give **evidence** to go along with common knowledge stuff.

1) Class affects an individual's chances from birth. The chances of a child dying before their first birthday are much higher if they're born into a lower social class.

2) When a child goes to school, their chances of achieving good results are better if they're in a higher social class.

3) When they go on to work they're more likely to become unemployed if they're from a working class background — **Goldthorpe and Payne (1986)**.

4) If they stay in work they're more likely to be paid less in a lower class occupation than in a middle class occupation.

5) An individual is more likely to suffer ill health and poor medical resources if they're working class. The **Black Report (1980)** and **Acheson Report (1998)** document this in detail.

6) Finally, social class affects how long a person lives.

Infant Mortality Rates in the UK (per 1000 live births)	1991	2001
Professional class	5.1	3.6
Unskilled Manual Class	8.2	7.2
Overall rate	5.3	4.6

Social Trends 33, (2003)

% achieving 5 or more A-C GCSE grades	2002
Higher professional	77%
Routine workers	32%

Social Trends 34, (2004)

Gross Weekly Incomes 2002	
Non-manual (men)	£608
Manual (men)	£366

Social Trends 33, references 2002 New Earnings Survey

Average Age at Death 1997-99	Men	Women
Professional class	78.5	82.8
Unskilled manual class	71.1	77.1
Overall	75.0	79.7

There's more on health inequalities according to class, gender, and ethnicity on p.84-87.

There are **Health Inequalities** between **Women** and **Men**

1) Women made up 55% of the UK population in 2001 (the last census).

2) On average women live five years longer than men. In 2001 average age at death was 75 years for men and 80 years for women. In fact, **death rates** are higher for males than females in all age groups.

3) Men in the UK are more likely to **commit suicide** than women, again in all age groups. There's not yet been a great deal of sociological research into the causes of elevated male death rate and suicide rate — a little, but not much.

4) Women are more likely to be **diagnosed** with mental health problems. Some sociologists say this is because of more stressful lives, while others say it's to do with sexism within the medical profession.

In a 2000 survey of people aged 18-74, **20% of women** had enough **symptoms** in the week before the survey to be diagnosed as having a **neurotic disorder**. This was compared to **14% of men**.

Neurotic disorders = depression, anxiety, phobias, obsessive-compulsive disorder

(Office of National Statistics — Psychiatric Morbidity Among Adults Living in Private Households, 2000)

UK women experience **Inequalities** in **Life Chances**

There's more on the theory about gender inequalities on p.132-133.

1) Women **earn less** than men and are **less likely** to be in the **top jobs**. There's still a "glass ceiling". In sociology-speak, the labour market is "**vertically** segregated in terms of gender" (men on one level, women on another).

- In 1996, **23%** of board members of **British government bodies** were women.
- After the labour election win of 1997 there were many **new women MPs** (they were known at the time as "Blair's babes") but even with this increase only **18% of MPs** were women
- In 1994-5 **93%** of all **professors** in English universities were **men**.

(Office for National Statistics, 2000)

2) Some **occupations** are almost exclusively **female** — e.g. primary school teaching. There are **more women** than men in **clerical** jobs, in **retail**, and in **catering**. There are more **male** than female **building site foremen**. In sociology-speak, the labour market is "**horizontally** segregated in terms of gender" (men on one side and women on another, on the same level of the class hierarchy). Some of these "feminine" jobs may be lower paid than equivalent masculine jobs.

Differences in Opportunity

Ethnic Minorities are more likely to experience Discrimination and Inequality

1) **8%** of the current UK population belong to an **ethnic minority** — Social Trends 33, (2003).

2) People in households headed by someone from an **ethnic minority** are more likely to be at the **bottom** of the **income scale** than those where the head of household was **white** — Social trends 33, 2003.

It's important to distinguish between different ethnic minority groups.

3) **Bangladeshi** and **Pakistani** groups have the **highest unemployment** rates in the UK.

> In the UK in 2001-2002, **21%** of **Bangladeshis** were unemployed and **16%** of **Pakistanis**, compared with **4%** of the **white** population, **6%** of the **Chinese** population and **7%** of the **Indian** population.

(Annual Labour Force Survey, reported in Social trends 33, 2003)

4) **Bangladeshis**, **Pakistanis** and **Black Caribbeans** were **least likely** to be in the **highest socio-economic group**, (higher managers and professionals).

> In 2001-2002, **3%** of the **top social class** were **Bangladeshi**, **4%** were **Pakistani** and **5% Black Caribbean**, compared to **11% Chinese**, and **34% White** (made up of **8% White British**, **10% White Irish** and **16% Other White**)

(Annual Labour Force Survey, reported in Social trends 34, 2004)

5) People of **Bangladeshi**, **Black African** and **Other Black** origin were **most likely** to live in housing in the **social rented sector** (rented from the council and housing associations). Whites and Indians were most likely to own their home.

> In 2001, **48%** of **Bangladeshis**, **50%** of **Black Africans** and **50% of Other Black** were in social rented housing, compared to **8% Indian** and **17% White** British. **79%** of **Indians** and **71%** of **White British** were owner-occupiers.

(2001 census)

Important **public inquiries** have found evidence of **racism** in modern Britain, in many areas of life. The **Gifford Report (1989)** found evidence of **widespread racism** in the police force. The post-Brixton riot **Scarman Report (1981)** said Britain wasn't institutionally racist, but public policy often had **unintended consequences** that **disadvantaged ethnic minorities**. The **MacPherson Report (1999)** into the investigation of the Stephen Lawrence murder said that the police force was institutionally racist, and said that the recommendations of the Scarman Report had been ignored.

Both the Young and the Old face Inequality in Life Chances

1) Young people have **lower wages** than average — this is partly to be expected, as they lack job experience. Young people are more likely to be **unemployed** than the average.

2) Old people also have **low incomes**, because of **poor pension provision** and **ageism** in employment.

3) Britain has an ageing population. The number of people aged **65 and older** has increased by **51%** since **1961** — **Social Trends (2003)**. There are now more over 65s than under 16s. These social trends have led to a changing position for older people in society.

4) **Pressure groups** campaign for fairer treatment of older people. They have a powerful voice with politicians because they make up a large section of the voting public and a powerful voice with business and industry because they make up a large section of the **spending** public. There have been campaigns to stop **ageism** in the **workplace**, improve **pension** levels, and improve **care** and **housing** rights and resources.

Practice Questions

Q1   Define the term life-chances.

Q2   Give examples of how social class can affect opportunities open to an individual.

Q3   Give an example of social inequality affecting a) men and b) women.

Q4   Which ethnic groups are most likely to be unemployed?

Q5   Give an example of social inequality affecting young people.

Exam Question

Q1   "Structured inequalities affect the opportunities and experiences of every individual in the UK." Discuss with reference to one or more of the following topics: education, work and leisure, families and households, poverty and welfare.   (40 marks)

See, it's all fair after all — women are paid less, but get to live longer...

If you're a stats geek, the Office of National Statistics website will ring your bell. They have huge mountains of statistics on just about every sociological factor you can think of. If stats aren't your thing, just learn the stats on these pages. You need some statistics to back up your argument in the exam — they don't give high marks for wild guesses and flights of fancy.

Changes in the Class Structure

No system of social stratification is fixed and static. The British stratification system has undergone considerable change in the 20th century — alongside the changes in society. I sense you switching off again — stop it at once.

There's been a **Change** in **Work** patterns

1) Britain in the 20th century has seen a **decline in manual jobs** and an increase in non-manual jobs. The 1997 Labour Market Trends report shows that between 1983 and 1997, production jobs fell from 5,644,000 to 4,245,000.

2) Much of this trend is related to the increase in the service industries such as **leisure** and **entertainment**. The Welfare State also created a new sector of non-manual jobs. The **NHS** is the **largest employer** in **Europe**.

3) **Women** have become an **equal part** of the **workforce**. During the 20th century there's been a **dramatic increase** in the number of **women** who have **paid jobs**. Since 1971 it's gone up from 56% of women to 70% of women.

There have been changes in **Income** and **Wealth Distribution**

1) Statistics show that in the 20th century there was a steady pattern of both **income** and **wealth** being more **widely distributed** across the British population — until the 1980s when the trends were reversed.

2) There are still **big differences** in income in the UK, and the change in distribution has largely been from the upper class to **middle classes**, not to the poorest.

3) Wealth is harder to measure (not all wealth has to be declared). Most wealth remains in the hands of a **minority**.

4) Despite increased wealth of the population, the **gap** between rich and poor remains.

The **Ruling Class** has **Changed** — opinions differ on just **How Much**

The New Right say that the ruling class has disintegrated.
Peter Saunders (1990) argues that the increase in the number of people **owning shares** in the UK has led to power being spread more widely. The small minority in power has been replaced with a **nation of stakeholders**.

Marxists insist the ruling class is alive and kicking.
1) **John Scott (1982, 1991)** agrees with Saunders that **more and more people own shares** in the UK but argues this hasn't led to a break-up of the ruling class. Most individuals own a **few** shares but hold **very little** real **power**.

2) Scott, and **Westergaard and Resler (1976)** say there's still a **power elite** who own **vast amounts** of **shares** and control business and the economy.

3) Scott says the **lifestyle** of the ruling class has changed — it's not all about "Hooray Henries" any more. However, changes in the lifestyle of the ruling class shouldn't be confused for a change in the **power** they hold. Wealth and power is still passed on through families — in 1990, 104 of the 200 richest families had inherited their wealth.

The **Middle Class** has **Grown**, but may be **Breaking Up** into **Several Classes**

1) The rise of the **professions** such as teaching, law and medicine have been cited by Functionalist and Weberian sociologists as evidence of an expanding middle class.

2) **Embourgeoisement** means working class people taking **middle class jobs** and **becoming middle class**. It was popular in sociology in the 1950s and 1960s to explain how the highest paid working class people became middle class in **lifestyle**, **wealth** and **values** as they became more affluent. This concept was used to predict a future where British society would be **largely middle class**. But reality wasn't quite so straightforward.

3) **Goldthorpe et al (1968)** tested the embourgeoisement thesis by interviewing car workers in Luton. They concluded that affluence had **not** made the workers middle class, and clear differences remained between them and the non-manual middle class workers — e.g. their attitudes to work and possibility of future promotion.

Some say the middle class is fragmenting into several middle classes with different life-chances and experiences.
1) **Goldthorpe** says there's an **Intermediate Class** of low grade non-manual workers who have little in common with middle class professionals. In terms of wages, perks, and relationship with employers, these groups are totally distinct.

2) Marxist **Harry Braverman (1974)** says many non-manual workers have been de-skilled by technology, so that they now have more in common with the working class in terms of job security and wealth. This is **proletarianisation**.

3) **Roberts et al (1977)** interviewed "middle class" workers about their view of their own class position and found wide variations in how groups saw themselves. They concluded the middle class is divided into smaller strata which have distinct values and positions in the structure of society — "the middle class are being splintered."

4) Influential sociologist **Giddens (1973)** disagrees — he says there's a **distinct middle class**. The middle class is distinct from the working class because its members can sell their "**brain power**" as well as, or **instead** of, their **labour power**.

Changes in the Class Structure

The 20th Century has Weakened and Divided the British Working Class

The decline in the **traditional working class** sectors of **manufacturing** and **heavy industry** in the 20th century has reduced the **size** of the British **working class**.

	1911	1971
manual work as % of employment	75%	49%

Routh (1981, 1987)

1) **Ralph Dahrendorf (1959)** argues that instead of uniting, the working class has disintegrated.

2) He said that the working class has been divided into groups of **skilled**, **semi-skilled** and **unskilled** workers, and that this is because of changes in technology.

3) Dahrendorf is criticised by **Penn (1983)**, whose research into cotton mills in Rochdale suggests that the working class has been divided into skilled, semi-skilled and unskilled since at least the **1850s**.

4) **Crewe (1983)** argues that the working class is splitting into groups with different concerns and interests, so it can no longer be considered a "real" class. He says that there's a "**new working class**" who live mainly in the South, work in the private sector and own their own homes. They have very different life experiences to the "old working class" who live mainly in the North, in council houses, and work in the public sector.

The idea that the working class is on its way out has been criticised, particularly by Marxist sociologists.

1) Marxist sociologists say that the working class can change its occupation and still be working class.

2) **Beynon (1992)** points out that the old working class jobs have been replaced by new occupations which are **equally badly paid** with poor conditions and rights — e.g. call centres, fast food outlets and hotels. Beynon says that **cooking burgers** is **manual, repetitive labour**, just like working on an assembly line in a factory.

3) Marxists argue what hasn't changed is the **status**, **rights** and **power** that go with the employment — the lack of these things is what makes it working class.

Remember the connection to **globalisation** (see glossary) — part of the reason that manufacturing working class jobs have vanished in the UK is because they've **moved abroad** to cheaper labour markets. There's an "**international division of labour**". Globally, the **working class** includes workers in **South East Asia** and **China** who have few rights and low pay.

Some Sociologists say there is an Underclass beyond the working class

The idea that the most **disadvantaged** groups in society are a **separate group** from the working class isn't **new**. Marx referred to the "lumpenproletariat" (beggars, pickpockets) and the "relative surplus" (people who aren't part of the regular labour market, but who do casual labour when needed). The idea of an underclass has gained support in the late 20th century.

1) The New Right see the underclass as dangerous to society. American sociologist **Charles Murray (1989)** defines the underclass by **behaviour** — **uneducated**, **delinquent** and **work-shy**.

2) **Runciman (1990)** defines the underclass as people who are **permanently dependent** on **welfare benefits**.

3) **Giddens (1973)** defines the underclass as those who are **most disadvantaged** in the job market — e.g. illegal immigrants. He says there's a **secondary job market** of **low paid** jobs with **low job security**, which are the best the underclass can get.

Practice Questions

Q1 Identify 2 long term trends which have affected the British class structure in the 20th century.

Q2 Explain Saunders' argument that the ruling class is no longer relevant in modern Britain.

Q3 Explain what sociologists mean by the terms embourgeoisement and proletarianisation.

Exam Questions

Q1 Examine the argument put forward by some sociologists that the working class has become so divided in the 20th century that it can no longer be considered a "real" class. (12 marks)

Q2 Evaluate the reasons put forward by sociologists for changes in the British class structure in the twentieth century. (40 marks)

Breaking up is so very hard to do...

There are a ridiculous number of sociologists on this page. I know it's a Sociology book, but still. I mean, for heavens sake. It starts off OK until we reach Peter Saunders, and then they just start closing in on you. Scott starts agreeing and Goldthorpe starts testing and then Giddens disagrees and Penn criticises Dahrendorf... please, sociologists, just give it a rest. Seriously.

Social Mobility

Social mobility is all about how easy it is for people to change class. Like if you just go next door and start doing history.

Learn these **Definitions** of **Mobility**

Social mobility = the movement from one strata (class) to another.

Intra-generational mobility = social mobility of the same person within their **lifetime** — i.e. whether they stay in the same class **all their life**.

Inter-generational mobility = Social mobility **between generations** — i.e. whether a person stays in the same social class as their **parents**.

Absolute Mobility = how much social mobility there is in the society as a whole.

Relative Mobility = how much social mobility different social groups have relative to each other.

Upward mobility is fun.

One general rule to remember — the amount of **social mobility** is higher in societies where status is **achieved** than in societies where status is **ascribed** (given at birth). The amount of social mobility shows how **meritocratic** a society is. High mobility shows that people can **achieve** positions on **merit** regardless of the class they were born into.

The **First** major study of **Social Mobility** in Britain was by **Glass** in 1954

Glass (1954) compared social class of fathers and sons

David Glass used statistical data and analysis to compare the class of fathers and sons. He found there was a high level of social mobility — two thirds of sons were in a different social class from their father. This mobility was equally split — one third upward and one third downward.

Yes, that's a long time ago, but it's a classic study — and a springboard for all the research that's happened since.

But, the social mobility was mostly short-range. Most sons moved to the next class up or the next class down. (Glass categorised seven classes). The study also found that the upper class had fewer people moving in or out of it than the other classes.

Conclusion: The evidence was Britain was a society with unequal opportunities for individuals of all classes to reach the top.

The **Oxford Mobility Study** found **Higher** rates of **Social Mobility** in 1972

This study was conducted by **Goldthorpe et al** and used Goldthorpe's seven class scheme (see p.41). You'll see this referred to as the Oxford Study, the Goldthorpe Study or the Nuffield study. Whatever the name, it's the same study.

Goldthorpe (1980) also compared social class of fathers and sons

This study was done in 1972, but not published until 1980.

Results:	There were higher rates of social mobility than in 1949 — half of all sons were in a different social class from their fathers. More of this movement was to a **higher social class** than down to a **lower** one.
Conclusion:	Opportunities for working class individuals had improved in the second half of the 20th century. This has been used by Functionalist sociologists to show that Britain has become a more open and meritocratic society.
However:	Closer analysis showed that the chances of getting into the higher classes were much greater for those whose fathers were already there. There was some movement but relatively the upper classes were still better off.

A neat summary of the probabilities of upward mobility and downward mobility is given by **Kellner and Wilby (1980)**. The data revealed a **1:2:4** rule of "relative hope" — whatever the chance of a **working class** son being in the **professional class** as an adult, it was **twice** as much for an **intermediate class** son and four times as much for an **upper class** son. So, this study has also been used by sociologists to show Britain is an unfair society.

Upper class people tend to be **Born Upper Class**

There's a much greater chance of **higher class** individuals **staying** in that class than **working class** individuals **moving up**. The top classes in the UK remain very **static** — the majority of members come from families who have been in the upper class for **generations**. The elite recruit the sons of those already in the elite (elite self-recruitment).

1) **Stanworth and Giddens (1974)** found that of the top company positions in over four hundred British companies, only 1% were occupied by individuals with working class origins.

2) **Goldthorpe and Payne (1986)** did a follow-up to the Oxford study, looking at mobility rates during the **economic recession** of the 1970s. They concluded that mobility rates had **increased generally** but the chances of reaching **top classes** remained **unequal** in favour of those already there.

3) The **Essex study** of social mobility by **Marshall et al (1988)** looked at 1984 data and found that social mobility was increasing, but it was mainly short-range. Working class children are less likely to get top jobs. The **Essex study** also showed that working class people who got upper class jobs were less likely to retain them than upper class people.

Social Mobility

Other sociologists say the Social Mobility Data shows Britain is Meritocratic

There **aren't many** sociologists who interpret the data as evidence of **equality of opportunity** but there are some.

1) The main man is the New Right thinker, **Peter Saunders**. He uses the Essex study and The National Development Survey to conclude that the **opportunities** are there for social mobility but the **individual** has to get off their backside and take them.

2) Saunders argues the inequality that exists results from differences in the **talent** and **hard work** of the individual — not their class of origin.

> "Class destinations reflect **individual merit** much more than class background." — **Saunders (1996)**

3) Saunders has been **criticised** by many sociologists. His **methodology** is criticised — he **doesn't include** the **unemployed** and **part-time employees** in his analysis.

4) Saunders' views have also been criticised because **class bias** at school could mean that school achievement reflects class background rather than ability. **Labelling** and **stereotypes** at school might discourage **working class** pupils from applying themselves to their studies.

See the AS course, or the OCR section on education, p.72.

Savage and Egerton (1997) analysed the **same** development survey as Saunders, but came to a very different conclusion.

They found that those with the same ability didn't all have the same chances of ending up in the higher classes. Other factors such as **social networks**, **confidence** and **cultural advantages** helped upper class children get to the top — e.g. they argue that educational qualifications and tests are based on middle and upper class culture and values. (This is covered in the AS course).

What about the girls — Women's Social Mobility wasn't studied until 1981

1) One of the biggest problems with the usefulness of the study of social mobility is that almost all major studies failed to take any account whatsoever of the class position of **girls** and **women**.

2) The first time women were included in a study was in 1981. **Heath (1981)** went back and looked at the statistics for 1971 and 1975 and compared **fathers'** and **daughters'** social class positions (still no mothers). He found that in classes one and two, **daughters** were much more likely to be **downwardly mobile** than sons.

3) **Goldthorpe and Payne (1986)** concluded that women's mobility rates varied according to which class they were in — just the **same as men**. They argue from this that the non-inclusion of women in previous studies didn't affect the overall results. Class overrode gender.

4) The **Essex study (1988)** looked at male and female mobility and found that women moved both up and down into the **routine non-manual** group — most routine non-manual work was done by women regardless of their class of origin.

5) **Savage and Egerton (1997)** looked at male and female mobility and found that class affected opportunity less for daughters than it did for sons. This may be because middle class sons can access an "**old boys' network**", or because of remaining sexism in traditional upper middle class jobs.

Feminist sociologists used to argue that as long as a woman's class is defined largely by the **male** she lives with (social class is defined by the occupation of the **Head of Household**, usually the **male** breadwinner), social mobility studies will reveal **very little** of significance about the impact of gender on social mobility. In **2000**, government statistics switched from a scheme that measured women by the **man's job** to a scheme which measured women by their **own job**. So, some **more useful studies** might come along soon — it'll be possible to see how a mother's occupational class affects her kids.

Practice Questions

Q1 Explain the different types of social mobility sociologists have studied.
Q2 What did the Oxford mobility study find out about social mobility?
Q3 What's meant by saying that the upper class is "static"?

Exam Question

Q1 Identify and explain two difficulties faced by sociologists when attempting to accurately measure social mobility. (8 marks)

I'm upper class — I have to go up three flights of stairs...

This may not be your favourite topic. You may be pining for the heady days of 'Section 1: Power, Politics and Protest'. Thing is, you've got an exam coming up, and this could be a good opportunity to get some marks squared away. Learn the studies — the Oxford study, Goldthorpe and Payne's follow up and Savage and Egerton are three good ones to learn and remember.

Defining Crime and Deviance

*This section is for **AQA** and **OCR**. OCR people just have to learn what's in this section. AQA people have to be able to relate it to other areas of sociology from the AS course as well as the A2 course — e.g. health, the mass media, families etc.*

Here are some **Definitions** of **Crime** and **Deviance**

> **Deviance** = behaviour which goes against the **norms**, **values** and **expectations** of a **social group** or **society**.

> **Crime** = behaviour which **breaks laws** and is **punished** by the **legal system**.

Crime is deviant, but **not all deviance** is **criminal**. Think about it — it's hard to think of a criminal act which isn't also viewed as deviant but it's easy to make a long list of **non-criminal deviant behaviour** — picking your nose in public and eating it, cross-dressing, barking like a dog during a job interview, swearing at the referee, cheating at poker, etc.

Downes and Rock (1988) gave this definition of **deviance**: "Deviance may be considered as **banned** or **controlled** behaviour which is likely to attract **punishment** or **disapproval**."

Brian decided that cross-dressing was the best form of deviance for him.

Crime and Deviance are Socially Constructed

1) Both crime and deviance are **culturally determined**. What is considered criminal varies less than what's considered deviant.

2) **Deviance changes** with **time** and **place**, as values, norms and social expectations change. 100 years ago, it was deviant for women to wear trousers. Postmodernist **Michel Foucault** wrote three books about how **criminal** deviance, **sexual** deviance and **madness** have changed throughout history.

3) Also, what's **deviant** for some groups in society is **conformity** for another. **Subcultures** have **different norms** to mainstream society.

The same act can be seen as **deviant** or **non-deviant** depending on the situation — See **Plummer (1979)**.

> **Societal deviance means acts which are seen by most of society as deviant, in most situations**
> * **Swearing** at an **authority figure** — even people who do it know it's deviant.
> * Random acts of **extreme violence**. ← *Even in manga cartoons, this is the mark of a true nutcase.*
> * **Child abuse** — considered universally wrong by society.

> **Situational deviance means acts which can be defined as deviant or normal, depending on the circumstances**
> * Being **naked** — OK in your **own home**, deviant on the **High Street**. 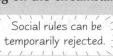 *Social rules can be temporarily rejected.*
> * Wearing **fishnet and PVC** from head to toe — OK in a **goth** **or fetish club**, deviant at **work** in an accountant's office.
> * **Killing** someone — OK if you're a **soldier at war** killing enemy soldiers, otherwise deviant.

Social Order and Social Control create a Consensus of how to behave

1) By definition, **most behaviour** in society isn't **criminal** or **deviant**. **Social order** and **social control** maintain the **status quo** and create a **value consensus** of how to behave. People are **socialised** to follow social norms.

2) Some norms become **second nature**. For example — when having a **face-to-face conversation**, people manage to stand the right distance apart, look at each other when they're talking without staring excessively, be polite and tactful, not talk for too long — all **without really thinking** about it.

3) Other norms are followed because we're **consciously aware** that they're a norm — e.g. stopping at a red traffic light.

4) **Sanctions** are **rewards** and **punishments** that **reinforce** social norms.

	Positive sanctions — these **reward** people for **conforming** to a norm.	**Negative sanctions** — these **punish** people for **deviating** from a norm.
Formal sanctions — carried out by an **official agency**.	• A **certificate** for passing an A level exam. • A **medal** for bravery in the armed forces. • A **cup** for winning a sporting final.	• A **fine** for breaking the law. • **Points** on a driving licence. • A **yellow card** from the referee.
Informal sanctions — carried out by the **public**.	• A **pat on the back**. • Saying **"well done"** for good behaviour.	• Deliberately **ignoring** someone. • A **telling-off** for bad behaviour.

Defining Crime and Deviance

Sociologists are interested in **Social Causes** of **Crime** and **Deviance**

Sociologists are interested in **crime** and **deviance** as a **social phenomenon** — it's part of understanding society.

The key questions about crime are:

Studying deviance is less clear-cut, because there's **deviance** and **social control** in all areas of sociological study

- Does crime have a **purpose**?
- What are the **causes** of crime?
- **Who** commits crime?
- What is the **extent** of crime?

This is all discussed on the next few pages.

There are **Non-Sociological Theories** of why **Crime** exists

Sociologists are not the only ones interested in understanding crime and deviance in society. The first theories regarding why crime and deviance exist in society were first established in the **19th century** and were based on the **psychological** or **physiological** characteristics of the individual deviant.

Physiological theories say that criminals are physically different

1) 19th century Italian doctor, **Cesare Lombroso (1876)** became famous for his theory that criminals were **genetically different**. He stated there were **outward signs** of the criminal personality such as a large jaw or extra fingers or toes.

2) Don't dismiss physiological theories as staying in the 19th century, though. They've moved with the times. **Moir and Jessel (1995)** argue **hormonal** and **chemical imbalances** make individuals more likely to be criminal. They say these imbalances affect **men** more than women, explaining why statistics show most crime is committed by men. Here's a **quote** from Moir and Jessel: "The male mind — whether for reasons of evolution or something else — is wired and fuelled to be more criminal."

Psychological theories say that criminals are mentally different

1) Others argue criminals are **psychologically** different from the rest of the population. Again, these theories started in the 19th century but have travelled through to the 20th century.

2) **Bowlby (1946)** argued that individuals who are **deprived of maternal love** in the first years of life are likely to **develop personality traits** which lead them to commit **crime**.

3) **Eysenck (1964)** concluded from his psychological research that individuals who commit crime have **inherited psychological characteristics** which **predispose** them to crime.

The **21st century** versions of physiological and psychological theories argue there is a **gene for crime** which some individuals **inherit** and others don't.

For the **non-sociological theories** the cause of crime lies within the **individual**. For **sociology** the cause of crime lies in **society**.

Practice Questions

Q1 Give an example of a behaviour which is deviant but not criminal.
Q2 What is situational deviance?
Q3 Give an example of a formal negative sanction and an example of an informal positive sanction.
Q4 Give an example of a psychological theory of crime.
Q5 Give one difference between physiological and psychological theories of crime.

Exam Question

Q1 Outline and assess the view that "The cause of crime lies within the individual." (60 marks)

Naughty, naughty, very naughty...

There's something about the word "deviance" that conjures up men in PVC suits cavorting in vats of custard. Or is that just me... Anyway, point being that deviance isn't limited to weird sexual deviance. It actually covers all behaviour that doesn't conform to social norms. Conformity is rewarded and deviance is punished. Remember, some deviance depends on the situation.

Theories of Crime and Deviance

All sociological theories regarding crime and deviance are trying to say why crime exists. Structural theories of crime all argue the cause of crime lies in the structure of society, but they disagree on a lot more than they have in common.

Functionalists *argue crime and deviance are* Useful *and* Necessary *in society*

You might well wonder how on earth crime can be useful. Functionalists say it's because it has a **function** in society:

1) Crime and deviance reinforce the **consensus** of values, norms and behaviour of the majority non-deviant population — people can join together in outrage.

2) **Durkheim (1897)** said deviancy allows for **social change** to occur. Durkheim and the Functionalists who came after him argue that all societies need some change to remain healthy and stable. If society reacts positively to deviant behaviour it starts the process for that behaviour to be seen as non-deviant in the future.

3) **Durkheim** said crime moves from **functional** to **dysfunctional** when the level of crime is either **too high** or **too low**.
   - Too high, and it threatens social order. • Too low, and there's no social change.

Albert Cohen (1966) *identified two ways that deviance maintained* Social Order

1) He argued forms of deviance such as **prostitution** provide a **safety valve** for releasing tension without threatening social stability.

2) Secondly, he argued deviant behaviour is used as a **warning device** by society to **identify** emerging **social problems**, which can then be dealt with, e.g. civil disobedience, protests, and truancy.

Merton said Crime *is a* Response *to* Failing *to* Achieve *society's cultural goals*

1) Functionalist **Robert Merton (1968)** concluded from his American study that the vast majority of individuals share the same goals but don't have equal access to the means of achieving these goals.

2) He identified the main cultural goal in American society as **success** and **wealth**. He said that the main (institutionalised) means of achieving that goal was through the education system. When individuals fail or are excluded from this system, this creates **anomie**. ← *Anomie = a lack of values, and feeling of purposelessness.*

3) Merton argues that individuals who fail at the standard route to success select **alternative** and **deviant** means of reaching success and wealth — e.g. **crime**.

4) Merton says they may also **retreat** from society — e.g. by **dropping out**, **drinking** to excess or taking **drugs**.

5) They may also **rebel** against society, and engage in **protest** and revolution to try and change society.

Subcultural *theories say* Cultural Values *of some groups* Encourage Deviance

Some deviance is **conformity** to norms and values – just **different** norms and values to **mainstream society**.

Cohen said delinquent gangs provide prestige for adolescents frustrated at their lack of status in society

Albert Cohen (1955) said that working class boys suffered from a lack of opportunities to succeed in mainstream society, largely due to cultural deprivation. This leads to dissatisfaction with their position in society — which Cohen called **status frustration**.

This tension is **released** by joining or creating groups which have **alternative values** to achieve status. These values tend to be the **reverse** of those of mainstream society — behaviour deviant in society becomes **normal** and **valued** in the subcultural group. For example, **petty crime** or **drug-taking** might be valued by the group.

1) **Cloward and Ohlin (1960) combined** the ideas of **Merton** with the ideas of **Cohen**. They believed there was a **legitimate opportunity structure** (passing exams and getting a job, as Merton said), and an **illegitimate opportunity structure** (being in a gang and committing crime, e.g. theft and vandalism).

2) They also argued that access to the **illegitimate** opportunity structure is **no more equal** than access to the **legitimate** system. In some areas, there are criminal gangs which provide adolescents a deviant route to success and status, and in some areas there aren't. This explained why **not all** frustrated working class boys turned to **crime**.

3) Cloward and Ohlin said where there's **no access** to criminal gangs, frustrated adolescents form their own **violent gangs**.

4) They also said that adolescents who have **failed** in **both** the legitimate opportunity structure and the illegitimate opportunity structure **retreat** from society and turn to drink or drugs.

The subcultural theories have been criticised for **assuming** that the majority of people aspire to the **mainstream goals** of success and wealth. **Taylor, Walton and Young (1973)** point to deviant groups such as **hippies** who **don't share these goals**.

Theories of Crime and Deviance

Miller thought crime and delinquency come from *Working Class Cultural Values*

W.B. Miller (1962) said that general **lower working class culture**, not subcultural gangs, was what encouraged lawbreaking behaviour. According to Miller, values passed from generation to generation encourage **working class men** to break the law. Delinquents are simply conforming to the "**focal concerns**" of their culture. "Focal concerns" are the main things that are valued in that culture, e.g. exciting thrills and macho toughness.

Miller was **criticised** right from the beginning. **Bordua (1962)** said that the idea that the working class live their lives **isolated** from the rest of society is **flawed to begin with**.

Miller's ideas have been supported by recent **New Right** sociologists. **Charles Murray (1990, 1993)** believes that there's an underclass in both British and American society with a **distinct culture** and **value system** which **encourages** deviant behaviour.

Individuals drift from *Mainstream* culture to *Deviant Subculture* and *Back Again*

1) **Matza (1964)**, on the other hand, argued that most delinquents **conform** to society's norms and values like everybody else for most of the time, but that under certain circumstances they can convince themselves that the law **doesn't apply** to them.

2) He thought that there was an **alternative** culture running **alongside mainstream culture** (or underneath it — he called the alternative culture "**subterranean values**"). According to Matza, this alternative culture values **spontaneity** and doesn't value responsibilities, so it provides a **break** from the usual commitments of life.

3) Matza argues individuals **drift** into this subculture at times of **stress** and **isolation** but most of the time remain outside of it, **conforming** to **mainstream** culture.

Marxists see *Crime* as an *Inevitable Consequence* of *Capitalism*

1) Traditional Marxist criminology says that the **rich** and **powerful** decide what is considered deviant and criminal in society to **suit their own interests**. No surprise for Marxists that the most common group convicted of crime is the working class — Marxists say the system is rigged against them.

2) Crime such as robbery and property theft is seen by traditional Marxists like **Bonger (1916)** as an inevitable response to the **extremes** of **wealth** and **poverty** in capitalist society. They see the individual as "**forced**" into crime by the structure of society.

3) The neo-Marxist position is best represented by **Taylor, Walton and Young (1973)**. They looked at previous studies as well as conducting their own, and agree with Marxists that crime is caused by the **inequalities** of capitalist society.

4) The new bit of their thinking is that is they reckon that individuals choose crime as an **active attempt to change their lot**, rather than being "**forced**" into crime almost subconsciously, as previous theories suggested. Their "fully social theory of deviance" concludes that the cause of crime lies in **every aspect** of the structure of capitalist society.

See p.63 for details of the "fully social theory of deviance".

Because Marxists see the "system" as the cause of crime, much Marxist sociology has looked at the systems of **power**, **control** and **punishment**, i.e. the **police**, the **law** and the **courts**. This is covered on p.62-63.

Practice Questions

Q1 Why did Merton think people committed crime?
Q2 What is meant by "status frustration"?
Q3 What did Miller say was the cause of crime?
Q4 What do Marxists think causes crime?

Exam Questions

Q1 Examine the ways in which subcultures may be relevant to the study of one or more of the following: education; poverty and welfare; work and leisure; mass media. (12 marks)

Q2 "The cause of crime lies in the structure of society not the nature of the individual." Consider this statement referring to at least two different sociological perspectives. (40 marks)

Society made me do it...

Unlikely to stand up in a court of law, that one. I wouldn't recommend defending yourself by quoting Merton and Cohen. It didn't work for me after all that unpleasantness with the goat smuggling. Anyway, I'm not going into all that now. The past is the past. And I was actually doing society a favour — I was acting as a warning device that goats are not fairly distributed in the UK.

Measuring Crime

Measuring crime isn't straightforward. Different statistics use different techniques and reach different, conflicting conclusions.

Police *crime figures* Don't *reflect the* Full Extent *of* Crime *in Britain*

Police crime figures have been recorded and published annually in Britain since 1857. For the first hundred years, these were largely taken as an accurate record of all crime but then sociologists began to question how reliable police stats are.

(1) **Firstly**, official police records only report crimes **known to the police**. Not all crime is **reported** to the police.

1) Individuals don't report crime if they **don't have faith in the police** to investigate and solve it.

2) Crime won't be reported to the police if the victim is **intimidated** by the perpetrator. Many communities have **gangs** of criminals who **threaten** anyone who reports their crimes, including witnesses as well as victims.

3) Much sexual crime is not reported because of the embarrassment, fear and shock of the victim.

4) Some victims see the crime against them as trivial — or fear the police will see it as trivial.

(2) **Secondly**, the police **don't record all crime** that's reported to them. Police officers use their own discretion to decide whether an incident is a crime **worth reporting** — if there's enough evidence to say a crime has really been committed, if the incident is serious enough to be a crime, etc. This makes crime reporting unreliable — some officers will record an incident, while others may consider it too **trivial** or lacking in evidence.

(3) **Thirdly**, not all offences **count** as crimes to be recorded by the police. For example, police weren't required to record all common assaults until 1989. **Official rules** and definitions **change**. In **1998**, **new guidelines** allowed police to record a lot more incidents as crime. This alone increased the level of crime recorded by 15%.

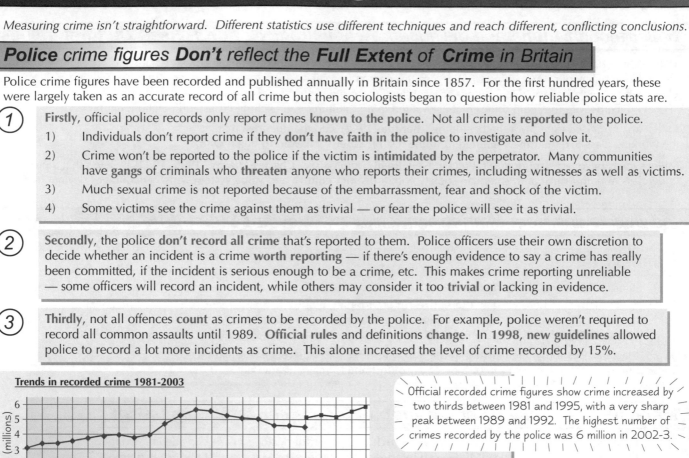

Trends in recorded crime 1981-2003

crimes (millions) — 0 1 2 3 4 5 6

1981 1983 1985 1987 1989 1991 1993 1995 1997 1999 2001 2003

◆ old rules
■ new rules post 1998

Official recorded crime figures show crime increased by two thirds between 1981 and 1995, with a very sharp peak between 1989 and 1992. The highest number of crimes recorded by the police was 6 million in 2002-3.

Victim Surveys *include crime* Not Reported *to the* Police

A victimisation (or victim) survey is an anonymous survey of individuals asking for details of crimes committed against them (even if not reported to the police) within a set time period, usually the last year.

1) The most significant victim survey in Britain is the **British Crime Survey** (**BCS**), which interviews a **sample** of the population (approx 14 000), and asks them about their experiences of being a victim of crime over the past year. All answers are confidential and can't be passed on to the police. The survey results are applied to the whole UK population.

Trends in crime: BCS 1981-2003

crimes (millions) — 0 5 10 15 20

1981 1983 1985 1987 1989 1991 1993 1995 1997 1999 2001 2003

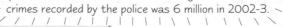

2) The BSC is respected for giving a fuller picture of crime in the UK. It indicates a significant level of unrecorded crime. In 1997, **44%** of crimes were **reported** to the police. **97%** of **vehicle theft** was reported but only **57%** of **robbery** and **26%** of **vandalism**. Also, **46%** of crime **reported** to the police wasn't **recorded**, because of a **lack of evidence**.

3) The **gap** between BCS and police figures has **reduced** since changes to **police recording criteria** in the late 1990s. Both victim surveys and police figures reveal the same **broad trends**. Crime **rose** in the **1980s** and **1990s**, and since **2002** there's been a **small reduction** in the overall crime level.

4) There are **problems** with reliability of victim surveys:

- Even the largest **victim surveys** only interview a **small sample** of the population.
- BCS doesn't survey all crime. It doesn't include crimes against a business, for example.
- **No under 16s** are interviewed for the BCS.

1) Sociologist **Jock Young (1988)** questioned the validity of victim surveys by pointing out that **each respondent's definition** of what's criminal is **different**, so the same incident would be mentioned by one person and not by another.

2) Also, some people are **more willing** to **reveal their experiences** than others.

3) Young accepts that victim surveys have a place in research, but maintains they **don't** give a **true, full picture** of crime.

Measuring Crime

Self-Report Studies ask people about Crime They've Committed

1) Self-report studies ask respondents to reveal crime they've committed. They're **less widely used** than victim studies.

2) Self-report studies are anonymous and representative of the population, like victim studies.

3) The obvious reliability problem is that the respondent may not trust that the evidence won't be given to anyone else, including the police.

4) However, they have been important in researching who commits crime.

> An analysis of 40 self-report studies by **Steve Box (1981)** indicated that **juvenile crime** was not a **working class** problem as had been widely argued. **Middle class** juveniles committed crime too but were less likely to get caught.
>
> Similar results have been found in the **adult** population. **Maguire (1997)** concluded **most respondents** admitted committing **some crime** at some point in their life. This is evidence against the argument that certain social groups are more likely to commit crime than others (there's more about this idea on pages 58-59).

Official Statistics show Fear of Crime is Rising

1) Statistics show that public **fear** of being a victim of crime is rising.

2) Public assessment consistently **overestimates** the actual amount of crime in Britain. People believe that the crime rate is going up faster than it really is. Also, far more people fear becoming a victim of crime than ever will become a victim of crime.

3) This stark difference between the level of crime and fear of crime has been attributed to the way crime is reported in the media. **Tabloid** papers often use **alarmist headlines** about crime and deviance to grab the attention of readers. It's been argued that these **exaggerate** the chances of being a victim of crime — which creates fear or panic in the population .

4) The Home Office Statistical Bulletin (2003) revealed that those individuals who read **tabloid newspapers** were twice as likely to be worried about crime compared to those who read broadsheets or didn't read any newspapers.

5) **Fletcher and Allen (2003)** identify several factors which affect the fear of crime, including locality, health, age, perception of disorder and whether a person has previously been a victim of crime.

Pantazis and Gordon found the poor are most likely to fear crime

Pantazis and Gordon (1999) analysed household surveys and found households with the **lowest incomes** were most likely to **fear** crime, but households with the **highest incomes** were actually the most likely to become **victims** of crime.

This is due to the consequences of crime being **more severe** for people who are **too poor** to **insure** their property, or buy **replacements**.

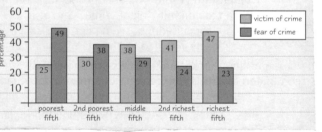

Practice Questions

Q1 Name two types of statistics published each year on levels of crime in Britain.

Q2 What crimes are not covered by the British Crime Survey?

Q3 What's a self-report survey?

Q4 Which social groups are most likely to fear crime?

Exam Questions

Q1	Identify and explain two ways in which official statistics may underestimate the level of crime in the UK.	(8 marks)
Q2	Examine the problems faced by sociologists trying to measure the level of crime in the UK.	(12 marks)

What's that old saying about lies and damned lies and that other thing...

There are quite a lot of statistics just on these pages. Once you scratch the surface of various government statistics it's amazing just how many figures there are out there. Try not to get too bogged down in detail, but do learn the central trends and which type of study they come from. Each type of study has its own supporters and its critics — make sure you can say why that is.

Patterns of Crime

Crime is not equally distributed in the UK. There are age, gender, class and ethnicity differences.

Young people are Convicted of More Crime than Older People

Most crime is committed by teenagers. The peak age for criminal activity is 18 for men and 15 for women (Social Trends, 33).

1) It's argued that young people commit more crime because their **lifestyles** take them to **environments** where **crime takes place**. The vast majority of crime is **property theft** — young people are more likely to be on the **streets** or in **clubs**, which is where **pickpocketing** and **mugging** often happens.

2) This is supported by the evidence that **young people** are most likely to be **victims** of crime too — if you're aged between 16-25 you're six times more likely to be a victim of crime than those aged 75 and older. It's not age itself, but the **likelihood** of being in areas where **opportunities for crime** arise which is the significant factor.

3) Young people may actually commit more crime, or it may be that they get **caught more** than older people. Crime committed by the **young** is typically more **visible**, e.g. vandalism, so it's likely to be witnessed, and the perpetrator is more likely to be caught. "White-collar crimes" such as **fraud** are more likely to be committed by **older people** but these offences are more **hidden** and don't take place in the public arena.

4) **Social stereotypes** that young people commit crime lead to police **suspecting** and **monitoring** young people more than older social groups — increasing their chances of being caught.

5) Young people are more likely to be **convicted** once in court — partly because they can't afford expensive **lawyer's fees**.

Men are Convicted of More Crime than Women

Women make up only **6%** of the prison population. (HM Prison Service)

58% of male prisoners released from prison are **re-convicted within 2 years**. (Social Trends, 1998)

In 2001, **167 per 10 000** of the **male** population were **found guilty** or **cautioned** for an offence compared to **3.7 per 10 000** of the female population.

1) Men are **suspected**, **charged** and **convicted** of crime of all types more than women. This pattern crosses **all other social factors** such as **age**, **class**, **ethnicity** and **region**.

2) The subcultural theories of **Miller (1962)** and **Merton (1968)** argue that the **culture** and **lifestyles** of **young men** encourage and lead to crime (remember, most crime is committed by the young.)

3) **Heidensohn (1986)** says gender socialisation prompts men to be more **aggressive** which makes them more likely than women to commit violent crime. She also says that **women** are **socialised** into **not being criminal** in the same way as men are socialised into seeing criminal activity as acceptable. **Abbott and Wallace (1990)** argue young women are more closely watched by their families and given **less freedom** outside the home, reducing their **opportunities** for crime. Criminal behaviour would be seen as highly **deviant** as well as criminal for women.

4) **Ian Marsh (1986)** reckons that men commit more crime because they have more opportunities to do so. He said that where females have similar opportunities to males they seem as likely to break laws. An example of this is handling stolen goods — women have more opportunity to sell, buy or use stolen property than to steal goods in the first place.

5) There may be an **underestimation** of female crime because the police and courts are **less likely** to **suspect** women or give women a **custodial sentence**. The stereotypes of men as criminal work as a form of **sexism** against men, which allows female criminal activity to go **unchecked**. **Campbell (1981)** did a **self-report survey** which unearthed a lot **more female crime** than the official statistics. However, she did include more trivial crimes than the official statistics do.

Urban areas have much More Crime than Rural ones

In 2003-2004, Metropolitan (urban) police forces recorded 43% of all crime.

In 2002, less than 2% of people living in rural areas became victims of burglary.

In 2003-2004, 60% of all robbery in UK took place in three urban areas (London, Manchester and West Midlands).

This table shows the percentage of households which have been **victims** (at least once) of **vehicle theft**, **burglary** and **violent crime**. The data's from the British Crime Survey, 2004.

There's **more crime** in **cities**.

Area type	All vehicle theft	All burglary	All violent crime
Inner city	15.3	5.3	5.8
Urban (towns and outer part of city)	10.3	3.3	4.4
All non-rural (cities, towns, suburbs)	10.8	3.6	4.6
Rural	6.5	1.9	2.7
All households/all adults	9.7	3.2	4.1

Sociologists argue most crime takes place in cities because there are more **opportunities** to be involved in crime in cities. Higher density populations mean more chances for **robbery** and **property crime**. Most young people live in urban areas and they are the most likely to commit crime. It's hard for criminals to remain anonymous in close-knit rural **communities**.

Patterns of Crime

Most criminal convictions are of people with a *Working Class Background*

There are more **working class** people in **prison** than any other social class.
Home Office figures also show that the majority of people who appear in **court** are working class, regardless of whether they're found guilty or not.

The idea of an upper class person in prison is so rare and contrary to cultural norms, that a Lord convicted of fraud can find himself on a "celebrity" reality TV show.

1) **Sub-cultural theorists** such as **Miller** argue this reflects the working class sub-cultures which often have crime as an accepted or rewarded activity.

2) **Marxists** argue the system of law and order is run by the **ruling class**, against the interests of the working class. They say parts of the working class are criminalised by a biased system — see p.62-63.

3) Middle class crime is treated more leniently by society. Fraud and white collar crime is often undetected and seen as "victimless crime" by the public. Consider public response to benefit fraud compared to tax or insurance fraud. There's more about **Marxist** opinions of why this is on p.62-63.

An *Ethnic Minority Background* increases your chances of arrest and conviction

	Population of the UK	Police "stop and search" England and Wales	Arrests for serious offences, England and Wales	Male prison population	Female prison population
White	92%	74.3%	84.3%	75.7%	69.1%
Asian	4%	7.3%	4.8%	3.4%	0.8%
Black	2%	14.6%	8.8%	16%	25.3%
Mixed and Other	2%	3.7%	2.1%	4.8%	4.7%

2001 census, and the Home Office "Statistics on Race and the Criminal Justice System" (2004)

1) Some have argued that **police racism** results in higher suspicion against black people in general. The Macpherson Report (1999) concluded that the police were institutionally racist. The court system has also been accused of automatically favouring white middle class defendants. There are few black people in either the police force or the legal system.

The stop and search, arrest and prison figures are based on <u>what a person looks like</u>. The census records what a person <u>identifies themselves</u> as.

2) **Hall et al (1978)** and **Gilroy (1987)** argue that young black people have been labelled as criminal by modern British society and have become a **scapegoat** for social problems in society.

3) Hall also says that high levels of **unemployment** among young black men leads some young black men to **opt out** of **mainstream society** and turn to **crime**.

Similar in some ways, but Hall blames the system and New Rightists blame the person.

4) New Right sociologists favour a **subcultural** explanation for the differences.

5) **Ethnic minority** households are **more at risk of crime** than other households — e.g. the British Crime Survey says they're more likely to be mugged than white groups, and slightly more likely to be victims of vehicle theft. Pakistanis and Bangladeshis were more likely to be **burgled**. The survey found ethnic minority respondents were **more worried about crime** in 2000 than white respondents.

Only **23% of reported crimes** in 2003 were **solved** — i.e. someone was convicted for the offence in 2003 (2004 Social Trends). The social profile of who committed the **unsolved** and **undetected** crimes could change these patterns considerably.

Practice Questions

Q1 Which social groups are most likely to be convicted of crime in Britain?
Q2 What evidence is there that crime is more prevalent in urban areas?
Q3 Briefly state the two explanations that Stuart Hall gives for increased arrest and criminality among the black population.

Exam Question

Q1 Examine sociological explanations for 76% of the UK male prison population being white. (12 marks)

Avoid committing crime — be an old woman and live in the countryside...

Of course, that's easier said than done for many of us, particularly young men. But just because a task is difficult does not mean you shouldn't strive to achieve it. Being young, male, working class, black and living in an urban area puts you at the highest risk of being convicted, or of being a victim, of crime. There are loads of possible reasons for this — make sure you understand them.

Social Reactions to Crime and Deviance

Social Action theorists (Interactionists) say that social reaction is really what defines deviance in the first place. Great.

Interactionists *say that* Deviant *folk aren't really* Different *from everyone else*

Interactionist study of crime and deviance starts from the standpoint that deviants are **not characteristically different** from the rest of the population. They are deviant because their chosen behaviour is **labelled deviant** by others in society.

Interactionists therefore think that there aren't any **universal causes** of deviance or crime to be "discovered" by sociologists.

Interactionists stress the view that deviance is **relative** — it varies over time and place because it is defined by each society and by each situation within the same society.

Interactionists are also called social action theorists.

Becker (1963) argues deviance is behaviour which has been labelled deviant by the reaction of others

1) This may sound like common sense, but interactionists like Becker were the first sociologists to **challenge the assumption** that sociologists should focus on what **causes** people to act in deviant and criminal ways.

2) Instead, interactionists studied how an act or behaviour comes to be **labelled as deviant** by the rest of society, and the consequences of that label or reaction.

3) The **same behaviour** gets **different reactions** depending on the social situation. Becker thought there's therefore nothing intrinsically deviant about the act itself. For example, **nudity** is normal and acceptable in the privacy of your own home but seen as deviant (and criminal) in a public space.

4) The **reaction** of those around you is what makes you **recognise** your behaviour as deviant. Becker said "Deviance is not a quality that lies in the **behaviour** itself but in the **interaction** between the person who commits an act, and those who respond to it."

Being Labelled *as* Deviant *can* Affect Future Behaviour

Interactionists argue we form our self-identity from **interpreting** how others respond to us and **internalising** the reaction. A **label** has a **positive** or **negative** effect on the individual and it helps to define them in their **own eyes** as well as in others' eyes. Becker calls this a **"self concept"**.

1) Becker argued that a **self concept** of being deviant can **increase deviant behaviour**. For example, if a person is **shamed** by the reaction of others who know they have been in trouble with the police, they may return to criminal activity or **join a criminal group** to escape the rejection they feel. This then reinforces the label of criminal and it becomes even harder to remove and a bigger part of their identity. Becker called this process the **deviant career**.

2) The **label** of **criminal** is **not easily removed** by society, whatever the actions of the individual — it becomes their **master status** (see glossary). On release from prison many individuals find it hard to obtain work, housing and positions of trust because of the reaction of others to their status as an **ex-offender**.

3) **Jock Young (1971)** used his study of drug users in Notting Hill to demonstrate the process of becoming deviant.

The marijuana users developed a **deviant self concept** because their drug of choice was **illegal**.	The **deviant** element became their **main identity** in society. They were "hippies" first and foremost.	The **negative response** of those around them and the police made the drug-taking more **significant** to their lives.	Their drug-taking **increased**.

4) **Goffman (1961)** wrote about a deviant career in **mental illness**. He said the **negative label** of being **mad** is **imposed** on the patient by society and psychiatry, and that the patient must eventually **conform** to it.

Lemert (1951) *distinguished between* Primary *and* Secondary *deviance*

Primary deviance = the initial deviant act.

Secondary deviance = deviant acts committed after the individual has **accepted the label** of deviant.

1) Lemert argued **most people** commit some acts of **primary deviance** in their lives but that it was of **little significance**.

2) When there's a **societal reaction** (a reaction from society as a whole or groups within society such as family, peers, police and the media) the individual is **labelled** as **deviant**.

3) Lemert argues that when the individual **feels the weight** of the label "deviant" or "criminal", they sometimes commit **more** of the deviant behaviour. For example, once a person is labelled an **alcoholic**, they might drink more because well, they're an alcoholic, and alcoholics drink. Lemert called this **secondary deviance**.

Public reaction to an individual labelled deviant can be very powerful. Sometimes, individuals **commit suicide** once their deviance has been discovered — e.g. it's not uncommon for suspects in Internet child pornography raids to kill themselves.

Social Reactions to Crime and Deviance

Critics argue people are not as Passive as Interactionists suggest

1) **Ronald Akers (1967)** criticises both Becker and Lemert for presenting individuals as **powerless** to make decisions or take control of their own identity. **Deviance**, according to **Akers**, is not something which **happens** to people but a **choice** that individuals make.

2) **Taylor, Walton and Young (1973)** argue many forms of behaviour are **widely viewed** as deviant — so deviants **know** they are breaking the law or social rules **before** any **societal reaction** but they **still do it**.

3) Marxist critics accuse interactionism of **ignoring the role of power** in defining crime and deviance. Certain groups have the **power** to influence what is classified as **criminal** or **socially unacceptable**.

4) **Gouldner (1973)** accused interactionists of being **fascinated with deviance**, and even suggests they enjoy observing "cool" deviants, and hanging out with the "underworld". He thinks interactionists aren't interested in changing society.

The Media plays a powerful role in Amplifying Deviance in society

Interactionists such as **Stanley Cohen (1972)** argue the media helps to **create** the deviance it predicts or anticipates.

> **The Amplification of Deviance**
> 1) Media presents a **distorted view** of the level of crime.
> 2) This distorted view creates **public concern**.
> 3) Related pieces of crime and deviance are **over-reported** and given more prominence than they'd otherwise have.
> 4) This keeps the issue or problem **high** on the **public agenda**.
> 5) The public want **something done** about the problem.
> 6) The police are more **aware** or sensitive to the problem so they **discover more crime**.
> 7) Police records **reinforce** the idea that there is **more crime** and **deviance**.

1) The risk of being a victim of crime is **amplified** by over-reporting by the media. This creates a public response of **panic** or **outrage**. Cohen refers to this as a **moral panic**.

> Definition of a **moral panic**: "When a **condition, episode, person** or **group** of persons emerges to become **defined** as a **threat** to **societal values** and interests." **Stanley Cohen.**

2) Cohen famously developed his theory from a study of conflicts between **Mods and Rockers** in 1964, but there are plenty of **new** examples, especially with the increased power of the media — e.g. gun crime, "bogus asylum seekers", benefit fraud, Roma (Gypsy) encampments.

3) The state response to a moral panic in society is to introduce **stricter** forms of **social control** through legislation.

4) **Hall et al (1978)** claim that the national concern about **mugging** in the early 1970s was a **moral panic**. The media claimed that mugging was a new kind of crime, but Hall et al point out that violent street robbery had been going on for a long time, and wasn't rising particularly fast at the time of the moral panic. (See p.63 for more on this.)

Practice Questions

Q1   Why are interactionists less interested in the causes of crime than other sociologists?

Q2   Explain how the reactions of others are significant in the interactionist understanding of deviance.

Q3   What is "amplification of deviance"?

Q4   Define the term "moral panic".

Exam Questions

Q1	Outline and assess to what extent the media plays a significant role in creating deviance in society.	(60 marks)
Q2	Outline and assess the view that societal reaction is a major cause of deviance.	(60 marks)

Sigh. If you will insist on running naked through the streets...

It's interesting how people react to deviant behaviour. Some people scream and shout, others run away, and others pretend it's not happening. Well, according to Becker and his merry bunch of interactionists, it's the reaction that people have to deviance that makes it deviant. They even went as far as saying that reaction can make deviance more deviant. Give a dog a bad name...

Deviance and Social Control

Deviance is controlled by society, and kept to a low level. Which is good, as it means you're less likely to be mugged by a naked nose-picker.

Social Control keeps Order in Society

Functionalist sociologists argue that deviance must be kept to a **low level**. They say that a small amount of deviant activity can actually help maintain social order because it unites the rest of society in disapproval of the deviant behaviour. Functionalists say social control **benefits everyone** in society.

Marxist sociologists agree social control is essential to keep order. They say capitalism is an **exploitative** system which requires systems of social control over the population to **prevent rebellion and revolution**. Marxists say social control **benefits the ruling class** and works against the interests of the majority working class.

Marxists say Social Control is maintained through Hegemony

1) **Informal social control** is achieved through socialisation where individuals are **taught** to accept ideas and norms which support the status quo in society. These ideas are supported by **institutions** of the state such as the **education** and **legal** systems.

2) This ideology (set of ideas and values) are presented as **common sense** and neutral. However, according to neo-Marxists such as **Gramsci**, they're really designed in the interests of those in power.

3) Alternative ideas are overwhelmed by the **dominance** of this **ruling class ideology**.

4) The ability to **informally control** ideas and values in this way is **hegemony**.

5) Part of capitalist class hegemony is the **belief** that the legal system operates in the interests of **everyone** in society. Traditional Marxists argue the legal systems are actually methods of **formal social control** over the population. They claim the legal system backs up the ideas and values of the ruling class ideology.

Marxists say the Capitalist State passes Laws which benefit the Ruling Class

1) According to Marxism, laws **aren't the will of the people**. They're a reflection of ruling class interests.

2) Other than the most serious crimes of murder, rape and violence, the vast majority of law in the UK is **property law**. **Chambliss and Mankoff (1976)** wrote that most of this law serves to keep **working class** people **away** from the property and land of the rich. The ruling class uses the law to protect **private property** because **capitalist exploitation** is built upon it.

3) The vast majority of the population have **no power** or **say** in the creation of **laws** and **punishments**.

4) The **lack of legislation** in some areas of life is also a demonstration of the law as an instrument of the ruling class.

5) Canadian sociologist **Laureen Snider (1993)** argues legislation regulating **large companies** is **restricted** in capitalist societies because it could **threaten ruling class interests**. For example, legislation regarding health and safety, pollution and fair trade are passed to a **minimum level** and often **weakly enforced**. **Tobacco companies** have put huge **pressure** on governments **not to pass laws** making them **legally responsible** for the deaths of smokers.

6) **Pearce (1976)** suggested that even the laws which supposedly protect the working class (e.g. health and safety laws, consumer laws) are really in ruling class interests. He said the system needs healthy, safe and loyal workers.

Marxists say Ruling Class law-breakers are Less Likely to be Punished

Marxists also say the laws which exist are not enforced equally in capitalist societies.

1) **Laureen Snider (1993)** argues that working class crimes such as burglary don't cause as much harm in society as corporate crimes such as breaking health and safety law.

2) Marxists suggest that **ruling class ideology** successfully presents the burglars as the "real criminals" and a threat to society, largely through the media. Meanwhile **corporate law breakers** get very **little media condemnation** and are treated more **leniently** by the legal system.

3) Also, if company bosses are charged they have the **money** to buy the **best legal advice**.

4) The work of **Chambliss (1978)** is good evidence for this. He studied crime in the American city of Seattle and found those in power were able to use it to conduct criminal activity and to avoid prison. He found an organised crime syndicate which included elite businessmen and politicians who used money and influence to bribe officials.

Gordon (1976) argues **selective enforcement** of the law and **selective reporting** in the media gives the impression that criminals are largely working class. He thinks this not only diverts attention from ruling class crime but also **divides the working class** when the working class criminal becomes the target of anger rather than the system itself.

Deviance and Social Control

Traditional Marxists are Criticised for overlooking Other Effects on Crime

1) Traditional Marxists stated clearly that the cause of crime lay within the nature of the **capitalist system**. Their assumption that if you ended capitalism you'd end crime is **rejected** by many. There's **crime** in **socialist societies** like Cuba, and **some capitalist societies** such as Switzerland have very **low crime rates**.

2) Feminists accuse traditional Marxist theory of **ignoring** the role of **patriarchy** in rule creation and social control.

3) More recent Marxist-influenced theory such as left-realism (see glossary) reckons traditional Marxism focused too much on **corporate crime**. They dispute the argument that other crimes such as burglary are **insignificant**, especially as the **victims** are usually **working class**.

Radical Criminology argues criminals Choose to break the law

Taylor, Walton and Young's *The New Criminology* (1973) says crime is a choice

Background: *The New Criminology* was an attempt to present a thorough and considered **Marxist analysis** of crime, largely because Taylor, Walton and Young thought other Marxists, including Marx, had **failed** to do so. The main aim of *The New Criminology* was to move the sociology of crime on from the idea that society should be trying to **remove** deviant behaviour to a need to **understand** and **accept** it.

Theory: Taylor, Walton and Young argued that criminals were not **passive** individuals unable to control their economic situation as **traditional Marxists** had stated. Instead, crime was a **conscious**, **meaningful** and **deliberate choice** individuals made to try and **change society**.

Much crime is a **deliberate fight against capitalism**. Taylor, Walton and Young point to political action groups such as the **Black Panther** Movement who use criminal means to **agitate** the system. Robbery is also seen by the new criminologists as a potential means of **redistributing wealth**. (Robin Hood, anyone..)

Conclusion: Sociology needs a "**fully social theory of deviance**". Deviance needs to be explained from **different viewpoints**, which consider how society is **organised** and at the same time **how** and **why** individuals **choose** to be deviant.

Seven Aspects of a full social theory of deviance, from Taylor, Walton and Young's *The New Criminology*.

1) How **wealth** and **power** are **distributed**.
2) The **unique circumstances** of each **individual act**.
3) The **nature** of the **deviant act** itself.
4) **Reactions** of the **rest of society** to the deviant act.
5) Who has the **power** to **make rules** about the **treatment** of deviance or **response** to deviance.
6) The **effect** being **labelled deviant** has on an individual.
7) How all these factors **interlink**.

Hall et al's (1978) study of the **moral panic** over **mugging** in Britain is a good example of a fully social theory of deviance in practice.

Hall et al analyse the **social** and **economic** and **political** conditions as well as the **motivations** of the **media** and the **government** and conclude that the **combination** of these factors all coming together at the same time led to a **moral panic**.

In brief: there was an <u>economic crisis</u> and a <u>crisis of hegemony</u> (unions and militants threatened state power), so the state wanted to exercise more control. The police <u>arrested more people</u>. The media picked up on this, and presented (black) muggers as a <u>threat to society</u>.

Practice Questions

Q1 Give two examples of how traditional Marxists argue capitalism creates crime.
Q2 According to Snider, how does the law protect ruling class crime?
Q3 According to Taylor, Walton and Young, why do people commit crime?

Exam Questions

Q1 Outline and assess the view that the law is an instrument of the ruling class. (60 marks)

Q2 Examine how the concept of deviance might be relevant to the study of one or more of the following topics: health, mass media, poverty and welfare, families and households. (12 marks)

It's not my fault — capitalism made me do it...

Again, not recommended as a defence in a court of law. It didn't work for me when I insisted on running naked through the streets. Anyway. It's the usual suspects here — Functionalists and Marxists. The Marxist theory of criminology is useful to learn. There are a lot of studies, and if you can explain and analyse them in the exam then you'll get plenty of marks.

Solutions to the Problem of Crime

There are two theories focused on finding a solution to crime that have had a significant influence on social policy in Britain and America. One from the left (New Left Realism) and one from the right (New Right Realism). Wonder which one copied.

New Left Realists *said policy must accept that crime is* Real *and* Rising

In *What is to be done about law and order?* **(1984)**, **Lea and Young** launched their **new theory** of crime and how to reduce it. They criticised other leftist writers (especially Marxists) for overlooking the reality of crime in Britain by focusing on the problems within capitalism.

> **Lea and Young said left wing sociological debate and social policy on crime must start accepting that:**
> * Crimes **other than white-collar crime** are a **problem**.
> * There has been a **rise in crime** in Britain since the Second World War.
> * Being a **victim** of crime is a very **significant event** in an individual's life.
> * **Fear of crime** is a real factor in shaping modern urban lifestyles, especially for **women**.

Kinsey, Lea and Young (1986) *recommend changes in* Policing Policy

1) **Kinsey, Lea and Young (1986)** say that British policing policy needs to be centred on **creating** and **maintaining good communication** between the **police** and **local communities**.

> The public **report most crimes** to the police.
> The public **provide most evidence** to solve crimes. = The police **need** the public.

2) Kinsey, Lea and Young say the public should have a **key role** in deciding **police policy**. They propose setting up **Police Authorities** which are **democratically elected** from the public. These authorities should formulate policing policy and direct police action.

3) This would create **consensus policing** where the police are acting on the instructions of the local community, rather than in isolation from them.

4) Kinsey, Lea and Young say the key role of the police should then be "**full and proper investigation of crime**" which they reckon has been reduced in recent years.

5) They say the police need to improve their **detection** and **clear up** rates. At the time they were writing, only 12% of recorded crime was cleared up. This figure has improved since then.

New Left realists say Relative Deprivation *is a factor causing* Crime

1) **Lea and Young (2002)** argue that a sense of **relative deprivation** is a major factor leading to crime. When an individual feels deprived in relation to similar social groups, they can turn to crime to "solve" the problem and acquire the resources to remove the feeling.

2) It's not actual deprivation but the **feeling of being deprived** relative to someone else that triggers this response. This explains why crime occurs in all social strata — the rich can feel deprived next to the super-rich.

3) **Lea and Young** says these feelings of deprivation are compounded by the **consumer culture** of modern Britain — **advertising** and the **media** present individuals with images of what they **could** have and what others have got.

4) Therefore, a rising standard of living can lead to a rising crime rate.

New Left realists say Social Inequality *must be fought in order to* Reduce Crime

Left Realists identify **deprivation** and to a lesser extent **marginalisation** as causes of crime. They say that in the long term, order will come from a **fair** and **just** society. **Left Realists** stress the need for **all social agencies** to have a direct aim of removing inequality. They include the **general public** in this — everyone's responsible.

> Left Realists use the "**square of crime**" to show the **interactions** between **four elements** which affect crime — the state, the public, the offender and the victim. Left realists argue that all four elements should **work together** to understand and reduce crime.

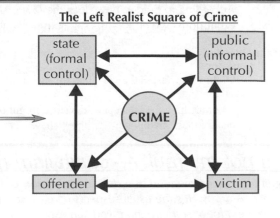

The Left Realist Square of Crime

New Left Realist work has influenced **Labour** government **social policy** since **1997**. Remember Tony Blair's phrase "tough on crime, tough on the causes of crime" — it sums up the New Left Realism theory pretty well.

Solutions to the Problem of Crime

Critics say that if New Left Realism was Correct there'd be More Crime

1) **Hughes (1991)** says the Left Realists haven't explained why **some people** who experience **relative deprivation** see **crime** as a **solution** and others don't. He argues there would be a lot **more crime** if **relative deprivation** was the main cause.

2) Critics also say that Kinsey, Lea and Young didn't collect enough data to develop a full theory of crime. Their theory only focuses on **property crime**.

No one wants to end up here

New Right Realists have influenced American Social Policy

1) **Wilson (1975)** believes individuals commit crime because the **gains outweigh** the chances of being **caught and punished**. In order to reduce crime, Wilson says it's necessary to issue **harsh punishments** for the smallest crimes — so the benefits won't outweigh the punishment any more. Punishment should be a **deterrent** to future offenders.

\ \ \ \ | / / /
~ Wilson was a social ~
– policy advisor to the –
– Reagan government of –
/ the USA in the 1980s. \
/ / | | | \ \

2) This has been put into action in the social policy of **Zero Tolerance**, first in America and now in parts of the UK (e.g. Middlesborough).

3) **Wilson and Kelling (1982)** say that damage to a neighbourhood has to be put right straight away, or problems of crime and deliquency quickly get out of hand. This is called the "One Broken Window" idea — their article says that tolerating just one broken window sends the message that you can get away with crime.

4) Wilson and Kelling actually advocate **taking resources and police supervision away** from areas where law and order has **broken down** — this sounds wrong, but Wilson says that once social order has gone it's almost impossible to regain it, so it's not worth **wasting resources** on trying. He recommends **diverting police** to areas which **aren't too far gone**, to **prevent breakdown** of social order in those areas.

Wilson and Hernstein (1985) claim there's a **biological predisposition** to crime in some individuals — but with the right **socialisation** they can be trained away from it. They argue that **single-parent families** are more likely to have "criminal children" because their socialisation hasn't been complete.

Murray (1997) claims that the higher the **risk** of going to **prison**, the less likely people are to commit crime.

New Right Realism has been Criticised

1) Critics of New Right Realism have been many and varied. The New Right argument that criminals are biologically different is rejected by many as coming from theories that have already been discredited.

2) **Jones (1998)** questions the assertion that resources put into run-down areas are wasted. He argues that investment in these areas makes a positive difference to the communities who live there.

3) **Matthews (1992)** didn't find any evidence that tolerating broken windows leads to crime.

4) Critics also say that crime has risen in the USA despite Zero Tolerance policies, and the prison population is rising because of them — e.g. the "three strikes and you're out" policy which means three serious offences automatically result in **life imprisonment**.

Practice Questions

Q1 Give an example of a sociological theory being used in social policy.

Q2 How does New Left Realism differ from Marxist criminology?

Q3 What do New Left Realists say causes crime?

Q4 Give two examples of things that New Right Realists say would reduce crime.

Exam Questions

Q1	Outline and assess the Left Realist argument that different policing strategies would reduce crime.	(60 marks)
Q2	Outline and assess the view that relative deprivation can trigger a criminal response.	(60 marks)

A kid broke my window playing football last week — give him life in prison, I say...

Both these new approaches are quite different to the old sociological theories, which just tend to blame society. The New Left are quite harsh on Marxism, and say that it ignores the effect of crime on ordinary people. Right wing politicians and New Right Realists have been quite firm in their claim that prison works, but just like everything in sociology, there's no broad agreement.

Suicide

*There's an awful lot of sociology on suicide, for two reasons. Firstly, it's a totally individual act, so it's a big task for sociology to explain. Secondly, it's been a focus for exploring issues of sociological methodology since Durkheim used his study of suicide to explain the "rules" of sociological research and enquiry. These pages are just for **AQA**.*

Durkheim's study of Suicide is one of the most Important Sociological Works of all time

Durkheim wrote in the **1890s**, and was one of the very **first sociologists** — right at the forefront of establishing and defining sociology as a scientific discipline. Durkheim argued that it was not only **possible** to apply **scientific principles** to **social phenomena** but that it was **essential** to apply scientific principles in order to produce **useful sociology**. His 1897 book *Suicide: a study in sociology*, uses his scientific methods to explore suicide.

1) Durkheim chose suicide **deliberately**, because as the most **individual**, **private** and **psychologically driven** act it was considered by most **not** to be a **social** phenomenon.

2) If sociology **could** identify **social factors** and **causes** of suicide, this would demonstrate the **power** and **impact** of **society** on **individual behaviour**.

3) Durkheim followed the **methodology** laid down in his earlier book, *The Rules of Sociological Method*, in his suicide study. This methodology was **rigorous**, **systematic**, **detailed** and **scientific** analysis.

4) Durkheim said that if this **scientific methodology** is followed then "**social facts**" can be discovered in the same way as **scientific** research reveals **laws** or **facts** of the **natural world**.

Analysis of Statistics found some groups were More Likely to Commit Suicide

1) Durkheim's analysis of the **official statistics** on suicide revealed some **social groups** were **more likely** to commit suicide than others. He looked at a large amount of data from **different societies** and from **different cultural** and **social groups** within the same society.

2) Social **patterns** of **suicide** rates demonstrate suicide is **not a random individual act**. **Social factors** play a part.

Correlation between suicide and other "social facts".
- Suicide rates were higher in predominantly **Protestant** countries than in **Catholic** ones.
- **Jews** were the religious group with the **lowest suicide** rate.
- **Married** people were **less likely** to commit suicide.
- **Low suicide rates** were found in countries after a **national upheaval** or **crisis**.
- Those with more **education** had a **higher suicide rate**.

Durkheim used "social facts" (statistics) as his raw data and then analysed the data to draw conclusions on the cause of suicide. He didn't question the reliability or accuracy of the statistics — that all came later...

Durkheim concluded there were Four Forms of Suicide

Durkheim concluded there were four different forms of suicide, related to how much **integration** and **regulation** there was in a society.

Social integration means **socialisation** into the **norms, values** and **lifestyles** of social groups and society.

Moral regulation means the **control** that **society** and **social groups** have over an **individual's behaviour**.

Durkheim's **four types of suicide** relate to **dysfunctional** integration or regulation.

Form of suicide	Cause	Example
Egoistic	**Not enough integration**. The individual isn't successfully integrated into groups or society.	More suicide in Protestants compared to Catholics because Protestants had a **looser social network/belief system**.
Anomic	**Not enough regulation**. Society has insufficient control over individuals.	Often in periods of **economic depression** or **very rapid expansion**, the suicide rate rises. People find it hard to adapt.
Altruistic	**Too much integration**. An over-integrated individual sacrifices their life for the group.	**Followers** who commit suicide after the death of their **leader**. Terrorist **suicide bombers** are a modern example.
Fatalistic	**Too much regulation**. The individual is too highly controlled by society.	Suicides of **prisoners** or **slaves**.

Durkheim has been Criticised by other Positivist Sociologists

Positivists try to use scientific methods. See p.136-137

Halbwachs (1930) largely supported Durkheim's conclusions but he pointed out that the impact of **rural** versus **urban** lifestyles on suicide rates hadn't been considered.

Gibbs and Martin (1964) argued that Durkheim hadn't used vigorous enough scientific methods even though he'd stressed how important they were. The key concepts of **integration** and **regulation** weren't **defined** closely enough to be **measured statistically**. Gibbs and Martin query how anyone can **know** what "**normal**" levels of integration and regulation are.

Suicide

Interactionist Sociologists have devised Alternative Theories of Suicide

Interactionist sociologists say social reality isn't a series of "social facts" for sociologists to discover, but a series of different **meanings** and **interpretations** that each person brings to and takes from each situation.

Durkheim's work is **fatally flawed** from this perspective because he relies on the **unquestioning** use of official **statistics**. According to interactionists, **statistics aren't fact** — they're a **social construction** based on the definitions of the people who compile them. In other words, statistics give you **one picture** of society, not the **only picture**.

Douglas (1967) said there was a need to categorise suicides according to their **social meanings** because the **triggers** and **response** to suicide are **different** in **different cultures**.

Douglas identified **four social meanings** for suicides in modern industrial societies.

1) **Transformation** of the **soul**.
2) **Transformation** of the **self**.
3) Achieving **sympathy**.
4) Achieving **revenge**.

Baechler (1979) used **case studies** for his research into the meanings behind suicides. He concluded suicide was an action **chosen** by individuals to **solve a problem** when all other solutions had **failed**. Suicide is one response to the social circumstances an individual is in.

He also established four main types of suicide.

1) **Escapist** — an attempt to **remove oneself** from an **unbearable** situation.
2) **Aggressive** — a means of harming or **hurting** other people.
3) **Oblative** — a means to **achieve a wish**, such as to join a loved one who's already dead.
4) **Ludic** — **knowingly taking risks** likely to result in death.

Atkinson suggests the key question is "How do deaths get Categorised as suicide?"

There is a **social process** involved in a death becoming **labelled** as a **suicide**.

1) **Atkinson (1978)** studied coroners' courts and suggested that coroners use their own **interpretations** and **definitions** in order to define a death as **suicide**.

2) He thought that coroners had a **"typical biography"** of a suicide victim to compare the case against — the more factors **fitted**, the more likely they'd record the death as suicide. For example, **young single men** were more likely to be labelled suicide than **middle-aged married men**.

3) Atkinson concludes suicide statistics are **not facts** but reflections of **coroners' interpretations**.

Coroners don't have to record a death as suicide, murder or accident. They can record an open verdict if they aren't 100% sure.

Critics of Atkinson have said that although the suicide statistics are **socially constructed** they follow a **clear set of criteria** which are **shared** and therefore there will be **consistency** in the figures.

Practice Questions

Q1 What are the two reasons why the study of suicide is so important to sociology as a discipline?

Q2 What did Durkheim mean by "regulation" and "integration" in society?

Q3 What does Atkinson suggest about the social construction of suicide?

Exam Questions

Q1 Evaluate the importance of Durkheim's study of suicide within the discipline of sociology. (40 marks)

Q2 Outline and assess the view that suicide statistics tell us more about the values and interpretations of coroners than they reveal about the causes of suicide. (60 marks)

On a more cheerful note, section five has just ended...

This all ties in with the stuff on sociological method in Section Eleven (yes, this book goes all the way to eleven). Suicide, although a terrible downer, is something that sociologists find deeply fascinating. Never let it be said that sociologists aren't an odd bunch. The key is to understand Durkheim's theory, where he got his data from, and why he's criticised by interactionists.

Education and Socialisation

*This section is for **OCR**. AQA people have already covered Education in the AS course. We won't be seeing them again until section 11. Slackers.*

Socialisation is the Passing On of Culture

1) Remember, **culture** includes knowledge, skills, roles, norms and values. It's **passed on** through **socialisation** from generation to generation.

2) Socialisation **transmits culture** — it **teaches** children knowledge, skills, roles, norms and values. Socialisation also **reproduces culture** — it makes children **copy** knowledge, skills, roles, norms and values.

3) There's only one **agent** of **primary** socialisation — the **family**. In early childhood, individuals learn the **skills**, **knowledge**, **norms** and **values** of society. Children **internalise** norms and values by **imitating** their parents or guardians. Children are **rewarded** for socially **acceptable** behaviour and **punished** for socially **"deviant"** behaviour.

4) **Secondary socialisation** comes after primary socialisation and **builds on it**. It's carried out by **various institutions**, including **education**, **peer groups**, **religion** and the **mass media**.

Education Socialises children by passing on Knowledge and Skills

The education system aims to pass on **knowledge and skills** such as reading, numeracy and basic science, and skills which pupils will need in the world of **work**.

Learning these skills is a part of socialisation, but sociologists suggest that **education socialises individuals** in **other ways** as well. Education passes on **core values** such as working hard to succeed, respect for authority, and cooperating with others.

Behold the tools of socialisation!

Durkheim said education Integrates Society by passing on Norms and Values

1) The Functionalist **Durkheim (1925)** said education helps **create social order** based on **cohesion** and value **consensus**.

2) He said that children must learn to **identify** with society. Education teaches children to identify with wider society by teaching them the **history** of their society — e.g. children in the **United States** learn about the Founding Fathers, about the Constitution, and about American values as personified by the life story of **Abraham Lincoln** (raised in a humble log cabin, went on to be President). They even start each day by **swearing allegiance** to the American flag.

3) Durkheim said that school teaches children to **interact** with each other, and with adults, by **following rules**. He said school rules should be enforced **strictly**, because pupils should be **rewarded** for acceptable behaviour and **punished** for deviant behaviour. He also thought that children had to learn that **rules benefit society**.

4) Durkheim saw school as **society in miniature** — in other words, it's an agent of **cultural reproduction**.

Parsons saw education as the Main Agent of Secondary Socialisation

1) The Functionalist **Parsons (1959)** saw education as a **bridge** between **family** and **society**, preparing children for their role in society.

2) Families treat their children as individuals and love them unconditionally, but in society people are judged by **universal standards**. Schools start to judge children by universal standards — e.g. **good behaviour**, following school **rules**, and doing well in **exams**.

3) Parsons said that schools pass on **universal values** — **achievement**, **hard work**, and **equality of opportunity**.

4) Parsons says that school is **meritocratic** — the best students rise to the top. This means that education can **allocate** people to **roles** in society. Schools test pupils' talents, and see which pupils are suited to which kind of job.

Davis and Moore said education allocates roles based on achievement

1) **Davis and Moore (1945)** say that every society sorts its members into different positions. They think that there are **rules** for this — called **"principles of stratification"**.

2) They believe that education **sorts people out** according to their **talents** and **abilities**. According to Davis and Moore, those who do **best at school** will do **best in society**.

There's plenty more about this on p.42, if you want to read more around it.

Functionalist views of Education and Socialisation have been Criticised

1) Functionalism is deterministic — it assumes that all pupils get the "message" of shared values. Critics like **Hargreaves (1975)** say education **doesn't succeed** in transmitting **shared values**. Children ignore rules, or feel they **don't belong**.

2) Evidence of **differential achievement**, in terms of class, gender and ethnicity, suggests that education **isn't meritocratic**.

3) There **isn't** a close relationship between academic **achievement** at school, and **earnings** at work.

4) There's even **doubt** that the education system grades people according to ability. Some say **intelligence** doesn't have much impact on academic achievement.

5) Functionalism doesn't consider that education might transmit **ruling class** values. It **doesn't explain conflict**.

Education and Socialisation

Marxism Says Education Legitimises Inequality through Ideology

1) The neo-Marxist **Althusser** sees education as part of the **"ideological state apparatus"**.
   In other words, it's a tool of capitalism which is used to justify, maintain and reproduce class inequalities.
   According to Althusser, education transmits and reproduces an **ideology** about what it **means** to be
   working class, what it means to be middle class, and what everyone's **place in society** ought to be.

2) Marxists say education makes sure that the **ruling class** continue to get the **best jobs** and most **powerful**
   positions in society, and makes sure that the **working class** continue to do **poorly paid** manual jobs.

3) Marxists also say that education is used to pass on the **belief** that society is **fair**.
   This means that pupils **accept their lot** and aren't ever motivated to change society.

4) The belief that education is a fair **meritocracy** is also used to **blame** pupils for not succeeding.
   Children at the bottom feel they only have themselves to blame — that they must be "thick".

5) Marxists agree with Functionalists that education passes on culture — but Marxists say this culture is ruling class
   culture. Education is a tool of cultural **hegemony**. **Bourdieu** used the concept of **cultural capital** (language, skills,
   knowledge and attitudes) to explain how the middle-class get into the top positions. There's **plenty** on this on p.72-73.

6) Marxists think education produces a **docile** and **obedient** workforce. **Bowles and Gintis (1976)**
   say there's a close link between school and work — see p.70-71 and 78 for more on this.

Marxist views of Education and Socialisation have also been Criticised

1) Marxist views of education are **deterministic** — they assume that all pupils get the "message" of ruling
   class ideology, and that all working class pupils learn to be good little workers. They ignore pupils who
   disagree with or **ignore** everything their teachers say.

2) Even some **Marxists** and neo-Marxists **disagree** with the traditional view of education as a tool to create
   an obedient workforce. Neo-Marxist **Paul Willis (1977)** found that some kids aren't obedient. They form
   an **anti-school subculture** and cope with school and then adult work by mucking about. See p.78.

Liberals tend to believe Education is about the Individual, not Society

Liberals believe that education should develop children as individual human beings. The benefit to society in general should
be secondary. Liberal educationalists such as **Dewey (1953)** argued that children should learn by experience, so they could
develop the ability to think for themselves. This view influenced progressive child-centred education in the 1960s and 1970s.

Functionalists, **New Right theorists** and **Marxists** all criticise liberal/progressive educationalists. **Functionalists** and **New Right
theorists** say that the progressive style of education **failed** to teach children either **skills** or **cultural norms**. **Marxists** say that the
liberal, individualist view **ignores inequalities in society**, which Marxists say are the sources of **inequality in education**.

> Radical **Ivan Illich (1971)** agrees with both Functionalists and Liberals about the role of education. He
> believes education should **teach skills**, and **also** encourage children to **develop as individuals**. Illich
> believes that schools **aren't much good** at teaching **skills**. He also believes that schools **repress pupils'
> individuality**. Illich recommends doing away with school ("deschooling society") altogether, and
> replacing it with a system where children and adults learn skills from people who use them in daily life.

Practice Questions

Q1 According to Durkheim, what is the function of education?

Q2 According to Davis and Moore, what is the function of education?

Q3 Give two examples of Marxist criticisms of the idea that education is meritocratic and fair.

Q4 Why do New Right sociologists criticise liberal and progressive educationalists?

Exam Questions

Q1 Outline and assess contrasting views of the role of education in socialisation.	(60 marks)
Q2 Outline and assess the view that education is meritocratic.	(60 marks)

So, what norms were you socialised into today...?

*Sociologists sometimes over-analyse. Take education — so far on this page it has been the means of passing on core values,
a way of creating social order, the main agent of secondary socialisation, a tool of capitalism and various other things. I mean, it's
just school. Still, thinking is a well paid indoor job with no heavy lifting, and if you learn all this stuff you could do it too.*

Institutional Processes

Sociologists are very interested in processes that go on in the classroom, such as streaming and stereotyping. Weirdos.

Schools teach a *Formal Curriculum* of subjects

1) In **1988**, the **Education Reform Act** set up a compulsory **National Curriculum** of Maths, English, Science, History, Geography, Technology, Art, Music, and PE, and a foreign language for 11-16 year olds.

2) The National Curriculum was narrowed in 1994 to focus on **three core subjects** — **Maths**, **English** and **Science**.

3) Some sociologists criticise the National Curriculum as **ethnocentric**. **Conrad MacNeil (1990)** said that the history part of the National Curriculum focused on British **colonialism**, and ignored the negative effects of colonialism.

The *Hidden Curriculum* is what pupils *Learn* through *Experiencing* school

The phrase "hidden curriculum" was first used by **Jackson (1968)**, to refer to
things that children learn at school that aren't part of the formal curriculum.

1) The **hidden curriculum** teaches pupils to **sit down** and **be quiet**, even when they're bored.

2) **Accepting authority** and doing as **teacher says** is part of the hidden curriculum.

3) The hidden curriculum teaches pupils to **work on their own**.

4) The hidden curriculum also teaches children about being **part of a group**. It passes on cultural norms about being part of a group — cooperating with other children and adults, identifying with the school.

5) The hidden curriculum teaches pupils an **attitude** to learning. It teaches them **how to learn**.

The hidden curriculum is taught partly by the way school is organised.

1) School is somewhere **separate** from home, so kids learn that education is something **special** that happens somewhere special — not at home, not out in public, but in school.

2) The classroom is organised with children sitting at **desks**, and **facing the teacher**, who stands at the **front**. This teaches children that the teacher is an **authority** figure. It also teaches them to **sit** and **be passive**, as the teacher passes on knowledge to them.

The hidden curriculum is also taught by the way subjects are organised.

1) Knowledge is **compartmentalised** into **subjects**, and these are taught separately. There's not much connection made between science and history. Knowledge is **fragmented**, if you want to be fancy about it.

2) **Timetabling** sends messages to children about the **importance** of subjects. "Core" subjects like Maths and English might get five or six hours a week, while History, Geography and Music might get an hour each.

The hidden curriculum is also taught by the way teachers act towards pupils.

1) Teachers **interpret** pupils' behaviour as "naughty", "disruptive", etc.

2) Pupils learn to **please** their teacher.

Marxists and *Functionalists* see the *Hidden Curriculum* as a *Tool* for *Socialisation*

Marxists **Bowles and Gintis (1976)** believe that hidden curriculum acts entirely in the interests of capitalism, by training children to be **obedient** little workers, ready to be cogs in the machine of industrial capitalism, as it were...

1) The hidden curriculum teaches children to be **obedient**, **dependable**, **punctual** and **hard-working**. In their study of children at an American high school, they found that kids who **kept their heads down** and never caused trouble got **good grades**, whereas **independent**, **creative** students got **bad grades** — even if they were academically **bright**.

2) It teaches pupils to **accept authority**, which prepares them for a **subservient** relationship with **bosses**.

3) The hidden curriculum teaches pupils to be motivated by **external rewards** like good grades and qualifications, rather than by the **fun** of the work itself (because, of course, there is **no fun**). This prepares them to be motivated by **wages**, rather than the fun of the work itself (because, you've guessed it...).

4) The way that the hidden curriculum compartmentalises knowledge is connected to the way that **work** is broken up into **separate jobs**. Individual workers do individual tasks, and don't have **knowledge** of, or **power** over, the production process. The capitalist **class** can **control** the workers — it's the principle of **divide and rule**.

Functionalists have a much more positive view of the hidden curriculum. They see it as a way of transmitting and reproducing culture for the good of society. Functionalists see it as **beneficial** that children learn to sit still and listen.

Institutional Processes

Interactionists stress the importance of *Labelling* pupils as good or bad

Interactionists focus on **teacher-pupil relationships** at school. Sociologists such as **Hargreaves**, **Becker**, **Rist** and **Keddie** have looked at the way that teachers judge pupils and **label** them as "good", "lazy", "troublemaker" etc.

Children who are **positively labelled** get more out of school than children who are **negatively labelled**. This is called the **self-fulfilling prophecy** theory.

1) Teachers spend more time on pupils labelled "bright", and expect **higher quality work** from them. Teachers **don't expect much** from pupils who they've labelled as "thick".

2) The pupils' **ideas about themselves** and their work are **affected** by the **teachers' behaviour**. Pupils labelled as "thick" believe that they **can't achieve much**, and **don't bother trying**. So, they end up **not achieving much**.

Hargreaves et al (1975) looked at how teachers classify pupils

Speculation:	Teachers **guess** what **type** of pupil a child is, according to the following criteria: **appearance**, whether they **do as they're told**, apparent **ability**, **enthusiasm**, how they **get on** with other kids, their **personality**, whether they're **deviant** (naughty).
Elaboration:	Teachers refine their initial impressions of pupils based on more data.
Stabilisation:	After a few weeks, teachers feel they know the pupils. The pupils' actions are seen in terms of the type of pupil the teacher thinks they are.

Becker and **Rist** found that labelling isn't as **gradual** as Hargreaves suggests.

1) **Rist (1970)** found that children in a kindergarten were **permanently** labelled on the **eighth day** of school. Children were sat at three separate tables — supposedly on grounds of ability.

2) In Rist's opinion, the children had actually been labelled on the basis of **class**. Children with a **neat appearance** and a "nice" **middle class background** got onto the "fast learners" table.

3) **Becker (1971)** found that teachers tend to evaluate pupils in terms of an **ideal student**. This included ideas of **ideal work**, **ideal conduct**, and **ideal appearance**.

Streaming puts children into *Classes* depending on *Ability* — or on *Labelling*

Streaming puts children into different classes, depending on how well they're perceived to do at school. The **top stream** are given the most **academic** education. The bottom stream are given a more **basic** education. Top stream kids are prepared for **university** education, while bottom stream pupils are prepared to go straight into **employment** — usually low paid employment.

1) **Ball (1981)** found that pupils' behaviour changed according to what stream or band they were in. He thought this was because teachers had stereotypical views of different bands — the top band were supposed to be best behaved, the bottom band were least able, but supposedly quiet, and the middle band were supposed to be **worst behaved**.

2) **Keddie (1973)** studied a humanities course for pupils of all abilities. She found that teachers' attitudes depended on the stream that pupils were in. Teachers also transmitted more knowledge to A stream pupils than C stream pupils.

3) Keddie also looked at the **pupils' experience** of the class. She thought A stream pupils were more likely to take the teachers' word on trust. C stream pupils objected when teachers said things that didn't match their own experience. It appeared to Keddie that A stream pupils were more willing to **play the game**, and were rewarded for this.

Practice Questions

Q1 What is the hidden curriculum?

Q2 Give three examples of things the hidden curriculum teaches pupils.

Q3 What is the self fulfilling prophecy effect?

Q4 According to Keddie, which stream contained pupils who didn't question what they were taught?

Exam Question

Q1 Outline and assess the view that teachers' stereotypes of pupils affect pupil experiences of education. (60 marks)

Kids are taught to sit quietly and work? I think my teachers would disagree...

There must be more to school than learning facts — otherwise we could all stay at home and read books instead. Interactionists are very big on the interaction between pupils and teachers in the classroom. They think this explains a lot about social inequalities in education. Learn all this lot, and then you can start applying it to the stuff on the next six pages.

Inequality of Achievement: Class

Sociologists have investigated how social class affects how well people do at school. The middle classes do better than the working classes, but the upper classes don't seem to get a mention. Probably posh schools refuse to let grubby sociologists in.

Social Class *tends to affect* Educational Achievement

1) Pupils from **professional** backgrounds are significantly **more likely** to enter **higher education** than those from unskilled backgrounds.

2) Pupils from **middle class** backgrounds are more likely to study **A-Levels**, whereas **working class** pupils are more likely to take **vocational** subjects.

3) Pupils from disadvantaged backgrounds are **more likely** to **leave school at 16** and **less likely** to start school being able to **read**.

4) Pupils from **unskilled backgrounds** on average achieve **lower scores** on SATs and in GCSEs and are more likely to be placed in **lower streams** or **bands**.

I wonder if class affects how well you do in a school of fish...

Eysenck (1971) and **Saunders (1996)** have suggested the relative intelligence levels of different social groups account for differences in educational attainment. But it's very **difficult** to isolate whether IQ or social factors are the key to achievement. Some sociologists think that IQ tests are **culturally biased**, and measure things that **middle class** kids are more likely to know.

Processes Inside School — Labelling, Streaming *and* Subcultures *are factors*

1) **Negative labelling** of students can lead to a **self-fulfilling prophecy of failure**. **Becker (1971)** and **Keddie (1973)** say that teachers tend to evaluate pupils in terms of an **ideal student**, by looking at appearance, personality, speech and social class.

2) Negative labelling can mean students get put into **lower streams or bands**. **Ball (1981)** found that the pupils in the top bands were from **higher social classes**. Teachers had **higher expectations** of them and they were **taught in different ways**. Keddie found that pupils from middle class backgrounds tended to be in the top stream, and get access to higher levels of knowledge.

3) As a response to negative labelling and frustration with low status, pupils may form **anti-school subcultures**. **Hargreaves (1975)** found that those in the **bottom streams** were more likely to be non-conformist. **Woods (1983)** responded by saying that there are lots of different reactions to school, but **non-conformist** reactions were more likely to come from **working-class** students.

These explanations are useful when looking at day to day experiences in schools. The problem is that they don't explain how **factors outside of school** (e.g. poverty, cultural deprivation) can influence achievement.

Labelling theory is also too **deterministic** — it says that once you're negatively labelled that's it, you'll fail. This isn't always the case. Pupils can **resist negative labelling**, and work extra hard to **prove the teacher wrong**.

Material Deprivation Outside School *can affect achievement*

The theory of **material deprivation** says that **economic poverty** is a big factor in low achievement at school.

1) In 1997, the **Joseph Rowntree Foundation** classified **one in ten** children as **poor** — which was defined as being in a family that couldn't afford at least three things other families took for granted.

2) **Halsey (1980)** found that the **most important factor** preventing working class students staying on at school was **lack of financial support**.

3) **Douglas (1964)** found that children in **unsatisfactory living conditions** (poor housing, lack of nutritious food, overcrowding) didn't do very well in ability tests compared to kids from comfortable backgrounds.

4) **Unemployment** or **low income** means less money for books, the Internet and school trips. Low income families can't afford **nurseries** and **private schools** and they can't afford to support their kids through **uni**.

5) Poverty and unsatisfactory living standards may cause **health problems** and **absence from school**.

Cultural Deprivation Outside School *can affect achievement*

The theory of **cultural deprivation** says that **working class culture** and **parenting** aren't aimed at educational success.

1) **Douglas (1964)** thought **level of parental interest** was the most important factor affecting achievement. Middle class parents are more likely to visit schools for open evenings. Bear in mind that **working class parents** may not go to open evenings because they work **inconvenient shifts** — not because they aren't interested.

2) Some sociologists say that working class kids don't have the **knowledge** and **values** that help achievement. **Museum visits**, **books** and **parental knowledge of education** may help middle class pupils to succeed.

3) Some **styles of parenting** emphasise the importance of education more than others.

Inequality of Achievement: Class

Some sociologists say **Class Affects Attitudes** to **Education**

1) **Sugarman (1970)** said that pupils from non-manual backgrounds and manual backgrounds have **different outlooks**. The pupils from **manual** backgrounds lived for **immediate gratification**. The pupils from **non-manual backgrounds** were **ambitious** and **deferred their gratification** — they invested time in studying and planned for the future.

2) **Hyman (1967)** said that the **values** of the working-class are a **self-imposed barrier** to improving their position. He said that the working-class tend to place a **low value** on education.

> ethnocentric = believing your group/nation/culture is superior to others.

But...

Material and cultural deprivation theories **don't** explain how **factors inside school** affect achievement.

Cultural deprivation theory **generalises a lot** about differences between middle class and working class life. It **ignores** working class families who **do** place a high value on education, and tends to **assume** that working class families have **no culture** at all, or that working class culture can't be **relevant** to school. This is **ethnocentric**.

The **method** may be **unsound**, e.g. attending parents' evenings might not be a good measure of parental interest.

Bernstein found **Working Class** pupils were **Linguistically Deprived**

1) **Basil Bernstein (1970)** found that working class pupils in the East End of London weren't comfortable with the style of language required by school. They used a **restricted code** — short forms of speech.

2) **Middle class students** knew how to use the same **elaborated code** as the **teachers** — a much more wordy style of speech with everything made very explicit. In terms of **language**, the working class kids were at a disadvantage.

Bernstein's theory is **criticised** for painting with a very broad brush.
There are **linguistic variations** within the middle class and within the working class.

Cultural deprivation theorists have developed Bernstein's ideas to say working class speech patterns are **wrong**. **Labov (1973)** disagrees, arguing that the elaborated speech code is just **different**, not better.

Marxist **Bourdieu** said schools require **Middle Class Cultural Capital**

1) **Bourdieu (1967, 1974)** reckons middle class students are at an advantage because they have the right kind of "**cultural capital**" — the right **language**, **skills**, **knowledge** and **attitudes**.

2) He thought that the **more cultural capital** you have, the **more successful** you'll be in education — and he believed that working class pupils don't have **access** to cultural capital.

3) **Middle class** families **pass on cultural capital** and **expectations** from parents to children. This is **cultural reproduction**.

4) Bourdieu said that working class pupils **knew** the system was **biased** against them, so they **left school** rather than staying on in further and higher education.

Bourdieu was criticised for being too **deterministic** — not all working class students fail, even if they lack cultural capital.

Also, **Halsey (1980)** found that **material factors** are **more important** than cultural factors. Pupils may feel they have to get a job as soon as possible after leaving school. Nowadays, tuition fees may discourage pupils from going on to university.

Practice Questions

Q1 Give two facts about social class and educational achievement.

Q2 Name two factors inside school that explain the links between social class and achievement.

Q3 For Halsey, what was the most important factor preventing working class students staying on at school?

Q4 Briefly outline the findings of Sugarman's 1970 research into class attitudes to education.

Q5 Who initially used the term "cultural capital"?

Exam Question

Q1 Outline and assess the view that the education system is biased against working class pupils. (60 marks)

Immediate gratification sounds good to me...

Just a quick word of warning. In the exam you could get a question like "Assess how factors inside and outside school affect levels of achievement". This is a very broad question. You'd need to look at home and school factors for ethnicity, gender AND class. This means you'd need to have revised pages 74-77 as well as these two pages. So get on with it.

Inequality of Achievement: Gender

Gender is another factor that can influence how well people do at school. Since the 1980s, things have changed. Sociologists used to talk about female underachievement. Now there are worries that boys are falling behind. Geez Louise, make your minds up...

Here are **Six Facts** about **Gender** and **Differential Educational Achievement**

1) Girls get better results at all levels in National Curriculum tests.
2) Girls get better results in most subjects at GCSE.
3) Girls are more likely to pass their A-levels.
4) Women are more likely to go on to university.
5) Men seem to have most success at the highest levels of University. A higher proportion of male students get first class degrees and PhDs.
6) Girls tend to go for communication based subjects like English and Sociology and boys tend to go for technical ones like maths and physics.

it's so BORING...

Statistics are all very well, thought Jodie, but it doesn't mean I have to like school.

Understand the **Old Explanations** of **Girls' Underachievement**

There were three explanations for why **girls didn't do as well as boys** before the 1980s:

1) **Biological explanations** said that **girls matured earlier** so they did better at younger ages, and boys would **catch up** and overtake girls by age 16. **Sociologists** point out that there's not much difference in IQ between boys and girls, so biology can't be a factor.

2) Sociologists said that **gender stereotyping** started before kids got to school. **Toys** and **media representations** of women helped to socialise girls into the **mother/housewife role**.

3) **Behaviour in the classroom** was also used to explain why boys did better. **Stanworth (1983)** said that classroom interaction **disadvantaged girls**. Girls got **less attention** from teachers and were often **negatively labelled**. **Spender (1983)** argued that education was **controlled** and **dominated** by **men**. She said the curriculum was **male-centred**, boys got more attention and boys got away with being disruptive in class.

Other sociologists didn't reproduce Spender and Stanworth's findings.

Factors Inside School explain why Females Now Do Better

1) **Mitsos and Browne (1998)** say teaching has been **feminised**. Women are **more likely to be classroom teachers**, especially in primary schools. This gives girls **positive role models**.

2) **Textbooks** and **teaching resources** have changed and are less likely to include sexist **stereotypes**.

3) The National Curriculum **forced** girls to do **traditionally "male"** subjects. For example, more girls started to do **science**. Other Local Education Authority and government initiatives tried to encourage girls to do science, technology and maths, e.g. WISE (Women In Science and Engineering) and GIST (Girls into Science and Technology).

4) **GCSEs** include more **coursework** than earlier qualifications. **Mitsos and Browne** argue that coursework suits girls better because they put in **more effort**, are **better organised** and can **concentrate** for longer than boys (that's quite a sweeping generalisation though...)

Factors Outside School explain why Females Now Do Better

1) Policies such as the **Equal Pay Act** and **Sex Discrimination Act** have helped to create **more equal opportunities** in wider society. This has **changed values** of society and attitudes in school.

2) **Sue Sharpe (1994)** found that girls' priorities have changed. They now want **careers** — and qualifications. More women go out to work, so girls see lots of **positive role models** in work. Girls nowadays often want to be **financially independent** — they don't just want to marry a rich man any more.

The Equal Pay Act (1971) makes it illegal to pay men and women different money for the same work. The Sex Discrimination Act 1975 means employers can't discriminate on the basis of gender.

3) **Boys** tend to spend their leisure time being **physically active**. **Girls** are more likely to spend their leisure time **reading** and **communicating**. This means girls develop **language skills** that are useful for most subjects.

4) The **feminist** movement caused a **change in female expectations**, and made more people **aware of inequality**. People are now more careful about negative stereotyping, sex discrimination and patriarchy.

Inequality of Achievement: Gender

Here are some *Reasons* why *Boys Underachieve*

1) Boys may be having an **identity crisis**. The rise of **female independence**, the decline of the **breadwinner** role for men and the rise in **male unemployment** might mean that boys don't see the point of education. This may lead to anti-school subcultures.

2) **Interactionists** say that teachers have **lower expectations of boys**. Teacher expectations may lead to a **self-fulfilling prophecy** of poor behaviour. **Negative labelling** may explain why they're more disruptive. Boys are more likely to be sent out of class or **excluded** from school — which cuts the time they spend learning.

3) The **feminisation** of **teaching** means that boys don't have as many **role models** in school.

4) **Reading** is often seen as "uncool" or "girly". Boys who **avoid books** don't develop **communication skills**.

5) Boys may **overestimate** their ability, which means they don't work as **hard** as they need to to get good grades.

Some sociologists say that there's been a bit of a **moral panic** about males underperforming.

Weiner et al (1997) say that there's a **backlash** against female achievement. They also say that the concern about **male underachievement** is more specifically about **underqualified working class males** turning to **crime**.

Subcultures help to explain *Gender* and *Achievement*

Negative labelling and putting students into different **streams** or bands can cause some pupils to rebel against school's values. They form **subcultures**. These can be either **pro** or **anti-school** subcultures.

1) In the 1970s **Willis** studied a group of boys who **rejected school** and formed an **anti-school subculture**. They **coped** with their own underachievement by having a **subculture where it didn't matter**, and where having a laugh was more important. See p.78 for more on Willis.

2) **Mac an Ghaill (1994)** says that **subcultures are complicated**. There are **lots of different types**. Boys may join a **macho lad subculture** because of a crisis of masculinity. But boys could also join **pro-school subcultures** and be proud of academic achievement.

There are different ways to *Explain* links between *Gender* and *Subject Choice*

Girls tend to go for **arts and humanities**. Boys tend to go for **science and technology**.

1) **Subject choice** may still be influenced by **gender socialisation**. The ideas of **femininity** and **masculinity** create different **expectations** and **stereotypes** of what to study. Kids often see Biology as "the science that it's OK for girls to do" — as opposed to Physics and Chemistry.

2) **Kelly (1987)** found that **science** is seen as a **masculine subject**. Boys dominate the science classroom, and Kelly claims this puts girls off studying science.

3) **Parental expectations** and **teacher expectations** may encourage girls to follow what they see as the traditional "**normal**" choice for their gender. There's a pressure to **conform** to a social norm.

4) **Abraham (1995)** studied a comprehensive school and found that some pupils formed **subcultures** that **rejected** school expectations of **masculinity**, **femininity**, and **gendered subject choice**. Boys in the mixed "**gothic punk**" subculture rejected ideas about "boys' subjects" and "girls' subjects", and preferred art and music to science and technology.

Practice Questions

Q1 Give two facts about gender and educational achievement.

Q2 Which sociologists studied how classroom interaction disadvantaged girls?

Q3 Name one inside of school factor that explains why girls now do better than boys.

Q4 Who found that girls' priorities have changed?

Q5 Give one reason why boys and girls choose different subjects.

Exam Question

Q1 Outline and assess the view that the education system is institutionally sexist against boys. (60 marks)

Girls are DOOMED... no wait, boys are DOOMED... no wait... ah, forget it...

Obviously a lot of boys do really well in school. These pages are just talking about overall trends (which seem to change every decade or so anyway). So don't give up hope, you readers with Y chromosomes out there — you can still get an 'A' grade in your Sociology A2 exams no matter what Mitsos and Browne say...

Inequality of Achievement: Ethnicity

Ethnicity is another factor that can influence how well people do at school. Quick reminder — ethnicity means the shared cultural traditions and history which are distinct from other groups in society.

Some **Ethnic Groups** do **Better** than **Others**

These figures are from **Modood et al (1997)** — the Policy Studies Institute's fourth survey of ethnic minorities in Britain.

All these statistics are averages. If you look at someone and say "she does well cos she's Chinese" you might be wrong.

Higher levels of achievement

1) The survey found that **Chinese**, **African Asians** and **Indian** groups were more qualified than whites. **Afro-Caribbean women** were more likely to have **A-levels** than white women.

2) Ethnic minorities were **more likely than white pupils** to continue into **further education** (from ages 16-19).

3) People from ethnic minorities who were **born in the UK** had much **higher qualifications** than people who moved to the UK from abroad.

Lower levels of achievement

1) **Bangladeshi** and **Pakistani women** were least well qualified. **Afro-Caribbean**, **Pakistani** and **Bangladeshi men** were least qualified.

2) **Pakistani** and **Afro-Caribbean** groups were **less likely** to get onto **university** courses, and **more likely** to get into **less prestigious universities**.

3) **Afro-Caribbean boys** are **more likely** to be **excluded from school**, more likely to be put in **lower streams** and more likely to do **vocational** courses.

African Asians means people of Indian origin who lived in Kenya and Uganda and then moved to Britain in the 1970s.

There are big **variations** between the **average achievement level** of different ethnic minority groups. There must be something behind it all — probably more than one factor, and probably some **social** and **economic** factors.

Some people say that **intelligence is inherited** — i.e. people underachieve because they've inherited low IQ. HOWEVER... **IQ tests** can be **biased**. Sometimes they ask things that aren't really a test of brains, but really a test of **cultural knowledge**. The **Swann Report (1985)** found that if you took into account social and economic factors there were **no significant differences in IQ** whatsoever between different **ethnic groups**.

Processes Inside School — **Labelling**, **Curriculum** and **Prejudice** are factors

Labelling theory says that teachers have **different expectations of different ethnic minority groups**. **Gillborn (1990)** found that teachers **negatively label black students**. Afro-Caribbean students were seen as a **challenge** to the school **authority** — and are more likely to be excluded from school. Gillborn calls this the "myth of the black challenge". Teachers had high expectations of Asian students. Negative labelling could result in a **self-fulfilling prophecy of failure**.

Mac an Ghaill (1992) also found that teachers saw Afro-Caribbean boys as a threat, and saw Asian girls as having more potential than Afro-Caribbean girls. Black girls were encouraged to do non-academic subjects.

There's also an issue about whether the school curriculum is **ethnocentric** — i.e. that it might fit the mainstream, white, middle class culture better than other ethnicities. It could be **Europe-centred** too. Languages in the National Curriculum are mainly **European** — kids usually learn French and German, not Gujarati or Chinese. **Assemblies, school holidays** and even **history lessons** may not fit with the culture and history of particular groups.

Some sociologists see British education as **"institutionally racist"**. This is where **policies** and **attitudes** unintentionally discriminate against ethnic minority groups. **Wright (1992)** found that even though members of staff said they were **committed to equal opportunities**, Asian girls got **less attention** from teachers and felt their cultural traditions were disapproved of (e.g. staff assumed Asian girls' parents wouldn't allow them to come on a school trip). **Afro-Caribbean boys** were more likely to be punished and **sent out of class**.

Some sociologists say that these factors may lead to a **low self esteem** for ethnic minorities. **Coard (1971)** said that black students are made to feel inferior in British schools.

Low Self Esteem exists — *but it Isn't Really All That Widespread*

1) **Mirza (1992)** found that black girls had **positive self-esteem** and **high aspirations**. The girls experienced discrimination but had **strategies** to minimise the effects. It **wasn't low self-esteem** that affected their achievement — it was being **unwilling to ask for help**. Mirza found that teachers often tried to help in **counterproductive** ways, e.g. by not letting a girl enter an exam because the teacher thought the girl was overworked at home.

2) **Fuller (1980)** found Afro-Caribbean girls in London **resisted negative labelling** and **worked hard** to gain **success**.

3) Negative labelling and racism can affect pupils' reactions to school. Pupils may join either a **pro-school subculture** or an **anti-school subculture** to maintain their self-esteem, depending on their experience of school.

Inequality of Achievement: Ethnicity

Factors Outside School — Language Difference affects achievement

1) **Language** was a barrier for kids from **Asian** and **Afro-Caribbean immigrant families** when they **first arrived** in the UK.

2) The **Swann Report** found that **language didn't affect progress** for **later generations**.

3) **Driver and Ballard (1981)** also found Asian children whose **first language** was **not English** were **as good at English** as their **class mates** by the age of 16.

4) **Interactionists** would say that language might not be a barrier, but **dialects** or having an **accent** might **influence teacher expectations** and lead to **negative labelling**. For example, a teacher might **assume** that a child isn't good at English because they have a foreign accent and put them in lower sets.

Factors Outside School — Family Difference affects achievement

Some studies say that **family life varies** for different groups and this can influence achievement.

1) **Driver and Ballard (1981)** say that the **close-knit extended families** and **high parental expectations** increase levels of achievement in **Asian communities**.

2) Some sociologists say that the underachievement of Afro-Caribbean boys is connected to high levels of **single-parenthood** in Afro-Caribbean households, and a lack of male role models.

3) **Pilkington (1997)** found that although there are high levels of **divorce** and **single-parenthood** in Afro-Caribbean households, and very low levels of single parenthood in **Asian** families, **both** had more children staying on at school after 16 than **white working class** families. He also said that **economic** factors and **racism** were as important as cultural factors.

4) **Mac an Ghaill (1992)** found that a group of Afro-Caribbean and Asian pupils saw their **parents** as their main source of **inspiration**.

Ethnicity Combines With Social Class to affect achievement

On their own, the inside school factors and outside of school factors may not seem all that convincing. If you bring **social class** and **material factors** into the equation you get a more complex explanation.

1) The **Swann Report** found that **socio-economic** factors affected the lower levels of achievement of **Afro-Caribbean** pupils.

2) **Pakistani**, **Bangladeshi** and **Afro-Caribbean** groups are more likely to be in **lower class positions** such as routine occupations (assembly line workers, factory workers) and elementary occupations (cleaners, labourers). This may result in poor housing, periods of unemployment, poverty and **material deprivation**.

3) **Chinese**, **African Asian** and **Indian** groups are more likely to be in **higher class** positions and **less likely** to experience material deprivation.

If you were answering an exam question on this, you'd need to bring in stuff from p72-73 about class and achievement.

Practice Questions

Q1 Give two facts about ethnicity and educational achievement.

Q2 Why do sociologists dislike genetic explanations about intelligence and educational success?

Q3 Name one inside of school factor that explains the underachievement of some ethnic minority groups.

Q4 How does language affect educational achievement?

Q5 Give an example of how social class combines with ethnicity to affect achievement.

Exam Question

Q1 Outline and assess the significance of inside of school factors in explaining the educational achievement of different ethnic minority groups.

(60 marks)

The Swan Report found that waterfowl tended to underachieve in schools...

Remember that not all ethnic minorities underachieve — so don't go storming into your exam answer with a pre-prepared rant that it's all about white / black racism. There are always several different factors that affect each ethnic group. Also, remember that other factors like class and gender (see page 74) also influence how someone does at school.

Education and the Economy

After leaving education, pupils enter the world of work. Sociologists have various theories about this transition from school to work, and various theories on what the relationship between education and the economy ought to be.

Functionalists *say that education must* Teach Skills *required by the Economy*

1) The Functionalist view of education says that employers use qualifications to **sort** school leavers into jobs that suit their level of **ability**. According to **Davis and Moore (1945)**, school is the place where people's ability is **tested** and **graded**. Remember, Functionalists think education is a **meritocracy**.

2) Functionalists also think that the job of education is to teach the **skills** that are needed by the economy.

But...

This view has been criticised, especially by Marxist sociologists such as **Harry Braverman (1974)**. Braverman said that work had become more and more **deskilled** and **automated**. This would mean that education was actually teaching people **far more skills** than they **needed** in order to work in the economy. There is, after all, not a great deal of skill required to work in a **fast food** outlet. However, the economy also requires computer database analysts, electricians and accountants — which all require skill. The question isn't just **how much skill** the economy needs, but **what skills** the economy needs.

There's more about teaching **job skills** on p.79 and p.80.

Marxists *say education* Prepares Working Class *children for* Work

1) Marxists believe that education is an **apparatus of the state**, which has the purpose of providing an **obedient workforce**. According to Marxism, the capitalist system **demands** a willing and obedient workforce to do low paid jobs in order that the capitalist class can maximise profits.

2) In the Marxist view, education is more about **transmitting the right sort of attitudes** towards work than about transmitting actual measurable **skills**.

Marxists **Bowles and Gintis (1976)** say there's a close link between school and work, and a **correspondence** between **pupil experiences of school** and **adult experiences of work**. This link is called the **correspondence principle**.

1) Pupils have to accept the **hierarchy** at school. Work also has a hierarchy.
2) Pupils are **motivated by exam success** to do **boring work**.
   Workers are **rewarded with pay** to do **boring work**.
3) The **school day** is broken into **small units**. So is the **work day**.
4) At school and work, **subservience** (following the rules) is **rewarded**.

Bowles and Gintis say that the **hidden curriculum prepares people for work** — see p.70.

Paul Willis (1977) *says school* Doesn't *prepare children to* Work Hard

Willis's study "Learning to Labour" researched working class pupils

Background:	Willis studied a school on a working class housing estate in a small town in the Midlands. He focused on a group of **12 white working class boys** — called "Willis's lads". His aim was to see how the pupils **interacted** with school, and to find out what their **attitudes** to **school** and **work** were. He wanted to find out "**why working class kids get working class jobs**". Willis was a **neo-Marxist** who was also influenced by Interactionism.
Methods:	Willis used **observation**, **participant observation**, **group discussions**, **informal interviews** and **diaries**.
Findings:	The lads had an **anti-school subculture**. They were deliberately opposed to the values of hard work and conformity that the school was trying to transmit. The lads felt **superior** to **conformist** pupils, and to the teachers. They aimed to do as **little work** as possible, to **skive off lessons** as much as possible, and to **muck about** as much as possible. They didn't often confront teachers' authority head on, but tried to see how much they could **get away with**. The lads' subculture was **sexist** and **homophobic** — they saw boys who worked hard in lessons as effeminate. They were also **racist** towards ethnic minorities.
Conclusion:	Willis thought that the lads were **nothing like** the **obedient worker** that Bowles and Gintis wrote about. However, Willis thought the lads' **experience of school** and attitude towards schoolwork actually **prepared them very well** for work as adults. They went on to **unskilled** or **semiskilled manual jobs**, which they saw as "real work" (as opposed to office jobs). The **anti-work, having a laugh subculture** was carried on to the lads **first jobs**. Just like in school, they didn't challenge the boss head on, but tried to **get away with** as little work as possible **without getting the sack**. The work culture was **sexist, homophobic**, and somewhat **racist**.

Education and the Economy

Some sociologists say *Globalisation* makes education more *Important*

1) There's increasingly a **global economy**. In the global economy, both nation states and businesses have to be **internationally competitive**. 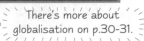 There's more about globalisation on p.30-31.

2) **Education** is an important factor in international competitiveness. British workers are no longer competing with other workers in the UK, but with workers all over the world — who may be **educated** under a **better system**.

3) **Post-Fordists** (see glossary) say that work is becoming more **flexible**. According to **Brown and Lauder (1997)**, because the demands of the global economy change rapidly with changes in technology, it's better to have a general education, than to be taught specific skills. Specialised high-level skills go out of date, but a good set of **basic skills** and the right **attitude to learning** can be applied to learning skills for lots of different jobs.

New Right Sociologists blame *Skills Shortages* on *Schools*

1) **New Right** theorists **agree** with **Functionalists** that the job of education should be to teach people the skills that are **needed by the economy**. However, New Right thinkers accuse education of **failing** to do this.

2) New Right sociologists blame a **skills shortage** on the **education system**. They say that education in the 1980s was teaching pupils an **outdated curriculum** which didn't serve the **needs of industry** — e.g. not enough computer skills, and not enough stress on learning the right businesslike, professional **attitude**.

Industrialists tend to complain that many school-leavers and graduates enter the world of work without basic job skills and IT skills.

3) The New Right suggest teaching children a more **business-oriented** curriculum. The 1988 Education Reform Act introduced **City Technology Colleges**. These are inner city schools for 11-18 year olds, sponsored by private industry. They teach technology, to meet the needs of industry.

Conservative governments were influenced by New Right ideas.

The solution to problems in education, according to New Right theorists such as **Chubb and Moe (1988)**, is to "**marketise**" education. They say parents should have **more choice** about what school to send their children to, and that **public funding** should be based on the number of pupils, which would reward popular schools. The idea is that schools have an incentive to improve standards.

The New Right believe in the power of the <u>market</u> to raise standards — they say <u>competition</u> makes things more <u>efficient</u>.

The New Right also favoured **standardised testing**, and school **league tables**. This would help parents **decide** which schools to send their children to, and **encourage competition**. The **1988 Education Reform Act** introduced testing at ages 7, 11, 14 and 16, and the results of these tests were published in **league tables**.

Feminists say *Education* prepares pupils for *Gendered Job Choices*

Subject choice in school tends to be **gendered** (see p.74-75). According to feminists, this prepares boys for stereotypically male jobs, and girls for both stereotypically female jobs and for the housewife/mother role.

This gendering of subjects and skills was pretty darn **explicit** back in the 1950s, 1960s and 1970s. **Girls** did **home economics** (cooking), and **needlework** classes, while **boys** did **woodwork** and **metalwork** — almost entirely without exception. Today, this gendering is less explicit. Resistant materials is still seen as more male, while Food Technology is seen as more female.

Feminist sociologists think that boys and girls are **encouraged** towards **gendered work experience** and **career choices**.

Practice Questions

Q1 In what way did Braverman criticise the Functionalist view of education and the economy?

Q2 What is meant by the correspondence principle?

Q3 Why does Willis disagree with Bowles and Gintis?

Q4 What did the New Right blame the education system for?

Exam Question

Q1 Outline and assess the view that the role of education is to prepare pupils to contribute to the economy. (60 marks)

At my school, the girls did the Waitress Race on sports day...

In the 'Waitress Race', the girls had to run while carrying trays of drinks. The winner was the first girl to finish without spilling all her drinks. We were clearly being prepared by a patriarchal hidden curriculum to grow up to be very fast waitresses. The boys meanwhile got to do the sack race and have fun. Not that I'm bitter or anything.

Educational Policy

So now you're learning about why you're learning what you're learning, and it's just really... boring. Sorry.

Until the late 1970s, Education was Academic

1) Until 1965, the education system was divided into **three parts**. **Grammar** schools taught the most able 20% (who passed an exam called the 11+) and prepared them for university. **Secondary moderns** gave a basic education to the 75-80% of pupils who failed the 11+ examination. **Vocational** education was limited to **technical** schools.

2) The curriculum of **grammar** schools and **secondary moderns** was based around **academic** subjects. The aim of education was to give pupils a good grounding in Maths, English, History, Geography, etc. Grammar school pupils also studied Latin and Ancient Greek — languages with very little direct **vocational** relevance.

3) **Social Democratic** theorists such as **Halsey (1980)** were very **critical** of the tripartite (three part) system. Halsey said that secondary modern schools didn't develop potential, and didn't produce a highly educated and skilled workforce.

During the 1960s and 1970s, the aim of education was to develop children's **creative thinking** and **critical thinking**, through the **academic curriculum**. Some sociologists argue this is at odds with the aim of providing a **skilled workforce**.

In 1976 the Push for Vocational Education Started

In a **1976** speech, **Labour** Prime Minister **James Callaghan** said he thought British education and industry was in decline because schools didn't teach people the **skills they needed in work**.

Conservative governments between **1979** and **1997** developed this idea, and introduced policies to create a closer link between school and work. This is called **new vocationalism**.

The Government introduced Vocational Qualifications

1) In the late 1980s, **National Vocational Qualifications** (**NVQs**) were introduced. They have four levels, from GCSE standard to graduate standard, and they cover specific job knowledge and skills.

2) In 1993, **GNVQs** were introduced — a vocational alternative to GCSE and A level **qualifications**, aimed at broad job fields, e.g. catering. They're designed to make the transition from school to work easier.

3) Recently, **key skills** qualifications have started. These are supposed to be useful for **all jobs**.

The Government introduced Youth Training Programmes

1) The **Youth Opportunities Programme** (YOP) was introduced in **1978**, and run by the Manpower Services Commission (responsible to the Department of Employment). It provided one day a week **off the job training**, which included teaching **good attitudes to work**, punctuality and discipline.

2) **Youth Training Schemes** (YTS) replaced YOP in 1983. YTS started as a year long job training scheme for 16-17 year old kids leaving school. In 1986 it was extended to a two year scheme.

3) YTS was scrapped and replaced by **Youth Training** in 1990, which was a lot less **time-consuming** than YTS.

The introduction of the **New Deal** in 1997 means unemployed young people must attend courses aimed at getting them into work, or back into education. They're offered various options — a subsidised job, full time education, or a job in the voluntary sector. If they don't take one of those options, they lose their right to benefits.

New Vocationalism has been Criticised

1) Marxist sociologist **Phil Cohen (1984)** argues that vocational education aims to teach **good work discipline**, not skills. Other people say that this isn't necessarily a problem if it results in equality of opportunity, or economic growth.

2) Some sociologists such as **Dan Finn (1987)** say that vocational training provides **cheap labour** and that governments encourage people into training schemes to **lower unemployment statistics**.

3) **Finn** also points out that a lot of **young people** have **part time jobs** so they **already have work skills**, and don't need vocational education schemes.

4) **Marxists** also argue that vocational education **legitimises class inequality** — they say it perpetuates the idea that middle class kids get educated and working class kids get trained.

The Vocational and Academic sides of the curriculum have to Balance

As mentioned on p.79, post-Fordists believe that a **broad education** is better than a **specific vocational education**, because it prepares young people for the new **flexible** world of work. After all, there's no point spending your whole school career training as a motor mechanic if the internal combustion engine ends up obsolete by the time you're 30... Also, **traditionalists** favour a strong **academic** curriculum.

Not that this'll happen, it's just a silly example

Educational Policy

Social Democratic theory says education should promote Equality of Opportunity

Social Democrats believe in equality of opportunity, and a more equal society. They think education must provide **equality of opportunity**, and it must develop the **potential** of all pupils. Some social democratic theorists also think that if education provided **real equality of opportunity**, it could make society more **egalitarian**, by **increasing social mobility**.

Social Democrats also think that education encourages **economic growth**, by making sure everyone fulfils their potential.

The **Labour** government of Tony Blair have followed **social democratic** principles (and some post-Fordist principles).

> **Gillborn and Mirza (2000)**, wrote a report for the Government called *Educational inequality, mapping race, class and gender*, which starts with the statement: "**Equality of opportunity** is a **vital issue** of **social** and **economic importance** to the whole of society".

Educational Policy has tried to Smooth Out Inequalities

1) **Cultural deprivation theory** influenced **compensatory education** in the 1960s. The idea is that if cultural deprivation affected educational achievement, then **equality of opportunity** wouldn't be enough — working class kids would **still fail**. Compensatory education tried to give **more resources** to schools in deprived areas to raise their level of achievement, and try to achieve more **equality of results**.

2) In 1998, the Government introduced **Education Action Zones**. These were set up in areas where **material** and **cultural deprivation** was **high**, and educational **achievement** was **low**. Education Action Zones get money from the **Government** and the **private sector**. This is used to **pay teachers** more, and set up **homework clubs** to provide **culturally deprived** children with a quiet place to do homework, with access to books.

1) In the 1980s, **feminist sociologists** drew Government attention to **girls' underperformance** at school. Educational policy encouraged teachers to watch out for **gender stereotyping** in the classroom and in teaching materials.

2) The **National Curriculum** forces all pupils to do a **mix** of traditionally "male" and traditionally "female" subjects.

1) The **Race Relations Amendment Act (2001)** says all educational establishments have to have a **policy** on **race equality**.

2) They also must monitor and assess the **impact** of their policies on **pupils**, **staff** and **parents** of different **ethnic groups** — schools must monitor pupil achievements to see if there's a **pattern of ethnic inequality**.

← This has been slightly controversial — some education professionals think it creates too much paperwork and wastes time.

New Right sociologists Oppose the focus on Inequalities

New Right sociologists say that education has **tried too hard** to iron out educational inequalities at the expense of teaching skills. They think that the education system has **dragged down** the achievements of **able pupils**, instead of raising the achievement of pupils at the bottom of the class. They also think that the drive to reduce inequality has **failed** to make sure that the **least able** pupils at least get some decent **qualifications**.

Practice Questions

Q1 Give two examples of vocational qualifications.

Q2 Give two criticisms of new vocationalism.

Q3 What is compensatory education?

Q4 Why are New Right sociologists against changing policy to improve equality of opportunity?

Exam Question

Q1 Outline and assess the view that new vocationalism is essential to provide the economy with skilled workers. (60 marks)

Enjoy education while you can — it beats working...

I had no idea there's been so much thought put into this education thing. I mean, you just go to school and they bore you for a few years. Then you pick some GCSEs to do, and do them. And then you can pick some GNVQs or some AS levels. And do them. I didn't realise they were all tearing their hair out about whether we were having real equality of opportunity. It's quite sweet really.

The Social Nature of Health and Illness

*Most people believe they're unwell if they don't feel like they normally do. Sociologists see health as more than just not feeling poorly. Well, they don't like things to be simple, do they... The whole of section seven is just for **OCR**.*

Sociologists see Health as More than absence of Illness

"Health" is defined in everyday language as an **absence** of **physical symptoms** of illness. This view is based on the **biomedical** (or **biomechanical**) model of health which is current in modern Western societies. There's more about this on p.90, but in a nutshell it's the idea that disease is something that's **physically wrong** with the body, and that it's a doctor's job to fix it.

Some sociologists favour the **social model** of health, which sees health and illness as "**social constructs**" serving the interests of a powerful **medical elite**.

> A "social construct" is an idea that's created by a society — rather than an idea based on objective, testable facts. It's specific to the values and norms of a particular society, but people living in that society usually accept it as natural.

The Social Model argues that Illness and Health are products of Society

There's a **social process** of becoming ill, being defined as a patient, and getting treatment.

1) Firstly, people who feel some kind of body discomfort can either interpret it as **illness**, or as **normal**. For example, a headache after a night's heavy drinking would probably be written off as a normal hangover.

2) People who feel ill can **choose** to **put up with it**, **treat themselves** with traditional or alternative remedies, or go to the **doctor**. **Society** affects their decision — **family members** may encourage the ill person to see the doctor, or the person may have to go to the doctor to get a sick note if they want time off **work**. **Class**, **gender** and **ethnicity** can affect the decision to go to the doctor.

3) The doctor has to **diagnose** the illness. The **doctor-patient relationship** affects the way that doctors diagnose illness. They may give a different diagnosis to a patient who provides lots of **information** about their symptoms. **Middle class** patients are more likely to be comfortable communicating with their doctor. The doctor may have a stereotype of the patient, e.g. a hypochondriac, which may affect the diagnosis.

4) The doctor then has to decide to **intervene**, and treat the illness. Treatment depends on **fashions** in medicine, as well as advances in medical science. Some conditions which used to be treated (e.g. anaemia) are now left to run their own course.

5) Diagnosis and treatment give the person's condition or illness a **label**, which affects how medical professionals and the rest of society treat the patient. See the next page for more about how this works.

Definitions of health and illness vary with time

1) **The medical elite** (doctors) **haven't always dominated** the definition and treatment of illness and disease — it's a modern phenomenon. In modern society, illness is only recognised as illness if it has been **diagnosed** by the medical elite.

2) **Definitions of health and illness** are therefore "social constructs" — they're **specific** to the **values** and **behaviour** of modern society. This means that health and illness aren't actually always related to real **physical symptoms**.

3) **Definitions** of health and illness **change** throughout time. For example, homosexuality used to be defined as a mental illness, but it isn't any more. On the other hand, obesity has become a medical condition. Some kinds of childhood behaviour are now classified as mental health disorders.

The Social Model of Disability says that Society Disables People

1) The **biomedical** view of disability sees a disability as a **physical impairment** that needs to be fixed by medical science.

2) The **social model** looks at the **environmental** and **social** factors which disable an individual, e.g. lack of access, rights and opportunities. For example, a person using a **wheelchair** might feel more disabled by the **lack of a wheelchair ramp** than the fact that they can't use their legs to walk. This idea is called **disableism**.

physical environment	**Public spaces** and **workplaces** often don't accomodate disabled people. There may be a lack of **wheelchair access**, lack of **instructions in Braille**, etc.
stereotyping and media	Some non-disabled people see disabled people as **dependent** and mentally impaired, and may speak to a carer rather than to the disabled person. Disabled people are also stereotyped as asexual. **Barnes (1992)** found that the media portrays disabled people either as **tragic and pathetic**, or as **amazing and brave**. Disabled people rarely appear on TV or in newspapers.
discrimination	Disabled people are **more likely** than non-disabled people to be **turned down** by a potential **employer**.

The social model of health **challenges** the idea that **wellness** is the normal state of affairs. Individuals with an illness are seen as "**living with**" their condition instead of having something "**wrong**" with them.

The Social Nature of Health and Illness

Many Sociologists see Mental Illness as a Social Construct

1) Definitions of mental illness **vary with time** — for example, in the 16th century, it was often defined as possession by evil spirits, and treated by priests rather than doctors.

2) Mental illness isn't as well **understood** as physical illness. Some sociologists say that society tends to treat the mentally ill as **deviants**, and even as **dangerous**. A diagnosis of mental health is often seen as a cause for shame.

Scheff and Szasz believed that mental health was about social roles and labelling

1) **Thomas Scheff (1966)** thought that **mental illness** was a kind of **rule-breaking**.

2) He saw mentally ill people, especially schizophrenics, as breaking **residual norms**. Residual norms are basic rules that are usually taken completely for **granted** — e.g. looking at someone when they talk to you, controlling body movements, understanding what people say.

3) When someone suddenly **stops** following these rules, and behaves "weirdly", they're labelled as **mentally ill**.

4) **Thomas Szasz (1971)** reckoned that **mental illness doesn't really exist**. His reasoning was that illness had to be physical, and mental illness is about odd behaviour, not physical symptoms. So, it's moral rather than medical.

5) **Szasz** thought mental illness was a **label** used for **social control** of deviant people. There's more about this on p.92-93.

R.D. Laing was a psychiatrist who wrote in the late 1960s. He believed that "mental illness" is really a natural response to being in an unbearable situation. He also thought that mental illness needn't always be a negative thing. He had an idea that **mental breakdowns** could turn into **mental breakthroughs**.

Labelling affects the Identity and Treatment of the patient

1) A **label** can **help** the patient get more medical **treatment**. Some say it **legitimises** their condition, and makes it OK for them not to be firing on all cylinders.

2) A label can affect the way **society** treats the patient. For example, the label "disabled" acts as a **master status** — disabled people are often seen in terms of their **impairment**. A diagnosis of schizophrenia or HIV can result in **stigma**.

1) **Erving Goffman (1961, 1970)** saw mental illness as a **stigma** caused by **negative labelling**.

2) Goffman was particularly **harsh** on the **role of mental health institutions** in **reinforcing negative labels**.

3) He thought that individuals in psychiatric institutions have to learn to **conform** to their label as "mentally ill". He said they **lose their old identities** in the process. Goffman calls this process a "**deviant career**" — see p.92.

Functionalists see illness as Deviant — doctors Control this deviance

1) According to **functionalists** like **Talcott Parsons (1951)**, illness is "**deviant behaviour**" which **disrupts** work and home life — you're not supposed to take time off from your social obligations.

2) Parsons said that sick people take on a "**sick role**". While a person is sick, they're allowed to stop functioning in their **normal role**. They don't have responsibility for making themselves better — but they are **expected** to **want to get better**, and to do whatever the doctor tells them.

3) Doctors are in charge of **confirming** that the patient is **actually ill**. Doctors **allow** the sick person to take limited time off, and **make them better** by using their **expert medical knowledge**.

Practice Questions

Q1 What is a social construct?

Q2 What is meant by disableism?

Q3 What effect does the label of "mentally ill" have on a patient, according to Goffman?

Q4 What is the sick role?

Exam Question

Q1 Outline and assess the view that health and illness are socially constructed. (60 marks)

If it's all a product of society, why does my throat hurt...

You've probably been brought up with the biomedical view of health without even realising it — it's the traditional "doctors and hospitals are great and they will cure you" point of view. But in Sociology, the biomedical view is just one of the alternatives — and you need to understand the others as well. Sociology's quite cool this way — nothing goes unquestioned.

Health Inequalities

There are inequalities in health depending on social class, gender, ethnicity and region — all the usual things that sociologists study, then.

Watch out — *Inequalities are Hard to Measure*

It's difficult to measure **morbidity** — it's almost impossible to tell how many people are **ill** at any one time, because people have **different definitions** of **illness**, and different ideas of what's **serious** enough to go to the doctor with.

> **Morbidity** = amount of **illness**
> **Mortality** = amount of **death**

Some sociologists say that **inequalities** are just **products** of the **statistics**. It may be that the statistics aren't really comparing **like** with **like**. Statistics may be **socially biased**.

See p.40 for more about social classifications.

For example, pre-2001 data that used the old **Registrar General**'s social classifications may be **misleading** because social class V had shrunk so much that it was hard to make statistically significant comparisons with other social classes.

Studies show Working Class people have Relatively Poor Health

1) The **working class** have a **higher infant mortality rate** than the national average. The **wealthiest social groups** have **lower infant mortality rates** than the national average.

These statistics are from the Social Trends report that the Office of National Statistics produces.

2) **Working class** people are statistically **more likely** to suffer from **serious medical conditions** such as heart disease, strokes and cancer.

3) **Working class** people are more likely to **die before retirement** age than the average.

4) According to government statistics from 1999, people born in **social class I** (professional) can expect to live for **seven years longer** than people born in **social class V** (manual workers).

Cultural Deprivation Theory blames Bad Health on Working Class Values

1) **Cultural deprivation theory** says that the **working class** lead **relatively unhealthy lifestyles** with relatively poor diets, more smoking, less exercise and more drinking.

2) Their poor health is therefore blamed on their **values** and their **choices**.

3) Cultural deprivation theory also says that the working class are less likely to take advantage of NHS **public health measures** such as **vaccinations**, **health screening** and **ante-natal care**.

4) Some claim that **middle class** people are better **informed** about health, so they tend to lead **healthier lifestyles**. **Parmenter et al (2000)** found that middle class people knew more about healthy eating than working class people.

> **Cultural deprivation theory** suggests that society needs better **health education** to make people more **aware** of health issues. It's resulted in lots of **government initiatives** through the **Health Education Authority** — trying to get people to give up smoking, eat less fatty food, etc.

Material Deprivation Theory blames Social Factors

The **Black Report (1980)** and the **Acheson Report (1998)** linked increased morbidity with low income, poor housing, unemployment and poor education. Sociologists who **disagree** with **cultural deprivation theory** point out that **working class behaviour** is more likely to be caused by **material deprivation**. They don't think it's an expression of different cultural values.

1) **Healthy diets** can be **expensive**, and **gyms** are often **very expensive**.

2) **Smoking and drinking** may be related to **stressful lives**, not **cultural values**.

3) Working class people are **less likely** to be able to afford **private health care**.

Social Administration Theory blames the way the NHS is Set Up

Dixon, Le Grand et al (2003) investigated use of the NHS by different classes

Their conclusion was that the **middle class** get far **more benefit** from the **NHS** than the working class. The benefit the middle classes got wasn't in proportion to their actual health needs.

Dixon and Le Grand found that the middle class were 40% more likely to get a **heart bypass** operation than the working class. Also, the working class were 20% less likely to get a hip replacement despite being 30% more likely to need one.

Even with something as simple as **consultation times** in GPs' surgeries, Le Grand found that professionals were likely to get on average two minutes more of a doctor's time than working class patients.

Research by **Cartwright and O'Brien (1976)** suggests that **middle class patients** tend to have a **better relationship** with their **doctor** than working class patients. Working class patients said they **felt** that the **doctor doesn't listen**.

Health Inequalities

Marxists Blame the Exploitative Nature of the Capitalist System
now there's a surprise...

OK, remember that Marxists define **capitalism** as "**commodity production**" (a commodity is a product for sale in the marketplace, for profit). Marxists tend to see healthcare in capitalist societies as **just another commodity**.

According to **Doyal and Pennell (1979)**, the **pursuit of profit** has **negative health consequences** for the working class:

> 1) **Physical health consequences**
>
> **Industrial accidents** and **industrial diseases** are far more common in the **working class**. **Keeping workers safe** from these risks would **cost money** and **eat into profits**.

> 2) **Economic consequences**
>
> Capitalism **keeps wages low to keep profits high**. Marxists say this makes the working class **poor**, and poor people have higher health risks.

> 3) **Psychological health consequences**
>
> **Workers** doing **repetitive tasks** on a production line are more likely to suffer from **stress related** health problems than workers with more varied roles.

Critics of the Marxist view point out that people in **communist countries often have poor health**, and that **Western capitalist society** has made a lot of **advances in health care**.

There are Regional Variations in Health and Health Care

1) There's variation in health and death rates across the regions of the UK. The **south east** is generally **healthier** than the north. **Scotland** has particularly high levels of poor health.

2) **Social administration theory** blames **unequal distribution** of **NHS resources**.

   - NHS **money** is **shared out unequally** between different areas of the country.
   - **Specialist** hospitals, e.g. heart hospitals, **aren't spread out equally** across the country.
   - There's a **north-south divide** in the **supply of health care**, as well as in people's health.

   > **Julian Tudor Hart (1971)** wrote "The availability of good medical care tends to **vary inversely** with the **need** for it in the population served". In other words, those with the **most** need for health care get **least**, and those with the **least** need get **most**. This is called the **Inverse Care Law**.

3) Tudor Hart's conclusion can be seen as **out of date** — a tremendous amount of reform to the structure of the NHS has gone on between 1971 and the present day.

4) **Some sociologists** have criticised his conclusions by saying he **didn't have evidence**. There isn't a simple relationship between NHS funding and good health in a region. Scotland gets more funding than England, but has poorer health.

Cultural deprivation theorists blame regional inequalities on **regional culture**, often combined with **working class culture**. For example, the high rate of **heart disease** in Scotland is blamed on Scottish fondness for **fried food**.

The Scottish Executive have funded a **healthy living programme** for Scotland, encouraging **exercise** and **healthy eating**.

Practice Questions

Q1 Why is it difficult to measure morbidity?

Q2 According to cultural deprivation theory, why do working class people have poorer health than middle class people?

Q3 What do Marxists blame for poor health among the working classes?

Q4 What is meant by the Inverse Care Law?

Exam Question

Q1 Outline and assess theories of inequalities in health and health care provision in relation to social class. (60 marks)

Inequalities and inverse square law? Is this a page from a maths book...

*No it's not, and it's inverse **care** law, a play on words that would be considered hilarious in Sociology circles. No, not really — I'm just fed up because an awful lot of this Sociology business seems about blaming some system or another for the World's problems. It can get a bit wearing. Favourite scapegoats are "working class values" and "the capitalist system".*

Health Inequalities

There are gender and ethnicity related health inequalities as well. You didn't think I was just going to leave it at class, did you?

There are **Patterns of Inequality** between **Men** and **Women**

- **Women** tend to **live longer** than men.
- More **women** are **long-term ill** or **disabled** than men.
- **Women** visit the doctor **more often** than men.
- **Women** are more likely to be diagnosed with a **mental illness** than men, and more likely to be prescribed drug treatment for mental health symptoms.
- A lot more men die between the ages of **16-35** than **women**.
- **Men** are up to four times more likely than women to commit **suicide**.

> These statistics are from the Social Trends report that the Office of National Statistics produces.

1) Some people say that the statistics don't **necessarily** mean that men or women are healthier.

2) For example, the statistic that says **women** visit the **doctor** more often than men — that includes visits to the doctor that are to do with contraception, reproduction, pregnancy, childbirth, etc. **Pregnant** women have to go to the doctor several times during pregnancy for blood tests, scans and the like. Women have to go for **cervical smear tests** once every few years — this pushes the number of female visits up too.

3) Also, the fact that women **live longer** might partly explain women's higher rate of **degenerative diseases** and **mental illness** — there are **more old women** than old men, and these are illnesses that old people often get. **Alzheimer's disease** might account for some of the mental illness diagnoses.

Feminists *blame* **Gender-role Socialisation** *for* **Health Inequalities**

Melanie tried to be more masculine, but all that happened was she kept getting her teeth knocked out in fights.

1) The **mother/housewife role** is seen by feminists as something that makes women ill. **Radical feminists** suggest mental illness in women is caused by **patriarchy**. They say women have low social status, the stress of housework and child care and the stress of social isolation.

2) **Hilary Graham (1984)** said that because women as mothers are **responsible** for the family's health, they're more **aware** of health and illness, so they use health care more than men.

3) **Annandale and Hunt (1990)** compared the health of a sample of men and women according to gender role. Men and women with more "**masculine**" personalities (assertive, mathematical, etc) had **better health** than men and women with "**feminine**" personalities (intuitive, caring). This suggests there's **something** in **gender** which affects health, as well as something in biological sex.

1) **Doyal (2001)** argues that the difference in death rate between young men and young women could be because men are socialised to be **aggressive** and **take risks**. A lot of deaths in this age range are in road accidents or from violence.

2) Doyal points out that men are a lot more likely than women to be **killed** or **injured** in **industrial accidents**. Men dominate **high-risk industrial jobs** — for example, construction jobs are seen as "men's jobs".

3) Men are socialised to be **tough**. They may see asking for medical help as a sign of **weakness**, and prefer to "take it like a man" when they're ill. This may also result in bottling up mental health problems instead of seeking treatment, which could influence the high **suicide rate** among young men.

Marxist Feminists *blame* **Women's "Dual Oppression"**

1) **Marxist feminists** think that women's stress and illness is caused by their "**dual oppression**" as **housewife** and **worker**.

2) They also believe that labelling women as **stressed** or **depressed** or otherwise **mentally ill** has the effect of taking attention away from women's **domestic environment**. According to Marxist feminists, women's **oppression at home** is the **true cause** of their symptoms of stress or depression. It's in the interests of capitalism to keep women working hard in the home.

Some *Feminists* see *Labelling* as a particular *Problem* for *Women*

Joan Busfield (1983, 2001) thinks that women might be diagnosed with more than their fair share of mental health problems because of **sexism** in the **male dominated medical elite**. She thinks that doctors **label** and **interpret** behaviour differently depending on whether it's a man or a woman doing it. For instance, an **angry, stressed, upset woman** might be labelled **mentally ill** but an **angry, stressed, upset man** might just be "**overworked**".

Health Inequalities

There are **Patterns Of Inequality** according to **Ethnicity**

Ethnic minority health needs were identified as **relatively high** in a report published by the **Department of Health in 1992**. Remember, "**relatively high**" doesn't mean "shockingly sky-high" or "loads higher than the white population". It means anything from a **tiny bit more** to a **lot more** than the **average population**.

1) **Heart disease** is significantly higher in men and women of **Indian** origin.
2) **Afro-Caribbean** people have higher incidence of **stroke** and **HIV/AIDS infection**.
3) **Afro-Caribbeans** are more likely to be admitted to psychiatric hospital than the rest of the population. This is particularly the case for **young black men**.
4) **Suicide** rates are **relatively high** amongst **Asian** women.

Cultural Deprivation Theory blames the **Patient**

1) **Cultural deprivation theory** says that the Indian diet is unhealthy, because it's high in carbohydrates and it uses ghee (butter fat) which is high in saturated fat.
2) Some people from ethnic minorities, especially the elderly, **might not speak enough English** to communicate well with health care staff.
3) Cultural deprivation theory also says that Asian mothers are less likely to go to **ante-natal classes**.
4) **Some ethnic minority groups** tend to see illness and disease as a part of life you can't do much about — and **don't bother** to go to the doctor.

The assertions of cultural deprivation theory have been **criticised**. For example, Indians don't serve everything swimming in ghee, and the Indian diet is high in **fresh vegetables**, which is considered **healthy**. Also, **language** isn't a problem for **second and third generation immigrants**.

Social Administration Theory blames the **NHS**

Some sociologists think that **ethnic minorities** have **relatively poor health** because they're **less likely** to get the **full benefit** from NHS services. **Various possible reasons** have been suggested for this:

1) The **cultural values** of the NHS might be **different** from those of some ethnic minority groups — e.g. female patients being examined by a male doctor. Some advisers say the NHS **needs to adapt to take these values into account**.
2) Health care facilities may not provide information in **languages** other than English.

Culley and Dyson (2001) argue that **language** used by health care staff to describe ethnic minorities may be **inappropriate**. Referring to "black" and "white" may not match up with the patient's own **identity**.

Marxists say it's because **Ethnic Minorities** are more likely to be **Working Class**

Marxists say ethnic minorities are more likely to be in **low-paid manual jobs**, and most likely to be in **poor quality housing**. For Marxists, it all comes down to **social class position**, and what they see as ingrained class inequality.

Practice Questions

Q1 Give two examples of ways that male gender roles could be said to contribute to high mortality in males.
Q2 What is meant by "dual oppression"?
Q3 Give an example of how the inverse care law applies to ethnic minorities.

Exam Question

Q1 Outline and assess sociological explanations of gender differences in health and morbidity. (60 marks)

So that's why all the Desperate Housewives were bonkers...

Hang on though — that doesn't make sense. How can being a Housewife make you mad and ill? They just have affairs with the gardener and stalk the plumber and go shopping and have their nails done. I've seen them. The only one who got stressed was the blonde one, and then she just hired a nanny. Oh, what's that? I think it's a lynch mob of radical feminists heading this way...

Health Policy

The National Health Service was set up to give free and equal health care for all. It was mostly a success. Mostly.

The NHS was set up to provide Equal Health Care

The **NHS** was set up in 1948. It aimed to provide **free** and **equal** health care for **everyone** in the country. Unfortunately, although the NHS was **generally a success**, it **doesn't give 100% equal health care** to all.

Marxists disagree among themselves about whether the NHS has succeeded

Ian Gough (1979) saw the NHS as a **good achievement** that the **working class** gained through political action. He pointed out that health provision for workers was pretty lousy before **1947**.

Vicente Navarro (1976) wasn't keen on the NHS. He thought that the NHS and biomedical elite played an **ideological** role — drawing attention **away** from the **social** and **environmental** causes of disease and illness (see p.82-83 for more on the biomedical elite, and the social model of illness).

Navarro also suggests that the NHS helps give the **illusion** that capitalist society is a **caring** society.

Sociologists and politicians often claim that there's a **two-tier system** in the NHS — which means that it provides a **lower level of care** to some, and a **higher level of care** to others.

Politicians have introduced **lots of reforms** to try to **make the NHS work better** and **make it cost less money**.

In the 1980s the NHS was Reformed to make it more Efficient

In the **1980s**, Mrs Thatcher's Conservative government tried to **reform** the NHS to make it **more efficient** and **less expensive** (a lot of taxpayers' money is spent on the NHS). In 1991, they introduced an **internal market**.

1) In the internal market, **health care providers competed** with each other.

2) **GPs** could choose to become fundholders. This meant they were **responsible for their own budgets**. They could buy drugs and services from hospital trusts.

Private health care benefits the wealthy directly, but the idea was to benefit the poor indirectly.

3) The idea is that **competition drives prices down** — it's an **economics** thing. More **hospital management** was brought in to manage and supervise these changes.

4) The government also **encouraged private hospitals** and **private health insurance schemes**. This was to take some of the **pressure** off the NHS by getting people who could afford private care to go private.

5) In **1988**, the **Griffiths Report** criticised **long-term hospital care** for the elderly and mentally ill. **Care in the Community** was introduced to take old, mentally ill and disabled people out of institutions and put them into the care of their families, and the general community. This **cut costs**, and gave patients more **freedom**.

6) Private sector companies put competitive bids to the NHS to provide support services, e.g. catering and cleaning, and the NHS authorities **had** to take the **cheapest bid**. This was called **Compulsory Competitive Tendering**.

Positive Consequences of the Internal Market

1) There's **more choice** for "health care consumers" (patients).

2) **Competition** tends to **drive down costs**.

3) Health care became **more responsive to local needs**. Fundholders could buy the services they thought were best.

4) Patients of fundholders could get **hospital referrals** faster.

Like most things in Sociology, there are pros and cons, and lots of different opinions.

Negative Consequences of the Internal Market

1) **Fundholding GPs** could pay **extra** to **bump their patients up the queue** to be seen at hospital, leapfrogging patients of non-fundholders. This is definitely a **two-tier system**.

2) **Inner city GPs** look after **more people** and **sicker people** than GPs in **middle class** areas. **Money has to go further**, so inner city GPs can't afford the same quality of treatment — again it's a **two tier system**.

3) Increased numbers of **NHS managers** and **accountants** could be a big **waste** of money. Doctors found that fundholding created a lot of **paperwork**, which a lot of them felt was a waste of their time.

4) **Competition** between health care providers means that **two hospitals very close together** might offer almost exactly the **same services**. This can also be seen as a **waste** of money.

The Conservative NHS reforms were **criticised** by **social democrats** as a three-tier system — they said the richest used private health care, the middle classes used suburban GP practices where the fundholder had money to spare, and the poorest tended to be with cash-strapped inner city GPs.

Verdicts on **Community Care** were mixed — the old **mental hospitals** were thought to oppress patients, and Community Care was thought to provide **freedom**. On the other hand, care in the community allowed for the needs of **some patients**, e.g. **elderly** dementia patients, to be **neglected**.

Health Policy

Since *1997* the *Government* has introduced *New Reforms*

The Acheson Report (1998) found that there was **still health inequality**, in spite of general improvements in health since the NHS was founded. ← *This is a good reference to put in an exam answer about health inequality.*

1) In **1999**, the Labour government scrapped the idea of fundholding, and set up **Primary Care Trusts** — groups of GPs and nurses responsible for local health care budgets. They're midway in scope between the old health authorities, and the fundholding GP practices, and aimed to have the advantages of fundholding without the disadvantages.

2) The government set up the **National Institute for Clinical Excellence** (**NICE**) specifically to ensure **equality** of **NHS treatment** across the UK. NICE produces guidelines for patient care, and is responsible for approving new drugs.

3) New Labour were in favour of the **Private Finance Initiative**, which allows private investors to pay for building new hospitals. Some sociologists think it's the first step towards a **privatised NHS**.

4) In **2003**, the Labour government planned to set up **foundation hospitals**. These would be free to opt out of government guidelines, raise their own money and set their own priorities for how to treat patients.

5) The plans for foundation hospitals were **criticised**. Critics pointed out that only the **top hospitals** would be able to become foundation hospitals — they'd get better funding so they'd be able to attract better staff. They claimed this was a kind of **two tier system** — the best hospitals would be given more money to get even better.

6) New Labour have put more focus on **prevention** of illness. The New Labour government increased the amount of **health education** programmes. There's a national stop smoking campaign, a national campaign to eat five portions of fruit or vegetables a day, and initiatives to get people to do more exercise.

In 2003, the Government set **targets** for reducing health inequalities in terms of **life expectancy** at birth and **infant mortality**.

Official evaluation said that the **life expectancy** target **might not be met**, because action was too focused on the **very young** and the **very old**, and not enough was being done to keep **young adults** and the **middle aged** healthy.

Sociology influences *Health Policy* and *Social Policy*

New Right sociologists believe that the **free market** is the best way to run a health care system. This point of view influenced Conservative governments of the 1980s. New Labour have kept some elements of the free market within the NHS.

Cultural deprivationists believe that **education** is essential to change unhealthy habits. This point of view has influenced New Labour governments since 1997.

Material deprivationists believe that **relieving poverty** is the best way to fix health inequalities. The Acheson Report recommended increasing benefits given to pregnant women, children and the old, and improving housing.

Most *Formal* and *Informal Health Care* in the UK is Provided by *Women*

1) Around **75%** of all **NHS workers** are **women**.

2) However, only **25% of doctors** and **13% of consultants** are **women**. **Over 90%** of **nurses** are **women**.

3) Studies have also discovered that the vast majority of **informal care** of **children** and **elderly relatives** is carried out by women. **Hilary Graham** argues that care in the community reinforces and legitimises exploiting women as low-paid carers.

Practice Questions

Q1 What is meant by "GP fundholding"?

Q2 Other than GP fundholding, give two examples of post-1979 Conservative health reform.

Q3 Give three examples of post 1997 Labour health reform.

Q4 Who provides most informal care in the community, men or women?

Exam Question

Q1 Outline and assess changes in health care policy since 1979, and assess their impact on health inequality. (60 marks)

Material deprivationist — a posh way of saying someone's a nudist...

There have been a lot of health care reforms since 1979, and yes, you are expected to know the main changes. You should be able to write down two subheadings — "Conservative reforms, 1980s and 1990s" and "Labour reforms post-1997", and jot down the main reforms under each heading. If you can write down some pros and cons of each reform, that'd be just the thing.

The Role of Medicine

Sociologists have different views about the role of the medical professions. The medical professions, on the other hand, have no views about the role of sociologists. They're too busy healing people. Or killing them. Depending on your point of view.

The **Biomedical Model** says **Health** and **Disease** are **Physical** things

The **biomedical** or **biomechanical model** is based around the idea that health and disease are **natural phenomena** which exist in an individual's body. **Disease** is something **physically wrong** with the body, and health is the **absence of disease**. The interaction of the individual and the social world is **not relevant** in the biomedical model. Health professionals generally follow the **biomedical model of health**.

Nicky Hart (1985) notes five key characteristics of the biomedical model

1) Disease is **physical**. **Social** factors **aren't relevant**.

2) Doctors are an **elite**. They are the only people who are sufficiently **qualified** and skilled to **identify** and **treat** illness.

3) The human body is like a **machine**. It can be **repaired** by **drugs** and **surgery** when it breaks down.

4) Illness is **temporary**. **Wellness** is the **normal** state of affairs.

5) Treatment is **special**. Treatment takes place in **recognised health care environments** (doctor's surgery, hospital, clinic, etc), which are **distinct** from the environment where the patient got ill.

Medical Intervention hasn't done a lot of good — according to **McKeown**

1) **McKeown (1976)** claims that **medical intervention** by the biomedical elite **hasn't had much impact** on improvements in health over the last 200 years.

2) McKeown thinks that big health improvements have been mainly down to **social factors** — things like **sewage disposal**, supply of **clean water** and **improved diets.**

3) The **social changes** that McKeown says changed people's health all happened in the **19th century** — before the medical elite came to dominate health.

4) McKeown uses evidence like **life expectancy** and **infant mortality statistics**. He points out that life expectancy went up and infant mortality went down **before** biomedical techniques came in. For instance, mass immunisation for TB (a biomedical approach) only happened after the death rate for the disease had already gone down.

The bathroom — where social health <u>really happens</u>.

Illich Says the **Medical Elite** Actually **Cause Bad Health**

1) **Illich (1975)** defines **health** as the **capacity** to cope with the **human reality** of **death**, **pain** and **sickness**. This is a very different definition to the mainstream biomedical definition.

2) Illich believes that medicine has **gone too far**, and started to "**play God**" — trying to **wipe out** death, pain and sickness. OK so far... he then says that **trying to control death and illness** is a bad move which **turns people into consumers** or even objects. In his opinion, this messes up people's natural capacity for health and **makes people ill**.

3) Illich uses the word **iatrogenesis** to mean this kind of illness that's caused by modern medicine. He says there are **three types of iatrogenesis**:

> 1) **Clinical iatrogenesis** — the **harm** done to patients by **ineffective** treatments, **unsafe** treatments or getting the **wrong diagnosis**.
>
> 2) **Social iatrogenesis** — the idea that **doctors** have **taken over control** of people's lives, and individuals can't make decisions about their problems. More and more of people's problems are seen as **suitable** for **medical intervention**. This is called the **medicalisation of social life**.
>
> 3) **Cultural iatrogenesis** — the **destruction** of **traditional ways** of **dealing** with and making sense of **death**, **pain** and **sickness**.

Illich thinks the **worst** is **cultural iatrogenesis**. He puts it like this: → "A society's image of death reveals the level of independence of its people, their personal relatedness, self reliance, and aliveness."

According to Illich's view, dying has become the ultimate form of **consumer resistance** (when you're dead, you can't buy any more Nike trainers, I'd imagine). **Death** isn't seen as something normal. It's become a **taboo**.

The Role of Medicine

Functionalists *see Medicine as* Altruistic

Doctors sanction the sick role — they **allow** the sick person to take limited time off from their social obligations. Doctors **make the patient better** by using their **expert medical knowledge**. **Parsons** thought that doctors **always** put the **patient's needs** before their own needs.

Critics of Parsons say the medical profession don't always put patients first — they say private medicine is proof that doctors are self-interested. However, it can't be denied that doctors treat patients, and give people sick notes so they can take leave.

Marxists *see* Medicine *as an* Institution *which* Supports Capitalism

Marxists believe that the medical profession only do good for the **capitalist** class — they **keep class inequalities going**. Marxists such as **Doyal and Pennell (1979)** say that the medical profession have a **conservative** role in society.

1) Doctors keep the workforce **healthy** and **productive**. **Healthy** workers can **work harder** and won't have to take **time off sick**. This means **more profits** for the capitalist class.

2) Doctors **check** that **workers** aren't spending too much time on **sick leave**. They say **how long** a worker can **stay off work**.

3) Marxists believe that doctors **hide the real social causes of illness** (poverty, class inequality etc.) by focusing on the individual and their physical symptoms.

Some Marxists think that **doctors** are **agents** of **large drugs corporations** — they believe that health care exists mainly to produce **profits** for drugs companies.

Weberians *see the* Medical Profession *as* Self-Serving

Weberians think that doctors **arrange** things so that they **keep** their **high status** in society.
They suggest that the medical profession is **self-serving**.

A Weberian is a follower of German sociologist, historian and economist Max Weber (1864-1920).

They argue that the medical profession has managed to **shut out** other forms of healing such as homeopathy, aromatherapy, faith healing and other types of **alternative medicine**. This makes modern medicine a monopoly.

Feminists *see the* Medical Profession *as serving* Patriarchal Interests

1) Feminists see medicine as yet another way that patriarchy can keep **control** over women. Feminists **Abbott and Wallace (1990)** say that women who deviate from a feminine norm are controlled by being diagnosed as **mentally ill**.

2) Female illnesses like post-natal depression, pre-menstrual syndrome and the menopause are neglected by medical science. Women who have symptoms of these illnesses may be stereotyped as malingerers, or "stressed".

3) Women tend to have **subordinate** roles in medicine — **nurses** and **auxiliaries** tend to be **women**, **consultants** tend to be **men** (see p.89). Some feminists think that the role of being a nurse has been made to look like being a "doctor's handmaid" — a female servant obeying the male doctor.

Practice Questions

Q1 What does McKeown claim is responsible for improvements in health in the last two hundred years?

Q2 What does iatrogenesis mean?

Q3 What three types of iatrogenesis does Illich identify?

Exam Questions

Q1 Outline and assess the view that "Health and sickness are defined by the powerful." (60 marks)

Q2 Outline and assess the extent to which the NHS can be described as a patriarchal institution. (60 marks)

If doctors make you ill, do teachers make you thick...?

Blimey, this iatrogenesis idea is a bit radical — it's actually the doctors' fault that we're ill... Still, you can kind of see some reasoning behind it. Oh, and as ever, you need to be able to compare and contrast Functionalist (all for the best), Marxist (all set up for the benefit of the bosses), Weberian (all for the benefit of doctors) and feminist (all unfair to women) views.

Medicine and Social Control

If health is socially constructed, then can it be used as social control? That's a serious question, not a conspiracy theory.

Reproductive *healthcare can* Exercise Social Control

1) **Oakley (1984)** has said that the process of childbirth has been "**medicalised**". In other words, women giving birth are treated like there's **something wrong with them**. **Control** over giving birth is taken away from women and given to **men**. Male doctors are often in charge, not midwives or the women who are actually giving birth.

2) Doctors decide what kind of **contraception** a **woman** can use. Doctors also decide whether to give a **man** a **vasectomy**. This **control** over **contraception** choices follows **social** and **moral** factors. Doctors are unlikely to sterilise **young** men or women who might change their minds about not wanting kids. Doctors may refuse to fit an IUD to a woman if they believe she's not in a standard **monogamous** relationship (this makes **sense**, considering the risk of sexually transmitted infections — but it's still a **judgement** about the patient's sexual morals).

3) The contraceptive pill carries some **health** risks, but it's widely prescribed. Radical feminists argue that the pharmaceutical industry pressurises doctors to restrict women's access to other forms of contraception.

Being pregnant carries much worse health risks than being on the Pill, so there you go...

4) Doctors also control access to **reproductive** technology — e.g. IVF. **Single women** find it hard to get **IVF**. **Lesbian** couples who want to have children usually have to rely on a sperm donation from a male friend.

5) Contraception **redefines** the body — it means that women's reproductive organs are no longer primarily for having **babies**, but they have become a source of **pleasure**. Some feminists say that contraception **liberates** women from constant **childbearing**. Others say that contraception **legitimises** women's role as **sexual objects**.

Access to abortion is seen by some sociologists as social control

1) **Married women** may be **discouraged** from having an abortion — they fit into the social norm of women who "should" be having babies, especially if they're **middle class**.

2) **Single** women, especially **poor** single women may have easier access to abortion.

3) In **Nazi Germany**, abortion and sterilisation were used explicitly as a form of **social control**. Women from social groups that the Nazis thought were **undesirable** were **forced** to have **abortions**, or sterilised without their consent. Disabled women, e.g. deaf women, were sterilised.

Mental Illness *is seen by many sociologists as* Social Control *of* Deviance

1) **Thomas Szasz (1971)** thought that what we call "mental illness" is a **label** society uses to **control non-conformist behaviour**. He said that people who behave in a way that the rest of society sees as **unacceptable** or **dangerous** are defined as "mentally ill".

2) People who are labelled as "mentally ill" can be admitted into psychiatric hospitals against their will. Szasz compared **forced treatment in mental hospitals** to the **persecution of witches** in the Middle Ages.

3) Feminists see the diagnosis and treatment of **depression** in women as a kind of **social control**. They claim that women who **deviate** from a feminine norm (by complaining of mental stress) are diagnosed, and prescribed **psychotropic (behaviour altering) drugs** to **control** their deviant behaviour.

4) **Young black men** are more likely to be sectioned under the Mental Health Act (put in mental hospital against their will) than any other social group. Young black men are often stereotyped in a **racist** way as **aggressive** and a **threat** (see p.76). This may affect the way they are treated by some medical professionals.

Goffman (1961) studied patients and staff in psychiatric institutions

Goffman described how patients respond to being labelled "mentally ill" — how they're controlled and how their identity is redefined. He called this the "deviant career".

Withdrawal — Patient doesn't communicate with other patients — doesn't believe he / she belongs with them.

Rebellion — Patient refuses to cooperate with staff.

Cooperation — Patient plays along with the staff idea of how a mental patient behaves. Patient starts to "act crazy".

If a patient said "I don't belong here, I'm not mad" the staff would think "that's just what a mad person would say, you must be mad".

This is what happens to Jack Nicholson's character in the film One Flew Over The Cuckoo's Nest.

The staff respond to the patient's "crazy" behaviour by **punishing** the patient — they take away the patient's liberty and privacy and they don't let the patient make choices. This is called "**mortification of the self**". It ends up with the patient losing their personality.

The patient becomes **institutionalised**, which means they can't manage on their own outside the institution. After this, the staff can start from scratch, building up a "sane" conformist personality.

Medicine and Social Control

There's *Ideology* about the *Human Body* — *including ideas of a "Body Norm"*

1) In society, there's quite a bit of attention paid to how people **look**, and how **healthy** they **appear**.

2) In consumer societies like the modern West, beauty and health are big business. Sociologists say that the body is treated as a **commodity** — people have the idea that they can **buy** a better body by spending money on diets, exercise equipment or cosmetic surgery.

3) In Western societies, there's a "**body norm**" of being **thin**, **pretty** and **young-looking**. According to **Naomi Wolf (1991)** the female body norm is oppressive to women. Some people think that attempting to conform to the norm contributes to **eating disorders** e.g. anorexia nervosa and bulimia nervosa.

4) Medicine defines some things like obesity, teenage spots and the ageing process as medical conditions which can be treated. This "**medicalisation**" of **previously normal** parts of life is criticised by some people. Definitions of the body norm can affect people's **opinion** of their **own health**.

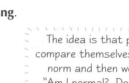

The idea is that people compare themselves to the norm and then wonder "Am I normal? Do I have something wrong with me?"

5) **Cosmetic surgery** is criticised by some feminists as the "**medicalisation of beauty**", and also as a **social control** over women.

6) Some sociologists suggest society is **intolerant** of **everyone** who **deviates** from the body norm — e.g. the old, the overweight and the disabled.

7) Some people think the body norm is **racist**. The **beauty ideal** is not only young, thin and pretty — she's also **white**.

Discourse, for Foucault, means rules about language. Discourse dictates how a topic can be talked about. See p.99 for more on discourse.

There's *Ideology* about *Sex* and *Sexuality* as well

Postmodernists like **Michel Foucault** were big on the idea that **discourse** has the power to socially control deviance. The example of AIDS shows how this can work in real life.

1) **Medical discourse** (talk and language) about **sexually transmitted diseases** has an undercurrent of **morality** and social control.

2) **AIDS** in particular has social and cultural meaning attached to it. In the 1980s, AIDS was characterised as a "gay plague" by the British media. The word "plague" is particularly negative — it conjures up ideas of **uncleanliness** as well as death. Homosexuality was therefore associated by the media and the public with uncleanliness and death.

3) AIDS patients were **stigmatised**. There was a common belief that people with HIV and AIDS "**deserved**" it. Discourse about the illness focused on the **morality** of socially deviant behaviours which allowed the transmission of HIV — in particular **anal sex between men** and **intravenous drug use**.

4) A distinction was drawn between "**good**" AIDS victims, who had contracted HIV through **blood transfusion**, and "**bad**" HIV victims, who had contracted the virus through sex (particularly **gay sex**, *particularly* **promiscuous gay sex**) or **sharing needles** used to inject drugs.

5) Discourse about HIV and AIDS was used, especially in the 1980s, to **punish homosexuality**. Gay and bisexual men in particular were directly blamed for the spread of AIDS.

Practice Questions

Q1 How could access to contraception be used to control women?

Q2 How could access to abortion be used as social control?

Q3 What is the "deviant career"?

Q4 How can cultural norms of beauty and health negatively impact on an individual's view of health?

Q5 How did the discourse around HIV/AIDS affect society's views about homosexuality?

Exam Question

Q1 Outline and assess the view that medicine is a tool for controlling social deviance. (60 marks)

This topic always makes me feel a bit paranoid...

Phew, there's some more strong stuff here. Word of warning — some of these views are controversial. Not everyone agrees that the contraceptive pill is part of a patriarchal conspiracy, for example. Yep, I thought you'd be surprised. By the way, lots of the stuff on body image and health ties in with the Media part of the AS course, so it might help to have a look through your old notes.

Defining Culture

*This section is for **OCR**. Ignore it if you're studying AQA. OK, remember the idea of culture from AS... Now you're in A2, it's time to look at some of the complications. For a kick off, in developed Western countries (like the UK) there's not only the one type of culture and there are lots of ways to look at culture — Folk vs Urban, High vs Low, Popular culture, Global culture...*

Remember the **Definition** of **Culture**

Culture means the **shared customs**, **values**, **knowledge**, **skills**, **roles** and **norms** in a society. It's the way of life of a social group. Culture is **socially transmitted**. That means it's **passed on** through **socialisation**.

Mass Culture replaces Folk Culture

Folk culture is the culture of **pre-industrial society**. It includes things like folk dances, folk songs, fairy tales, old wives' tales, traditional folk medicine and agricultural rituals. It's mainly passed on through word of mouth. Various sociologists have looked at the ways **culture changes** as people move from **small country villages** into **larger towns** and **cities**.

Just try and tell me folk culture is dead... I dare ya, punk...

1) **Robert Redfield (1947)** said that "**folk societies**" were based on strong extended families, **supportive communities** and a **local culture**. In **urban** societies these were **not present**.

2) **Georg Simmel (1950)** argued that **urban societies** showed a **reduced sense of community**, and that urban people were more **individualistic** and **selfish**.

3) Theorists from the **Frankfurt School** (see p.96) said that this reduced sense of community was linked to the development of a **mass culture**. They said that the **media** had become a **strong agent of socialisation**, and it was wiping out the differences between local cultures. Instead, it looked more and more like there was just **one big culture**, shared by **everyone**.

4) These days, the term **mass culture** is used not just to describe the effects of the **media**, but also refers to **fashion** and other types of **consumption**. If you buy a well-known brand of trainers, or eat lunch in a famous burger chain, you're taking part in mass culture.

You can also **Divide** culture up into "**High Culture**" and "**Low Culture**"

The **elite** (better educated, with more money and power) tend to have a **distinct culture** from the **masses**.

1) Shakespeare, opera, sophisticated restaurants and arty French films are the type of things that are associated with "**high culture**".

2) Meanwhile, the masses enjoy **low culture** — e.g. soap operas, reality TV, musicals, fast food and Hollywood films.

This is all linked to the ideas of "class taste", cultural deprivation and cultural capital — see p.131.

3) High culture is generally considered more **difficult to appreciate** and the audience is seen as **educated** and having "**good taste**". Aspects of high culture are seen as **good for society**, though they don't make much money compared to a lot of low culture, so the government **subsidises** them.

4) In recent years a lot of **funding for high culture** has come from a **low culture event** — the National Lottery. Some customers have been hostile to the idea that the lottery is used to pay for "arty" dance and theatre companies. They suggest it's **elitist culture** — most lottery punters **wouldn't get to see it** and probably **wouldn't like it** if they did.

Many sociologists say there's **No Such Thing** as "**Low Culture**"

1) The ideas of **mass culture** and **low culture** are very **negative**. Some sociologists have argued that this view is based on an **elitist perspective**. For example, **Bourdieu (1984)** says the **whole idea** of "high culture" is just a way of giving **status** to **elite groups** — he says that status is maintained by passing on **cultural knowledge**.

2) Marxists argue that high culture is just ruling class culture, and that the ruling class have imposed their idea of culture on the rest of society, and defined it as "better" than working class culture. Some Marxists argue that so-called "low culture" is just as **complex** and **sophisticated** as "high culture". For that reason, they prefer to use the term "**popular culture**", which is more of a positive idea.

3) Important work on popular culture has been done by the **Centre for Contemporary Cultural Studies** (**CCCS**). They analyse popular culture products like TV, magazines and youth fashions, finding **meanings** within them.

Popular Culture theorists emphasise that the Audience is Active

"**Mass**" and "**Low**" culture are both concepts that are based on the idea of a **passive audience**. They assume that the audience are being **manipulated** by the media and don't have much control.

"**Popular**" culture is a concept that is based on the idea of an **active audience**. This audience shapes and changes the culture. The CCCS has done a lot of work on the way this happens in youth fashions and subcultures.

Defining Culture

There's also a Global Culture

Giddens (1990) says that **technological change** has led to globalisation. Goods can be **transported** across the world, and **information** can be very quickly transmitted across the world. This has meant that cultures that were once local have become global. For example, British and American pop music is everywhere. American and Indian films are popular internationally.

1) **Klein (2001)** and **Sklair (1995)** point out that a few large **transnational corporations** (TNCs), e.g. Coca-Cola, Nike and Time Warner, are involved in the majority of cultural production, making cultural goods that are consumed all over the world. **Sklair** argues that TNCs and the global media have **more power** than individual **nation states**.

2) Critics of globalisation worry that these TNCs will replace all cultures with Western culture — they refer to cultural globalisation as **cultural imperialism**. **Klein (2001)** says there's already a trend towards **cultural homogeneity** (everyone having the same culture, wearing the same trainers, eating the same burgers, drinking the same fizzy drinks).

3) Supporters of cultural globalisation argue that it's a **two way process**. Western culture is transmitted to new societies, and other identities and cultures get passed back to Western societies — e.g. **Bollywood films** shown in Western mainstream cinemas. Postmodernists argue that this allows people to consume a **plurality** of cultures. They think that globalisation leads to **hybridity** (a **pick and mix**) of cultures rather than one culture being imposed over another.

A Cultural Industry is... an Industry that Creates Culture

In pre-industrial times, people mostly **made their own things**, or made things for their **community**. Now that we live in a capitalist industrial society, we **buy things** that have been made by **industry**.

In pre-industrial times, people **made their own folk culture** — singing folk songs, telling stories round the fire, even... morris dancing. In our capitalist industrial society, we **buy cultural goods** that have been made by the **cultural industries**.

Some of the most important examples of the cultural industries are:

- The **fashion** industry
- The Hollywood **film** industry
- The **news** industry
- The **music** industry
- The **advertising** industry
- The **broadcasting** industries (radio and TV)
- The **magazine** industry

All of these industries create and sell things that fit into people's **cultural lives** — the stuff they **think about**, and **talk about**, and in many cases the stuff that helps them to **define who they are**. Some theorists, e.g. **Featherstone (1991)**, call this "**Symbolic Consumption**" — see below.

Symbolic Consumption means Buying Things that help Define who you are

1) In modern industrial societies, **hardly anyone** buys any product based on its **function** alone.

2) For example, most **trainers** are just comfortable shoes — so choosing a pair should be pretty easy, right... yeah, right. The thing is, when most people choose a pair of trainers, they have to make sure that they're the **right brand** and the **right style**. You don't just buy the shoes, you buy what the shoes **stand for** — their "**symbolic value**". What you're actually buying is part of your **identity**.

3) That means that **most industries** in the modern world have actually become **cultural industries**. They're selling things that have some kind of "**cultural meaning**" attached. Any industry that makes things with a **brand image** that **means something** to people, or **stands** for something, is involved in **cultural production**.

Practice Questions

Q1 What is folk culture?
Q2 What is mass culture?
Q3 What is globalisation?
Q4 Give an example of symbolic consumption.

Exam Question

Q1 Outline and assess the view that high culture is superior to popular culture. (60 marks)

If I watch Pop Idol on top of Ben Nevis, does that make it high culture...

Culture is everywhere, apparently. Even something as simple as preferring Coke to Pepsi, or Burger King to McDonalds is seen by sociologists as a case of symbolic consumption. In fact, a sociologist would probably see this very book as a cultural product. You need to be up to speed with the terms on these pages, because you'll need them to analyse different views of culture in the exam.

Theories of Culture

Some approaches focus on the idea that those in power use popular culture to control those who aren't.

Cultural Decline approaches suggest everything is Getting Worse

The idea that culture is getting worse isn't new. Back in **1869**, **Matthew Arnold** argued that **low culture** (he called it "philistine culture") was **taking over**. Later on, the literary critic **F.R. Leavis (1930)** wrote a great deal about the idea that high culture was in decline. Like Arnold, he felt that **low culture** was **dominant**, and that this was leading to **serious social damage**.

You can still find people expressing Leavis's sort of ideas in books and newspaper columns.

A lot of cultural criticism doesn't come from sociologists, but from <u>art critics</u> and <u>literary critics</u>.

The **cultural decline argument** says there's a **cycle of degradation**. It goes like this:

1) **High Culture** is **refined** and improves its audience as people.

2) **Mass culture** has **bad values**. It encourages **swearing, violence, uncouth behaviour** and general **lack of respect**.

3) Society gets worse because almost **nobody** is exposed to **high culture** and almost **everybody** is exposed to **mass culture**.

4) As **society** gets **worse**, **mass culture** gets **even worse** in response, and in turn brings society down **even further**.

Many critics feel that this is a **snobbish** and **elitist** perspective, which encourages the idea that some people in society are **naturally superior** to others. For example, as you'd expect, **Marxists** have mostly been pretty **unsympathetic** to the cultural decline argument. On the other hand, some influential Marxists were very **pessimistic** about **mass culture** too, but for different reasons.

Marxism says that the working class are Oppressed by Capitalism via Culture

1) Many Marxists say it's all done with **ideology**. They say everyone is **tricked** into accepting the idea that everything about society is **just fine**. Marxists from the **Frankfurt School** decided that the **Mass Media** were the main way of transmitting **capitalist ideology**. (The Frankfurt School were a group of sociological thinkers from 1930s Germany.)

2) They argued that mass culture **helped capitalism** to oppress the working classes by **destroying community** and **individuality**. It also encouraged **acceptance of authority** and **discouraged** people from **thinking for themselves**.

3) In this way, capitalism used **mass culture** to **prevent revolution** from ever happening.

> Some examples the Frankfurt School pointed out were:
> * **Hollywood films** that distracted ordinary people from social issues, giving them **false dreams** of **glamour** and **adventure**.
> * **Newspaper horoscopes** which suggested that a person's life experiences were down to **luck** or **fate**, rather than social structures or personal actions.
> * TV and radio **advertising** that reinforced the values of capitalism.

Marxists said capitalism creates False Needs and Commodity Fetishism

1) **Capitalism** is based on **selling things**. According to Frankfurt School sociologists **Adorno and Horkheimer (1944)** mass culture encourages you to think you **"need"** to **buy things** which you don't need at all, such as a cupboard full of shoes, or an iPod. You **don't** actually **need** these things in the same way you need **food** and **water** and oxygen, but it's **good for capitalism** if you **think** you do. That's **false need**.

2) The next bit is **commodity fetishism** — which is when people become **obsessed** with having particular products, and with the **details** of those products, and become keen to pay a high price to own them. An example of this is when a new mobile phone comes out and everyone wants it, or when a clothing label is in fashion.

3) **Adorno and Horkheimer** said commodity fetishism was like a **religion**.

4) According to them, the really clever trick is that **capitalism creates desires** that **only capitalism can satisfy**. This means we all end up thinking **capitalism** is a **good** thing, because it gives us **exactly what we want**.

> So, to sum up, the **Frankfurt School** took a **pessimistic** and **negative** approach to mass culture, which said:
> * Mass culture is used to **dull the minds** of the **working classes**.
> * Mass culture promotes **capitalist ideology**.
> * **Commodity fetishism** encourages **economic activity**.
> * The population are **passive victims** of mass culture.

Theories of Culture

Not All Marxists agree with the Frankfurt School

1) The Italian thinker **Antonio Gramsci** (1891-1937) said that the idea of a **single mass culture** was too **simplistic**.

2) **Gramsci (1971)** accepted that capitalism creates a big **dominant culture**, and he used the term **hegemony** (see glossary) to describe this. But Gramsci went on to say that society produced lots of **oppositional cultures** that stood **against** the values of hegemony.

> Gramsci wrote most of his theories in prison, in the 1930s. His prison notebooks were published much later. That's why the date of publication is well after he died.

3) Gramsci also believed that **hegemony** had to **tolerate** oppositional cultures, rather than stamping them out. By **allowing opposition** to exist, he said, capitalism could encourage the **illusion** that it was a **fair** and **free** system.

4) He had a big influence on the work of Marxists like **Stuart Hall** of the **Centre for Contemporary Cultural Studies**. Hall says that **youth subcultures** help working class youths to **resist capitalist values**.

5) Hall, and other neo-Marxists who take a more positive, optimistic view of modern culture, prefer the term **popular culture** to mass culture.

1) **Stuart Hall (1992)** argues that people in contemporary societies have **fragmented identities**. This means they have **several identities** instead of one solid identity. Hall said that people were members of "several overlapping **imagined communities**" including national, gender, ethnic, religious and political identities.

2) Hall links this with the rise of **new social movements** such as feminism, black power, and the green movement. He also links this with **globalisation** — as a response to cultural globalisation, people have constructed new identities such as "Black British", "British Muslim", "Somali living in London" etc.

3) The way people **use culture** reflects their **fragmented identity**. Some sociologists have looked at the way that British Asians pick and mix aspects of traditional **Indian** and **Pakistani** culture, black **hip-hop culture** and British **urban** culture to make a **hybrid culture**.

Feminism links popular culture to Socialisation and Patriarchy

Where Marxists see the mass media as promoting **capitalism**, feminists have concentrated on representations of **gender roles**. During the 1970s and 1980s, many feminists researched the relationship between **popular culture** and **gender socialisation**.

Most of these studies suggested that popular culture **stereotypes** women into roles — such as housewife or sex object. These roles are then **reinforced** in society.

1) **Ferguson (1983)** and **McRobbie (1978)** studied magazines, showing how they promoted traditional female roles.

2) **Radical feminists**, such as **Andrea Dworkin (1981)** in her study of pornography, suggest that many images of women in popular culture encourage and justify **violence** against women.

3) More recently, some feminists have argued that popular cultural representations of women can also be **empowering**. For example, **Camille Paglia** has written a lot about Madonna's public image as a strong female role model.

Tania Modleski (1982) argues that a lot of **mass culture** and **low culture** has been traditionally aimed at women — e.g. **romance novels** and **soap operas**. She argues that snobbery and elitism about low culture can also be seen as **sexism** against women.

Practice Questions

Q1 Explain what is meant by "cultural decline".

Q2 How do the Frankfurt School view popular culture?

Q3 What is meant by "commodity fetishism"?

Q4 Explain how popular culture could be said to stereotype women.

Exam Question

Q1 Outline and assess one sociological theory of popular culture.	(60 marks)

Bling: good thing or bad thing...

According to the Frankfurt School, I didn't really need that Von Dutch baseball cap after all. If only Theodor Adorno could have texted me to tell me. Sigh. Anyway, make sure you know the nuts and bolts of these theoretical approaches, because you'll need them if you want to get the top level marks. Without mentioning relevant theorists, you aren't going to win the examiner over.

Theories of Culture

Get ready for some hardcore theory. This is the stuff that really shows those examiners that you know what you're talking about. Modernism, Poststructuralism and Postmodernism – it can look brain-bursting to start with, but once you get the key ideas, it all just falls into place.

Modernist sociologists believe society can be understood Scientifically

Modernism is a word that's used to mean many different things. In Sociology it refers to the "**classical sociological**" approaches of **Marx** and **Durkheim**. Those two certainly didn't agree about everything, but they had some similar **beliefs** which meant that they can both be seen as modernist.

- They both believed that society was a **structure** — an organised system.
- They both believed that **social structures controlled individuals**, never the other way around.
- They both believed in the idea of **progress** — society improving over time.
- They both believed a **scientific approach** could explain society.

> Marxism and Functionalism are also known as <u>structuralist</u> viewpoints because they focus on structure.

In Modernism there are Two Opposing Views of Culture

1) The **Marxist** perspectives start from the idea that culture creates **false consciousness**. Marxists believe culture is all set up to reinforce the **class structure** and to **distract** the working classes from realising that they're being **oppressed**. According to Marx, this helps prevent **revolution** from taking place.

2) Marx thought that the working classes would eventually **realise** that they were being tricked and the **false consciousness** created by capitalist culture would be replaced by **class consciousness**. Then **revolution** would come. The **Frankfurt School** perspective described on p.96 is a good example of Marxist modernism.

1) Durkheim's **Functionalist** perspective describes culture as a kind of **social glue**. It bonds people together by creating shared interests and purposes.

2) It also helps to **socialise** people into appropriate behaviour. This prevents society from breaking down into chaos.

It should be pretty clear that **Marx** and **Durkheim** saw culture as doing basically the **same thing** — **controlling people**. The difference was, Marx thought that this was a bad thing, while Durkheim believed it was necessary and good.

Semiotic Analysis looks for Hidden Structures of Meaning

1) An important approach to popular culture is semiotics. This perspective is based on the ideas of the linguist **Ferdinand de Saussure** (1857-1913). Saussure was a **structuralist** — he thought that meaning was found in the **structure** of language, rather than in the **individual words** of a language.

2) According to semiotics, society is full of **signifiers** (words, symbols and images) — which create **meanings**.

3) Meanings can be either **denoted** or **connoted**. **Denoted** (or denotative) meanings are **obvious**. **Connoted** (or connotative) meanings are **suggested** — you don't see them right away, and may only notice them **subconsciously**.

4) For example, a **picture** of a gun **denotes** a gun. A picture of a gun **connotes** all sorts of things — **power**, **masculinity**, **death**, **gangsters**, **fear** and so on.

5) Quite a lot of **sociological work** on culture now involves **semiotic analysis**, looking for the **connotative** meanings of cultural objects. This can be from all kinds of perspectives. For example, **Dick Hebdige (1979)** took a **Marxist** approach to his semiotic analysis of **Punk** (see p.102) while Ann DuCille's analysis of the Barbie Doll (see page 104) was focused on **feminism** and **ethnicity**.

Postmodernism rejects Modernist ideas and argues that Culture is Diverse

Postmodernism rejects the idea that **culture creates social unity**, and says there are lots of **different cultures**. Stuart Hall says this **pluralism** is what gives people **fragmented identities** (see p.97) — people construct their identity from different and sometimes contradictory bits of various cultures. In postmodern culture, "**high**" and "**low**" culture get **mixed** together.

Postmodernism says signifiers are more powerful than the things they signify

1) In other words, the **name** and **image** we give to something has more meaning than the thing itself.

2) There are lots of examples in popular culture — e.g. **brands**. Look at the counterfeit "label" goods on any street market in the country. The **only selling point** for a cheaply made, **fake Gucci watch** is the **name** on the product.

3) **Baudrillard (1981)** suggests that in the postmodern age **symbols** have become **commodities**, and that we no longer buy products for what they **are** but for the things they **represent**.

Theories of Culture

Poststructuralism is an Important aspect of Postmodernism

1) According to poststructuralists, people are **controlled** by **language** and other signifiers.

2) Poststructuralism says language has **no fixed meaning**, so there is no absolute truth. **Poststructuralism** says that there are **no real structures**, only **interpretations**.

3) **Baudrillard (1983, 1988)** said that the development of media communication has meant everyday life is stuffed full of **images**. Baudrillard claimed that audiences experience these images so **intensely** that they reach a state called "**hyperreality**" where the image seems to be **more real** than **real life**.

4) **Baudrillard (1988)** argued that the sheer **amount** of images and messages, and the way that people are so **fascinated** with them and **mesmerised** by them, causes people to **lose their grip** on **reality**. He thought that images seemed to refer back to other images, instead of to something **real** and concrete.

Think of virtual reality — computer games, reality TV, theme parks, soap opera — none of it's real life.

It is fake grass! It is a fake shoe! It is a fake ball! Help us, Jean Baudrillard, you're our only hope.

Poststructuralist Michel Foucault analysed Discourse

1) One essential idea of poststructuralism was introduced by **Michel Foucault (1971)**.

2) **Discourses**, for Foucault, are **sets of rules** about how language is used. They say how a topic can be talked about, who can talk about it, and where it can be talked about.

3) Foucault said that **discourse** about a topic **constructs** that topic. That's because it controls the way that you can talk about the topic, and it even controls the way you can **think** about the topic.

4) For example, there are discourses of **medicine** and **law**. These discourses are used to **maintain power**. For example, a patient has to do as the doctor says. The doctor has power.

Discourse	What it refers to	Who can use it	Where it's mainly used	Labels it can give to people
Medical discourse	The human body, biological science	medical professionals	medical institutions	patient
Legal discourse	Laws, crimes, justice, punishment	lawyers	courts	accused, convicted, criminal, prisoner

5) There are discourses in **popular culture**. For example, these may be discourses about celebrity, or about the public. There are discourses about literature. There's a powerful discourse about **sexuality** — Foucault argued that this discourse includes an urge to "confess" sexuality and talk about it all the time.

You can see this in popular culture, where pop performers like Britney, Kylie and Madonna wear sexy clothes and produce sexually loaded videos, where journalists write articles about the sexually suggestive content of pop videos, and where people are interested in rumours of celebrity affairs.

6) In Foucault's view, the audience or consumers of culture are **involved** in these discourses and **shaped** by them.

7) However, **Willis (1990)** and others have pointed out that in postmodern culture, people are now able to **choose their own cultural context**, and don't just accept the ideas they receive. This wouldn't necessarily mean that people are totally immune to all discourses, though.

Practice Questions

Q1 What does modernism mean?
Q2 What is meant by "semiotic analysis"?
Q3 What is meant by "hyperreality"?
Q4 What are discourses?

Exam Question

Q1 Outline and assess the view that there is a greater diversity in the construction of identity in contemporary society. (60 marks)

Ooh dear me, think I need a sit down...

Yes, poststructuralism strikes again. The Modernist viewpoints ought to be familiar — it's only old Functionalism and Marxism all over again. Semiotics is where it gets sticky — make sure you've got denotation and connotation straight. The poststructuralist side of postmodernism can be summed up by saying there are too many images to cope with or to know for sure what's real.

Leisure and Identity

This part is all about who you are, how you know who you are, how others know how you know who you are, and how you know how others who know you (and others who don't know you) know who you are. Oh, and how popular culture and leisure activities fit into it all.

One concept that keeps coming up in relation to *Popular Culture* is *Identity*...

This can be a bit of a slippery concept, so best nail it down right at the start.

1) At a basic level, your identity is the sort of stuff that would appear on an identity card — name, age, physical appearance, distinguishing marks, place of birth. These are **easily checked**, hard to change **facts** about who you are.

2) In **Sociology**, identity has a **deeper** meaning. It refers to the **way we see ourselves**, and the **way others see us**. This sort of identity comes from things that are more **complicated**, and sometimes **less fixed**, than your height and age. Social class, ethnicity, friendships, work, gender and sexuality are all factors that contribute to a person's identity.

Identity is influenced by *Popular Culture*

1) Many theorists and researchers have looked at the ways in which **individual identity** is influenced by popular culture. Mostly, these theorists have taken a **social action** perspective, emphasising the **differences** between individuals and how they **interpret culture**.

2) According to **Blumler and Katz (1974)**, people use the media to meet their needs. They called this the "**uses and gratifications model**". Individuals **decide** which media to experience, based on what they **want** to experience.

3) They classified people's use of the media into categories. "Personal identity" and "social interaction" were two of their categories. For example, they found that some viewers of TV quizzes liked to **compare themselves** with the contestants (personal identity) and would **talk about** the shows **afterwards** (social interaction).

Morley (1980) studied reactions of different social groups to media

Morley showed the same episodes of current affairs programme Nationwide to different social groups. He demonstrated that different social groups created **different semiotic readings** of the same product:

- **black** viewers were likely to see the programmes as **racist**.
- **union** organisers were likely to see them as **anti-union**.
- **management** trainees were likely to see them as **pro-union**.
- **university** students drew attention to the way the programmes were **constructed**.

The uses and gratifications model suggests that popular culture is **involved** in personal identity, but doesn't create it. Blumler and Katz are opposed to the structural control ideas of **modernist** sociology, and emphasise that the **individual** has **agency** — i.e. they can **decide what to watch** on TV, and can decide to **ignore** ideology in the media. Morley's Nationwide study points to the influence of other factors, such as class and ethnicity, on the ways individuals engage with popular culture.

Some argue that *Identity* is increasingly linked to *Leisure*

Traditional patterns of employment helped create a strong sense of identity through **work**, **family** and **location**. When people often expected to stay in the same skilled or semi-skilled job for a lifetime, and when work was closely linked to family and community traditions, it was easier to build your sense of **identity** around your **job**.

People have become more **geographically** and **socially mobile**, jobs are **less secure**, and families (traditional, extended and nuclear) are **less stable**. **Willis (1990)** suggests that work is now **less satisfying** because it often requires little **skill**. All of this leads to people using their **free time** to gain satisfaction and build their identity. Willis argues that in our **leisure time** we do the "symbolic work" that creates our identities.

Postmodern sociology says *Class*, *Gender* and *Ethnicity Don't Mean* so much

1) Traditional sociology has looked at the way patterns of leisure and identity are linked to **social class**, or **gender**, or **ethnic** background.

2) In recent years, sociologists have suggested that people do not feel constrained by these social determinants, and are now much more likely to build their identities through **symbolic consumption**.

3) Some examples of this include "new man" (caring, sensitive, does the housework), "ladettes" (young women who take on some features of traditional masculine identity) and "wiggers" (white people adopting aspects of black identity). In all of these cases, individuals use leisure time and products from the culture industries to build identities for themselves. **Consumption**, some say, has now become **more important** for society than **production**.

4) Some sociologists, such as **Chris Rojek (1995)** have concluded that **culture**, rather than social class, is the best way to understand patterns in leisure.

5) **Ken Roberts (1999)**, however, has pointed out that important patterns in leisure are **still related** to **social class**.

Leisure and Identity

As leisure expands, the Culture Industries also Expand

1) The **classic Marxist explanation** of this is that the culture industries exist just to **make profits**. They **control** and **exploit** consumers in their free time, making them **think** that they need **expensive leisure pursuits and entertainment**. Workers keep working in order to buy cultural commodities and spend money on leisure.

2) The **cultural decline explanation** (see p.96) says that people are encouraged by popular culture to waste their time on **vulgar worthless activities** when they could be improving themselves with **education** and **high culture**. According to this view, greedy companies are making easy money by providing cheap, trashy entertainment.

3) **Willis (1990)** says that these two views are actually quite similar and **equally wrong**.

   Willis suggests that capitalism has acted exactly as you would expect — of course it's tried to **profit** from the increased desire for leisure in modern audiences. However, the audience **wants** all this material because it **needs to be creative**. Now that work is often **less creative** than it used to be, people find ways of being creative and finding identity through leisure. Willis refers to "**symbolic creativity**" — a pick and mix approach to the culture industries that allows people to construct their identity from little bits of high culture and little bits of mass culture.

4) In the **consumer society**, work only exists to give people the **money** they "need" to spend on **building their identities**.

Symbolic Communities are constructed through Culture and Leisure

1) **Cohen (1985)** suggests that communities are now "**symbolic communities**". Instead of the traditional idea of a group of people **living near each other** and providing mutual support, a community can now be any group of people who are **connected** to each other. For example, supporters of a football team, work colleagues, users of a website.

2) **Jenkins (1996)** argues that groups such as **football supporters** use the symbols and rituals of the group to **define themselves** as people. He said that there are **three important elements** to this:
   - Defining yourself and others as belonging to the group.
   - Defining who is not a member of the group (the "other").
   - Being defined by other people in the group as "one of us".

3) The idea of symbolic communities is closely connected to Willis's idea of **symbolic creativity**.

   1) **Lifestyle shopping** makes us feel like **individuals** — because we choose the products that we buy to express our identity. For example, you might feel that your limited edition Hello Kitty bag really says something about **you**.

   2) **Lifestyle shopping** also helps us to belong to **symbolic communities** — because we choose products that have symbolic meanings which other people share. When you see another person in town with a limited edition Hello Kitty bag, you might feel a sense of **kinship** with them.

Rojek says the study of Leisure should be Decentred — All Culture's important

Chris Rojek (1995) says we need to **decentre leisure** — i.e. we should start looking at wider culture.

1) He suggests that **too much sociological thinking** about leisure has centred on leisure itself.

2) In his view, **leisure is important**, but it's not a thing that exists on its own. He claims that leisure can only be understood as **one aspect** of the **whole culture** that surrounds it.

3) So, to understand leisure in a society, Rojek says we need to build up a detailed understanding of that society's culture.

Practice Questions

Q1 How do sociologists define identity?

Q2 What is the uses and gratifications model?

Q3 What is meant by a "symbolic community"?

Exam Question

Q1 Outline and assess the view that individuals now build their identities through symbolic consumption. (60 marks)

It says it's about leisure but it looks like work to me...

For you, I'm afraid this is work. You need to learn the key bits of the sociology of leisure and identity, in case you get a leisure question in the exam. You'd also find it useful for discussing youth culture, fashion, music, masculinity or femininity — you might have to write about symbolic creativity and symbolic communities, or male sports fans and symbolic communities.

Youth Culture

Youth culture is particularly interesting to sociologists, partly because it's often visible and "spectacular", partly because it's often rebellious.

Youth culture can be **Compliant** or **Oppositional**

1) From a **Functionalist** perspective, youth culture is an essential stage in **secondary socialisation**.

2) **Parsons (1951)** saw the media as a way by which social roles were communicated to the young. This is quite apparent in modern day sport, where people like the basketball player **Michael Jordan** and the boxer **Prince Naseem Hamed** are promoted by the media as **good role models** for the young. These are examples of youth culture as obviously **compliant** to the values of society.

This gets tricky if the "role model" does something unacceptable...

3) On the other hand, many media role models, in the music industry for example, seem to be quite hostile to the values of conventional society.

The **CCCS** have taken a **Neo-Marxist Approach** to the study of **Youth Culture**

A lot of sociological work on youth culture has been influenced by Gramsci's ideas about hegemony and counter-culture (see p.97). Theorists like the **Centre for Contemporary Cultural Studies** (**CCCS**), who follow Gramsci, are known as **neo-Marxists**.

1) According to the **CCCS**, youth subcultures are often **counter-cultural**. This means that they **oppose** the values of **hegemony**. Some youth subcultures seem to do this pretty explicitly. For example, 1970s punks seemed to stand against every aspect of capitalism. ⟹

Punk values	Hegemonic values
Music that's **easy** to **learn** and **play**	Music requiring lots of **practice**
Homemade fashions	Fashion as a **commodity**
Aggression	**Non-aggression**
Resistance to authority	**Compliance** with authority
Rudeness	**Politeness**
No future plans — "no future"	**Deferred gratification**
Anti-patriotism	**Patriotism**

2) **Dick Hebdige (1979)** saw punk as an example of the way a subculture could be a **working class movement** against capitalism.

3) Hebdige also points out that over time, these counter-cultures are normally **absorbed** into **mainstream popular culture**. He said they **begin** by **challenging capitalism**, but end up as part of the capitalist media machine. In 1977, spitting, swearing Punk bands such as the Sex Pistols were portrayed in the media as a threat to society's very existence. Nowadays Punk Rock has become much more mainstream and acceptable, e.g. Busted and McFly. These are good-looking, well-behaved boy bands, manufactured by the record industry and promoted strongly in the tabloid press.

Youth Culture may not be as **Rebellious** as it **Seems**

1) A lot of youth subculture is based on **rebellion** — against social norms and against adults.

2) On the other hand members of most subcultures also need to consume products of the culture industries, like clothing and music. In other words, the so-called "rebellious subcultures" are mostly **marketed** by **mainstream adult society**. Even subcultures which start on the street quickly become part of **capitalist society**.

3) This fits in with Gramsci's belief that hegemony needs to include some counter-cultural groups. Mainstream society allows young people to rebel within limits, and the culture industries profit from the "rebellion".

Gangsta Rap is an example of a **Paradoxical** subculture

Black American academic **John H. McWhorter (2003, 2004)** has strongly criticised this music from a cultural decline perspective. He says its values and language discourage aspiration and education, particularly in urban black youth. On the surface, it looks really rebellious:

- The lyrics are often **pro-crime** and **anti-police**.
- **Violence** and the use of **guns** are encouraged.
- **Promiscuous casual sex** is **boasted** about.
- There is a lot of **swearing** and other explicit language.

On the other hand, from a Marxist point of view, you could say that gangsta rap actually **reinforces hegemony**:

- It **encourages consumerism** because the music is sold by **big record companies**.
- It **encourages consumerism** because it is associated with **expensive clothes**, footwear and jewellery.
- It **reinforces stereotypes** about two **oppressed groups** (**black urban youth** and **women**).
- A large proportion of its audience are **privileged** (**white middle class boys**).

Youth Culture

Sociologists have concentrated on Spectacular Subcultures

Hebdige, and sociologists like him, have been drawn to so-called "**spectacular subcultures**", such as Hippy, Mod, Punk and Hip-Hop. These subcultures show a spirit of rebellion by wearing very **distinctive clothes** and focusing on a **specific musical style**. They're interesting to sociologists because they're highly visible and seem to be taking a counter-cultural stance.

Young people construct identity through fashion

Spectacular subcultures use fashion to make themselves look **different** from **mainstream society**, e.g. a goth's black eyeliner and ankh pendant immediately identifies and defines them as a goth.

Joanne Entwistle (2000) argued that young people use clothing to **express themselves**, and also use clothing to **emphasise** the way they use their **bodies**. For example, **baggy trousers** could be used by members of a **hip-hop subculture** to **emphasise** a shuffling way of **walking** which is common to that subculture.

Young people construct identity through music

1) Sociologist of music **Simon Frith (1981)** said "the sociology of rock is inseparable from the sociology of youth".

2) Rock music began in the **1950s**, when young people started to have more freedom and more disposable income.

3) Young people organise themselves into peer groups based on the **music** they listen to, regardless of what **social class** they belong to.

4) **Frith and McRobbie (1978)** said that popular music can be looked at in terms of **gender**. Rock music is more aimed at boys and young men, while pop is aimed at young girls. Most successful rock performers are men.

Willis says Ordinary Youths are Creative Too

Members of spectacular subcultures are a **minority**. This could lead you to think that the **majority** of young people, who **don't belong** to such a **subculture**, are basically **victims of the mass media**. Sociologists like **Willis (1990)** have criticised this idea.

1) Willis believes that "**ordinary youths**", meaning all of those young people who don't belong to any distinct subcultural group, are also very **creative** and **individual**.

2) Willis points to the way young people **choose** from a **wide range** of **cultural products** such as music, fashion, TV and magazines and **mix them up**. Far from being manipulated by mass culture, young people make "selective and active use" of mass culture. Willis calls this "**symbolic creativity**".

3) According to Willis, this is a way for young people to **create their individual identities**. For example, an "ordinary youth" might listen to **speed metal** at home but dance to **garage** when she goes clubbing; she could wear clothes drawn from **skater fashions** some days and **80s glam** on others. She might play **women's football** and support a US **baseball** team. Willis considers this just as **individualistic** and **creative** as someone who takes the **whole package** of a subculture, even if that subculture seems to reject the culture industries.

4) The creative use of music, sport and fashion means that every individual can belong to various **symbolic communities** — usually several at the same time.

Yes, she chose this sweater in a process of symbolic creativity.

Practice Questions

Q1 How does the CCCS view youth subculture?

Q2 How does Dick Hebdige interpret Punk?

Q3 What does Willis mean by "ordinary youth"?

Exam Question

Q1 Outline and assess the view that young people construct their own identities. (60 marks)

OMG teen angst LOL...

Since the 1950s, when people first started to see teenagers as a distinct social group, they've become a major focus for the culture industries. You lot consume huge amounts of music, TV, movies, sport and fashion. You bet this has attracted the interest of the sociologists. Make sure you can contrast the analysis of spectacular subcultures with Willis' symbolic creativity approach.

Femininity and the Culture Industries

There's been a lot of feminist research into the effects of cultural products as an agent of secondary socialisation for girls. The idea is that cultural products create and reinforce expectations of femininity.

Feminists say **Culture Industries** create **Narrow Images** of **Femininity**

According to feminist researchers like **Gaye Tuchman (1978)** and **Marjorie Ferguson (1983)**, women are constructed in cultural products to be:

- **Domestic** rather than career oriented.
- **Subservient to men**.
- **Thin and pretty** — cultural products tend to be based around a narrow and often unachievable image of the ideal female body.

There are **limited roles** in the media for women.

1) **Tuchman (1978)** thought there were only two roles portrayed in the media — **domestic** and **sexual**.
2) **Meehan (1983)** categorised **ten stereotyped roles** for women in **American TV drama** — the Imp, the Good Wife, the Harpy, the Bitch, the Victim, the Decoy, the Siren, the Courtesan, the Witch and the Matriarch.

Barbie is an **Excellent Example** of a **Limited Female Role Model**

Many feminists have made **negative comments** about the way Mattel's very successful doll, Barbie, helps to **socialise pre-teenage girls**. Black American feminist **Ann DuCille (1996)** points out that Barbie is promoted as "a role model for girls". She criticises the marketing of this doll as a **bad influence** on girls in general and especially on black girls.

- Barbie's body and clothing are based around **male sexual fantasy** ideals of femininity.
- Barbie's "lifestyle" teaches girls to want a life based around **clothes, cosmetics and consumption** along with "the **right boyfriend**".
- Barbie has a history of encouraging black girls to see **whiteness** as an ideal. For example, even the black Barbies still have features like **long combable hair** that aren't anything like natural Afro-Caribbean hair. DuCille says this encourages black girls to see their **own hair** as **inadequate**.

If Barbie were scaled up to 5' 9" tall, she'd have a 38 inch bust, 18 inch waist, and 33 inch hips — that's a darn small waist for those bosoms.

Women's Magazines traditionally present **Narrow Images** of **Femininity**

1) **Ferguson (1983)** looked at a wide range of **women's magazines**. She found the magazines gave **advice and training** on **being feminine**. She called this a "**cult of femininity**" which **reinforced stereotypes** of women as **sexual, domestic** and **romantic**.
2) **Angela McRobbie (1978)** analysed the **teenage girls' magazine** Jackie and showed how features about **fashion, makeup** and **dieting** encouraged girls to aspire to a **specific idea of beauty**.
3) **Naomi Wolf (1991)** criticised women's magazines for **fuelling consumption** of **beauty** and **diet products** in the desire to **conform** to a specific beauty ideal.

Feminists say **Romantic Fiction** reinforces **Expectations** about **Femininity**

1) **McRobbie (1978)** argued that **romance** stories in teenage girls' magazine **Jackie** encouraged readers to believe that women's role was to **get a man**, and then **keep him** by submitting to him. She thought they pushed girls away from thinking of themselves as independent.
2) **McRobbie** also claims that romantic fiction is **anti-feminist**. She says the stories break down female solidarity, both by showing women **competing** for men, and by depicting the company of a boyfriend as better than the company of "**bitchy**" girl chums.
3) McRobbie's analysis was criticised as too pessimistic. **Frazer (1987)** found that girls had a **critical reading** of the romantic stories — they **understood** that the stories were **fantasy**, and that the stories represented **stereotypes**.

Romance has always been a very **important** aspect of popular culture for women.

- **Cartoons** aimed at little **girls** (e.g. Aladdin and Pocahontas) have **romantic** plots.
- The lyrics of **pop songs** for **female** audiences are usually based around **romance**.
- "**Chick flicks**" tend to be **romantic comedies** or **straight romances**.
- Magazines aimed at middle-aged and older women often contain **romantic short stories**.
- Romantic novels from publishers like Mills and Boon are very popular with female readers.

Modleski (1982) claimed that on one hand, romance stories presented the heroine as **powerful**, and capable of turning a **rough, tough man** into a **down-on-one-knee romantic hero**, but on the other hand, they presented a **dangerously positive view** of the **domineering male**. Modleski said that **abused women** who read romances believed that their abusive partner would one day become like the **soft-centred heroes** of their favourite romantic novels.

Femininity and the Culture Industries

Many feminists say Cultural Images treat the Female Body as a Commodity

1) **Laura Mulvey (1975)** wrote that in cinema films, the female body was presented to give men erotic pleasure, and a feeling of **control** over women. She called this the camera's **male gaze**.

2) Other feminists have looked at similar ideas. For example, **Joan Smith (1989)** said that popular culture was full of representations of women as **sexually available**.

> Smith describes the way **Page Three** of the **Sun** newspaper presents images of young women. The topless models on Page Three aren't just undressed, they're also posed to **look out at the reader** in a deliberately "**inviting**" and **flirtatious** way. Smith says that the Sun is selling a dangerous **myth** of female sexuality based on **passivity**, lack of **demands** on the male and **perpetual availability**.

Some Sociologists believe all that is Changing

You might have noticed that most of the work on representation was done quite a **while ago**. In recent years, there have been some **important changes**.

1) **David Gauntlett (2002)** points out that culture industries are always **keen** to **respond** to new ideas — like **feminism**.

2) There are also far more females working as **producers**, **writers** and **managers** in the media than there were in the 1980s.

3) **Angela McRobbie (1999)** wrote that "**popular feminism**" had become important. This means some of the **big ideas** of **feminism** are being promoted in **popular culture** products like **pop songs** and women's magazines.

McRobbie is much more positive about today's teenage girl magazines than she was about Jackie back in the 1970s...

4) **Gauntlett** calls popular feminism "a **radio friendly remix**" of the original feminist ideas — he means that it is simplified and leaves out the difficult parts, but may be seen as more exciting and more relevant to young people.

5) **Popular feminism** presents the idea that women should be financially independent, tough, educated, self-confident individuals who **don't need a man**. It also emphasises the importance of **female friendship** and **support**.

6) Popular feminist icons can be criticised for continuing to present **traditional ideas** of **female beauty**. The **exception** to this is the **riot grrl** subculture of the early 1990s, which combined punk with feminist ideas, and deliberately **rejected** and **subverted** traditional ideas of **femininity**.

One very good example of popular feminism is '<u>girl power</u>', as promoted by the <u>Spice Girls</u> in the mid-1990s. This was continued by artists like Destiny's Child, as well as in various magazines aimed at younger women, and in the Buffy the Vampire Slayer TV series.

Some feminists worry that the popularisation of feminist ideas through popular culture has led young women to **believe** that **feminism has "won"**. Feminists argue that **gender inequality** and sexism **still exist**. McRobbie suggests that the conflict between popular feminism and traditional, critical "academic" feminism should be resolved through debate.

Women are Aware of Social Constructs in Culture and the Media

Seiter et al (1989) found that female viewers gained pleasure from interpreting **soap opera** and reading it as a text. They weren't passive viewers, soaking up any **ideology** presented by the soap opera.

Ien Ang (1985) studied viewers of the TV soap Dallas. She found that different people interpreted the programme in different ways. She also found that viewers saw Dallas as obviously **made-up**, but **emotionally realistic**. Several of Ang's respondents were aware of the ideology that Dallas was lowbrow, trashy TV, but still watched it — some agreed with the ideology and watched Dallas to feel **superior**, and others watched Dallas in an "**ironic**" way.

Practice Questions

Q1 How does Anne DuCille interpret Barbie?

Q2 According to Angela McRobbie, what were the main characteristics of Jackie?

Q3 What is meant by "popular feminism"?

Exam Question

Q1 Outline and assess the view that popular culture reinforces traditional ideas about femininity. (60 marks)

Come on Barbie, let's go party...

Popular culture is changing all the time. You'll impress the examiner if you can apply the ideas and theories to some up-to-date examples — e.g. a song that's in the charts at the moment, a recent film or an advert currently on TV. Only do this if you're sure your examples fit with the ideas of the theorists and researchers you're writing about, though.

Masculinity and the Culture Industries

*There's been more work done about femininity and culture than on
masculinity and culture. That's not to say there's nothing to learn, though.*

Sociologists talk about a **Crisis** in **Masculinity**

According to the likes of **Mairtin Mac an Ghaill**, there's a **crisis in masculinity**.
The idea is that **traditional roles for men** are **disappearing** and this has left a lot of blokes with
a major **identity crisis**. Like most important social changes, it involves popular culture.

Sport has been a **Key Element** of popular culture for **Men**

1)   It's pretty obvious how playing and/or watching **sports** fits in with "**traditional masculinity**". Sport is **physical**
        and **competitive**, and it requires **toughness**, **strength** and **skill**. These are all traditionally **masculine traits**.

2)   In Britain, **cricket** and **rugby union** were considered sports for the **upper** and **middle classes**,
        while **football** and **rugby league** were traditionally **working class** sports.

3)   So for many men, sport has been part of their **gender identity** and their **class identity**.

Sports Audiences are **Changing**

These sorts of changes have often made the male sports audience **uncomfortable**.

1)   **Anthony King (1997)** investigated the effects of changes in football on traditional
        male fans, whom he calls "**the lads**". He suggested that in the past, supporting a
        football team had been an important part of **working class masculine identity**:

    - For many men, the **team they supported** was a big part of their sense of **who they were**.
    - Supporting the team was also linked to men's sense of **status**.
    - By visibly supporting the team (going to matches and wearing team colours)
      men could **prove** that they possessed **important male qualities** such as **loyalty**.
    - If necessary, men could show they were tough enough to **fight** for their club when confronted by opposing fans.

2)   **Standing up** to watch the match in an all-male crowd was **important**. King found that the new **all-seater**
        stadiums were **disliked** by "the lads" because they took away the ability to stand and sway together while
        singing and chanting. This was a traditional way of bonding with other "lads".

3)   "Traditional" fans are often also hostile to other new developments, such as **increased**
        female audiences at matches, and **controls on alcohol** in and around the football ground.

4)   Football clubs have tried to **increase middle class audiences** by methods such as creating **family areas**.
        They have also increased ticket prices. This has led to **male working class fans** feeling **excluded**.

Some sports audiences have become feminised. For example, a relatively **high proportion** of the audience for **televised**
snooker is **female**, compared to other sports. **Before** snooker was **televised**, it was a "**man's**" sport. It was played in
snooker halls which had a very masculine **atmosphere** and were not considered appropriate places for women.

Although TV sports audiences are becoming more and more feminised, **adverts** in the ad breaks of sports programmes are
still aimed at men. They advertise traditionally masculine products such as cars and beer, in a way that appeals to
traditional masculinity — a beer ad may picture men enjoying sport, with women in a secondary role (e.g. as a waitress).

Popular Culture provides **Models** of **Masculinity**

Just as **feminists** have looked at the way the media creates **stereotypes of femininity**,
various sociologists have investigated the types of **male role models** it offers.

1)   **Connell (1987)** argues that there is a rank order of "**gender types**" in society.

2)   Taking the idea of **hegemony** from Gramsci (check out p.97 for more about hegemony), he argues
        that the **strongest** male gender type, the one with the **most power**, is "**hegemonic masculinity**".
        Hegemonic man is **heterosexual**, **married**, in **paid work**, **powerful** and **physically tough**.

3)   According to Connell, **gay men** are at the **opposite end** of the power scale and have the **lowest** status of all men.

4)   As Gramsci says, **culture reinforces hegemonic ideas**, so **hegemonic masculinity** is **promoted**
        through popular culture by **role models** like the action film stars Bruce Willis and Vin Diesel.

5)   Connell also recognises that changes in society mean that the **role of men** is **altering**. He sees this as a process of
        undermining gender hegemony. Popular culture has reacted to these changes, for example by using **gay men** like
        Graham Norton as key presenters in **mainstream television**. This may suggest that gender hegemony is changing.

Masculinity and the Culture Industries

According to Rutherford, there are now Two Main Models of Masculinity

Jonathan Rutherford (1988) said that in response to changing male roles, the media now offered two opposite ideals of masculinity:

1) **Retributive man** — he **defends traditional masculinity** by attacking all "traitors to manhood". In films, characters played by Sylvester Stallone and Arnold Schwarzenegger are examples of this type of role model.

2) **New man** — he is **sensitive** to the needs of others and talks about his feelings. He is a gentle, supportive father, willing to change nappies. The footballer David Beckham and the character of Ross in the long running American drama Friends both provide this type of role model.

Rutherford suggests that the **body** of the "new man" is **presented to women** in a style linked to the way **women's bodies** were traditionally presented to the **male gaze** (see p.104-105). Images of men as "sexy and sensitive" are now common in advertising and in culture products associated with popular feminism, such as Cosmopolitan and More magazines.

Lad Mags are a Reaction to the Crisis of Masculinity

In recent years a number of **popular cultural products** have appeared which seem to be reactions to a crisis in masculinity. This means TV series like **Men Behaving Badly** and **Jackass** as well as magazines like **Loaded** and **FHM**. These products seem to offer simple male role models, based on things like **binge drinking**, **sexual promiscuity** and **sick jokes**.

1) According to **Gauntlett (2002)**, Loaded and FHM may **look like** they are trying to create an **old-fashioned** essentialist image of the **hegemonic masculinity**, but they're **really** aimed at helping men to **cope** with constructing a **new masculine identity** much closer to the so-called "**new man**".

2) For example, there are a lot of pictures of semi-naked women, but interviews with these women usually ask what they want from a boyfriend or husband. Where men's magazines before the 1990s would concentrate **solely** on traditional male interests like **cars**, **politics** and **pornography**, the new ones are full of stuff you'd expect from women's magazines — stuff like **relationship**, **lifestyle** and **health advice**.

3) Gauntlett says these magazines **recognise** that **masculinity** is basically a **role**, and offer their readers **advice** on **how to play that role**. He says they have a similar function to **self-help books** such as *Iron John* and *Men are from Mars, Women are from Venus*, which try to teach people how to cope with changing gender roles.

4) Men's magazines have been criticised for treating women as machines, with articles that compare the reproductive organs of the reader's female partner to a car engine, or suggest how to "fix" what's "wrong" with her sexual response. However this can be seen as a **step forward** from **not bothering** about women's sexual pleasure at all. Gauntlett suggests that the idea that women have to be compared to cars can be seen as "a joke at the expense of men".

5) On the other hand, the **latest generation** of lads' magazines (**Nuts** and **Zoo**) have moved away from health and relationship content towards **sports** and **bikini-clad girls**. They can be seen as moving the discourse of masculinity back to traditional, hegemonic masculinity.

Practice Questions

Q1   What is the "crisis in masculinity"?
Q2   According to King, what did traditional male football fans dislike about all-seater football grounds?
Q3   What is meant by "hegemonic masculinity"?
Q4   According to Rutherford, what two opposite ideals of masculinity are offered by the media?
Q5   How does Gauntlett see magazines like Loaded and FHM?

Exam Question

Q1   Outline and assess sociological explanations of the relationship between leisure and the construction of a masculine identity.

(60 marks)

Howay the lads...

There are a lot of images of masculinity in popular culture, and they all carry some sort of meaning — just the same as images of femininity do. They can all be analysed. You may not agree with the idea that there's a crisis in masculinity (not all sociologists do), but some new representations of men have come about in response to the idea that there is a crisis in the land of blokedom.

Key Concepts in Welfare

*This section is for **OCR**. And so's the one after it, so I'll see you AQA folk on p.136. You lucky sons of guns.*

Welfare means looking after Social Needs and sorting out Social Problems

Welfare can be explained as looking after the **personal** and **social needs** of individuals in society. Society needs to find solutions to social problems to protect social order and fulfil responsibility towards the individual. This role and responsibility is shared between individuals, families, communities and the state. How much the state does and how it does it are the big debating points.

1) **Social policy** means **government policy** to deal with **social problems**. It includes the government's plans for things like housing, health, education and employment. Social policy is not created in a vacuum but in a **political context** — e.g. economic policy will influence social policy.

2) The **Welfare State** is the **policies**, **institutions** and **practices** set up and run by the **government** to take responsibility for the welfare of its citizens. It covers housing, education, poverty, health, work and unemployment. Currently in Britain these are provided by various **social institutions** — the **NHS**, **schools** and **colleges**, **job centres** and **benefit agencies**, **social work offices**, etc.

However, it's important to note that the **role of the state** in welfare **varies** over **time** and **place**. **Contemporary Britain** has one of the most **comprehensive** and **expensive** welfare systems. At other times in history there was little state support for individuals and families in need, so **charity** was the main source of help. Similarly in other parts of the world the state provides different levels of support and assistance. A state or government could choose a social policy of **not providing** state welfare.

The detail of the British welfare system and its history is covered on p.112-117.

1) From a **Functionalist** perspective, value consensus means that social problems will be those concerns which are shared by the **majority** of the population.

2) For example, **prostitution** is **widely seen** as **undesirable**, and therefore a social problem.

3) **Merton** argued that social problems occur when a **minor adjustment** to the social system is needed. This argument says that social problems are more frequent in modern society because the pace of change is fast.

1) From a **Marxist** perspective, **social problems** are issues which those in the **ruling class** find **threatening**, or **not in their interest**. Marxists say the ruling class use their **power** to establish these issues as **problems** in society.

2) For example, a **Marxist** view of the different treatment of **marijuana** and **tobacco** by the law would say it reflects the **large profits** made by members of the **ruling class** from **tobacco companies**.

3) Marxism says social problems are the **inevitable consequence** of the exploitative nature of **capitalism**.

The Collectivist model says Society is responsible for the welfare of Individuals

The **collectivist** model says **all citizens** have a **responsibility** for **each other's wellbeing**. Under collectivism, the **government organises** this **welfare** on **our behalf**. We **all pay** (through **taxes**) when we can and we **all benefit** (through **services**) when we need to. This was the thinking behind the setting up of the **Welfare State** in Britain in the 1940s.

These are the principles of the collectivist model of welfare:

1) Services must be available **free to all**, regardless of income. This is called **Universalism**. Universal services and benefits are designed to ensure the welfare of everyone is covered — you may pay some people who don't need the benefit but no-one is missed out. **Child Benefit** is a good example — it's paid to all families, whether they're rich or poor.

2) Services should be **Institutional** — this means they're controlled and monitored by the government. The idea is that the government must ensure fair consideration to all groups in society.

3) Individuals have the **right** to expect **care** and **support** from the government.

4) Individuals have a **duty** to **contribute** towards the care and welfare of others in society. Under the collectivist model, the strong support the weak.

5) Taxes should be **progressive**. This means you **pay more** if you **earn more** or are **wealthier**. Income tax is a **progressive tax** — you pay a different rate depending on how much you earn.

They're called progressive because they move the redistribution of wealth forward — the rich pay proportionally more than the poor.

The collectivist model is designed to provide welfare as a **social right** for every individual on an **equal basis**. This social welfare is intended to enable **social unity** and **cohesion** in society and to ensure a **healthy** and **productive workforce** to keep the whole thing ticking over nicely.

Key Concepts in Welfare

The *Individualist* model says *Each Individual* is responsible for their *Own Welfare*

The **individualist model** says each individual must make sure they **manage their lives** to cover their own welfare needs. It says that the State should be involved as **little as possible** in individual lives. This was the thinking behind the Welfare policies of the British government in the 1980s.

These are the principles of the individualist model of welfare:

1) There should be a **limited range** of welfare services and benefits.

2) Benefits should be given **only** to those in most **desperate need** and on **lowest income**. This is **selective** rather than universal. A **means test** is used to see if an individual or family has a low enough income to qualify for a benefit or free service. **Dentistry** and **eye-care** are good examples of means-tested benefits — they're only paid for by the government if the patient is living on a low income, e.g. state benefits or a pension.

3) Individuals **only** have the **right** to support from the government when in **desperate need** and only for a short period of time.

4) Individuals have a **duty** to **support themselves**.

5) More taxes should be **equal**, where **everyone pays the same** regardless of wealth. For example, Value Added Tax is paid at the same rate by everyone. These taxes have been called **regressive** taxes (the opposite of progressive taxes) because the **poor** pay a **higher percentage** than the rich of their overall wealth and income.

The individualist model is designed to provide welfare **only** to those who **need it most**. By using **means-testing**, benefits and service bills will be **cheaper** and enable resources to go to those who **really need** it. The aim is to get individuals motivated to take **responsibility** for themselves, which promotes **prosperity** in society.

Welfare Policy is about the *Balance* between *Individual* and *State* responsibility

The two models of social welfare policy are **adjusted** and **adapted** to the requirements of different societies and governments. Those decisions are based on **political beliefs** about how much the state should be involved in our lives. The bigger issues of **power**, **control**, **equality** and **justice** are all tied up in these decisions.

Too little state involvement — individuals and families in poverty suffer **without support**. A **severely disadvantaged** sector of society lives in standards below the rest of society.

Too much state involvement — individuals **stop taking responsibility** for themselves and a culture of **dependency** on the state develops. **Choice** is **taken away** from individuals by the **state**, which is characterised as the "**nanny-state**".

The concept of **welfare citizenship** is about the individual's **rights** and **responsibilities.**

Practice Questions

Q1 What is social policy?
Q2 Explain the difference between a universal and a selective model of welfare.
Q3 What is meant by "means-testing"?
Q4 Give an example of a means-tested benefit currently available in Britain.
Q5 Why is VAT called a regressive tax?

Exam Questions

Q1 Outline and assess the role of the state in welfare provision. (60 marks)

Q2 Outline and assess the view that a universal system of welfare benefits both society and the individual. (60 marks)

Q3 Outline and assess the argument that welfare policy can create a "culture of dependency". (60 marks)

Welfare — often well unfair for a lot of people...

Hmm, sociology is okay and everything, but it can be a bit repetitive. Have you noticed this? I mean, here we are on page 109 and look who it is — the same old Marxists and Functionalists. Can't we have some new schools of sociological thought, like the Bingbongists and the Ooglyooglyooglyists? I don't want to complain too much though — at least it's not Maths.

Theories of Welfare

There are three main theories of welfare — the Social Democratic, the New Right and the Third Way. It's worth mentioning the Marxist view of the Welfare State as well, although most thinking about welfare falls into one of the three main theories.

Social Democrats believe the State should Provide Welfare to All

Social Democrats believe **inequality** in **wealth and income** is the root cause of poverty, so they want government policy to **intervene** to make society more **fair**, and establish **equality of opportunity**.

They believe that the state **should** work to stamp out poverty — and that the state **can** work to stamp out poverty.

Social Democrats believe that **all citizens** have the **right** to welfare benefits.

1)   **Mack and Lansley (1985)** suggested a big increase in benefits. They conducted a public opinion poll in which British people said they were **prepared to pay higher taxes** to get rid of poverty.

2)   Social Democrats see part of the solution to poverty in the **labour market**, and say that **social policy** must have the job of **reducing inequalities** in the labour market.

3)   The poor are most often unemployed or low-paid. Social Democrats suggest that **social policy** needs to **improve wages** and **conditions** and to **protect workers' rights**. The **National Minimum Wage** and **Working Families' Tax Credit** brought in under the Labour government of 1997 are examples of this kind of intervention.

4)   British sociologists **Walker and Walker (1994)** argue for an **"active employment strategy"** where the government would actually **create work** for the unemployed.

> Social Democratic theory has been **criticised** by people on the **right wing** and on the **left wing**.
>
> 1)   **New Right** theorists argue that welfare causes dependency (see below). They think the Social Democratic policy of **strengthening the Welfare State** and increasing the power of social policy would make people more dependent, and less able to look after themselves.
>
> 2)   On the left wing, **Marxists** say the **state serves the interests** of those in **power**. They argue that it's in the interests of the ruling class to keep the working class poor. Marxists reckon that the state **couldn't** ever do anything that would **really help** the poor.

The New Right believes in the Reduction of the Welfare State

1)   The **New Right** think that a **generous Welfare State** actually **makes people poorer**.

2)   British New Right thinker **Marsland (1989)** thinks all **universal benefits** (paid to everyone regardless of wealth) should be abolished because they **encourage dependency**. He says that benefits should only exist to support those in the **most desperate need** for the **shortest possible time**, and argues that this will encourage people to be self-reliant.

Marsland thinks that this dependency hurts poor people the most, and claims it takes away their <u>self-reliance</u> and their <u>freedom</u> to do things for themselves.

3)   Right wing sociologists like Marsland would prefer everyone to **make their own money** and **decide how to spend it**, instead of paying lots of **tax** or getting **benefits** from the state.

4)   **Marsland (1989)** said society would gain twice over from welfare cuts — individuals would have **less tax** taken off them by the **state** because the welfare system wouldn't cost so much any more, and the state would be able to **invest in industry** instead of spending money on welfare, which would make the whole country more wealthy.

5)   The New Right say that in a strong economy, **private welfare providers** can compete for business, giving individuals **choice** and **value**. They reckon the **free market economy** is the **best way** to ensure services are provided at the **lowest prices** and the **best quality**.

6)   American sociologist **Murray (1993)** recommended a **"moral"** benefits system to discourage people from forming **single parent families**. He thought that unmarried mums should get no benefit at all.

The New Right view has been criticised by many sociologists, especially left wing sociologists.

1)   **Bill Jordan (1989)** and **Frank Field (1989)** claim that **means-tested benefits** create **more** of a culture of **dependency** than universal benefits. He says that restricting welfare to the unemployed means that some people are **worse off in a job** than on benefits. **Dean and Taylor-Gooby** did research which supports this idea. Respondents to their survey said that losing means-tested benefits was a problem when starting work.

See p.118 for more on <u>Field's argument</u> about <u>social control</u> of the <u>underclass</u>.

2)   **Dean and Taylor-Gooby (1992)**, and also **Walker (1990)** found that people didn't tend to stay on benefits for long, and they believe that Murray and Marsland were wrong to claim that there was a **culture of dependency**.

Theories of Welfare

Since 1997, the New Labour Government has had a "Third Way" Approach

When New Labour took power in Britain in 1997, it claimed its social policies would reduce poverty significantly. Their philosophy **combines** both the **New Right** and the **Social Democratic** theories — so it was called "**the Third Way**".

The theme was that the poor need "**a hand up not a handout**". The "hand up" part means the state should have **social policies** which **help the poor** — rather like the Social Democratic theory. The "not a handout" part means people **shouldn't depend** on benefits — rather like **New Right theory**.

The Third Way is based on a concept of **citizenship**, rights and responsibilities.
1) The Third Way says the **state** has a responsibility to **help people in real need**, and **individuals** have a **responsibility to help themselves**.
2) The "**New Welfare Contract**" of 1998 states that the **government** has to **help people find work**, make it **worth getting a job**, help with **childcare**, help the **poorest** old people and help those who really **can't work**.
3) It says that **individuals** have to look for work, be as **independent as possible**, support their own family, save for retirement and not defraud the taxpayer by claiming benefit when they shouldn't.

The Third Way included policies to get people from **welfare** into **work**.
1) **Social security policy** was changed so that people were **better off** having a **job** than being on the dole. Welfare benefits that had been **restricted** to the **unemployed** were opened up to people on **low incomes** as well.
2) The **New Deal** is a scheme to give the long term unemployed help in looking for work. It requires them to either:
   - accept a **subsidised job**,
   - do **voluntary work**,
   - take up **full time training** or **education**.

   Those who refuse all of those options are no longer entitled to benefits.
3) **Will Hutton (1997)** argued that the New Deal would not be **sustainable** if the economy **couldn't provide enough jobs**. He pointed to places where there were very **few jobs** available, and argued that **this** was what was keeping people out of work, not **dependence on welfare** or fear of being **worse off in work**.

Marxists argue that Welfare Benefits Don't Do Much to reduce Poverty

1) Marxist sociologists **Westergaard and Resler (1976)** argue that **welfare benefits remain low** to **make sure** that people **still need to get a job** even if they don't get paid much. If benefit levels were higher, wages would have to be higher to make it worthwhile to get a job. Westergaard and Resler say this is in the interests of the capitalist class — it keeps up the supply of cheap labour.
2) They also point out that most of the **money paid out in welfare benefits** has been **paid in by the working class in tax** or **subsidised by their low wages**. That means the working class are getting their own money back, not money from the rich. Westergaard and Resler say that the Welfare State "**redistributes within classes** rather than **between them**".

Practice Questions

Q1 Which theory sees welfare benefits as a universal right?
Q2 Why do the New Right think that the Welfare State can be too generous?
Q3 What does the Third Way have in common with Social Democracy, and what does it have in common with the New Right?
Q4 Why did Will Hutton say that the New Deal policy might fail?
Q5 What do Marxists believe about the Welfare State?

Exam Questions

Q1 Outline and assess the view that the role of the Welfare State is to redistribute wealth and resources. (60 marks)

Q2 Outline and assess the view that the Welfare State creates a culture of dependency. (60 marks)

Welfare good, welfare bad, welfare good, welfare bad...

I wish they'd make their flipping minds up. Some sociologists criticise the Welfare State because they think it encourages people to be lazy. Other sociologists support the Welfare State because they think it makes society more equal. New Labour's Third Way approach tries to combine all the good bits from the other theories... that's cheating a bit I reckon.

State Welfare Provision

It helps if you know the history of welfare in Britain. If you're taking Sociology, that is. Not if you're a mouse or a raisin.

In **Victorian Times** the poor were made to **Work** for their **Welfare**

1) Way back in the 17th century, the **Poor Law (1601)** set out to provide relief to the very poorest. It made provision to set the poor to work, and to offer relief to those who were unable to work — the very old and the disabled. The first **workhouse** was set up in **1697** and combined housing, provision of food and provision of work. Through the 18th century, more parish workhouses were established.

2) The **Poor Law Amendment Act (1834)** set out to deter people from becoming poor — it was based on the idea that poverty was a choice. The 1834 Act had two principles — making the position of being poor **less desirable** than the position of working, and making welfare relief **only available** in the **workhouse**.

3) 1840s reports into water borne disease led to provision of **sewers** and **clean water** through the Public Health Acts.

4) In **1870**, the **Education Act** provided for **primary school** education. Local school boards could use local taxpayers' money to build schools. In 1880, school became **compulsory** for all children under 10. It was only in 1891 that primary education became **free**, though.

During the **Early 20th Century**, some **Welfare Benefits** were introduced

1) In **1902**, **secondary schools** started to be **partly funded** by the state. Secondary schools still charged pupils school fees, and in **1907**, a **scholarship** scheme made it possible for poor children to go to secondary school.

2) In **1906**, the **school meals service** started, although it wasn't fully established until the Second World War. The school medical services started in 1907.

3) **Old age pensions** began in **1909**. The state paid a pension to people over 70, on a means-tested basis. This was replaced by a contributory state pension scheme in 1925. ← *These schemes favoured those who had been in regular employment.*

4) The **1911 National Insurance Act** provided compulsory **health insurance** and **unemployment insurance** for workers in some industries. However, the worker's family weren't covered.

5) The **1930 Poor Law Act** reversed the 1834 decision to **restrict welfare** to the **workhouse**. The workhouses were turned into **hospitals**, **old people's homes** and **children's homes**, to look after people who couldn't be looked after at home.

The **Beveridge Report (1942)** set out the modern **Welfare State**

1) During the 1939-1945 war, a series of reports revealed **poor conditions** and high levels of **sickness** in parts of the UK. A survey by **Rowntree** in 1941 found that 18% were still in relative poverty (see p.126).

2) The **Beveridge Report** of 1942 set out how social problems could be eradicated. Beveridge defined "**five evils**" — Want, Ignorance, Disease, Idleness and Squalor. The table below shows how the Welfare State proposed to fight them. Beveridge's idea was for the **state** to provide **social services** just like the state provides **public services** like roads. He wanted welfare to be for everyone, not just the poorest — from cradle to grave.

Want (poverty)	**Universal welfare benefits** for the unemployed, the old, the sick, the disabled and children.
Ignorance	**Free education for all**.
Disease	The **NHS** — universal right to see a doctor, free prescriptions, dental treatment and eye tests.
Idleness (unemployment)	Economic policies to promote **full** employment.
Squalor (poor housing)	A programme of **council house** building.

3) The British **Welfare State** was set up in the late **1940s** after the **Beveridge Report** was published. After the second world war, there was a mood of **mutual support** across classes because everyone had worked together in the war effort. There was hope for a better life after the war. This produced a climate for **reform**.

4) The Welfare State was designed to be free at the point where you actually needed it. For example, going to the doctor is free. People in work would pay into a **national insurance scheme** which would **pay for the Welfare State**.

> **Key Acts of Parliament**
> - **Education Act 1944** — Free compulsory secondary schooling up to the age of 15.
> - **Family Allowance Acts 1945** — This Act paid a regular sum of money to mothers of two or more children.
> - **National Health Service Act 1946** — Established free health care for all (the NHS actually started up in 1948).
> - **New Towns Act 1946** and **Town and Country Planning Act 1947** — Large numbers of council houses were built.
> - **National Insurance Act 1948** — Employees pay into a national insurance scheme to pay for the Welfare State.
> - **National Assistance Act 1948** — Abolished the Poor Law, and provided for the elderly, sick and disabled.

State Welfare Provision

The NHS became Less Universal because it was Expensive

By 1950, the NHS was costing the state over £350 million a year — this was much more than the government had expected. The NHS had to be made a little cheaper.

In **1949**, a small **charge** for **prescriptions** was introduced. In **1951**, **charges** were introduced for **glasses** and **false teeth**, and **prescription charges** were **raised**. In **1956**, the NHS started charging for prescriptions **per item**, instead of charging a flat rate no matter how many medicines you received.

Conservative Reforms aimed to Save Money and Reduce Unemployment

1) The Conservative government of 1979 believed that the Welfare State was wasting money. They agreed with the **New Right** point of view that the Welfare State was **too generous**, and encouraged people not to work. They made it very clear that they wanted to **get rid of the dependency culture** by **reducing benefits** and **allowances**.

2) They wanted to allow the **free market** (see glossary) a much greater influence in welfare provision, and believed that **privatisation** would make welfare provision much more **efficient**.

3) The government was also concerned that the Welfare State would become **too expensive** for the country to afford — especially as the **birth rate** was **declining**. A declining birth rate meant **fewer workers** paying tax and funding the system. An **ageing population** meant that the **demand** on the system to pay **pensions** was increasing.

4) To cut costs, they **removed** some **universal benefits**, and increased the number of benefits that were **selective** and **means-tested**.

5) The idea was that resources freed up by these welfare cuts would **boost the economy**, which would benefit society as a whole. Conservatives said the money at the top would "**trickle down**" to make **everyone** in society wealthier.

There have been a lot of Conservative reforms to reduce the size of the Welfare State and cut costs.

1) **Increase** in **selective benefits** — e.g. 1980 Housing Act, 1988 Social Security Act.
2) **Reduction** in **universal benefits** — e.g. general entitlement to free eye tests abolished.
3) **Privatisation** of welfare provision — e.g. local authority care homes closed, replaced by private care homes.
4) **Increase** in **voluntary** and **charitable** welfare provision — e.g. housing associations taking over council houses.

New Labour tried to Solve Problems and Save Money at the same time

Under **New Labour** governments of 1997 onwards, there's been an emphasis on trying to make the NHS and social security more **efficient** to **save money**, while **tackling social problems** at the same time.

After coming to power, the Labour government set up the **Social Exclusion Unit** to help deprived groups such as poorer single mothers, the unemployed, the homeless, and people living on the worst housing estates.

Most benefits and services cut by the Conservative governments **haven't been re-introduced**.

Labour governments of 1997 onwards have continued the move towards **welfare pluralism** — i.e. welfare provision from private, voluntary and informal sectors as well as from the Welfare State (see p.114).

Practice Questions

Q1 Where did the 1834 Poor Law Act say was the only place the poor could receive welfare?
Q2 Give three examples of welfare benefits introduced between 1900 and 1940.
Q3 Name four key Acts of Parliament that set up the Welfare State, and give their dates.
Q4 Give three examples of 1980s reforms to the Welfare State.

Exam Question

Q1 Outline and assess the view that the Welfare State has remained essentially unchanged since the 1940s. (60 marks)

Beveridge Report — nothing to do with tea, coffee or other drinks...

In your exam, you might be asked a straight question about the development of the Welfare State in Britain. You might get asked a question about the effect of post 1979 reforms — in which case you'll need to refer to the history to say what the Welfare State was like before 1979. If you're a mouse or a raisin you probably won't get asked anything at all, so count yourselves lucky.

Patterns of Welfare Provision

In the late 20th century, there were changes in who provides basic welfare for the needy.

There's a *Trend* towards *Welfare Pluralism*

1) The Welfare State was firmly established in the UK by the 1960s.

2) Since then there have been **extra** and **alternative** welfare schemes and providers. There has been a trend to move away from **total state provision** — this is partly forced by **lack of funding**, but it's also developed out of **individual choice**.

3) The modern Welfare State in the UK is a mixture of **state**, **voluntary**, **informal** and **private** care providers. This is called **Welfare Pluralism**.

4) There's been some welfare pluralism in the UK ever since the Welfare State began. In the later 20th century and into the 21st the number of non-state providers has really increased — and their roles have increased too.

Welfare pluralism	=	State provision	+	Private provision	+	Voluntary provision	+	Informal provision

Policies in the *1980s* and *1990s* moved *Care* from *Institutions* to the *Community*

1) The **Community Care** programme was a scheme to take patients out of institutional care and back into the community. This started with the **mentally ill**, with the Mental Health Act of 1983 which allowed psychiatric patients to appeal against being committed to psychiatric institutions. The **Community Care Act of 1990** included the physically disabled, the mentally disabled, mentally ill people and people with physical impairments (including the elderly).

2) One reason for this policy was that institutional care was very **expensive**. It was going to get more expensive for the taxpayer because the population was getting older — i.e. there'd be fewer people paying tax, and more elderly people requiring care.

3) Also, the Conservative government favoured the idea of **individual responsibility** and **choice**. Care in the community removed patients from the control of institutions, and allowed them the **freedom** to live independently instead of tying them into **strict routines**. Patients were no longer **institutionalised** (see p.119). Care in the community was welcomed by many patients' groups.

4) However, the scheme was **criticised** for not providing the necessary **resources** to care for some vulnerable adults. Some patients weren't given any **structured care** once they had been rehoused in the community. Patient groups pointed out that **good quality** care in the community could work out as **more expensive** than institutional care, and criticised the government for trying to use care in the community to **cut costs**.

5) Much of the care in the community was taken on by **family members** for **no pay**. **Gillian Parker (1985)** argues that community care meant care for free, usually by women. An Equal Opportunities Commission report (1982) concluded that community care was "**care on the cheap**".

There's been *Huge Growth* in *Volunteer Welfare Services* and *Provision*

Volunteer services are sometimes set up by individuals who think there's not enough state provision. Volunteer services sometimes provide extras that the state doesn't provide at all, and sometimes they compete with state services.

Housing, health, education and other welfare areas have seen an increase in the numbers of voluntary organisations — e.g. the **hospice** movement, **Housing Associations** and **refuge centres**. Don't forget **national charities** like the **NSPCC**, **NCH** and **Alcoholics Anonymous**.

It's good if you can use your own examples here — there are plenty to choose from...

> **Robert Page (1993)** argues that voluntary services now play a **significant** role in the modern welfare system in **four ways**:
>
> 1) They provide **back-up** if state services are overloaded.
>
> 2) They provide **cheap care** because carers work for no pay.
>
> 3) They provide **extra care** in communities where state-funded care isn't adequate.
>
> 4) They provide opportunities to use **new ideas** and practices because they're not restricted by **regulations** as much as state providers.

Patterns of Welfare Provision

More people are Paying for welfare Privately

1) This is welfare provision that individuals **pay for themselves**.

2) Many individuals opt for **private** provision **instead** of state provision if they can **afford** it, especially if **waiting times** for state services are seen as too long.

3) **Private health care** is no longer seen as exclusively for the very rich. Many people now have private health care as part of their salary package and providers such as BUPA advertise on TV.

4) Many working parents pay for childcare from **childminders** or **private nurseries**.

---

1) There's also been a shift towards **private welfare** within the **public sector**.

2) Large state agencies are using **private services** as part of **health**, **education** and **welfare** provision. Many state nursing homes have closed and the NHS and Social Services now **pay private homes** to provide care for the elderly.

3) Conservative reforms introduced an **internal market** to the public sector, to cut costs and make services more efficient. From **1988** onwards **hospitals** were required to offer all support services to external private contractors, and to employ the **cheapest contractor**, state or private. The same applied to some **school** services such as provision of **food** and **music tuition**. This was called **compulsory competitive tendering**.

4) In 2000 **compulsory competitive tendering** was **replaced** by the concept of **"best value"** — state agencies are now allowed to take into account factors **other** than the cost, but the decision is still **largely based on cost**.

Much Welfare Provision is still provided Informally by Family and Friends

1) **Before** the Welfare State, **family members** were the main providers of welfare in Britain. Family and friends **still** provide a lot of **free** care and welfare with little help from the state — this is called **informal care**. Informal care is usually **free** to the **recipient**, but **costs** the **provider** money.

2) One of the most common examples of informal welfare is **childcare**. **State** childcare provision often isn't **enough** for families where both parents work. **Private** childcare provision is very **expensive**. So **relatives** often help look after the children. The majority of this **informal childcare** is done by older women — **grandmas**, in other words. In fact, some families **move closer** to the **grandparents** just so the grandparents can help with the kids.

There's a Debate about the shift to Welfare Pluralism

Obviously, there is much **sociological** and **public debate** about whether the shift to greater welfare pluralism is a good thing.

1) Those on the **right** argue the Welfare State couldn't continue to provide for everyone, because the **costs** would be too high. They say the private and voluntary sectors are **preventing**, or responding to, a **crisis** in the Welfare State.

2) Critics (on the **left**) claim that the "crisis" in the Welfare Sate is a **myth** created to cut spending, and suggest that the UK government could afford to carry on providing welfare, especially if the **tax system** were more **progressive**.

Remember — <u>Progressive tax</u> = those who earn more or have more pay progressively more.
<u>Regressive tax</u> = tax where the poor pay a higher percentage of income than the rich.

Practice Questions

Q1 Explain the term "welfare pluralism".
Q2 What is meant by "care in the community"? Who provides most care in the community?
Q3 Give an example of private welfare provision.
Q4 Give an example of informal welfare provision.

Exam Question

Q1 Outline and assess the view that the Welfare State in Britain would be in crisis without welfare pluralism. (60 marks)

The bare necessities of life will come to you (with a price tag)...

This topic can come up in the exam as a direct question about welfare pluralism, or "hidden" in a question that doesn't specifically mention welfare pluralism. For example, a question about welfare provision post 1979 would need you to discuss welfare pluralism as part of your answer, alongside New Right influenced Conservative social policy, individualism and dependency. Blah blah blah.

Patterns of Welfare Provision

Changes in housing policy, social security policy and social work policy have had effects on social stratification.

Housing Policy has Changed since the 1940s

1) Between the 1930s and late 1960s there was a **consensus** on housing policy — both Labour and Conservative governments **built council houses**, first for the poor, then to **replace** the **housing stock**.

2) By the **1970s**, the Labour and Conservative views diverged. The Conservatives favoured a **free market policy** of encouraging **private home ownership**. The Conservative goverment of 1979 began allowing council tenants to **buy their council houses** at a **reduced price**. This was called the **right-to-buy** policy.

3) Social housing policy became more **targeted**. Eligibility for council housing was restricted to the most **needy**.

4) The policy of council tenants **buying their houses** massively increased the number of **home owners** in the UK. It also, obviously, **reduced** the number of **council houses** available for rent. The Conservative government weren't building as many new council houses either, so there was a **shortage** of council houses.

5) Also, the homes still in council ownership weren't of great quality — the **nicest council houses** sold off **first**. Central government reduced the budget it gave to local councils, so councils had **less money** to spend on **repairs**.

6) **Housing associations** are voluntary sector organisations who provide and manage social housing. From the 1980s to the present day, a lot of council owned homes have been sold to housing associations, who now have responsibility for managing social housing either on behalf of the council or privately.

> **Council housing** is also known as **municipal housing**. The policy of renting council houses and flats directly to tenants from all social sectors is part of an idea called **municipal socialism**.

Effects of the right-to-buy policy

1) **Poorer** people have **less choice** in housing and lower quality housing because there's **less good quality council housing** available. People who **own property** have seen the value of it **rise**. This has deepened some social divisions, but on the other hand the selling off of council houses allowed many council tenants to **invest** in their **own house** for the first time — making them **wealthier**.

2) Conservative social security reforms had an effect on access to housing for **younger people**, who were expected to live with their parents. Entitlement to housing benefit was **abolished** for **under 18s**.

3) **Le Grand (1982, 1987)** claimed that housing policy **didn't solve** inequalities. **Le Grand (1982)** claimed that although **poorer** households **benefited** from **rent rebates**, **homeowners** benefited **more** from **tax relief** on **mortgage interest payments**. In 1987, he argued that the change from rent rebates to housing benefit had helped the poor, while an increase in tax relief on mortgage payments helped the rich.

New mortgages stopped qualifying for tax relief in 2000.

Social Gatekeepers affect Access to Housing

"**Social gatekeepers**" such as local authority housing officers, private letting agents, estate agents and landlords can all affect an individual's access to housing. **Letting agents** and **landlords** can choose not to show a prospective tenant around a house or flat. Landlords can refuse to let, or claim that the property is already let. Housing officers can say whether or not an individual is eligible for social housing, and they have a certain amount of leeway in interpreting the eligibility rules.

The idea that managers act as **gatekeepers**, restricting access to choice, is called **urban managerialism**.

1) Nearly half of **single mothers** live in social rented housing. Eligibility rules prefer single parents to single non-parents.

2) People of **Bangladeshi**, **Black African** and **Other Black** origin are **most likely** to live in housing in the **social rented sector** (rented from the council and housing associations). Whites and Indians are most likely to own their home.

3) Some people believe that **perceived prejudice** on the part of **social gatekeepers** such as estate agents and landlords may limit the number of black citizens who own their own home or rent their home privately.

Rex and Moore (1967) studied access to housing in Sparkbrook

Approach:	Rex and Moore were Weberians, and looked at housing from a **market relation** point of view.
Findings:	They found that access to housing was **stratified**, from outright owner-occupiers at the top, through mortgage payers and rental tenants to lodgers at the bottom.
Conclusion:	They thought there was a group of people whose needs weren't met either by the housing market or by the Welfare State. These people had to find their housing through **informal** means, e.g. by renting from a friend or a family member.

Sparkbrook is an area of Birmingham.

1) Some Marxists believe that the desire to be a home owner is a **false need** — i.e. you don't really need to own your home, you just need a roof over your head. Marxists believe false needs are created to serve capitalism.

2) **Saunders (1990)** disagrees, and says that the desire to own one's own house is **so widespread** that it can't possibly be a delusion. Saunders also says that there's a link between housing tenure and **politics** — **homeowners** tend to be a little bit more **conservative** than tenants.

Patterns of Welfare Provision

Social Security has become More Targeted since the 1940s

The Conservative policies of 1979-1997 were designed to **reduce the size of the Welfare State** from a **universal** to a **targeted** system, influenced by New Right philosophy.

1) The **Social Security Acts** (1986 and 1988) contained the majority of the changes and represented the biggest shake-up of the Welfare State since Beveridge in 1942 (see p.112). After the new policies were implemented in April 1988, **80% of claimants** received **less** in welfare benefits.

- The **Social Fund** was introduced — grants for the poorest families to buy household essentials were replaced by **loans**.
- **Supplementary benefit** (for unemployment) was replaced with **Income Support**. A **higher rate** of income support was paid to the **disabled** and **parents**, and even more to **lone parents**. However, Income Support **wasn't paid** to **under 18s**, or to anyone who was considered to have made themselves **intentionally unemployed**.
- **Family Credit** was paid to families where the main breadwinner had a very **low income**.

2) In 1996, Income Support was replaced with **Jobseeker's Allowance**. In order to claim Jobseeker's Allowance, the unemployed individual had to **prove** that they were **actively looking for work**.

As with housing, **social gatekeepers** have a role in restricting access to social security benefits. For example, in order to claim incapacity benefit, the claimant must **convince** the state that they can't work. They have to complete a **long questionnaire** and have a **medical examination**.

Means-tested benefits require the claimant to **prove** they are **poor enough**. Potential claimants may see the process of claiming means-tested benefits as too complicated, and may not bother to claim. Stigma and embarrassment are also factors.

Personal Social Services have an impact on individuals

Personal social services aim to provide for the needs of **vulnerable** groups in society — e.g. children, the old, the physically disabled, the mentally disabled and people with mental health problems. Personal social services are also linked to the criminal justice system, and work with both offenders and victims of crime. Personal social services are provided by the **state** (through local authorities), **voluntary groups** and **informal providers**.

Social gatekeepers can affect access to personal social services. Individuals may have to go through an **interview process** to assess their eligibility. This is sometimes seen as **demeaning**, and can put people off asking for help from social services.

1) With an ageing population, the **elderly** are a key group in need of personal social services. However, many of these services have been **reduced** since the 1980s. For example, many **council residential homes** have been closed down, and entitlement to **home help** has been **reduced**.

2) One of the most contentious issues in welfare policy has been the introduction of means-testing for **personal care services** in England in the 1980s. The elderly are no longer entitled to free personal care if they have savings above a certain threshold.

3) Devolved governments in **Scotland** and **Wales** have reintroduced free personal care for the elderly. In England, it's a **political issue** — the elderly form a significant part of the electorate and so they're in a strong position to keep welfare on the political agenda.

Personal care means help with washing, getting dressed, feeding, etc. Nursing care is paid for by the state.

Practice Questions

Q1 What effect did the right-to-buy policy have on:
a) council house tenants who bought their homes and b) the council housing stock?

Q2 What is meant by "urban managerialism"?

Q3 Why are some people put off applying for means-tested benefits?

Exam Question

Q1 Outline and assess the evidence that the Welfare State has not removed social inequality in Britain. (60 marks)

I can't wait to tell my landlady she's a social gatekeeper...

It'll make her feel dead important, bless her. Well, the Conservative government has been pretty busy over the last couple of pages, and now you need to make sure you can remember all the changes they made to welfare provision. It doesn't matter if you agree with them or not — you just need to remember them, and what sociologists like Le Grand and Saunders thought about their effects.

Welfare as Social Control

Social control is a kind of hypnosis that some aliens can do using gamma rays. Well, okay, it's not. But it should be.

Social Policy *is the* State's *response to* Social Problems

1) The state can use **social** and **welfare legislation** to control groups or problems in society. For example, the **Child Support Agency** (CSA) was introduced in the 1990s to **control absent parents** who don't support their child financially. The CSA can **automatically remove child support** payments from the absent parent's **pay packet**. This is the welfare state **controlling** how an individual **spends their money**.

2) Some see this as **positive control** to ensure the care and wellbeing of the child. Others see it as the "nanny state" infringing civil liberties. Either way, it is **social control** — and pretty direct social control at that...

Marxists *say the* Welfare State *maintains* Social Control *of the* Disadvantaged

Marxist analysis of welfare argues state services and benefits are **useful** to the **ruling class** in two ways:

- Benefits only deal with the **extremes** of poverty, so Marxists argue they leave the **core inequality** unchallenged.

- Minimum care and benefits ensure a **healthy working population**, which Marxists say is essential to maintain profits for the ruling class.

In short, Marxists say that **social control** is an **aim** of welfare in capitalist societies.

Peter Taylor-Gooby (1985) argues that the British Welfare State has never **genuinely** attempted to **redistribute wealth** or eradicate inequality. He says it has kept the poor and unemployed just where capitalism needs them — ready to work and dependent on the state for a minimal income.

Marxist feminists argue that women are used as part of the welfare system to serve the needs of capitalism — women provide free care and labour in the role of **housewife** and **mother**. Marx said that women are part of the "reserve army of labour". This means they aren't part of the main labour force, but can be called on to do low-paid jobs when necessary.

The *Underclass is a* Socially Controlled *group*

The concept of an underclass has been used to describe groups at the **very bottom** of the social hierarchy, e.g. the very **long-term unemployed** and the **homeless**. The underclass is distinct from the working class in general.

1) **Frank Field (1989)** identifies three main groups who are reliant on **benefits** for a minimum income — the unemployed, the elderly and non-working single-parents. He says these groups have **limited opportunities** to **escape** their **dependence** on the state.

2) He argues that the welfare policy of the 1980s of **reducing** and **means-testing** benefits **kept families poor**. The policy of **removing all state benefits** from **working individuals** kept low paid families in poverty, and made it so that some **low paid jobs** actually **paid less** than **staying on the dole**.

3) Field says that the **media** then perpetuate ideas about the poor being **lazy** or **inferior** because they can't drag themselves up out of poverty. This **reinforces** the social position of these groups as a **separate underclass**.

4) Field clearly sees the underclass as **victims** of an **unequal system** which is controlling their destiny. He was part of the Labour government in 1997 which implemented **social policy** aimed at making sure **work always pays more than benefits** alone — e.g. **continuing benefits** for individuals who find **work**, and the **National Minimum Wage**.

Welfare socially controls *Women — although it has* Benefited Women

1) The introduction of **family benefits** in the Beveridge reforms had been campaigned for by **women** for many years.

2) In the **1950s**, benefits such as Family Allowance were generally seen as **helping women**, because childcare and welfare was viewed as a **woman's role** and responsibility. State provision **reduced the burden** on women.

3) The 1960s and 1970s saw women wanting **equality** and a role in society other than the housewife/mother role.

4) Welfare policies had a **positive** impact on women's equality — e.g. the Equal Pay Act and Sex Discrimination Act (1976, 1979) gave women the right to be paid the same as a man for the same job.

5) However, feminists argue the persistence of the stereotyped role of women as **carers** has **disadvantaged** women in the workplace.

6) Women still provide the majority of **informal care** for children, the elderly, the sick and the disabled. Community Care policies of the 1980s resulted in a huge increase in the number of **unpaid carers**, most of whom were **women**.

7) Women now make up half of the UK workforce but still do the majority of household tasks and take most of the responsibility for childcare. **Ferri and Smith (1996)** found two thirds of full-time working mums said they were responsible for cooking and cleaning.

Welfare as Social Control

Welfare socially controls the **Disabled**

The rules for claiming **incapacity benefit** require claimants to accumulate a certain number of points on a test — the less the claimant can do unassisted, the more points they get. The process of claiming **disability living allowance** is **long** and **complicated**, and some disabled rights groups see it as unfair. Some see the process of claiming as a form of social control.

Disabled rights groups campaign for **fairer** and **easier** benefit calculations.

However, the last ten years have seen a change from **assuming** disabled people can't work to **enforcing legislation** to make all **workplaces accessible**. All public buildings now have to provide disabled access whether for work or leisure.

Welfare Institutions socially control their **Patients**

1) Some welfare is provided in **institutions** where individuals live for short or long periods of time, including **hospitals, residential old people's homes** and **care homes**.

2) Sociologists have studied these institutions and observed a process of **control** over the individual, which leads to the individual losing the identity they had in the outside world.

3) **Goffman (1968)** is the main man for this theory. From his very famous study *Asylums*, he developed the theory of **total institutions**.

> Goffman studied a psychiatric institution, but his findings have been applied to boarding schools, old people's homes and hospitals. Life is strictly regulated in these institutions as well.

> Goffman argued that the **routine**, **order** and clear **hierarchy** of institutions make them a **society within themselves**. The new patient has to **adapt** to the social order and is given a **rigid** and **limited role** within it. Patients **lose control** over their everyday lives, because meals, bedtime and activities are all **strictly regimented**. This results in the institution having **total control** of the individual. The individual **loses** their **self identity**.

4) Remember, Goffman was observing institutions in the **past** and in the decades since he did his study, there's been a move towards more flexible approaches to care. However, many of the systems and **routine practices** haven't changed — it can be argued that they're **necessary** for a prison, hospital, or residential home to **function effectively**.

5) This social control of patients usually ends when leaving the institution, although some individuals become so "**institutionalised**" that they feel unable to operate confidently outside of the institution. A person leaving a psychiatric institution or a prison may find it tough to **cope** with the **huge amount of choice** in the outside world after living with very **limited choices**.

Welfare Bureaucracy can control social groups

Bureaucracy can have effects on individuals in **less extreme** circumstances.
Things you've learned in other parts of the course about interactionists and **labelling theory** are relevant here.

- In schools, pupils become what their teachers expect them to become. Hargreaves said that teachers' expectations can lead to self-fulfilling prophecies.

- Elderly people are restricted when stereotypical labels are used by institutions to select services and activities for them.

- The bureaucracy of claiming benefits and the label of being unemployed can control the behaviour and attitudes of people who are out of work.

Practice Questions

Q1 Give three examples of how welfare can act as a form of social control.

Q2 What is the underclass?

Q3 In what way do disabled rights groups claim that the welfare system socially controls the disabled?

Q4 What is meant by the term "total institution"?

Exam Question

Q1 Outline and assess the view that disadvantaged groups are socially controlled by the modern welfare system. Refer to at least two different groups in your answer. (60 marks)

Help! I'm being socially controlled...

It's the capitalists! They're giving me just enough benefits to make me able to work for a minimum wage! Or perhaps it's not the capitalists, in which case it's the men! They're disadvantaging me in the workplace and expecting me to do all the cleaning! Or maybe it's the welfare institutions! They're not letting me make any choices and assuming I want to play bingo all day! Help!

Distribution of Wealth and Income

*This unit is for **OCR** only, and it's a **synoptic unit** — which means it can include material from the rest of the course, e.g. Health, Education, Crime and Deviance, Popular Culture or Welfare. So revise what you've already studied alongside this section.*

Wealth equals Assets — which Doesn't just mean Cash

In Sociology, people use the term "wealth" rather than "money" because a lot of the stuff people own includes things other than fivers and tenners. **Buildings** and **land** are forms of wealth, as are **stocks** and **shares**. If you were doing Economics, you'd really have to understand how this works, but for Sociology you just need to learn a few basic points…

- Wealth gives its owner **long-term security**.
- Wealth can be converted to **money** if it is **sold** — selling an asset is called "realising" an asset.
- Wealth can be used to create **income** through **interest**, **rent** or **profits**.
- Much wealth is gained through **inheritance** and not **earnings**.

> **Wealth can be marketable or non-marketable**
>
> 1) **Marketable wealth** can be **sold** to **make money**. It's also **not immediately needed** by the person who owns it (i.e. selling it wouldn't leave them in desperate trouble). Examples of marketable wealth include stocks and shares, paintings and land.
>
> 2) **Non-marketable wealth** either **can't be sold** (e.g. some kinds of pension plan and insurance policy), or it's **needed** by the person that owns it (e.g. a farmer's tractor).
>
> 3) **Marketable wealth** is more **useful** and more **powerful** than **non-marketable wealth**.

Sociologists can Measure Trends in the Distribution of Wealth

Now here's an amazing statistic… According to the Inland Revenue, about 23% of the total marketable wealth in the UK is owned by 1% of the population. At the other end of the scale, **6% of the wealth** is spread out across the **poorest 50%** of the population. That's what sociologists mean when they talk about the uneven distribution of wealth. Maybe a pie chart will make all that clearer: ⟹

Wealth shared among poorest 50%
Wealth shared among richest 1%
Wealth shared among everyone else

71%   23%   6%

Official statistics seem to show that the **rich are getting richer** and the poor are getting poorer. This is **especially** the case if you don't include the value of an individual's **home** in their wealth.

% of wealth owned by:	1976	1986	1996	2002
wealthiest 1%	21	18	20	23
wealthiest 10%	50	50	52	56
wealthiest 25%	71	73	73	74
wealthiest 50%	92	90	93	94

% of wealth (except home)	1976	1986	1996	2002
wealthiest 1%	29	25	26	35
wealthiest 10%	57	50	63	75
wealthiest 25%	73	75	81	88
wealthiest 50%	88	89	94	98

There are Three Main Routes to becoming Wealthy

Every year, *The Sunday Times* publishes its "Rich List", based on the estimated value of the wealth of the 1000 wealthiest people in the UK. The list includes people who have got rich in one of three ways:

1) **Route to Riches number 1** is **inheritance** of **money**, **land** and **property**. For example, the **Duke of Westminster** is third on the list, with £5.6 billion. Most of this comes from valuable land in central London, inherited from family.

2) **Route to Riches number 2** is **success in business**. For example, **Lakshmi Mittal** and **Roman Abramovich** are the richest and second richest on the 2005 list. Mittal is a steel billionaire from India, with a fortune of £14.8 billion, and Russian oil billionaire Abramovich has a fortune of £7.5 billion.

3) **Route to Riches number 3** is success in **art**, **sport** or **popular culture**. For example, **J. K. Rowling's wealth** comes from sales of the Harry Potter books, merchandise and films. In 2005 she had £500 million, and was 96th on the list.

It's Hard to Measure Wealth Precisely

1) Wealth **isn't taxed** while its owners are alive, so the government doesn't collect information about wealth.

2) When people **die** and their wealth is passed on, it does get taxed. This information is used to work out the distribution of wealth. These figures aren't very accurate, though, because some wealthy people **hide** their wealth from the tax system. For example, to avoid **inheritance tax**, they pass on wealth **before** they die.

3) You can **estimate** the value of a painting or antique, but estimates often prove very wrong when they're auctioned.

4) The value of some assets, such as **shares**, can **change enormously** from day to day.

5) People also invest **overseas**.

Distribution of Wealth and Income

Income is Different from Wealth

Income is the money that comes into a household. It can be earned, unearned, or come from state benefits. **Earned** income is wages from a job. **Unearned** income includes things like interest on money in the bank, and share dividends.

Some people have **high income** but **little wealth**. If they lose their jobs they have little money to live on. It's also possible to have a lot of wealth but little income — if you own land you can't or don't want to sell, for example.

Income can be measured as **gross earnings** — i.e. before tax is taken off. Or it can be measured as **net earnings** — i.e. after tax is taken off.

The **government** measures gross earnings with the **Annual Survey** of **Hours** and **Earnings**. This calculates **median average hourly earnings**. It's based on a **sample** of **1%** of the working population and taken from Inland Revenue figures.

Income affects Life Chances, and it's Unequally Distributed in society

Income can have an important effect on an individual's opportunities in life. Generally, the **higher** your **household income**, the better you are likely to do in **education**, **health** and **status**. On average, children from **high-earning households** get better GCSE grades, and are more likely to take A levels and go to university. Higher income means you can expect to **live longer**.

1) In **1998**, the **Joseph Rowntree Foundation** found that the gap between the **incomes** of the richest and poorest was at its biggest since the end of the 1940s. Between 1979 and 1994-5, average income rose by **60-68%** for the **top 10%** of earners whilst it rose by **only 10%** for the **poorest 10%**. When **housing costs** were taken into account, the incomes of the poorest 10% actually **fell** by **8%**.

2) However, in **1999**, the government introduced a **National Minimum Wage**, which has increased the incomes of the lowest paid workers.

3) There are **regional differences** in income. People in **London** earn most on average, and people in **Northern Ireland** and the **North East** earn least. Incomes are rising fastest in the **North East**, **Wales** and **Northern Ireland**.

4) There are also differences between **men's average hourly earnings** and **women's**. The size of this gap varies by region. In London in 2004, women earned 75.9% of men's earnings, but in Northern Ireland, women earned 90.6% of men's earnings.

Sociologists study the Effects of Wealth and Income on Lifestyle

1) Lots of the data on distribution of wealth is **statistical** — it's based on **quantitative methods**. It's also possible to use qualitative methods, such as **informal interviews** or **participant observation** (see p.152).

2) Statistics can give you an idea of **how much wealth** there is in society, but they don't show you anything about the **experience** of **individuals**. For example, you could only find out if income changed people's **values** and **expectations** through **qualitative** methods.

3) Sociological work on income and wealth is either theoretical or quantitative. The **qualitative research** has been mostly done by **non-sociologists**. For example, the journalist **Polly Toynbee (2003)** published a study of life on the minimum wage, based on **observation** and **unstructured interviews**. She found that low pay went with bad working conditions, low self-esteem and a sense of hopelessness.

Practice Questions

Q1 What is wealth?
Q2 What is marketable wealth?
Q3 Describe how wealth is distributed in the UK.
Q4 What is income?

Exam Questions

Q1 Identify and explain two problems sociologists face when attempting to measure wealth. (12 marks)

Q2 Identify and explain two advantages of using informal interviews to study the lifestyles of wealthy individuals. (12 marks)

Well, we can all wish we had more cash...

...and more things like land and company shares. Measuring income is fairly easy — the Inland Revenue know exactly how much we're all paid. Measuring wealth is slightly trickier, because there are loads of different assets to consider and the assets can quickly change in value. However, the Sunday Times Rich List has a pretty good idea of how much they're worth.

Workplace Inequalities

People are always being forced to learn how to work in new ways in order to cope with change. It goes right back to the Industrial Revolution in the 18th century, when workers suddenly had to deal with factories full of big machines instead of little workshops and craft tools. Since then, there have been many times when patterns and types of work have changed.

Braverman (1974) linked Fordist Mass Production to Deskilling the workforce

Henry Ford, the American car manufacturer, invented **mass production**. Each worker on an assembly line performs a repetitive, simple task, over and over again all day. This means that **training** is **quick** and **cheap**, pay is **low**, and workers are **easy to replace**. Ford's methods were used a great deal during the twentieth century.

Marxist sociologist **Harry Braverman** said that by breaking down the work like this, Ford started a trend of **deskilling** the workers — i.e. manufacturing used to need skill, but doesn't any more. Braverman saw 20th century industrial workers as being **powerless** and **alienated**. He claimed that this would **get worse** as technology and mechanisation progressed.

Post-Fordism is Flexible and High Tech

1) In the **20th century**, the long-term trend was towards **non-manual** employment. **Manufacturing** and **extraction** industries (e.g. shipbuilding and coalmining) declined while **services** (e.g. retail and catering) grew.

2) **Bell (1973)** predicted the **post-industrial society**. He thought that white collar jobs in areas such as leisure, health care and education would become the **norm**. Manual work, such as mass production, would be done more and more by **machines**. This meant a "**knowledge society**" would develop, where most work was in professional, technical and scientific occupations.

3) According to **Piore (1986)**, in post-Fordist industry, **technological change** has led to a need for more **skilled**, flexible and specialised workers (often referred to as a "**flexible workforce**").

4) Under post-Fordism, there's **less hierarchy**, **more communication** and more **industrial democracy**. For example, workers can join **profit sharing** schemes and worker directors sit on **company boards**.

5) **Atkinson (1986)** suggests that post-Fordist industry organises workers in terms of **core workers** and **peripheral workers**. Core workers are **multi-skilled** and **highly motivated full-time** employees. Peripheral workers are low-paid **temporary** workers. Peripheral workers are disproportionately female and black.

The flexible workforce...

David Ashley (1997) summarised post-Fordism like this:

1) New **information technologies** play a leading role. Computers and the internet are now important.

2) The labour force is more **flexible**, **specialised** and **decentralised**. Workers are highly skilled and able to take on many different tasks. The new technologies mean they can work from various locations, and don't have to clock in to a factory or office every day.

3) **Consumer choice** is more important. Henry Ford made every car the **same**, in order to make them cheaply. Now companies have to **compete** to provide the most **attractive** product. More products are aimed at a discerning **niche market**, rather than the mass market. **Market research** is more important.

4) The **male** skilled manual **working class** is less important. This is linked to **feminisation** of the workforce. Modern jobs require "**female**" skills like networking, communication and multi-tasking.

5) There's more **flexitime** and **part time work**. Work can be treated flexibly to fit around other aspects of the worker's life. This fits changing social patterns and new forms of family life. Between 1971 and 1988 **male employment fell** by almost 1.8 million, whereas **female employment rose** by about 1.7 million. A large proportion of these jobs were in the **service sector**, which grew in this period.

6) **Globalisation** has affected the distribution of work. Much of the manual work is carried out in **LEDCs**. Service industries are concentrated in MEDCs.

The theory of Post-Fordism has been Challenged

1) **Anna Pollert (1988)** argues that the theory of flexibility is **over-simplified** and **inaccurate**. She says that the empirical evidence shows **no major reduction** in Fordist mass production.

2) Pollert also claims that the idea of a **peripheral workforce** isn't a **new** thing at all.

3) **Stephen Wood (1989)** questions the view that flexibility has led to workers needing greater **skills**. His study of two British steel rolling mills found that new technology **did not** lead to an **increase** in **skills** for the workers.

Workplace Inequalities

Most Work is **Segregated** — **Vertically** and **Horizontally**

1) Most organisations where people work are **hierarchies**. In other words, there are people who are **low-status** and **poorly paid** at the **bottom**, and people who are **high-status** and **highly paid** at the **top**.

2) Traditionally, these **hierarchies** contain a lot of **social inequalities**. This is called **vertical segregation**. Higher up the hierarchy, workers tend to be middle class, white, older men. Sociologists refer to the "**glass ceiling**", which means it **looks like** there's **nothing stopping** some groups of people (e.g. black women) from getting promoted, but they just keep on not getting promoted anyway.

3) **Horizontal segregation** is segregation on the **same level of a hierarchy**, and at the **same level of pay**. For example, two people work in a garage earning similar amounts of money. One's a **receptionist**, the other a **mechanic**. Guess which one's the woman...

There are **Gender** inequalities at **Work**

1) **John Lovering (1994)** found that **older companies** in manufacturing and public services tended to employ **men** in **high status** and **full-time** positions, while their **female** employees were **lower status** and often **part-time**.

2) Lovering did find evidence of **new attitudes** to gender, usually in **new companies**, or following **restructuring**.

3) The new **flexible workforce** includes a large number of **female part-time workers**, who fit work around family commitments. Since the 1970s, there's been a **large increase** in the number of **females** in employment.

There are **Ethnic** inequalities at **Work**

There's evidence of **racial discrimination** in the workplace.

The Policy Studies Institute researched responses to job applications

In a **1973-74** study, they wrote **fake job applications** and sent them out as coming from **white applicants**, and as coming from **black applicants**. The fake candidates were equally qualified and experienced. The "**white**" applicants were much **more likely** to get an **interview** than the "black" ones.

The study was repeated in 1977-79 and 1984-85, with **similar results**. Even after the **Race Relations Act (1976)**, which makes racial discrimination in employment **illegal**, discrimination was **still** taking place.

1) The Labour Force Survey in 2000 showed that non-white workers were less likely to reach **managerial** and **professional** jobs. This is more the case for some ethnic groups than others. People of **Indian** and **Chinese** background have a **better chance** of **promotion** than **Bangladeshis** and **Afro-Caribbeans**. This is likely to be due at least partly to employers having **stereotyped ideas** about particular ethnic groups — Chinese people are stereotyped as **intelligent** and **hardworking**.

2) There's **horizontal segregation** on ethnic grounds. For example, a **disproportionately large** number of **Bangladeshi** men work as **cooks** or **waiters**.

The new **flexible workforce** includes a lot of **temporary workers** on short term contracts. Contract workers in the public services and in **support services** are disproportionately from **ethnic minorities**.

Practice Questions

Q1 Who invented mass production?

Q2 What did Braverman mean by "deskilling"?

Q3 Name two sociologists who have written about "post-Fordism".

Q4 What is the difference between "horizontal segregation" and "vertical segregation"?

Q5 What did the three studies carried out by the Policy Studies Institute into ethnic discrimination all show?

Exam Question

Q1 Outline and assess sociological explanations of how work has changed in the twentieth century. (44 marks)

It's all work and no play...

Some of this probably seems like a bit of a history lesson, or a stray piece of Business Studies. It's important to know what changes have taken place in work since mass production began, because they've affected inequalities. Make sure you've got the difference between vertical and horizontal segregation sorted, then you can use the terms to describe various inequalities at work.

Workplace Change and Class

The traditional definition of "working class" is "people in manual jobs". Nowadays, more people work in services (see p. 122), which might make you wonder whether everyone's now middle class. Some say yes, some say no. Sociologists can't agree about anything...

Lots of sociologists believe that the Middle Class is Changing

1) **Savage et al (1992)** divided the middle class into **groups** according to how they got their life chances.

Type of middle class	Examples	Where they get their life chances from
1) Professionals	Lawyers, teachers, doctors	**Cultural assets** — from educational achievement and professional training. Also from **cultural capital**. (see p.131)
2) Managers	Bank managers, supermarket managers	**Contacts** and **experience** from **working their way up** in the company. Have more economic capital than cultural capital.
3) Self-Employed and small employers	Shop owners, IT consultants, small business owners	**Property assets** — from **business** success. Have more economic capital than cultural capital.

2) Savage et al claimed that the **middle class is changing**. The rise of **post-Fordism** has meant that self-employed consultants are becoming **more important**.

3) They also said that there's an **increasing division** between **private sector** middle class (marketing managers, accountants, etc) and the **public sector** middle class (teachers and doctors). The private sector middle class are becoming more important. **Entrepreneurship** is becoming more important, and private sector managers are gaining more cultural assets in the form of qualifications.

4) **Roberts et al (1977)** found wide variation in how middle class workers saw their own class position. They concluded the middle class is becoming **fragmented** into separate strata.

5) Influential sociologist **Anthony Giddens (1973)** disagrees — he says there's a **distinct middle class**, and they're different from the working class because they can sell their "**brain power**" as well as, or instead of, their **labour power**.

6) **Braverman (1974)** argues that the middle class has been **deskilled** and **proletarianised** — i.e. it's becoming **more like** the **working class**. Braverman says that non-manual jobs are being broken up and simplified (fragmented) or taken over by computers (mechanised). Because of this, much of the middle class, especially the lower end, has **lost social and economic advantages**. They, and their jobs, are becoming working class (proletarian).

Many sociologists also believe that the Working Class has Changed

1) **Crewe (1985)** distinguished between the **old working class** and the **new working class**.

2) Crewe characterised the **old working class** as **council tenants**, employed in **manufacturing** and the **public sector**, who belonged to a **trade union**.

3) He characterised the new working class as **home owners**, employed in **services** and the **private sector**, who **weren't likely** to belong to **trade unions**.

Fulcher and Scott (1999) said that there was once a **strong working class identity**. People **knew** they were working class and **agreed** on what being working class **meant**. Because the class has grown **smaller**, Fulcher and Scott say that **strong sense of belonging** has **gone**.

Zweig (1961) argued that skilled manual workers had become more like the middle class. This idea is called the **embourgeoisement thesis**. **Goldthorpe et al (1968)** set out to **test** the embourgeoisement thesis.

Goldthorpe et al (1968) studied affluent manual workers in Luton

1) These workers made **good money** compared with other members of the **working class**, but **not as much** as **middle class** groups.

2) There was **very little social mixing** between the classes. They lived in separate areas and didn't spend leisure time together.

3) **Differences** in **norms and values** still existed between the affluent manual workers and the middle class.

4) Most of the manual workers supported the **Labour Party** and **trade unions**.

5) They didn't see themselves as having a **career**, just a **job**.

Conclusion: Goldthorpe et al concluded that the working class were **not** going through **embourgeoisement**.

Fiona Devine (1992) repeated this study in 1986 and 1987. She found that people still saw themselves as working class. There was still a **working class identity**. She found **some changes** in attitudes, including **less support** for the **Labour Party**.

Workplace Change and Class

Upper Class Privileges are preserved through Inheritance and Culture

Upper class families **pass their wealth on** to the next generation. Equally important is "**cultural capital**" (see p.131). Upper class children **learn** the "correct" language, mannerisms, attitudes and values, and can "fit in". **Scott (1991)** argues that the upper class create an **exclusive social world** by marrying within their class, and through social institutions such as public schools, top universities and "gentlemen's clubs".

1) **New Right** sociologist **Peter Saunders (1990)** argues that the increase in the number of people **owning shares** in the UK has led to power being spread more widely. A **nation of stake-holders** has replaced the small minority in power.

2) **Scott** agrees with Saunders that **more and more people own shares** in the UK but argues this hasn't led to a break-up of the ruling class. Most individuals own a **few** shares but hold **very little** real **power**. Scott says there's still a **power elite** who own **vast amounts** of **shares** and control business and the economy.

3) Scott says the **lifestyle** of the ruling class has changed — it's not all about "Hooray Henries" any more. However, this doesn't mean the upper class hold less power. **Wealth** and **power** is still passed on through **family** — in 1990, 104 of the 200 richest families had **inherited** their wealth.

Scott divides the Upper Class into Three Groups

1) **Scott (1982)** said there were **three types** of traditional upper class:

2) Although the sort of upper class a person belongs to affects their status, the three types share **similar lifestyles** and **values**, and share **social** and **cultural ties**, so they form a **unified class**.

- **land owning** — the oldest form
- **commercial**
- **manufacturing** — the newest form

3) The new upper class can be divided into three new groups:

- The **Jet Set** (or **Pop Aristocracy**) are people who have become rich through the **media**, **sport** or **entertainment**.
- The **Landowning Aristocracy** have **inherited wealth** and large amounts of land.
- The **Entrepreneurial Rich** have wealth from business.

See the three "routes to riches" on p.120

Some sociologists claim that the Underclass is growing

Dahrendorf (1987) argued that the **underclass** was growing rapidly. This may be because of **globalisation**. A lot of manual work now goes **overseas**, so the demand for manual workers has dropped. As the labour market becomes more flexible, there's much more **insecure**, **temporary** or **casual** low-paid work.

Will Hutton (1995) put forward the 30-30-40 thesis, suggesting workers are divided into these categories:

- **30%** are unemployed or have low paid, insecure work.
- **30%** have some job security and quality of life.
- **40%** are privileged workers in secure and regular employment.

Hutton believes this situation is economically and socially **unstable** and could lead to a breakdown in social order.

Practice Questions

Q1   According to Crewe, what were the main differences between "old" and "new" working class?

Q2   What does the term "proletarianised" mean?

Q3   What is another name for the Pop Aristocracy?

Q4   How might globalisation lead to a growth in the underclass?

Q5   Who suggested the 30-30-40 thesis?

Exam Questions

Q1   Outline and assess sociological explanations for the importance of class as a source of identity in the contemporary UK.

(44 marks)

Q2   Outline and assess sociological explanations of the changes taking place in the middle class in the contemporary UK.

(44 marks)

Classy pair of pages...

Changes in work have made a few differences to social classes. Some sociologists think class differences haven't really altered all that much. It's tedious to learn all the theories and studies on both sides of the argument, but it really will help. Braverman and Goldthorpe are particularly good names to mention. Make sure you can give details of what they thought and why it's relevant.

Defining and Measuring Poverty

Measuring poverty is difficult. First you have to decide what counts as poverty — whether it's not having a TV, or not having enough food to eat, etc...

Absolute Poverty *is a Lack of the* Minimum Requirements *for* Survival

1) An individual is in **absolute poverty** if they don't have the income to afford the basic necessities — **food**, **warmth** and **shelter**. By this definition there are **very few individuals in the UK in poverty**.

2) **Rowntree** (1871-1956) set up the first major studies of poverty in the UK in **1899** and measured it in absolute terms. He made a **list of essentials** needed for life and recorded how many families could **afford** them. Those whose income was **too low** were classed as **in poverty**. He found **33%** of the population in York were in poverty.

3) There are criticisms of Rowntree's study. His definition of poverty assumed people ate every scrap of food they bought without wasting any and it assumed the **cheapest** options were **always available**. The lists of essentials were compiled by **experts** and **didn't match the lifestyle** of the folk he surveyed. He did listen to his critics though, and for two further studies (1941, 1951) he **added more items** to the list of essentials. By this time, **more people** could afford the basics on the list. His conclusion was that **poverty was disappearing fast** in 20th century Britain.

4) **Bradshaw et al (1987)** used a similar "**budget standards**" method to Rowntree, with some changes. They drew up their budget based on the way that families actually spent money. They found that welfare benefits only provided a very low standard of living — families couldn't afford a car, or books, and even by buying the cheapest lines of food, families couldn't provide a nutritional diet. *Some say this is cultural — for the cost of a burger and chips you could get proper fresh stuff.*

Relative Poverty *is a* Comparison *with the* Average Standard of Living

Many sociologists (especially left-leaning ones) favour the **relative** definition of poverty. **Relative poverty** shows whether someone is rich or poor **in relation to other people** in **society**, rather than whether they have basics like food and shelter. The **government** defines relative poverty in terms of **income**. An income of **less than 60% of the median** is defined as **poor**. Sociologists have come up with various ways of measuring relative poverty in terms of what people can afford to buy.

Townsend (1979) studied relative poverty in the UK
Townsend did his research in 1968-1969 and published his book in 1979.

Method	Townsend devised a "**deprivation index**" of 60 items central to social life in the UK. He selected 12 as essential to the whole population — the **level of poverty** was the **percentage** of the population **without** these. Importantly, Townsend didn't just focus on income and material basics but also the ability to have a **normal social life**.
Conclusion	Townsend's study concluded that in 1969, **22.9%** of the population were living in poverty.

1) A **big problem** in measuring poverty like this is that **not everyone agrees** on what the **essential items** are. Sometimes people don't buy something because they **can't afford** it, sometimes they don't buy it because they don't want it.

2) **Piachaud (1981, 1987)** said that the deprivation index reflected Townsend's **cultural bias** — it included things like Sunday roast dinners, which not everyone eats by choice. **Wedderburn (1974)** thought that the items on the index were **arbitrary**, and thought Townsend should have done a lot more research before coming up with the index.

3) Another problem is that **relative poverty levels** are **constantly changing**, as the economy grows and society gets wealthier. **Some sociologists** would argue that this makes it a **less useful concept** than absolute poverty.

Mack and Lansley (1985, 1992) took note of Townsend's critics

Method:	Mack and Lansley actually surveyed the **general public** for a list of items essential to social life in Britain and included items that **more than 50%** considered **essential**. They left out items which the rich were as likely to go without as the poor, which made their index more reasonable than Townsend's. The final index had **22 items**. They classed those **without three or more items** on the list by necessity as **poor**, and those **without seven or more items** as in **severe poverty**. Mack and Lansley asked respondents whether they were doing without an item **by choice**, or because they **couldn't afford** it. Townsend's survey didn't do this.
Conclusion:	Their 1983 survey found **7.5 million people** (13.8% of the population) were in **poverty**, and **2.5 million** were in **severe poverty**. You can't compare this with Townsend's survey, because the methodology is different.
Follow up:	Mack and Lansley did a follow up survey in 1990. They found public perceptions had changed, and added several **new items** to the index, including phone, TV, fresh fruit & veg every day, and home contents insurance.
Trends:	The numbers who were without at least three items on the list had risen to **11 million**. The numbers without seven items had gone up to **3.5 million**. More of the poor were **pensioners** in 1990 than in 1983. Many more **single parents** fell into the "poor" category in 1990 than in 1983.

Critics pointed out that it **wouldn't be valid** to **compare** their 1983 survey with their 1990 survey, because they'd added **new** items to the deprivation index. **Piachaud (1987)** also argued that the findings were **arbitrary**, because Mack and Lansley had **defined** poverty as lacking three items on the list. They could have chosen a **different number** and got **different results**.

Defining and Measuring Poverty

Poverty can be affected by Social Class

Unskilled manual workers and the unemployed are most likely to be poor.

Working class people often have a **disadvantaged education**. They're less likely to find employment that is **secure** and / or **well-paid**. They're more likely to fall into poverty at some point in their lives than middle class people.

Women are More Likely to be Poor

Government statistics measure households rather than individual men and women. However, they show that **lone parents** and **pensioners** are more likely to be poor. Both these groups are **mostly women**.

Townsend et al (1987) wrote about the **feminisation** of **poverty**. They identified four main groups of female poor:

1) Women whose **main role** is **looking after children** or other dependants.
2) **Lone women** with **children**, whether working or not.
3) **Elderly women** pensioners, especially those living alone.
4) Women with **low earnings**.

Caroline Glendinning and **Jane Millar (1994)** said that women have higher rates of poverty than men because...

1) Women are **disadvantaged** in the **labour market** (see pages 132-133). Their **primary role** is seen as **housewife and mother**. Women spend more time out of the labour market than men and they're more likely to have part-time jobs.
2) Within the household, male "breadwinners" often control the **money**.

Ethnicity and Poverty are often Linked

1) **Richard Berthoud's 1997 study** for the **Policy Studies Institute** found that ethnic minority households were much more likely to fall below average household income compared with white households.
2) Some ethnic minorities were better off than others. Only **34%** of **Chinese** households lived in **poverty**, compared with **82%** of **Pakistani** and **84%** of **Bangladeshi** households.
3) Ethnic inequalities in poverty are mostly caused by **labour market** disadvantages. Ethnic minorities find it harder to get secure, reasonably paid jobs (see pages 134-35).

These are based on the official measure — having less than 60% of the median income counts as poor.

Peter Alcock (1997) says that **material deprivation** is only **part** of the problem. **Social exclusion** also reduces the quality of life for ethnic minority groups. Social exclusion can involve poor access to health care and social services, poor quality schools, a stagnant local job market, etc. Alcock suggested that **racial harassment** can make social exclusion worse, because it causes its victims to feel **isolation** and **fear**.

Disability and Poverty are also Linked

Oppenheim and Harker (1996) suggest that exclusion from the labour market is responsible for this, and also claim that welfare benefits for disabled people are inadequate. **Alcock** also blames social exclusion.

Practice Questions

Q1   What is meant by "absolute poverty" and "relative poverty"?
Q2   Give two ways that Mack and Lansley improved on Townsend's measurement of relative poverty.
Q3   Are all ethnic minorities equally economically disadvantaged?
Q4   What is meant by "social exclusion"?

Exam Questions

Q1 Using your wider sociological knowledge, outline the evidence that supports the view that some groups are more likely to be in poverty than others.	(22 marks)
Q2 Identify and explain two problems facing sociologists attempting to measure relative poverty.	(12 marks)

Relative poverty — when your cousins are hard up...

It's hard to measure poverty, because first you have to decide just how poor is "poor". That on its own takes some research, and you'd better be prepared to explain your definition of poverty to other sociologists, who'll be lining up to tell you you've got it wrong. Once you've found out some data on poverty (or used someone else's) you can start analysing it for social inequalities.

Poverty and the Underclass

Some sociologists claim there's an underclass at the bottom of society, held back by a culture of poverty. Others disagree.

Oscar Lewis said Culture was the Cause of Poverty

Lewis (1959, 1961, 1966) studied the poor in Mexico and Puerto Rico

Lewis thought that the **values**, **norms** and **behaviour** of the **poor** were **different** to the rest of society and these values were passed on to the next generation. In other words, Lewis thought that the poor are **culturally different** from the rest of society.

He said individuals learn how to be poor and learn to expect to be poor through the subculture of poverty they're socialised into.

He reckoned that this culture of resignation, apathy and lack of participation in wider society initially starts as a response to poverty, but then becomes a culture which keeps people in poverty. He called it a "**design for life**".

1) Lewis's work was **controversial** and **criticised** from the start. Other research done at the same time in similar poor areas found **highly organised community facilities** and **political involvement**.

2) **Schwartz (1975)** concluded that the poor **weren't culturally different** from the well-off.

3) **Situational Constraints theory** says that the poor are constrained by their situation, rather than by their culture.

4) **Coates and Silburn (1970)** studied poor areas of Nottingham. They found that **some people** in poor areas **did feel resigned to being poor**, and that it wasn't worth trying to get out of poverty. But... they said this was actually a **realistic assessment** of an individual's situation, not **proof** of some kind of **alternative value system**.

5) Coates and Silburn's research supported the idea that poverty leads to **other deprivation** which can trap people into a **cycle of deprivation**. This means poverty is **practically hard to get out of**, not culturally hard to get out of.

New Right Theorists blame Dependency on Welfare for Poverty

1) **Charles Murray (1989, 1994)** described a sector of society which he thought had a **culture of dependency on the state** and an **unwillingness to work**. He called this group the **underclass**. Murray characterises the underclass as **lazy**, **delinquent** and prone to abusing drink and drugs.

2) Murray identified three factors — a **rising number** of **single parent families**, **rising crime** and **attitudes** of **resistance to work**. Murray accepts that not all poor people are workshy, but he thinks that a significant group of the poor just don't want to work.

3) In Murray's opinion, **Welfare State benefits** are **too high**. He says this means there's not much encouragement to get off welfare and get a job. British New Right sociologist **Peter Saunders** also thinks that welfare dependency keeps people in the underclass.

Workshy fops, skiers.

4) Another right-wing sociologist, **Marsland (1989)**, thinks that the **level of poverty** is **exaggerated** by other writers on poverty. He says society should **keep a small level of poverty** to **motivate** others to work. Marsland agrees with Murray that the **Welfare State is too generous** and encourages a **culture of non-work** amongst some groups.

The idea of Dependency Culture has been Criticised

Sociological **criticism** of Murray says his **evidence** for the existence of an underclass is **too weak**. **Walker (1990)** found **very little evidence** of **different values** and **behaviour** among the poor. His opinion was that **blaming** the poor **distracts** from the **real causes** of poverty such as the **failure of social policy**.

Dahrendorf (1987) describes the underclass as **lazy**, **hostile** and **deviant** — rather similar to Murray's view. However, Dahrendorf blames the **labour market**, rather than the poor themselves, for the existence of the underclass. Dahrendorf says that technological advances in manufacture have massively reduced the number of **manual jobs**. He accuses employers and educational institutions of excluding the underclass. This exclusion creates a **cycle of deprivation**.

There are Other Theories about the Underclass

Giddens (1973) defines the underclass as those who are **most disadvantaged** in the job market — e.g. illegal immigrants. He says that the best the underclass can get are **low paid** jobs with **low job security** in the **secondary job market**.

> The **Dual Labour Market** thesis claims there are two labour markets — the **primary labour market** provides **steady**, **well-paid** jobs, and the **secondary labour market** provides **low-paid** work with **very little job security**. See p.134.

Runciman (1990) defines the underclass as people who are **permanently dependent** on **welfare benefits**. **Frank Field**'s definition of the underclass (see p.118) follows this model.

Dean and Taylor-Gooby (1992) disagree. They suggest that it's important to take account of an individual's **future prospects**. An educated unemployed person might get a job soon. A lone parent could find a new partner. This means that the underclass is **unstable** — people don't stay in it for long. **Dean** argues that it's **not worth thinking** in terms of an **underclass**.

Poverty and the Underclass

Marxists blame the Capitalist System for Poverty

Marxists believe that the working class tends to be poor as a direct result of capitalist exploitation. They think that **poverty exists** because it **serves the needs of the capitalist class** in society.

1) First of all, Marxists say that low-paid workers provide a **cheap labour supply** for the **capitalist class** which keeps **profits high**.

2) Secondly, they argue that varying pay levels within the working class keep individuals **competing** against each other to get the best jobs. This **divides the working class**. Remember, the working class is the **majority** in a capitalist society. Marxism says that if the working class all **united together** they'd be a **threat** to capitalism. That's why they reckon it's in the **interests of capitalism** to keep the **working class divided**.

Marxists also argue that **welfare** benefits **don't do much** to reduce poverty. **Westergaard and Resler (1976)** argue that **welfare benefits remain low** to **make sure** that people **still need to get a job** even if they don't get paid much. They say this keeps up the supply of cheap labour (see p.111).

Marxist explanations of Poverty have been Criticised

1) Marxist explanations of poverty **don't explain** why some groups in society are much more likely to experience poverty than others. Marxists treat poverty (and just about everything else) as a **characteristic of capitalism**, and as something that the **working class as a whole** suffer. They don't look for much **detail** about the experience of poverty for **individuals** or **groups**.

2) Marxism **ignores** the effects of **gender** and **ethnicity** on poverty. It doesn't explain why women are more likely to be poor than men, or why Bangladeshi households are more likely to be poor than Afro-Caribbean households.

3) **Townsend (1970, 1979) rejects** the argument that the Welfare State doesn't do much good. He believes that **social policy** can and should **improve standards of living** within a capitalist system.

4) **Capitalism** creates **wealth** in the economy. This increase in wealth contributes to the **reduction of absolute poverty**.

Weberian Sociologists blame Inequalities in the Labour Market

1) **Max Weber** thought that an individual's **position in the labour market** was the key to their life-chances, wealth and status. The people whose skills were most **valued** and **needed** would always be the **wealthiest**.

2) **Townsend (1979)** has the view that the key **explanation for poverty** is the **low status** of some workers, which doesn't give them much power to improve their labour market situation.

Dean and Taylor-Gooby (1992) think that changes in the UK labour market have led to increased poverty.

1) There are fewer jobs in the **manufacturing** sector and more jobs in the **service** sector. **Manufacturing** jobs had **good job security** through the 1950s to 1970s (until UK manufacturing declined). **Service sector** jobs **don't have much job security**, and they tend to be **part-time** or **temporary**. Many service jobs are **low-paid**.

2) The **decline** in **trade union power** and **membership** has meant that workers are less able to **fight** for their rights.

3) Dean and Taylor-Gooby say this means **more people** are likely to experience **poverty** at some point.

Practice Questions

Q1 Give an example of an attitude which Oscar Lewis argues causes poverty.
Q2 What does Murray identify as the key processes which create an underclass?
Q3 Give an example of how poverty is helpful to the capitalist class, from a Marxist perspective.
Q4 What do Weberians say is the cause of poverty?

Exam Questions

Q1 Outline and assess sociological theories of the underclass. (44 marks)

Q2 Outline and assess sociological explanations for poverty. (44 marks)

Blame the system or blame the victim — it's the same old suspects...

These theories tend to either blame the poor themselves, or blame society as a whole. Each theory makes a certain amount of sense (even sociologists would get found out pretty quick if they wrote nothing but rubbish), but they don't all look at the whole picture. When you're asked to assess a theory, look at what it's missed out, and mention how other sociologists have criticised it.

Concepts of Class

There are material (i.e. economic) theories about class, and cultural theories about class.

Functionalists and New Rightists believe Class lets the Best rise to the Top

1) **Functionalism** says that society is a **meritocracy** — the most able people rise to the top.

2) **Functionalists** believe that the class system enables each individual to find their **right place** and **role** in society. People who do well in terms of the common values of society will be at the top of the class system.

3) According to Functionalism, **high status**, **power** and **high income** are **rewards** for conforming to society's values. **Inequality** is seen as inevitable.

4) **New Right** sociologists such as **Peter Saunders (1990)** believe that class **inequality** is a **good thing** because it **motivates** people to work hard. Saunders suggests that in a society with equal rewards for everyone, some people wouldn't pull their weight.

5) Saunders says that **inequality** promotes **economic growth**. Individuals are motivated to **start businesses** so that they can make money, and this **benefits society** by creating **jobs** and **wealth**.

6) Because the New Right see society as a **meritocracy**, they don't believe in trying to make society more **equal**.

Marxists see class as Divisive and Oppressive

1) Marx argued there are **only two classes** in society — the **proletariat** (working class) and the **bourgeoisie** (ruling class). Marx's view of class was entirely based on **economics** and **power**.

2) The **ruling class**, or bourgeoisie, **own** the **means of production** — the factories. The ruling class control both the **price** they sell goods for and the **wages** they pay the workers who produce the goods. By paying the workers **less** than they **sell** the goods for they make a **profit**, which gives them **wealth** and power to **control** society in their own interests.

3) The **working class**, or proletariat, don't own the means of production, so they have little power in society. They **depend** on the **ruling class** because the ruling class pay their wages, which is their only source of wealth.

Neo-Marxist theories of class try to explain the Middle Class

In traditional Marxism, there's **no middle class**. There clearly **is** a **middle class** in **modern society**.

1) Neo-Marxist **Erik Olin Wright (1985, 1990)** looked at explaining the middle class of salaried professionals which grew in the late 20th century. This group have **some control** over the **means of production**, and may **own bits** of it, but they don't control large sections of labour power. He called this class the **"petty bourgeoisie"**.

2) Wright argues that the petty bourgeoisie have **things in common** with **both** classes at **different** times. For example, they may own shares (which is **part-ownership** of the means of production) but may also lose their livelihood at the will of the ruling class (e.g. if they lose their job, or the share price falls).

3) Wright concludes that **class conflict** and **exploitation** are more **complicated** in the late 20th century than Marx predicted but class is **still** the basis of power and wealth in society, and it's still related to economic power.

Weber thought Class was based on Access to Material Resources

1) Weber said that there are **three distinct areas** or forms of **stratification** in modern society.

   - **Class power** is defined by Weber as **economic power** to access **resources** — being rich, in other words.

   - **Social power** is defined by Weber as having **status** and prestige, and being **respected** by others.

   - **Party power** is defined by Weber as having influence over **political decisions**.

2) **Weber** argued that an individual's **class power** and **class position** derives from their market position — i.e. their **economic chances**, and their ability to **control** their **wages** and **working conditions**.

3) An individual's **market position** varies partly depending on how in **demand** their skills and talents are — i.e. how much an employer is willing to pay for their services. Be careful though — market position isn't just an individual's ability to get a job. It also covers their **ownership** of **property** and **assets** (e.g. shares).

4) Weber's view was that the class system was a **complex** hierarchy of layers each with their own market position.

Neo-Weberian Theory influences modern Class Schemes

The big name in neo-Weberian theory of class is **John Goldthorpe (1980)**. Goldthorpe categorized people into **seven classes** based on occupation, with **three main classes** — service class ("white collar" professionals), intermediate class and working class.

In Goldthorpe's scheme, an individual's **class position** is the **market position** he or she has in the **labour market** — e.g. their income and promotion prospects.

> The current official government socio-economic classification system (the NS-SEC) is based on Goldthorpe's work (see p.41). You don't need to know lots of detail about it for OCR though.

Concepts of Class

Cultural Differences are also Relevant to Social Class

Cultural deprivation theory says that working class children are **socialised** into **different norms** and **values** than **middle class** and **upper class** children. Cultural deprivation theory is applied to several areas in Sociology.

1) In the sociology of **education**, cultural deprivation is used to explain why working class children don't do as well at school as middle class children.
2) The idea is that middle class children are **socialised** to **value educational achievement**, and middle class parenting views education as important — working class parents are less likely to go to parents' evenings.

1) In the sociology of **health**, cultural deprivation is used to explain why the working class have a higher rate of illness than the middle class.
2) Cultural deprivation theory says that the working class have **unhealthy lifestyles**, linked to a hedonistic attitude of **instant gratification**.

There's much more detail about this in the Health and Education sections — look at p.72-73 and p.84-85. Remember, this social inequality stuff is for the synoptic exam paper — that means you're supposed to bring in stuff from the rest of the course.

Bourdieu said the Working Class Lack Cultural Capital

1) Cultural capital is the **knowledge** and **social skills** you need to fit in to the top strata of society — including table manners, the "right" way to speak, and an appreciation of high culture.
2) **Bourdieu** said the upper class **maintains its position** (on top, that is) by passing on **cultural capital** (see glossary). He argued that **working class** families **don't develop** the cultural capital they need to climb the social ladder. His research found that people's **tastes** matched up quite well with their **social class position**, and that the way people **spoke** and **wrote** made a big difference to their **social mobility**.
3) Bourdieu divided cultural capital into **three forms**:

embodied	What the individual **knows** and what they can **do**, including knowledge about high culture. Can be improved by **education**.
objectified	**Cultural goods**, e.g. books, paintings and music. Can be **bought** with **wealth**, or **appreciated** with **embodied capital**.
institutionalised	**Education** system which provides recognised academic **qualifications**. Can be used to get a **high-paid job**.

4) **Savage et al (1992)** included **cultural assets** in their theory of divisions in the British **middle class** (see p.124). They thought that the middle classes got their life chances from a mixture of **property assets** (marketable wealth), **organisational assets** (management jobs) and **cultural assets**.
5) Cultural assets could be either **educational qualifications**, or "**class taste**".
6) **Upper** and **middle class culture** is sometimes characterised as "**high culture**", and seen as **better** than "**low culture**". See p.94 and p.96 for more on this.

Practice Questions

Q1 According to Functionalists and the New Right, why is class inequality a good thing?
Q2 According to Weber, what in society is responsible for an individual's class position?
Q3 What is meant by "cultural capital"?

Exam Questions

Q1 Outline and assess sociological explanations of class inequality in the UK. (44 marks)

Q2 Using your wider sociological knowledge, outline the evidence that cultural assets are responsible for class inequality. (22 marks)

Yes, that's a lot of theories, but then you did choose to do A2 Sociology...

It's important to understand these theories. Once you know what Marxists and Weberians say causes class, you can apply the ideas to different sociological topics — and you could well be asked to. Look out for the words "using your wider sociological knowledge". The cultural ideas about class are particularly relevant to Popular Culture, and also to Education and Health.

Gender Inequalities

Feminists examine society's gender divisions and argue that society is patriarchal, and has been set up to advantage men. In education, at work and in the family, women have fewer chances to succeed and are less free to make their own decisions. Feminism is a sociological and political movement which tries to explain all that and to change it.

Liberal Feminists *want women and men to have* Equal Opportunities

1) Liberal feminists, such as **Ann Oakley** in *Subject Women* (1981), say **everyone** should be treated according to **individual merit**, rather than **gender**. They want women to be given the **same privileges** and **opportunities** as men.

2) This involves **overcoming prejudice** (e.g. stereotypes about the roles of men and women) and preventing **discrimination** (e.g. women not being promoted or employed because they might get pregnant).

3) **Liberal feminists** say **sexism harms everyone**, men as well as women. For example, women find it hard to make progress in the world of work, while men are **forced** into **macho roles** that stop them from spending time with their families.

4) To promote **equal opportunities**, especially in education and work, liberal feminists believe in campaigning to **change laws** and **attitudes**. In Britain, they supported the introduction of the **Sex Discrimination Act (1975)** and the **Equal Pay Act (1970)**.

Radical Feminists *say there is* Conflict *between* All Men *and* All Women

1) From the radical feminist perspective, society is run in the interests of patriarchy — male power. **Shulamith Firestone** wrote about this in *The Dialectic of Sex* (1971). According to this view, men take most of society's rewards and privileges for themselves.

2) Another aspect of male power is to commit **physical** and **sexual violence** against women. The radical feminist **Andrea Dworkin** has written a lot about this.

It had a lovely big moat to keep all the men out.

3) Radical feminists argue that men also use their control of culture to create the belief that **gender inequality** and **patriarchy** are "natural".

4) Many radical feminists agree that there are **natural differences** between the sexes but they don't accept male domination. Often, they suggest that although men are more physically powerful, women are the naturally superior sex in some way.

5) Radical feminists are **not interested** in "equal rights". They **don't want** women to become **like men**. Instead, they want to **free women** from what they see as patriarchal control. For **some** radical feminists, the only solution is "**separatism**" — i.e. the policy that women should cut themselves off (sexually and socially) from men.

Marxist *and* Socialist *feminists see* Capitalism *as the cause of gender inequality*

1) From this perspective, **capitalists**, rather than men, are the main **beneficiaries** of **sexism**.

2) Marxist and socialist feminists, like **Michele Barrett** in *Women's Oppression Today* (1988), stress that **social class** has at least as much effect as gender on your life chances and experiences. They also suggest that in capitalism, **women's work** is **exploited** in **particular ways**. For example:

- Employers treat women as a "**reserve army of labour**" to be hired and fired as needed.
- Male workers try to **exclude females** from their **trades** and **crafts**.
- Husbands **exploit** their wives' **unpaid housework**.

3) Marxist and socialist feminists say that **equal relationships** between men and women will arrive only when **capitalism** is **abolished**. They also believe that a **struggle against capitalism** should **include** a struggle against **sexism** and **patriarchy**.

Black Feminists *say white feminists have* Ignored *problems faced by* Black Women

In *Ain't I A Woman?* (1981), **bell hooks** (yes, she does spell her name without capital letters) argues that because they benefit indirectly from living in a racist society, white feminists are not enthusiastic about tackling racism. She says that mainstream white feminism makes the **false claim** that black and white women face **exactly** the **same problems**.

Gender Inequalities

Postmodern Feminism says no Single Theory can explain things for All Women

1) **Postmodern feminists** point out that **every woman is different**. Some women are white, some black, some heterosexual, some lesbian, some working class, some middle class and so on. Women also change over the course of time as they go through different experiences.

2) Because of this, the postmodernists say, there's **no such thing** as a "**female experience**" shared by all women.

3) **Postmodern feminism**, unlike the other types listed on p.132, isn't really about **political** or **social change**. Instead, postmodernists such as **Judith Butler (1990)** try to explore the different meanings and experiences of womanhood. Butler writes about the **social construction** of **gender**, and argues that women and men can **pick and choose** the aspects of gender they want to express.

Sylvia Walby Updated the Theory of Patriarchy

Walby (1990) agreed that women's experiences were varied and complicated.

However, unlike the postmodernists, she believed that it was possible to draw together the main elements into a "**triple-systems theory**" of patriarchy. Basically, she said women are oppressed in three systems: **gender** (through patriarchy), **social class** (through capitalism) and **ethnicity** (through racism).

She then went on to explain that patriarchy had six "structures":

1) The **patriarchal mode of production** — patriarchy at home, where women are forced to do unpaid housework and childcare.

2) **Patriarchal relations** in **paid work** — which keep women out of well-paid high-status jobs, and in **low-paid, low-status** jobs.

3) **Patriarchal relations** in the **state** — which means that the **government** and **legal systems** favour **men**, not women.

4) **Male violence** against women — which includes rape, sexual assault, wife-beating and sexual harassment.

5) **Patriarchal relations** in **sexuality** — such as the **sexual double standard**, which calls a man a "**stud**" but a woman a "**slag**" for the **same behaviour**.

6) **Patriarchal relations** within **cultural institutions** — such as the way the **media** and the **education** system sometimes promote **gender stereotypes**.

Hakim said Patriarchy is "a Feminist Myth"

1) Feminism has been very influential in sociology, but not everyone accepts it. The influential British sociologist **Catherine Hakim** has been **very critical** of some feminist ideas, calling them "feminist myths".

2) She suggests that feminists have tended to make their **research findings** fit their **beliefs**. Although Hakim agrees that women have faced discrimination, she says the theory of patriarchy doesn't fit the realities. Her research suggests that women are quite strongly **in control** of their lives, and largely free to make their **own decisions**.

3) Hakim claims that some women are focused on a **career** rather than family, some are focused on **family** rather than career, and the rest **fit work around their family**. She says these preferences are what's behind patterns of **employment**.

Practice Questions

Q1 What are the aims of liberal feminism?

Q2 What is meant by "separatism"? Which type of feminists might believe in it?

Q3 Which type of feminism is least interested in social change?

Q4 Who called patriarchy "a feminist myth"?

Exam Question

| Q1 | Outline and assess feminist explanations of gender inequality in contemporary British society. | (44 marks) |

Ah, more sociological disagreement — always fun...

If you were just flicking through, and not really bothering to revise, you probably wouldn't realise that there are so many different kinds of feminism. So make sure you learn this lot properly. Remember that you can apply these ideas to any other topic that you've studied — e.g. the family, gender inequality in health, religion as patriarchal, representations of women in culture.

Ethnic Inequalities

Lots of evidence suggests that if you belong to an ethnic minority, you'll be treated unequally in society. That means you don't get the same opportunities as some other people. It's not fair, and now you're probably wondering why things should be that way. Tricky question, huh? Sounds like a job for a sociologist or two....

Functionalists think All Inequality is Necessary in society

Remember, according to Functionalism, if something **exists** in society, that means it **needs to exist** — it has a **function**.

Patterson (1967) and **Banton (1983)** have both said that society needs to have some disadvantaged ethnic groups, for these reasons:

1) They can take the jobs the dominant group **don't want** — jobs with **low pay** and **bad conditions**.

2) They can be **scapegoated** — blamed by the dominant group for social problems like **crime**.

3) Because some ethnic minorities are economically and socially disadvantaged, the **dominant group** can feel **superior**.

4) Functionalists say that ethnic minorities **eventually** absorb the dominant social values of the host culture, and get **assimilated** into society.

The New Right say Society is Meritocratic

Peter Saunders (1996) believes that most Western society is meritocratic. There is **equality of opportunity**, so individual ability is rewarded, and lack of ability means lack of rewards. In a meritocracy, your **strengths** and **weaknesses**, rather than your **ethnicity**, lead to your social position.

1) The New Right say that the underclass is disproportionately made up of **ethnic minorities**. Because they believe society is a meritocracy, they blame ethnic minority groups rather than society, or racism.

2) The New Right argue that some groups **fail to assimilate**, and some groups develop a **culture of poverty** (see Oscar Lewis on p.128).

3) Murray (1984) claims that some ethnic groups in the USA tend to form **single parent families** and **depend** on welfare benefits. Saunders claims that welfare dependency is also a problem for the underclass in the UK.

Other sociologists **disagree** with the New Right. **Anthony Giddens (1973)** says that **poor access to education** means ethnic minorities are **underskilled** and **underqualified**. They also suffer from **prejudice** and **discrimination**. These factors have led to the formation of an **ethnically biased underclass**.

Weberians see Ethnicity in terms of Labour Market Position and Status

1) Weberians agree that the **lower socioeconomic classes** include the **largest proportion** of **ethnic minority** people. Ethnic minorities are over-represented in **low-paid** jobs, and among the **unemployed**.

2) Weberians also say ethnicity is related to **status** — i.e. the prestige and respect you get from others in society. **Racism** and **discrimination** cause ethnic minorities to have **low status**.

3) The third element of class in Weber's approach is **party power**. Ethnic minorities are **under-represented** in **political parties** and **trade unions**.

4) According to this approach, ethnic minorities are **economically disadvantaged** (low socio-economic class) and **culturally disadvantaged** (low status).

Rex and Tomlinson (1979) use the term "underclass" to mean people who combine lowest social class and lowest social status. They feel this describes Britain's ethnic minorities. Following the dual labour market theory, Rex and Tomlinson state that there are **two types of job** and **two types of worker**:

Primary labour market	Secondary labour market
Secure jobs for skilled workers. Good wages, opportunities for training and promotion, good working conditions. These workers are highly valued by employers and have high status.	Less secure jobs for unskilled or semi-skilled workers. Poor wages, few opportunities for training or promotion, poor working conditions. These workers are not valued highly by employers and have low status.

Rex and Tomlinson's evidence shows that there is a **disproportionate number** of **ethnic minority** workers in the **secondary labour market**.

However, critics of Rex and Tomlinson argue that this only shows that ethnic minorities are **economically disadvantaged** on the whole. They claim it **doesn't prove** that they are part of an underclass, or even that an underclass exists.

Ethnic Inequalities

Marxism links **Ethnic Inequalities** to **Class Exploitation**

Most people in ethnic minorities are members of the working class. According to **Marxist** explanations, it's their **class**, **not their ethnicity** that is the primary issue. There are **three main approaches** to ethnicity in Marxism:

Westergaard and Resler (1976) believed in the Unitary Working Class

1) According to this model, ethnic minority workers are **no more exploited** than **white** workers.

2) Looking at this or that ethnic group is a distraction from the main issue, which is (according to Marxism) that **all** members of the working class are **exploited** equally by **capitalism**.

Stephen Castles and Godula Kosack (1973) believed in The Divided Working Class

1) Castles and Kosack say that the working class is **divided** — with **ethnic minorities unemployed**, or doing more of the **low-status, low-paid work**. They say this helps capitalism to oppress the workers.

2) According to Castles and Kosack, capitalist societies need to keep a **reserve army of labour**. Basically, this means that if there are **lots of people chasing work**, employers don't have to pay such **high wages**.

3) Castles and Kosack also suggest that ethnic minorities are used to **distract** the workers from the real cause of their problems. **Ethnic minorities** get the **blame** for problems such as unemployment and housing shortages. Instead of uniting to start a revolution, the working class **fights amongst itself**.

Annie Phizaklea and Robert Miles (1980) believed in Racialised Class Fractions

1) This model looks at the **subgroups** within the working class. For example, traditional working class **women** have **domestic responsibilities** that men don't share; **skilled manual** workers have **higher status** and **wages** than unskilled workers.

2) Phizaklea and Miles say that the working class is broken into many **fractions**, based on **three things** — **gender**, **skill level** and **ethnicity**.

Andrew Pilkington evaluated Weberian and Marxist approaches

1) **Pilkington (1993)** said that although there were differences between them, Marxist and Weberian approaches also have some major **similarities**. He points out that they **agree** on the idea that ethnic minority workers are mostly **trapped** in a life of **unskilled, low-status work**, and because of that they are **separated** from other (white) workers.

2) However, Pilkington believes that the Marxist and Weberian approaches are not supported by the **evidence**. Recent figures seem to support his claim that ethnic minorities are **not concentrated** into an "**underclass**".

3) In fact, certain minority ethnic groups have become **very successful** in the labour market — e.g. people of **African-Asian** background.

African-Asian = people of Indian origin who settled in Uganda and Kenya, and then moved to Britain in the 1970s.

It's often **hard to compare** approaches, because it's **hard to accurately measure** ethnic inequality in the first place. Different figures use **different ethnic categories**, and these categories may **not** match up with how people see themselves.

Practice Questions

Q1 Name two Functionalists who have written about ethnic inequalities.

Q2 What does the term "meritocratic" mean?

Q3 According to Giddens, which factors lead to the formation of an ethnically biased "underclass"?

Q4 Why, according to Marxists, does capitalism need a "reserve army of labour"?

Q5 What is Pilkington's main criticism of Marxist and Weberian approaches to ethnicity?

Exam Question

Q1 Outline and assess sociological explanations of ethnic inequalities in the UK. (44 marks)

Sociologists blame the usual suspects...

In other words, it's the fault of the labour market, capitalism, or the "victim". Functionalists even suggest that ethnic inequalities serve some purpose in society, although I must admit their definition of "purpose" seems to be stretching it a bit. Remember that not all ethnic minorities are poor, or trapped in low-paid work. One of the richest people in Europe is an Indian steel baron.

Research and Sociological Theory

*This section is for **AQA** and **OCR**. These first few pages about theory are just for **AQA**, though. The **OCR** stuff starts on **p.144**. The section starts with a page about "Is Sociology a science?". Before which, we have to ask, "What is science anyway?"*

Science uses Experiments and Observation to Test Theories

1) Scientists collect data through **experiments**, **observation** and **measurement** in order to **test hypotheses** (a hypothesis is an unproved theory).

2) Science values **objectivity** (an unbiased viewpoint). Scientific statements are **based on evidence** which has been collected using **systematic**, **logical methods**.

There are Different Philosophies of Science

Obviously, it couldn't all be that simple. There are **different views** about **what science is all about**.

The Logical Positivist view of science is called the hypothetico-deductive approach

1) The researcher **observes** something, and decides it needs to be **explained**.

2) The researcher thinks up a **hypothesis** to **explain** the observed phenomenon.

3) The hypothesis is **tested** by **experiments**.

4) If the experiments **agree** with the hypothesis, then the hypothesis becomes a **scientific law**. Scientific laws are **universal** — they explain all phenomena which are similar to the one which was observed in the first place.

This process is called verification, which means checking that something is true.

Rudolf Carnap (1936, 1966) and Carl Hempel (1966) are examples of logical positivist philosophers.

Popper (1959, 1963) argued that experiments should try to prove the hypothesis wrong — this is called "falsification"

1) The idea is that you can't ever **prove** a hypothesis **100% correct**, no matter how much evidence you've got — but you can prove it **wrong** with just **one** piece of evidence that **contradicts** it.

2) For example, the hypothesis "all swans are white" isn't proved correct by seeing one flock of white swans. You'd have to look at **every single swan in the universe** and see that they were all white to do that. But if you see just **one black swan**, that proves that "all swans are white" **isn't true**.

3) Popper believed that it wasn't possible to know **absolute truth**, because you can't prove things are correct.

Popper's view has been **criticised** by later philosophers of science who point out that an experimental result that disagrees with a hypothesis may be because of **experimental error** and **silly mistakes**. In Chemistry practicals, you may not get the **predicted result**, but that doesn't mean you've **proved chemistry wrong** — it usually means you've made a **mistake**.

Thomas Kuhn (1962) disagreed with both the logical positivists and Popper

1) Kuhn believed that science uses an **accepted body of knowledge** to solve puzzles. He called this "normal science". He was pretty critical of it...

2) He thought that scientists took a lot of **assumptions** about the world **for granted**. This assumed **way of looking at the world** is called a "**paradigm**". He said that what scientists do is **constrained** by the **paradigm** they take for granted. For example, for hundreds of years people thought that the sun went around the earth, and astronomical observations were interpreted according to the paradigm that the sun went around the earth.

3) Kuhn argues that **big leaps** of scientific progress come about when **evidence** which **doesn't fit the paradigm** builds up to the point where it **can't be ignored**. Then, scientists come up with a **new paradigm**. This process is called **scientific revolution**.

Paul Feyerabend (1975) went even further, and claimed that there **weren't** any **hard and fast rules** of scientific method. He argued that scientists make all kinds of **tweaks** to theories to make them work. He also disagreed with the idea that science tests hypotheses according to whether they fit observed facts, claiming that already-accepted theories **influence** the way scientists actually **observe** facts.

There's Disagreement about whether Sociology is Scientific

1) **August Comte** (lived 1798-1857) invented the word "sociology", and he thought of it as a science. He thought sociology should be used to develop a **rational theory** of **society**.

2) **Popper** (see above) said sociology **wasn't a science**, and that sociological concepts **couldn't be falsified** by experiments.

3) **Kuhn** argues that sociology **doesn't have a paradigm** — there isn't a consensus as to what it's about and how it's done. So in his view, it doesn't count as a science.

Research and Sociological Theory

Sociology is More Subjective than Traditional Science

1) **Objective knowledge** is the **same** no matter what your **point of view**. **Objective** methods provide **facts** that can be easily **verified** or **falsified**. Objective research is also **value free** (see below), and doesn't have any bias.

2) **Subjective knowledge** depends on your **point of view**. **Subjective** methods give data that **can't** be easily tested. Subjective research requires **interpretation**.

3) Sociology is **more subjective** than the physical **sciences**, but it aims to be at least partly objective.

4) Some **postmodernists** like **Lyotard (1984)** claim that it's **impossible** to be objective at all. Lyotard sees **knowledge** as something that people **construct**, not something that people **discover**.

See p.140 for social action theory and subjectivity.

Positivist Sociology tries to be as Objective as Possible

1) **Positivists** think sociology should be **scientific** and **analyse social facts**. Positivists define social facts as things that can be **directly observed and measured**, e.g. the number of followers of Christianity in Britain. Positivists claim that social facts are **external** to individuals, and constrain their behaviour.

2) Positivists look for **correlation in data**, and **cause and effect relationships**. To do this, they use **quantitative** methods like **questionnaires** (see p.150) and **official statistics**, which are **objective and reliable**.

1) **Interactionist sociologists** (also called **interpretivists**) reckon **sociology doesn't suit scientific methods**. They try to understand human behaviour from the point of view of the **individual**, so they use methods that let them discover the **meanings**, **motives** and **reasons** behind **human behaviour** and **social interaction**.

2) **Weber** (see p.163) said it's important to use **empathy** to figure out **why** an individual is doing what they're doing. He called this **"verstehen"**. Interactionists take this idea very seriously — they're big on empathy.

There's Debate over whether Research can be Value Free

1) **Value free research** is research that doesn't make **value judgements** about whether the things it researches are **good** or **bad**.

2) Value free research doesn't let the **researcher's own beliefs** get in the way. For example, questionnaires mustn't ask questions that **lead** the respondent towards a particular answer.

3) In order for this idea of **value freedom** to work, the researcher must **interpret** all data **objectively**.

4) Value freedom means that the **end use** of the research **shouldn't matter**. Research should come up with knowledge, and how that knowledge is used isn't up to the researcher.

Some sociologists say **sociology can't be value free**.

1) The decision to research in the first place is **value-laden** — someone has to decide that the research is worth spending money on. Some say that research which the **state** or **businesses** want to see is most likely to get funding.

2) It's difficult to **completely avoid bias** and interview effects (see p.153).

3) Some Marxist and feminist sociologists **deliberately choose research** with an **end use** that they **approve** of. They believe that sociology **should** make **value judgements** about society and **suggest** ways it could be **better**.

Practice Questions

Q1 What is a hypothesis?

Q2 What did Popper mean by falsification?

Q3 What is a paradigm?

Q4 Why do some sociologists say sociology can't be value free?

Exam Question

Q1 Explain why some sociologists say that the study of sociology is scientific. (10 marks)

Don't even get them started on "What is Art?"...

*If you're flagging, remember that Sociology can lead to all sorts of **good jobs**. My mum did a Sociology degree and she's worked as a researcher, writer, lecturer, civil servant, NHS board-member and charity organiser. And if those kind of jobs don't tickle your fancy then there's also things like housing and social work. If you want to be a lion-tamer though, you're in the wrong book.*

Consensus Structuralism

*Structural perspectives analyse society as a whole system made up of different parts that mesh together. Structural approaches can be either consensus or conflict based. Consensus structuralism is pretty much the same thing as **Functionalism** (which you already know and love). It stresses the harmonious nature of society, something Durkheim called "social solidarity".*

Functionalists use the "Organic Analogy" to describe the Nature of Society

1) The **organic analogy** is used by **Talcott Parsons (1951)** to show how society acts like a **living organism**. An organism has a series of **organs** that are **interconnected** and **interdependent** with each other, and Parsons says that likewise **society** is a set of parts that are all **interconnected**, and all **interdependent** with each other.

2) Functionalists describe change as **"evolutionary"**, which means that if there's a change in one part of society, other parts will **slowly evolve** to adapt to this change.

3) **Social ills** (such as excessive crime) have a **disabling** effect on certain parts of the organism (society), and they can gradually "infect" other parts.

> According to Functionalism, interrelations between the various parts of society can only happen because all members of society **agree** on **values** and **norms**. In other words, **society functions by value consensus**. These agreed values and norms are passed down from generation to generation through the process of "**socialisation**".

Functionalism says Society's Needs are met by Four Major Sub-Systems

1) **Functionalism** says all members of society have **needs** and **desires** that the **social system** must cater for. These needs can be broken down into **instrumental** needs and **expressive** needs.

2) **Instrumental needs** are **material** — e.g. the need to be fed, the need to have a home. These needs are supported by the **economic sub-system** (**industries**) and the **political sub-system** (**political parties** and **trade unions**).

3) **Expressive** needs are **emotional** — e.g. the need to **belong**. They're looked after by a **kinship sub-system** (marriage and family) and a **cultural sub-system** (which includes schools and churches).

Functionalism tries to Explain Everything

1) Functionalism, through the work of **Comte, Durkheim and Parsons**, was the first real attempt to create a theory to explain the operation of the **whole of society**. This kind of theory is called a **macro-theory** — i.e. a **large-scale theory** as opposed to a **micro-theory** or small-scale theory.

2) It's useful in showing how all the main institutions of society, such as the **education** system and the **family**, are **linked** to each other.

3) It helps to explain activities and actions that superficially seem **unusual** or strange. An example of this is Durkheim's study of suicide (1897). In this study, Durkheim argues that **social structure** and problems in the modern world cause people to commit suicide. In this case, what seems to be an **individual act** is actually part of a **wider social picture**.

There's plenty more about suicide on p.66-67. Go and read it — it's relevant to this section.

Functionalism is Criticised for Ignoring Conflict and Maintaining Inequality

1) Functionalism is criticised for its focus on **harmony** and **co-operation**. It fails to take into account the **differences** and conflicts between groups in society.

2) It tries to see a **positive purpose** in **all aspects of society** — even aspects which many people would view as harmful and negative (see p.134). Durkheim claimed that if a **social phenomenon** didn't fulfil a **function**, it wouldn't **exist**.

3) Functionalism has been seen by critics as a **conservative** approach to society that **upholds inequality** and injustice. Critics say the problems suffered by the working classes, women and ethnic minorities have not been adequately explained and justified by Functionalism.

4) Functionalism has an almost **fatalistic** approach to the nature of **inequality** in society — it's seen as inevitable. Functionalists such as Parsons talk about "**meritocracy**" which is the idea that people succeed or fail based on their own merits. This suggests that society is **already fair**, so it's pointless to make things more equal.

Functionalism says that these hairstyles have a purpose in society.

5) According to Functionalists, **conflict** in society is **minimal** because people **accept** the **inevitability** of inequality. **Conflict theorists** (see p.139) definitely disagree on this.

Conflict Structuralism

Marxism is conflict structuralism. Marxists acknowledge that society is made up of institutions that work together. However, they believe that there is a conflict of interests between two different groups in society: the bourgeoisie and the proletariat.

Marxism says *Capitalist* society has created *Two Classes* with *Different Needs*

1) According to **Marx (1867)**, the ruling class own the means of production, and the working class work for the ruling classes without owning or controlling the means of production.

2) Marx explained change in society as the result of a **conflict of interests** between the **classes**.

3) According to Marx, the ruling class own the **infrastructure** (the means of production) and sustain their control over it by utilising the **superstructure** (the **institutions** within society e.g. religion, the education system).

4) In Marxist thought, the job of the superstructure is to legitimise the position of the ruling class through **ideological messages** within the institutions of society — i.e. society's institutions are set up to stop the working class gaining power, and also to make it seem OK for the ruling class to own and control everything.

5) Marx claimed that the proletariat (working class) are lulled into a **false consciousness**, which means they aren't fully aware of the **oppression** they suffer and how to **break free** from it. Marxists argue that only through **revolution** will the proletariat see how they have been oppressed, and then a socialist/communist society will emerge.

Neo-Marxism focuses on *Ideology* rather than *Economics*

1) Neo-Marxists such as **Althusser (1969)** and **Gramsci (1971)** have redefined the focus of Marxism by looking at the role of **ideology** rather than economic factors.

2) For example, Gramsci argues that the ruling classes can only maintain power through **gaining the consent** of the working classes by manipulative use of **ideology**. Althusser talks about **ideological state apparatuses** — e.g. the education system.

Marxism is criticised for its *Structural Focus* and *Determinism*

1) Marxism is **deterministic** — it assumes that oppression is inevitable for the working class, until a revolution happens.

2) Marxism fails to see everyday life in any other terms than "**class conflict**". **Ethnicity** and **gender** are largely **sidelined**.

3) Additionally, the fall of Communism in Eastern Europe has been used as evidence for flaws in Marxist theory. However many people argue that Eastern Europe didn't have **true Communism** anyway.

4) The increased affluence and consensual nature of many Western societies highlights the **lack of conflict**.

Weber was *Critical* of *Marxism*

Weber said that there could be **conflict** between **all kinds of groups** in society. He **rejected Marx's idea** that the division between **owners** and **workers** was the **only important division**.

Weber claimed that people were divided by **class**, **status** and **political** grouping. Weberian conflict theorists such as **Dahrendorf (1959)** argue that conflict is **much more complicated** than Marx had claimed. Dahrendorf argues that conflict is based on power and authority, not economics.

Practice Questions

Q1 What are the four sub-systems in society, according to Functionalists?

Q2 What is the main difference between Neo-Marxism and traditional Marxism?

Q3 Why are Marxist methodologies likely to be similar to Functionalist ones?

Exam Questions

Q1 Assess the influence of Marxist perspectives on sociological research. (40 marks)

Q2 Compare and contrast Functionalist and Marxist theories on the nature of society. (40 marks)

I'm barely functional before my first cup of tea...

You'll probably be at least a little bit familiar with these theories from other AQA sections. It helps to have it all here, so that you can revise what you need to know for the Theory and Methods paper without getting it mixed up with other stuff. They can ask you about these theories, or about theories in general, so don't think it's something you only need to know for background.

Social Action Theory

*Social action theorists focus on the interaction between individuals and small groups, rather than on the big structures of society. Social action theory is pretty much the same thing as **Interactionism** (which you already know and love...).*

Social Action sees individuals as "Social Actors" who Act rather than React

1) Social action theorists see people as **making their own choices**, and taking their own **action**, rather than being **controlled** by **social structure** or **reacting** to social structure. They see people's actions as key to studying society.

2) It claims that society is **constructed** from people's meanings, interpretations, behaviours and negotiations.

The process of labelling is important for understanding how people interact on a daily basis. People observe the behaviour of others and classify that behaviour into various categories — e.g. responsible, or delinquent, or deviant. Social action theorists see labelling everywhere — in the family, in education, in health care, in the sociology of deviance, etc.

Social Action Theory sees Social Order as a Social Construction

1) Social action theorists argue that social order isn't something generated by **institutions**, either through consensus or conflict. Social order is **part of everyday life**, and they see everyday life as a series of **interpretations**.

2) They say social order is a social construction — a **product** of individuals' minds. They say people want to believe that there's order in society so they behave towards others in a way that **convinces** them that there **is** order. For example, they **follow social norms**, e.g. being **polite** to each other, **not stealing** from each other.

Social Action Theory rejects the idea that Sociology is Objective

1) The idea is that if you believe that people put their own meanings and labels on the world, you also have to accept that they can all put **different labels** and **meanings** on the **same action**. Every person will interpret an action (e.g. drinking alcohol regularly) slightly differently to others depending on the meaning they attach, e.g. one person might think it's a normal part of relaxing after work, and another person might think it's the first sign of alcoholism.

2) This means that sociologists **can't predict** people's behaviour as easily as structural approaches would suggest. People don't passively react to external stimulation in exactly the **same way** every single time. They act differently according to the **circumstances**, and according to their own **personal opinions**.

3) In other words, social action theory says sociology **isn't an objective science**. It's all very, very subjective.

Social Action Theory is Criticised for being so Subjective

1) Social action theory is **criticised** for its **subjective** and **relativist** nature. Critics worry that if the world is seen as subjective and based on assumptions and interpretations, then **nothing is true or false** — this would reduce sociology to a **mess of individual opinions**.

2) Structuralists argue that social action theory fails to properly address the **large scale structure** of society. They accuse social action theorists of concentrating too much on the **small scale**, and ignoring the **wider social context** that individuals act (or react) in.

3) Critics of social action theory also point out that social action theory doesn't really **explain social norms**. They're taken for granted as something we believe in, maybe because we want there to be some kind of social order.

This is a simplified version of Giddens' theory. The real thing is pretty abstract.

Structuration combines Structuralism and Social Action

1) Structuration theorists such as **Anthony Giddens (1984, 1987)** believe that there's a place for a strand of sociological theory and research that looks at both the **relationship between individuals** and their **social setting**.

2) Structuration theorists say that individuals are subject to **restrictions** and **pressures** generated by **social structures** and **social systems**, e.g. laws. But... they also argue that individuals **respond** to these in **different ways**. Individuals have an **awareness** of the social rules and structures and have **some level of choice** about how to react to them.

3) Structuration theorists say social structures are **open to change** — they can be **changed** by the actions of individuals.

Critics of structuration theory point out that institutions can **severely restrict** people's actions — not just affect them a little bit. Structuration theory assumes that if people want to change the world, they can manage it fairly easily. This is something that Marxists and feminists would disagree with.

Modernity and Postmodernity

Modernity refers to the Modern, Industrial, Ordered world

1) Modernity refers to the industrial world. It's linked to **urbanisation**.

2) It's also linked to the rise of **state bureaucracy**.

3) Modernity refers to a period of time when studies of the world were guided by **ordered**, **rational scientific** thinking. **Science** was seen as the answer, rather than the **traditional** sources of knowledge, such as religion.

4) Modernist sociological theories aim to **investigate** the world **scientifically**. They explain why societies have **evolved** to be the way they are, and explain why they're **arranged** in the way they are.

5) The Modernist theories are the **Structuralist** theories of **Marxism** and **Functionalism**. These are also called "**grand narratives**", which is a fancy way of saying "**big stories**", and "**metanarratives**", which is a fancy way of saying "stories that **make sense** of **other stories**". They're **big**, **all-encompassing stories** that explain **how** the world got to be how it is.

6) Modernist theories like Marxism claim a **monopoly of truth** — they claim that they're **objectively right** about the way the world is.

Postmodernism argues that Society has Progressed from Modernity

Postmodernists say that society today has **moved on** from the ordered industrial world of Modernity. They point to various **changes** in society:

1) **Work** has become more **flexible**, and service industries have partly taken over from manufacturing industries.

2) **Globalisation** has affected both **production** and **communication**. There's been globalisation of **consumption** and **culture**.

3) There's an emphasis on **consumption of cultural products**.

4) There's **pluralism of culture**, and **pluralism of roles**. People **interpret** society, and their own identities, in **different ways** according to the **circumstances** they're in (i.e. the same woman could have labels and roles of "mother", "wife", "friend" and "employer").

Postmodernists argue that sociology has moved into a time when "**metanarratives**" don't answer all the problems of the social world. Postmodernists say that there's a whole range of **competing theories** out there, which all have **something** to say about society. They argue that no one theory can claim a monopoly over the truth.

Postmodernism is Criticised by Structuralists and Social Action Theorists

1) Postmodernists emphasise the role of **culture** and the **media** in driving the creation of **identities**, **norms** and **values**. People no longer seek one answer to life but are happy to pick and choose values and identities.

2) This approach largely ignores the interactions between **individuals**, which **upsets social action theorists**. It also ignores the relationships between **social institutions**, which **upsets structuralists**.

3) Some sociologists **disagree** with the claim that we're living in a postmodern society. **Giddens (1990, 1991)** argues that we're actually in a state of "**high modernity**", with **high risk** of war, economic collapse or environmental disaster. He sees high modernity as like a **juggernaut** — a massive truck that's very powerful, and which could go out of control.

Practice Questions

Q1 Which is more important to social action theory — social structure or personal circumstance?

Q2 How does Structuration theory combine both structuralism and social action theory?

Q3 What is meant by the term "metanarrative"?

Exam Questions

Q1 Assess the influence of postmodernism on sociological study. (40 marks)

Q2 Evaluate the usefulness of structural and social action theories in a study of society. (40 marks)

When crossing the road, look both ways for the juggernaut of modernity...

Postmodernism is a lot easier to understand when you look at Modernism. Modernism has all these ideas about how the world should be, and how sociology should be, and postmodernism decides to do the opposite. Remember that you can be asked about the usefulness of social theories in general to explain society, and that includes all the theories on these pages and on p.138-139.

Impact of Sociological Research

Social policy focuses on social problems and how social institutions respond to them. Social policy analysts use sociological research to inform governments and other organisations, and influence their response to social problems.

Giddens *claims the study of sociology gives* Four Practical Benefits

Anthony Giddens (2001) believes that sociological research has four practical purposes:

1) An **understanding** of the world.

2) A heightened awareness of the needs of **individual groups**.

3) An assessment of **"what works"** — **evidence based policy**.

4) An increased **personal knowledge** of ourselves and others.

Note: fluffy bunnies and free lemonade are not on this list.

Sociological Research *gives* Policy Makers *insight into* Poverty *and* Inequality

1) The creation of the Welfare State after the second world war gave many the impression in the late 1960s that poverty had been largely eradicated from the UK.

2) However, **empirical evidence** from **Peter Townsend (1979)** and **Mack and Lansley (1985)** showed that poverty was a hidden problem. Later research by the Child Poverty Action Group reported that some groups experienced poverty more than others.

3) Sociologists then did more research to come up with theories of **why** certain groups were more vulnerable to poverty. **Social Democrats** blamed an **inadequate** welfare system, the **New Right** (e.g. **Marsland (1989)**) blamed **reliance** on an over-generous welfare system, and **Third Way** thinkers emphasised **citizenship** (two-way responsibility between the citizen and the state). See p.110-111 and 128-129.

4) These theories, plus **empirical data**, guided **social policy** about welfare, poverty and inequality.

Empirical evidence means data that's from observation and experience.

This link between sociology and social policy was particularly close in the case of **Frank Field (1989, 1996)**, who wrote about the underclass as a group denied citizenship rights, and suggested **social policy changes** to improve the living standards of the elderly and unemployed, and to get the unemployed back into work. Between 1997 and 1998, as a **Minister** in the Labour government, he actually **was** a **social policy maker**.

Some believe Sociology *should help* Improve Society

Will Hutton (1995) argues that New Right theories have influenced social policy too much. He argues for a **Third Way** based on sociological research, and believes that social institutions should be made stronger, to provide better services.

Philanthropist **George Soros** believes in working towards **open society** — a society with the rule of law, democracy, and respect for minorities. He's influenced by **Karl Popper (1945)**, who first came up with the idea of open society.

Weber *believed* Sociology *shouldn't tell decision-makers* How To Fix Society

1) Weber believed that sociology **shouldn't make value judgements** — it shouldn't tell policy makers **how to fix society**.

2) Weber argued that sociological research can tell decision makers whether a particular policy is likely to have the **desired result**, and what **social costs** the policy will incur. Weber thought that the policy maker should come up with the **policy first**, and **then** the researchers should go away and find evidence to work out the best way of doing it.

3) Weber thought it was important to have **good methodology** to give the most **useful information** to policy makers.

4) Critics of this view say policy should come **after evidence gathering**, not before. There's a danger that only evidence which **backs up** the policy will be found. Evidence which might suggest a **much better policy** might be missed.

Postmodernists *have* Diverse Views *on the link between research and policy*

1) Postmodernist **Zygmunt Bauman (1990)** believes that sociology **should** inform social research, and worries that society may **get worse** if sociological theories about **poverty** and **welfare** aren't listened to. He argues that **postmodern consumer society** is **marginalising** the Welfare State, and believes this to be a bad thing.

2) On the other hand, Lyotard is worried that **"scientific"** methods of sociological research could be used to construct **oppressive metanarratives**. **Lyotard** sees **modernist metanarratives** (see p.141) as leading to **strict doctrine** and **oppression**. (Go back and read about metanarratives on p.141 if you're getting confused...).

Impact of Sociological Research

Marxists think sociology is Too Close to the Capitalist System

1) Marxists believe that sociology is too closely intertwined with the **capitalist system** to make a difference to society. Since Marxists believe that capitalism is inherently flawed and oppressive, they suggest that sociological study is a **tool** used to **justify unjust social policy**.

2) Marxists believe that research is **controlled** by **ruling class interests**, which prevents it from being used to change the system to socialism. They point to the amount of **funding** for sociological research which comes from the **state** and from **industry** — they claim sociology is being **bought**.

3) An example would be the use of empirical data to show that the poorest in society are over-represented in prison. Marxist commentators argue that sociology is being used here to **justify social policy** designed to **further oppress** and **marginalise** the working classes by focusing on crimes committed by the poor rather than looking at the underlying reasons for crime (i.e. the nature of capitalism, according to Marxist theory).

Some Feminists believe Sociology Can't affect Gender Inequality

Feminists are in **disagreement** over whether or not sociological research can actually improve the lives of women in a patriarchal society.

1) **Liberal feminists** believe that sociological research and analysis has influenced governments and had **beneficial results** for women's lives. For example, the UK has developed social policy designed to improve the status of women and make them equal in all spheres of social life including employment and benefits.

2) However, **radical feminists** argue that liberal feminist sociology can't **make much difference** to the lives of women because society is **inherently patriarchal**. Radical feminists such as **Shulamith Firestone (1971)** believe that patriarchal society must be dismantled before women's lives can ever be improved.

3) Socialist feminists claim that social policy oppresses women in particular. They argue it **undervalues women's labour** (e.g. in the voluntary and informal welfare sectors) and assumes they will bear a double burden of work and housework. Socialist feminists propose changes to social policy based on their own research and ideology.

"I 'ad that Tony Giddens round the other day to sort out me social policy. 'E were bloomin' useless."

Some believe the Link between Sociology and Social Policy isn't all that strong

Governments take account of research, but they're **constrained** by **other factors**.

1) Firstly, governments often seek to implement social policy that's **popular** with the **electorate**. It's argued that policies which aren't clear vote winners don't get implemented.

2) Some groups in society may be marginalised because they **don't vote** in **large numbers**. Even if sociology focuses on these groups, they may still find themselves neglected if they don't have electoral power.

3) Governments must consider the **financial implications** of any policies they introduce. If a policy is **too expensive**, then no matter how persuasive the sociological research behind it is, it **isn't going to happen**. Also, **expensive policies** tend to make **voters worry** that **taxes** might have to **increase** to pay for them.

Practice Questions

Q1 What four practical benefits does Sociology have for society, according to Giddens?

Q2 What role did Weber think Sociology should have in relation to social policy?

Q3 How do Marxists criticise the link between Sociology and social policy?

Q4 What other factors affect government decisions on social policy, other than Sociology?

Exam Question

Q1 "Sociology has no effect on social policy". How far do you agree or disagree with this statement? (40 marks)

Sociology, eh — what's it all for...?

In an exam, remember that all arguments in this topic are broken into three camps: 1) sociology should actively try and influence policy, 2) sociology should try to change and replace the system, and 3) sociology shouldn't influence social policy. Some people criticise sociologists such as Giddens for overplaying the ability of sociology to influence government decisions and actions.

Choosing a Topic and Generating Questions

The first step in sociological research is figuring out what you're going to research. The second step is condensing your topic down into a single question, or a single hypothesis. These pages are for OCR.

Sociologists pick a Topic based on their own Preference and Knowledge

Well, obviously. But there's slightly more to it than the obvious, so here you go.

1) Sociologists often **specialise** in different fields of the subject and therefore will often choose a topic that they have experience or knowledge of — for example, **Steve Bruce** specialises in **religion**.

2) Sociologists try to pick a topic that they think they'll find **enjoyable** and **interesting** to research. It's best not to try a piece of research that you won't enjoy — it only leads to a poorly constructed report that may be either flawed or just plain boring.

3) Also, certain topics become popular in sociology at different times. For example, research in the **mid twentieth century** focused on **stratification** and the **class system**. **Nowadays**, the focus of sociologists has moved on to other topics such as **World Sociology** and **Medical Sociology**. To gain **prestige**, **funding** and public or academic **interest**, sociologists are more likely to focus their research on topics that are currently **in vogue**.

4) Sociologists and other academics who want to make a **change** in society prefer research that could help develop **solutions** to **social problems**.

5) Sociologists may feel that a particular issue is **neglected** by other researchers, so they'll research the issue to try and "**plug the gap**" — and encourage others to embrace the issue as well.

Funding and Cooperation for Research have an impact on the choice of Topic

1) There are a wide range of potential **sources of funding**. Some research is funded by **charities**, e.g. the Joseph Rowntree Foundation. Some is funded by **industry**. Some are funded by the **government**. A lot of quantitative studies are done **directly** by **government agencies**.

2) The organisation which funds the research often likes to have some say in the **choice of topic**, or the **way** that the topic is **researched**. Government agencies often do research into areas covered by current or proposed **government policy**. **Industrial** grant providers tend to fund research that gives their industry some **practical benefit**.

3) Additionally, a researcher needs to decide whether or not they will be able to get the **cooperation** of the groups they'll be studying if they choose a particular topic. If potential subjects refuse to give their help for the research, then the topic may not be viable.

The researcher's Career in Sociology is another factor in selecting a topic

1) Sociologists have their eye on their **careers**, just like everyone else. Researchers would jump at the chance to conduct a study that improves their **employability**. Interesting, original or popular topics that are well researched, with good clear results, improve an academic's chance of having their work **published**. Getting work published, particularly in one of the **big sociological journals**, really **improves a researcher's standing** in academia.

2) A quick way for a sociologist to progress in their career is to respond to another sociologist's work. The aim can be either to **prove** the other sociologist **wrong**, or to **add something** to their research. Practically speaking, this could mean investigating the same topic, but using slightly different methods, or investigating a different group of people.

3) This can mean that particular social groups are researched a lot. For example, **routine office workers** are frequently researched in order to test out **theories of stratification** — some systems classify them as working class and some as middle class. Each sociologist who wants to **disprove** or **add to** earlier research on classification has to research **yet another** bunch of routine office workers. Beekeepers **never** get this level of interest from sociologists.

Reviewing The Field is crucial to a good research topic

1) **Reviewing** and **critiquing** existing **data** and **literature** is an important feature in any sociological report. It requires the researcher to spend time reading **articles**, **publications** and other sources of information already produced on the subject.

2) The researcher then needs to **analyse** this material to help clarify the issues around the subject.

3) Reviewing the field gives the researcher useful information on the types of **methodology** used in **previous studies**. They can see whether specific methods, e.g. structured interviews, worked in the past. They can see if research samples were big enough, and form ideas about how big their own sample should be.

See p.146-153 for more on methodology.

Choosing a Topic and Generating Questions

Research Questions give Focus to sociological research

1) Once the researcher has chosen a broad topic area, they need to **narrow down** the focus of their research so they don't spread their work out too thinly and end up with not enough detail.
They do this by coming up with a **single research question** that their research aims to **answer**.

2) A good research question should focus on **one part** of the topic, and it should be **clear** and **easy** to **research**.

3) Questions should be as **value free** as possible. In other words they shouldn't be **biased**, or **suggest potential social changes**. So, "Should governments provide vocational education to 14 year olds?" isn't a good research question because it asks for a **value judgement** on social policy. "What are the attitudes of employers, parents and teachers towards vocational education for 14 year olds?" is **better**.

Hypotheses are Statements that make Predictions that can be Tested

1) A hypothesis is a **statement** that makes a **prediction**. A hypothesis acts as a **starting point** for research. The research will aim to either **show that the hypothesis is true**, or **show that it's false**. Having an idea and then testing against the evidence is known as the "hypothetico-deductive model" of research. Having a hypothesis and trying to prove it wrong is called the falsification model (see p.136).

2) A hypothesis states a **relationship** between **two factors** — e.g. "sociology teachers wear corduroy trousers" or "material deprivation causes educational underachievement".

Terms like "democracy" need to be Operationalised — i.e. Made Measurable

1) Sociology prides itself on giving names to **concepts** and **ideas** that aren't **easily explained** or measured. For example, it's **tricky** to measure terms like "democracy", "development" and "culture".

2) You end up measuring these concepts by measuring **something else** that's **linked** to the tricky concept — sociologists call this an **indicator**. This is called "**operationalising**" a concept. It means making it operational, or workable, by finding a way to measure it.

3) Researchers do this **every time** they conduct a piece of research, because you **can't research** something if you **can't measure** it. Each difficult concept needs an **indicator**, e.g. electoral participation or diversity of electoral results for democracy.

4) There's a **series of steps** that a researcher needs to go through in order to **operationalise** a concept properly:

Operationalising a concept	Example — "democracy"
1) Clearly **define** the concept.	**Rule by the people**
2) Define its **dimensions** — i.e. say what **other ideas** it's **made up of**.	**Voting, freedom of speech**
3) Define **potential indicators** to test the various **dimensions** of the concept.	**Electoral turnout, voting patterns**
4) Select the **most useful** indicators.	**Voting patterns**
5) Create **data collection techniques** for each indicator.	Compare successive **general election results**

5) Researchers need to be able to **justify** how they **operationalised** their concepts in their final report. This is often a **subjective** process and the way a researcher operationalises may be **criticised** by other sociologists.

Practice Questions

Q1 Give three factors to consider when choosing a topic for research.

Q2 Why is reviewing the field useful?

Q3 What is the "operationalisation of concepts"?

Exam Question

Q1 Examine the various factors to be considered when choosing a research topic. (14 marks)

Hey, you know, this is to do with your coursework...

This isn't only for your theory and methods exam paper. It's for your OCR coursework as well, because the content that you're marked on is exactly the same for both. Everything on these pages relates to YOU, and YOUR coursework. So make sure that you pick a decent topic that you'll enjoy, and that you come up with a clear, objective research question or hypothesis.

Choosing a Method and Designing Research

*This page is a spot of revision of AS material for **AQA** and **OCR**. There is some new stuff here, so don't skip over it.*

Remember the **Difference** between **Reliability** and **Validity**

1) Reliable research can be **repeated** to get the **same results**. Reliable data means data that **another researcher** would be able to get by using the **exact same methods**.

2) **Sociological research** isn't as reliable as research in the **natural sciences** (physics, biology, chemistry, etc).

1) Valid data is a **true picture** of what the researcher is trying to measure.

2) Even **reliable** data isn't always valid. For example, you could measure democracy by measuring voter turnout. This wouldn't always give a true picture, because it's possible to have **high voter turnout**, but **completely fixed elections** (e.g. under a dictatorship).

Research can be **Primary** or **Secondary** and **Quantitative** or **Qualitative**

Primary Data	Secondary Data
Information gathered by the **researcher themselves** — it's new, **original** and not taken from any existing data set.	Information gathered from **existing data sets** or **documents** — e.g. official statistics, diaries etc.
Primary data is as **valid** and **reliable** as the researcher's method makes it.	The researcher has to **trust** that the data is **valid** and **reliable** — this is easier if the researcher can find out the **original methodology**.
Collecting primary data can be **time consuming** and **expensive**.	Secondary data can **save** the researcher **time and money**.

Quantitative methods	Qualitative methods
These produce **numbers** and **statistics**.	These produce **stories**, and include people's **motivations**, and the **meanings** they give to what they do and think.
Can be **very reliable** — studies are easily repeated.	Qualitative methods **aren't reliable**.
May not be valid. Doesn't include anything subjective.	Can be **very valid**.
They allow the use of **large samples** (see p.147) so they can be **highly representative** of the population.	They're **time consuming**, so they only use **small samples**. This means they're **less representative** than quantitative methods.

Theoretical considerations **Influence** choice of **Method**

1) **Structural** theories like **Functionalism** and **Marxism** favour **quantitative** methods.

2) **Functionalists** argue that the social world acts similarly to the **natural world** and therefore all study should be similar to that of "natural science" — i.e. using **objective** and **quantitative techniques**.

3) **Marxists** explain the nature of society in **economic** terms which also tend towards "scientific" techniques of data collection — i.e. quantitative methods.

4) **Social action** theories favour **qualitative** methods, because social action theory is **subjective**.

5) For a social action approach, methods of data collection are more **small-scale** and **in-depth**. In order to analyse **why** people make the assumptions they make and act in the way they do, researchers **observe** and **question** them **at length**.

6) Social action theorists prefer techniques that give detailed **stories** and **meanings** — e.g. ethnographic studies, unstructured interviews (see p.151) and observation (see p.152).

7) **Feminists** sometimes take a **falsificationist** approach. Feminist researchers may choose to look for evidence that proves a hypothesis **wrong**— e.g. evidence that gender roles **aren't** shaped by biological sex differences.

Practical considerations **Influence** choice of **Method**

1) Some methods take a lot of **time** — **qualitative** methods tend to **take longer** than quantitative methods. Participant observation takes a very long time both to plan and to complete. Quantitative methods can take a long time — social surveys take a relatively short time to **complete**, but a **long time** to **interpret**.

2) **Funding** affects choice of method. The **researcher's time** costs money, **resources** such as computers cost money, and it costs money to send out **postal questionnaires** to large samples.

3) **Lack of access** to primary sources would mean that the researcher has to use **secondary** sources.

Choosing a Method and Designing Research

> Population means the bunch of people you're surveying, not all 60 million people in the UK.

Before you can Start — you Need a Sample

1) It's **too expensive** and **time consuming** for sociologists to involve the **whole population** in their research. They select a **sample**.

2) When they select the sample they usually try to make it **represent the population** — with similar proportions of people in terms of age, class, ethnicity and gender to the proportions in the general population.

3) With a **representative** sample, the researcher can make **generalisations**. They can make statements about the **whole population** based on what they've found out about by researching the **sample**.

Probability Sampling involves Random Selection

Probability sampling involves picking names out of a "sampling frame" at **random**. A sampling frame is a **complete list** of the population being sampled, which needs to be **accurate**, **complete** and without any **duplicate** entries — easier said than done. **Random**, **systematic** and **stratified random** are all kinds of probability sampling.

1) In simple **random sampling**, names are taken completely at random, e.g. randomly selected from a list by a person or a computer, so each member of the population has an **equal chance** of being selected.

2) **Systematic** sampling involves choosing a **starting point** in the sampling frame and selecting every nth value, e.g. every fifth name. There may be bias, if there's an underlying pattern in the sampling frame.

3) In **stratified random sampling** the population is put into **segments** called "strata" based on things like age, gender or income — for example age 18-24, age 25-34, age 35-44, age 55-64, age 65+. Names are selected at random from within each segment.

Non-Probability Sampling involves Human Choice

Quota, multi-stage and non-representative are different types of non-probability sampling.

1) In **quota sampling**, the selection is made by the **interviewer**, who'll have a quota to meet — e.g. "interview 20 women between 25 and 34". It's a bit like stratified random sampling, but it's not random — interviewers tend to pick people who look "nice", which introduces bias. It's quick and useful, though.

2) **Multi-stage sampling** means selecting a sample from **within another sample**. It's often used to select samples for opinion polls to measure voting intention. First, a selection of constituencies are selected to represent the whole country, then postcodes within that constituency are selected, then houses from those postcodes.

3) **Snowball sampling** means finding **initial contacts** and getting them to **give you more names** for your research.

4) Sociologists sometimes **deliberately** pick a sample who **aren't representative**, in order to try to **falsify** a hypothesis about social behaviour. For example, feminist sociologists trying to disprove the idea that gender roles are determined by biological difference deliberately looked for samples where women's roles **weren't different from mens' roles**, or weren't traditionally "feminine".

A Pilot Study is a Small-Scale Practice Run before the Real Research

1) A pilot study lets you **test** the **accuracy** of your **questions**, or **check** to see if there are any **technical problems** in your research design. Researchers do this to make the study **more valid** or **more reliable**.

2) You can also **test how long** the research will take and **train** your **interviewers**.

3) Pilot studies are **time consuming** and **expensive** and they create a **lot of work**. However, by showing that the project is feasible, they can help secure **research funding**.

Practice Questions

Q1 What does it mean to say that a study is: a) reliable, b) valid?
Q2 What is a sampling frame?
Q3 What is meant by each of the following — "systematic sampling", "quota sampling" and "snowball sampling"?

Exam Question

Q1 Identify and explain two methods of sampling that you could use for a postal questionnaire. (8 marks)

What about the free sample...?

Sampling is a very important part of research design. It's one of the things that rival sociologists will really pick on if they think you've got it wrong. Remember that it's important to have a representative sample if you want to generalise from your results at all. The more random your sample, the easier it is to repeat your survey — good news for reliability.

SECTION ELEVEN — SOCIOLOGICAL RESEARCH METHODS AND THEORY

Ethics and Safety in Research

Ethics are appropriate behaviours and procedures that sociologists must adhere to when conducting research. The British Sociological Association have published guidelines to help researchers to conduct ethical research.

Ethical Considerations can be grouped into Four Main Areas

1) **Consent** — all participants must have openly agreed to take part.
2) **Confidentiality** — the details of all participants and their actions must remain confidential and private.
3) **Avoidance** of **harm** — participants should not be physically or psychologically harmed by the research process.
4) **Avoidance** of **deception** — researchers should be open and honest about the study and its implications.

Participants should give Free, Informed Consent to their role in the study

1) The researcher should get participants' **consent** before they conduct their study. Sociologists should be **open** and **honest** about the work they wish to carry out. It's important that the respondent knows what they're signing up for.

2) **Children** or people with **learning difficulties** may **not fully understand** what participation would entail. This is problematic. It can be argued that **uninformed consent** isn't really consent at all.

3) Consent can be **difficult to obtain**, especially from **secretive** groups (e.g. Scientologists, the Freemasons, gangs) or when the research is about a **sensitive** topic (e.g. crime, sexuality).

But... studies can be **endangered** if the person studied is aware of the **real purpose** of the work.

Milgram (1974) was not honest with participants in his experiments on obedience

Background:	Milgram conducted a series of experiments in which volunteers were ordered to administer electric shocks to another person on the other side of a glass screen, when that person failed to give the correct answers in a memory test.
Deception:	• Milgram lied about the purpose of the experiment. He told the volunteers that they were doing an experiment about **memory**. *Many volunteers kept on giving punishment shocks until the actor pretended to pass out.*
	• The electric shocks **weren't real**. The person who the volunteers were "shocking" was an actor, pretending.
Results:	The results of the experiment were **very useful**. The experiment showed how people are ready to **obey** authority without **question**. This helped people understand how **ordinary people** take part in war crimes and genocide.

The experiment **wouldn't have worked** if the volunteers **knew** the real purpose of the experiment. If they knew that their **obedience** was being tested, they might have deliberately been less obedient. If they knew the shocks weren't real, they wouldn't have behaved in the same way. Milgram **had to be dishonest** for the experiment to work at all.

The general opinion is that this experiment **wouldn't be allowed to go ahead today** — partly because of the **deception**, but mostly because of the risk of **psychological harm**. Some participants were disturbed at how **easily** Milgram had **manipulated** them. However, Milgram **debriefed** all the participants afterwards so they all **understood** the study, and did **follow-up work** to check that they weren't psychologically harmed. He found that some participants saw it as a **valuable learning experience**.

Covert Studies are Criticised for not getting Informed Consent

1) Covert methods (e.g. **covert participant observation**, see p.152) **don't tell** the group being studied that they actually are being studied. They're often criticised for their **lack of honesty** and the absence of **true informed consent**.

2) Covert participant observers argue that to **negotiate access** into **sensitive** or **dangerous** groups such as criminals, the researcher often has to either **pretend to be part of the group**, or not inform the group of the **true purpose** of the study.

	### Laud Humphreys' "Tearoom Trade" (1970) was a covert observation of secretive homosexual activity
The group:	The group Humphreys wished to study were men who engaged in homosexual activities in **public places** (especially public toilets). They were **secretive** about their activities for three main reasons — homosexuality was **taboo** in mainstream society, sexual activity in public is **against the law**, and some of the men may have been married men leading a "**secret life**".
Covert study:	Humphreys probably wouldn't have gained access to this group if he'd openly and honestly informed them about the nature of the research and then sought their permission. Even if he did gain their permission, it's likely that they'd have **acted very differently** if they were aware that they were being observed. Humphreys therefore posed as someone who watches homosexual acts for a sexual thrill. This enabled him to gain the **trust** of the group and for him to observe **genuine actions**.

Not that sort of tearoom...

Other sociologists argue that work like Humphreys' shouldn't be conducted, even if they give valuable insights to Sociology.

Ethics and Safety in Research

Respondents have Rights to Privacy and Anonymity

1) All respondents taking part in a piece of research must have their **basic right to privacy** valued and **upheld**. The **data** gathered from them and their **personal details** must not be distributed to anyone **outside** the **research process**.

2) When the report is finally produced, respondents must be made **anonymous**. Any descriptions of people, geographical locations and institutions have to be written in a way that prevents readers from easily recognising the participants. **False names** may be used — in which case the researcher should **clearly state** that false names have been used, in case someone who **shares** the name is **mistakenly identified** as having taken part in the research.

3) Of course, if a researcher **breaches** trust and confidentiality, potential participants will be **put off** taking part in future studies. Research participants must feel they can **trust** the researcher, especially if the research is of a sensitive nature — e.g. a self reported crime study, or a sexual health survey.

Researchers must make sure that Nobody is Harmed by Taking Part in a study

1) Emotional and physical harm is **never acceptable** in sociological research and work is actively criticised and rejected if it has allowed harm to come to those involved.

2) For example a study into street prostitution could potentially be carried out through observation. It could be argued that the researcher is putting the prostitute into a **dangerous situation** just to gain useful data.

3) Researchers studying topics such as **mental health** or **geriatric care** may stumble across **situations** and **experiences** that cause individuals **harm** — e.g. inappropriate living conditions, or abuse by carers. There is an ethical question as to whether they should **stop** or **suspend** the research in order to **remove** the individual from the dangerous situation.

4) Some topics that are discussed may be **traumatic** for the respondents — they would need to be **informed** of the possible temporary mental and emotional harm before starting the study. Remember, it's important to make sure that all consent is **informed consent** (i.e. that the person fully understands all the implications and aspects of the research before they agree to take part.)

Some Sociologists can justify Bending or Breaking ethical rules

There's a lot of **good** that can come from sociological research. Many sociologists can **justify** breaking or slightly bending some of the **ethical rules** — if the data that they'll gather has a beneficial contribution to make to society. This justification becomes even stronger if potential ethical problems are minimised — e.g. if there's **minimal harm** and **full confidentiality**, but just a **wee bit of deception** (the basis of covert participant observation).

1) For example, **Nigel Fielding (1981)**, in a study of the **National Front** (an extreme right wing political party with a secretive hierarchy) argues that he needed to conduct covert research otherwise he wouldn't have been able to gain access to the group and gather information.

2) **"James Patrick" (1973)** was a false name given to a researcher conducting a study on **violent gangs** in Glasgow — to ensure his **own safety** and protection.

3) **Roy Wallis (1977)** wasn't entirely **honest** when researching Scientology. He didn't say he was a sociologist when he signed up to a Scientology course. If he had been honest, the Scientologists may have told him to go away. Wallis was also forced to **name** some of his sources, during a **legal battle** between the Church of Scientology and another researcher. This broke the rule on **privacy** and **anonymity**, but in this case Wallis had **no choice**.

Practice Questions

Q1 What are the four main ethical considerations a sociologist needs to assess in their study?

Q2 Why is covert participant observation seen as unethical?

Q3 Give two examples of reasons that sociologists give to justify breaking ethical rules.

Exam Question

Q1 Assess the importance of ethics when conducting sociological research. (40 marks)

Danger, sociologists at work...

Well, obviously you wouldn't decide to do a covert observation into how people react to being hit over the head. Because that would be wrong. The key point here is that sometimes there are justifications, but only when the research provides such useful information that it's worth bending the rules a bit. To be perfectly honest, this isn't likely to be the case with your coursework.

Quantitative and Qualitative Methods

*Although most of these methods were covered in the AS syllabus, they're on the A2 syllabus as well. These pages are for both **AQA** and **OCR**.*

> See the glossary for a recap on the difference between quantitative and qualitative data.

Questionnaires *mainly provide* Quantitative Data

1) When planning a questionnaire, the researcher must first operationalise their concepts (see p.145). Once they've come up with a bunch of indicators, they can plan questions which accurately test for those indicators.

2) **Closed questions** and standardised **multiple choice answers** give **quantitative** data.

3) You can do a questionnaire with **open ended questions** but it's harder to quantify the data into nice neat numbers. It's not impossible though — you have to classify the answers into **categories**. This is called coding (see p.154).

4) Questionnaires should use **clear**, **simple questions** which are **easy to understand**.

5) They should give **clear instructions** and have a clear layout.

6) **Multiple choice** questions must give an appropriate number of responses. The researcher doesn't want too many respondents to answer "none of the above" or "other".

Questionnaires have several advantages

1) Questionnaires are **easy to administer**, and they can collect a **lot of data** in a **short time**. Closed questions provide quantitative data which can be **quickly** analysed too.

2) Questionnaires are **reliable**.

3) Questionnaires are **anonymous** and don't require the respondent to sit **face to face with an interviewer**. This makes them suitable for **sensitive topics**. For example, the National Survey of Sexual Attitudes and Lifestyles was a **postal questionnaire** rather than a face to face structured interview.

4) A **large sample** can be given a questionnaire, so they produce **representative data** that can be used to make generalisations.

Questionnaires have limitations — they aren't very valid

1) Respondents **may not tell the truth**. They may lie, or they may be mistaken.

2) Questions may be **misleading** or **mean different things** to **different people**. This means they may not accurately measure what you **want to measure**.

3) Respondents can't give any **extra information**, even if it would be really helpful to the researcher.

4) Because the respondent fills in the questionnaire on their own, there's no one there to **explain** the questions if the respondent doesn't understand them.

5) Postal questionnaires have a **low response rate**. If it's **too low** it won't be a **representative** sample.

Pilot studies (see p. 147) are useful for questionnaires. Researchers can test if the questions make sense to the respondents.

Structured Interviews *are* Questionnaires *given* Face to Face

1) Structured interviews are questionnaires given to individuals or groups, face to face.

2) The main plus point over a postal questionnaire is that the interviewer can **explain** and **clarify** the questions.

3) Also, most structured interviews get a much **higher response rate** than questionnaires. People tend to agree to be interviewed — unless the research topic is sensitive or taboo.

4) However, they're **more expensive** than questionnaires — you need to **pay for the interviewer**.

5) In a structured interview, the interviewer has to **follow the list of questions** so they **can't ask for more detail** if the respondent says something **particularly interesting**.

Social Surveys *use* Questionnaires *and* Interviews

1) **Social surveys** collect information about a **large population**, using **questionnaires** or **structured interviews**.

2) There are three main types — **factual**, **attitude** and **explanatory**. Some surveys are a mixture of more than one type.

Type of survey	What it's for	Who conducts it
Factual	Collects descriptive **information**	**Government agencies** and sociologists
Attitude	Collects **opinions**	**Opinion poll organisations** and sociologists
Explanatory	Looks for **reasons** and tests out hypotheses	Sociologists

Unstructured Interviews give Qualitative Data

1) **Unstructured interviews** are **informal**, without a **rigid structure**. They use **open ended questions** and give **qualitati**_data, so they're quite **valid**. Interviews are **flexible** — they can be used to find out facts or attitudes.

2) In a **fully unstructured** interview, the conversation just develops **naturally**. Interviews can be **slightly structured** and slightly **unstructured** — i.e. the interviewer has to follow the questions in a set order, but they can let the respondent **elaborate** on any interesting points, and they can **ask** the respondent for **more information.**

3) Interviews can be done with **individuals** or small **groups**. Group interviews let the researcher observe **interaction**.

4) Because they're used with **smaller samples than questionnaires**, they're **not as representative**.
However, they're **more representative** than **participant observation**.

5) Unstructured interviews are good for researching **sensitive issues** where the interviewer has to gain the respondent's **trust** — for example sexuality, domestic violence, crime.

6) The interviewer needs to have **skill** so they can **probe** to **find out more detail** about the interviewee's **beliefs** and **opinions**.

See p.153 for more about interviewer effects.

7) There are a lot of **interviewer effects** in an unstructured interview. The interviewee may say what they **think** the **researcher wants to hear.**

8) It takes a **long time** to write up an **unstructured interview**. You have to write down a **whole conversation**, not just the **codes** for **multiple choice answers** (see p.154). It's possible to do some **limited coding** of responses — the researcher could code for a particular category of opinion expressed, for example the respondent saying "I'm worried about crime".

1) Interviewers usually use a **non-directive** style — they keep their own opinions to themselves, and they don't show any approval or disapproval of what the respondent says.

2) However, some sociologists choose to be more **aggressive** and **argumentative** in their questioning — more like a journalist. **Becker (1970)** took this approach when interviewing teachers, and claimed he'd got more useful information out of them than if he'd used the traditional non-confrontational approach.

3) **Ann Oakley (1981)** included unstructured interviews in her description of a "**feminist methodology**", and contrasted them with structured interviews, which she saw as masculine. She liked the respondent to get **involved** in the research process, and sought to get more from them by becoming **close** to them.

Pilot studies allow the researcher to find out what kind of question gets a **substantial response**. They let the researcher find out whether they need to **warm up** with a gentle **chat** to gain **rapport** with the respondent before asking more meaty questions.

Longitudinal Surveys are done over a Long Period of Time

Longitudinal studies are done at **regular intervals** over a **long period of time**, with the same people. They're often **large scale quantitative** surveys. Some are more **qualitative** — e.g. the TV programme *Seven Up*.

1) You can **analyse changes** and **make comparisons** over time.

2) You can study how the **attitudes** of the sample **change** with time.

3) It's **hard** to recruit a **committed sample** who'll want to **stay** with the study.

4) You need **long-term funding** and you need to **keep the research team together**, which may be problematic.

Seven Up was a TV documentary that asked 14 kids aged 7 what they thought about life, and what they wanted to be when they grew up. The programme makers came back to interview them every seven years.

Practice Questions

Q1   Give two advantages and two disadvantages of questionnaires.

Q2   Give two advantages of unstructured interviews compared to questionnaires.

Q3   What is a longitudinal survey?

Exam Question

Q1   Examine the advantages and disadvantages of interviews as a method of data collection.   (22 marks)

Top tip: never subcontract your interviews to Trappist monks...

It's worth giving these methods a good going over, even if you think you remember them from the AS course. There's a little bit more detail here, and you're supposed to take a more critical approach at A2 level. That means you don't just learn what each method is, you have to be aware of pros and cons, and how to figure out if it might be appropriate for a particular topic.

e and Qualitative Methods

eople, or they can observe them — with or without the subjects knowing
osite approach and just read about people through secondary data.

Quantitative Data

ne in a **controlled environment**. They analyse one variable in terms of another (see p.136).
ed by psychologists. Experiments can be very reliable and give quantitative data, but on the
not be valid because it's hard to reproduce real social situations in a lab.

2) **Fi...** are a response to the criticisms of lab experiments. They take place outside of the lab in **real social settings** ... involved are often **unaware**, which poses **ethical problems**. This method is used by **interactionist** sociologists. ey're highly valid, but much less controllable and reliable than lab experiments.

Observation provides Qualitative data about Behaviour in Real-Life Settings

1) In **covert observation**, the researcher **doesn't tell the group** they're being observed. The BSA advise that you should only use covert observation when there's **no other way** of obtaining the data.

2) **Overt observation** (direct observation) is when the group is aware of the research and they know who the researcher is.

3) **Participant observation** is when the researcher **actively involves themselves in the group**.

> 1) Participant observation gets the researcher **right to where the action is** — so they can **check out the dynamics of a group** from **close up**. The researcher gets **first hand insight** of people in **natural real life settings**.
>
> 2) **Participant observation** allows you to research the workings of deviant groups (see **Humphreys**, p.148).
>
> 3) The researcher may get too involved and find it **hard to objectively observe** the group. **Whyte (1955)** became so involved with the gang members he studied that he started to see himself as **one of them** — even though his research was **overt**. The researcher in a **covert observation** may be pressurised to join in with illegal acts if they're in a **deviant** group.
>
> 4) Participant research is extremely **flexible**. The researcher can change their ideas based on what they see.
>
> 5) Participant research **lacks reliability** — it can't be repeated. A covert observer may find it difficult to **record** the study accurately, and without imposing their own subjective values on it. However, interactionists say observation can be used to assist more objective methods. **Becker (1970)** used observation to collect information that he used to formulate a **hypothesis**, which could then be checked out in further research.
>
> 6) There are **ethical** and **practical** problems in **getting in**, **staying in** and **getting out** of the group.
>
> 7) The research usually includes a **small group** so it's not **representative** of the population. **Goffman (1968)** studied just **one** mental asylum.
>
> 8) It's **hard work, time-consuming** and **expensive**.

Overt researchers may have a "sponsor" who gets them into the group. Covert researchers must pretend to be just like the group members.

4) **Non-participant observation** is when the researcher **observes** the group but isn't actively a part of the group.

5) **Ethnography** is where the researcher studies the way of life of a group. It can include observation, interviews, and diary keeping. **Case studies** are detailed investigations of one thing — e.g. one person, one institution, or one event. **Life histories** are case studies of one person's whole life. Case studies can be used to falsify hypotheses. It's not possible to **generalise** from a case study — they **aren't representative**, because of their tiny sample size.

Statistics are a Secondary source of Quantitative data

1) **Hard statistics** are **objective**, e.g. statistics on births and marriages.

2) **Soft statistics** are more **subjective**. Statistics on **crime**, **poverty** and **unemployment** are soft statistics. In the 1980s and 1990s, the government **changed the method** used to **measure unemployment** over 20 times.

Secondary sources of Qualitative data include Documents and Mass Media

1) A document is **written text**. Documents can be **personal** — like **letters**, **diaries**, **autobiographies**, **memoirs** and **suicide notes**. Documents can also be **official**, like **school records**, **health** records or **church** records.

2) Documents can be **expressive** — to do with **meanings**, like a **suicide note**. Documents can be **formal** — like **official letters**. **Interactionists** like **expressive** documents because they're a big source of **qualitative data**.

3) There are **problems** with documents. They can be **difficult to understand** if they're old. They might be **fakes**. They might contain **lies** — especially personal documents.

4) The **mass media** is another source of **secondary data** about people and society.

5) Sociologists analyse **documents and the media** by looking at **content**, **themes** and **style of language** used.

6) **Content analysis** can be **quantitative** or **qualitative**. **Quantitative** analysis **counts** the number of times a theme comes up in the text, or the number of times something happens. **Qualitative** analysis looks at the **meanings** of the text.

The Context of Data Collection

The way in which data is collected can seriously affect its validity.

Data must be **Valid** — the **Collection Process** can make it **Less Valid**

1) Respondents in an interview may **forget** things, **exaggerate**, or flat-out **lie**.

2) They may try to show themselves in the **best possible light**. They may say they **wouldn't commit crime** when **really they would**. They may say they **recycle all their rubbish** when **really they don't**.

3) **Criminals** interviewed by **Laurie Taylor (1984)** later claimed that they'd **made up lies** to see if Taylor **believed** them.

Asking people about their **attitudes** to an event a **long time afterwards** often isn't valid. People **change their views** over time, and may **alter their description** of the past in the light of their **current beliefs**. For example, a middle-aged person may **falsely claim** to have been law-abiding as a youth when really they were a teenage delinquent.

There is a danger in **participant observation**, particularly **covert** participant observation, that the researcher will "**go native**". This means they get **too involved** and find it **hard to stand back** and **observe** the group **objectively**.

Interviewer Effects can Alter the way Respondents Behave

Interviewer effects are also called "researcher effects".

1) Respondents in interviews may give the sort of answer they **think** the **interviewer wants to hear** — or the **exact opposite**, if they're feeling stubborn.

2) Interviewers can give **subtle direction** towards certain responses — often **without realising** they're doing it.

1) Participants in experiments may try harder at what they're doing to get a **positive response** from the researchers.

2) This is called the **Hawthorne Effect** — first observed in an experiment at the **Hawthorne** electricity plant in Chicago, analysed by **Elton Mayo (1933)** in his work on motivation. The experiment was **meant** to test worker responses to **changes in variables** such as **workplace lighting**, but in fact **productivity increased** with **each variable change**, positive or negative. The workers seemed to be responding to the fact that they **knew an experiment was going on**.

3) These effects mean data from experiments may not be **valid**.

The presence of a researcher affects the **behaviour** of the participants **being observed**. Also, the observation must be **interpreted** by the researcher, and the researcher's interpretation may be **biased**.

Cultural Issues have an Impact on Validity

1) **Labov (1973)** found that **black American children** were much **more forthcoming** with a **black interviewer** than a **white** interviewer. He suggested that this could lead white researchers to think that the children had poor linguistic ability.

2) Ethnicity wasn't the only factor — the children were most forthcoming in an **informal setting**, where they could bring a **friend** with them.

3) Labov's explanation was that the children didn't speak up and show their abilities when they perceived the situation as alien, or **hostile**.

4) **Oakley (1981)** thought that **women** responded to a **friendly** interview style.

The **acceptability** of some sensitive issues **varies** between **social groups**. Some social groups may be less keen on **admitting embarrassing** or **socially undesirable** things, e.g. deviant behaviour, or mental health symptoms.

Practice Questions

Q1 Give two advantages and two disadvantages of participant observation.

Q2 What is the Hawthorne Effect?

Q3 Why did Labov suggest that children were more forthcoming in an informal setting, with a same-ethnicity interviewer?

Exam Question

Q1 Assess the usefulness of participant observation as a research method. (40 marks)

But what do they do if all the respondents decide to lie...

That covert participant observation stuff sounds a bit cloak-and-dagger to me, almost like being a spy. I don't think I'd be up to it myself — after a point you must get sick of pretending to be a gang member or a neo-Nazi or whatever and just feel like going home for a nice cuppa. And after all that trouble, you could find that interviewer effects ruin your results. What a life.

Quantitative and Qualitative Analysis

Once a researcher has gathered their data, they need to analyse it.
The way data is analysed depends on whether it's quantitative or qualitative. **This is for OCR.**

All **Quantitative** data needs to be **Coded** and **Collated**

1) Coding means the creation of a numbered category for a series of similar responses.

2) The responses to **closed questions** are **pre-coded**. The data merely needs to be **counted** and **grouped** according to the answer given.

3) Open questions require more work. Data from open questions and observations needs to be grouped into **categories** of **similar answers**.

4) Once all of the responses have been given a numerical code, the figures should be collated and transferred onto a **coding sheet**.

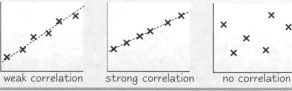

Do you like worms? Yes ☐ Yes=1
Please tick one box only No ☐ No=0

Yes=1 and No=0 are the answer codes

All **Quantitative** data can be presented in **Graph** and **Chart** form

1) Presenting complex data in a **table** or **chart** allows non-experts to **understand** the results fairly easily.

2) **Other sociologists** and **policy analysts** can confidently **use** the data in other reports and theories without having to do **too much work** themselves.

3) On the other hand, charts and graphs can **mislead** people over the significance of findings. With a **small sample**, freak results can look quite significant on the chart.

1) **Correlation** is a measure of how **closely** two variables are **related**, for example household income and number of children. Correlation may be **strong** (high), **weak**, or there may be no apparent correlation at all.

2) Correlation is **useful**, but it **doesn't prove** cause and effect by itself. Correlation could be coincidence.

weak correlation   strong correlation   no correlation

3) **Trends** are the long-term movement of a variable, for example household income over a number of years. Trends may be **upward**, **constant** or **downward**, but there are usually **fluctuations** around the trend.

4) The pattern revealed by data can be **extrapolated** into the **future**. You can identify the **trend**, and **assume** that the trend carries on. All you do is draw a line of best fit on the graph to show the trend, and keep the line going to project the trend into the future.

5) For example, a graph of average household size over time can show correlation between household size and time — say a **downwards trend**. Be **careful** though, as **trends don't often stay constant** for ever. If you kept extrapolating the trend of declining household sizes, you'd get to a point where the average household had **no people at all**, which clearly **makes no sense**.

It's very useful to figure out the **central tendency** of a set of data. The central tendency is another word for the **average** of a set of data — it's one single representative figure. **Mean**, **median** and **mode** are measures of central tendency. The **mean** is all the results ÷ the number of results, the **median** is the **middle** value when the figures are put in ascending order, and the **mode** is the **value that occurs most often** in the data. It's all **basic maths**.

The mean, median and mode aren't always the same. With household income, the mean is higher than the median and mode. The few people who earn millions push the mean upwards.

Some **Quantitative** data can be **Analysed More** than others

1) **Nominal data** is **classifications** that don't have a numerical figure attached to them — e.g. sex and ethnic origin. Analysis is limited to adding up the number of times an answer is given, giving a percentage of how many participants gave that answer, calculating the modal answer, and making a frequency table, or a chart.

2) **Ordinal data** can be put in rank order. You get ordinal data from a **coded multiple choice question** with **ordered answers** e.g. "How much do you agree?" Strongly agree = **1**, agree = **2**, neither agree nor disagree = **3**, disagree = **4**, strongly disagree = **5**. With ordinal data, you can work out percentiles, quartiles and the median — as well as everything you can do with nominal data.

Don't sweat about the maths stuff if you don't get it.

3) **Interval data** is numerical data that can be measured on a **scale** where the distance (or interval) between each point is **identical**, but with an **arbitrary zero** — e.g. temperature data, or IQ scores. You **can't divide** one value by another to get the **ratio** — e.g. 30°C isn't twice as hot as 15°C. But you can work out the mean.

4) **Ratio data** is numerical data on a scale with "true zero" — i.e. you can divide one value by another to get the ratio. Examples are age, income and number of children. Someone with 4 children clearly has twice as many as someone with two children.

Interval and **ratio** data are the most open to analysis — you can work out **all three** types of **average** as well as putting it all on a graph and figuring out the interquartile range. However, a lot of sociological data is nominal.

Quantitative and Qualitative Analysis

Qualitative data needs to be Collated but Not All the data gathered is Useful

1) Qualitative data needs to be collated in a way that makes it **useful** and **relevant** to the topic of research.

2) The nature of qualitative data means that a great deal of the information gathered may be **irrelevant** and useless for the research. Care must be taken when deciding what to include in the final data to be analysed.

3) A researcher can gather all the data through **tape recording** so that they have **every word** saved. The researcher doesn't need to **remember** exactly what was said, or rely on a **set of notes** from the interview or observation, which might have missed something out. The only problem is one of practicality — it means that the research process becomes more expensive.

4) Data can be categorised according to patterns and similarity. Some sociologists **make notes** as they're going along on what seems to be **useful**, and what's **linked** with what. Useful bits of data can then be **coded** and **included** in the final report.

5) A **full original data set** should be kept so the researcher can keep **referring back** to see **exactly** what was said or written.

Qualitative analysis involves looking for Themes and Interpretations

Qualitative content analysis of an interview or document looks at the symbols and meanings in the text. Qualitative analysis suffers from **interpretive bias**. The researcher may see what they **want to see**, instead of what the respondent **actually meant**.

Differences and similarities in the ways that different social groups **interpret** and **respond** to a situation are key to **social action** research and **standpoint** research (e.g. feminist sociology).

Qualitative Data is usually presented as an Essay

1) Qualitative data can't be presented as charts and graphs, so qualitative researchers present their data in the form of a **written discussion** or **essay**.

2) **Quotes** from respondents are often included to highlight particular points of interest.

3) Researchers detail **similarities** and **differences** between respondents — e.g. their **gender**, their **class** background, and the type of **work** they do.

4) The reports from qualitative researchers may not be as **highly valued** by **politicians** and other non-experts, because of their inability to **generalise** and provide **easy to comprehend findings** in nice neat tables and charts.

Triangulation means using Several Different Methods

1) Triangulation allows researchers to get the benefit of **both** qualitative and quantitative research.

2) Researchers can use **qualitative** research to **build up understanding**, and formulate a **hypothesis**. They can then use **quantitative** research to **test** their hypothesis. **Barker (1984)** used this approach in her study of the Moonies, using a combination of participant observation, questionnaires and in-depth interviewing.

3) **Quantitative** research can show that two factors are **correlated**. **Qualitative** research can give **insight** into **reasons why**.

Practice Questions

Q1 What is correlation?
Q2 What is extrapolation?
Q3 What is meant by the following — "nominal data", "ordinal data" and "ratio data"?
Q4 What kind of data is subject to interpretive bias?

Exam Question

Q1 "Only quantitative data is useful in analysing society." How far do you agree or disagree with this statement? (22 marks)

Bet you thought you were safe from Maths here...

And I bet you thought that figures were just figures. Oh no, siree. See, data from a coded question like "What's your ethnic origin" is numbers, but those numbers represent White, Afro-Caribbean, Asian, Chinese, etc. So you could work out the mode (most common ethnic origin), but not the mean. (White + Black + Asian + Chinese ÷ 4 makes no sense at all.)

Creating a Research Report

Writing the research report is one of the final stages in the research process and is one of the most crucial. It is the report that other sociologists will read and respond to— so it must be clear, coherent and detailed. The report needs to explain the process and the findings of the research. Many researchers follow a standard structure when creating a report.

Publication must be Honest and allow Criticism and Comment

1) In the quest for objectivity, researchers should be open and public when they **conduct** the research and when they **publish** their findings. Being open and public enables the researcher to **avoid accusations** of **falsifying data**, **over-emphasising insignificant findings** or using **dodgy methodology**.

2) Researchers should present their data and allow other researchers to build on it, criticise it or compare it to other work. This means that results get analysed in terms of **objectivity**, **validity** and **reliability**, and it allows others to **check** the researcher's **interpretations** to see if they are correct.

3) **Accountability to participants** is **crucial**. All participants should be given **access** to the final report.

4) The report should be **fair** and **representative** of their meanings, actions and beliefs.

5) The report must not **identify** the participants without their consent.

Researchers all tend to use the Same Report Structure

1) A **standard (common) report structure** can be **helpful** for researchers — it provides a **ready made logical structure** to the report. It helps them detail all the **processes** they undertook and the **findings** they unearthed.

2) A common, logical report structure makes reports **easy to use**. With a standard structure, readers of a report can easily figure out where to look for what they want. Readers can more easily **compare** and **contrast** the report with other reports.

3) A common report structure helps to make sure that researchers don't put too much of their own **biases** and **opinions** into the production of the final report. By including a series of standardised chapters to their work, they are prevented from spending the whole of their report criticising other work or promoting their findings too much. That's the idea, anyway.

A Good Report Structure includes about Nine Different Sections

According to **Walsh (2001)**, a good report includes **nine sections** that range from the **title** to the **appendices**.

1) **Title** — this should **concisely** tell the reader what the research is **about**.

2) **Abstract** — this is a **short summary** of the report (often known in official documents as the "Executive Summary"). It includes a **brief mention** of the aims, the methods, the findings and any conclusions.

3) **Introduction** — this includes **background reading**, research **aims**, **research question** and **hypothesis**.

4) **Method** — this details **how** the researcher carried out their work, how **scientific** it was and any **ethical** considerations.

5) **Findings** — these can be **statistics** or **graphics** or **words**, but **no analysis**. Raw data sets don't appear in the report.

6) **Discussion and conclusion** — here's where **discussion** and **analysis** of the findings goes. It must mention any patterns or anything unusual. Also, there should be a series of **conclusions** backed up by the data. This should state whether the aims have been fulfilled, and whether the researcher thinks the hypothesis is correct.

7) **Recommendations** — this says how the research could have been **extended** or **improved**.

8) **References or Bibliography** — all **sources of information** that have been **referred to** should be noted here (see below).

9) **Appendices** — This will include material that was important in the research process such as **tables** and **notes**.

Referencing your research Accurately is very important

1) Section 8 of the research report should be a **bibliography** — a list of **books** and **other sources** that have been used when creating and compiling the research report. **Books**, **articles**, **websites**, **programmes** and other sources should be **referenced fully**. That includes **publisher** and **place of publication** for **books**.

2) It ought to go without saying that researchers need to keep an **accurate record** of all sources they use, **as they're going along**. This **saves hassle** when it's time to **write up** the report.

3) The **Harvard** and **Chicago** systems of referencing are the most **common** styles and have the advantages of being **simple** to complete and easy to **understand**. Here's an example of each:

This is the Harvard style → Giddens, A. (1999) The Third Way: The Renewal of Social Democracy, Polity Press, Cambridge.
↗ publisher ↗ place of publication

This is the Chicago style → Giddens, A. (1999) *The Third Way: The Renewal of Social Democracy*, (Cambridge: Polity Press).
↗ name ↗ year ↗ title ↗ place of publication ↖ publisher

Reflexivity

Many people question how valid and/or reliable a piece of research is if the presence of the researcher has affected the results. Reflexive researchers acknowledge that their opinions affect their work, and take this into account.

Research can be affected by the **Background** or **Opinions** of the **Researcher**

1) An individual's **social background**, their **perspectives** on life, their **sociological viewpoint**, and their **culture** will all affect how they **perceive** the world around them.

2) This counts for **sociologists** in exactly the same way as it does to us **regular folk**. Sociologists **are** regular folk.

3) What the **researcher** observes or notes as relevant depends on **their idea** of what's useful, true and accurate.

Reflexive Research takes the Researcher's Opinions into Account

1) Reflexivity refers to the **understanding** that a researcher has that their research **will be affected** by their own **opinions** and **standpoints**.

2) Reflexivity forces the sociologist to see **social structures** and **norms** and ways of **interpreting** them as something they have **in common** with the people they study.

3) Sociologists aren't magically free of the effects of the social world. They can't necessarily be **value free** or **impartial**, but they **can** keep a **sense of self awareness** about their preconceptions.

4) **Bourdieu and Wacquant (1992)** saw reflexive sociology as a way of giving a **deeper** and more **meaningful** understanding of the social world. They thought that if the sociologist saw themselves as in the same boat as the people they studied, they'd understand them better.

5) Bourdieu and Wacquant argued that reflexivity could **help sociology** to be **more objective** — they thought it was very important to **keep an eye** on the way that researchers **actually obtain knowledge**, as it could help researchers avoid settling for poor methods.

6) Reflexivity rejects the **certainty** of Functionalist approaches, and rejects the "there's no truth" attitude of some **postmodern** approaches.

The **Reflexive Researcher** will try to **Guarantee Valid Research**

1) A researcher who's **aware** of **potential bias** can take steps to **avoid** it.

2) Reflexive work can often be found in **social action/interactionist sociology** (see p.140). Social action researchers use subjective methods that involve **interpretation**. Reflexivity techniques require the researcher to put themselves **in the place** of their participants for long periods of time to seek a **fuller understanding** of the **meanings** that participants put on their actions.

Reflexive researcher on the wall...
Oh, it's just a mirror. Never mind.

3) For example, **Barker (1984)**, in her study of the Unification Church (the Moonies), spent significant periods of time with **Moonie families** to gain their **trust** and understand their lives **from their point of view**. This allowed her to understand Moonie lifestyle without excessively imposing her **own interpretations** (which may have been different to theirs).

4) **Cicourel (1968)** actually spent time as an **unpaid probation officer** which enabled him to interpret the meanings attached to the definition of "delinquency" from the perspective of the probation officers.

Practice Questions

Q1 What are the benefits of making research open and public?
Q2 What nine sections should there be within a sociological report?
Q3 What are the most common forms of referencing in a report?
Q4 What is meant by "reflexivity" in sociological research?

Exam Question

Q1 Explore the influence of the structure of a sociological research report on its openness and honesty. (14 marks)

Holy cats! It's the end of another book...

Famous people who studied Sociology include Martin Luther King, Robin Williams and Ronald Reagan. So if you want to follow in the footsteps of an inspirational leader, a bad actor and a comedian (pick which you think is which) then you've come to the right place. You just need to pass those all important exams — and that means revising (and turning up on time with a pen).

Do Well in Your AQA Exam

*These two pages are all about how to do well in AQA exams. So don't bother reading them if you're not doing **AQA**.*

These pages describe what the AQA Sociology exam papers have been like for the past few years. We can't predict exactly what new exam papers will be like though — there may be a few changes. So it's important that when you take the exams, you **read the instructions and questions really carefully**. Don't assume they'll always follow the same pattern.

The A2 Exam is split into *Three Units* — units 4, 5 and 6

The A2 exam is split into **three units**, and each of these units is tested by one **1.5 hour exam**.

You'll have to answer **data response questions** (where you're asked questions about sources) and **essay questions**.

Unit 4 has three core areas — Power and Politics, Religion and World Sociology

1) You only have to answer questions on **one** of these topics. You might decide to revise more than one, so you can choose the best questions on the day. Knowing about more than one of these topics might also help you answer the synoptic questions in Unit 6.

2) Each topic usually has a compulsory **data response question** which is divided into **two parts** — (a) and (b). These questions are sometimes broken down into further subparts — (i) and (ii).

3) You also have to do an **essay question worth 40 marks** (there's usually a **choice** of two essay questions for each topic).

Unit 5 is the Sociological Theory and Methods unit

1) On this paper, there's usually **one compulsory data response question**, and a long **essay question**.

2) The **data response** question is usually divided into four **parts** (which may be divided into further subparts). You have to answer questions specifically about the items (sources), and some more general questions. This part of the paper is worth **20 marks** altogether.

3) The **essay question** is worth **40 marks**. You usually get a choice of two essay questions.

Unit 6 has a choice of two topics — "Crime and Deviance" or "Stratification and Differentiation"

1) Whichever topic you choose, there's a **compulsory three-part question** worth a **total of 60 marks** (some of these parts may be broken down into further subparts).

2) This unit is the **Synoptic Paper**, which means you need to use your knowledge from the **whole course, including your AS work**. You have to make **references** to and **links** with **other topics** (like "Education and Stratification", "Poverty and Crime") and with sociological **theories** and **methods**.

3) Each part of the question **tells you specifically** what kind of **synoptic links** it expects you to make.

4) This is the **only** unit which is tested synoptically — don't overlook it when you do your revision. The buzz word is **connections**. The examiners want you to demonstrate an understanding of how sociological issues and themes **overlap** and **interlink**, as they do in real life.

You Get Marks For...

AO just means 'Assessment Objective'

You Get Marks for *AO1 — Knowledge and Understanding* and *AO2 — Identification, Analysis, Interpretation and Evaluation*

1) In the A2 exam, more of the marks are for AO2 skills than they were at AS level.

2) This is significant. You must be able to draw on a wide range of studies and theories and **analyse** them in detail. However much knowledge you display, if you don't **analyse** and **evaluate** it you won't get high marks.

3) Remember — A2 is not just studying new and different topics from AS, but studying topics in **more depth**. Examiners want to see:

   - More evidence of **critical evaluation** and **interpretation**.
   - More reflective, **critical understanding** of sociological **theory** and **method**.

Do Well in Your AQA Exam

Take a concept and **Make It Work** for you

A way to build up those AO2 marks is to master the art of **writing about sociological concepts**. There are key concepts in every topic — here's how to **wring the marks out of them**.

1) **Define** the concept.
2) Give **examples** of it in practice.
3) Present **different viewpoints** on the same concept.
4) Present **evidence** for each viewpoint.

Use what you learnt in your **AS Level**

Don't make the mistake of **forgetting** all the Sociology you learnt to get your stunning AS grade. The key research and theories will be relevant to these exam questions, too — especially unit 6, the synoptic unit. Use it, don't lose it.

Oh... and don't forget **the basics**.

The AQA examiners really care about stuff like being able to read your handwriting — they're always going on about it in their examiners' reports.

- Write as **neatly** as you can.
- Use good **grammar** and **punctuation**.
- Check your **spelling** — especially of words to do with sociology.
- Make sure you **answer the question**.

Here's an **Example Essay** to show you what to aim for:

Assess the view that religion is in decline in the UK. (40 marks)

Mention relevant studies.

Evaluate how reliable data is — don't just take it at face value.

Discuss contrasting viewpoints.

Define the key term or idea that the question asks you about.

Have separate paragraphs about different aspects of a topic.

Bring in relevant examples.

Explain your opinion on the topic, based on the evidence in the essay.

Bryan Wilson (1966) describes a process of secularisation. This is a decline in the significance of religious belief, religious institutions and religious practice in society. Evidence about the influence of religion in society is often open to different interpretations; it is difficult to prove definitively that religion is in decline.

In the 2001 census, 72% of the people in the UK identified themselves as Christian. However, these 72% who identify themselves as Christian do not necessarily hold strong religious beliefs. Some may have been brought up nominally Christian, but have minimal belief in God or the teachings of Christianity.

Church attendance figures are often used to support the view that religion is in decline — the percentage of adults who go to church has fallen from 10% to 7% over the last 20 years. This is a questionable method of judging the extent of secularisation though, as it only deals with religious practice, not religious belief. It's possible to attend church without having faith, just for the social networking aspects, as Herberg suggested. On the other hand, it is possible to believe strongly in God, but never go to church. Grace Davie (1995) called the first situation "belonging without believing" and the second situation "believing without belonging". Davie claimed that belonging to a church and believing in religion are getting more and more separated.

Some argue that religious institutions have lost influence in wider society. Wilson argues that religion is only involved in symbolic rituals, "hatching, matching and dispatching", and doesn't have relevance to everyday life.

Steve Bruce (1995) said that the Church became less important to people as its functions were taken over by other, secular institutions. For example, the Church used to have a strong role in education and welfare — roles which are now primarily filled by secular, state organisations. On the other hand, Parsons claims that even though the Church no longer has all the functions it had back in the middle ages, religion can still have an influence on people's everyday lives.

There has been a trend towards religious pluralism (a greater variety of religions practised in British society). This is partly because of the immigration of ethnic minorities, and partly because of new religious movements (NRMs).

Immigrant groups often have a higher level of religiosity than the settled population. Religion contributes to a sense of community and ethnic identity. Davie claimed that identification with a religion was important to South Asian immigrants because it gave a strong sense of cultural identity. Bruce refers to cultural transition — when South Asian immigrants came to the UK, they quickly set up religious institutions to act as a support structure for the immigrant community.

Religious pluralism has also resulted from the growth of new religious movements (NRMs) since the 1960s. A large variety of groups and beliefs have been labelled NRMs, from the Moonies to Reiki healers. Many sociologists use the growth of NRMs as evidence to argue against secularisation. Sociologists have claimed that the conditions of modernity and postmodernity create insecurity and alienation, and that the growth of NRMs is a response to this. However, it is not easy to use the rise in NRMs as evidence against secularisation. Some NRMs are very vague in their beliefs, and may not count as religions at all.

In conclusion, it is difficult to accurately measure whether religion is declining. Personal belief is a complex topic; for example even if a person says they are Christian, they may not attend Church or believe strongly in God. The rise of NRMs since the 1960s suggests that many people do want some element of spirituality in their lives, but it is arguable whether this is the equivalent of a traditional religion.

Do Well in Your OCR Exam

*These two pages are all about how to do well in OCR exams. So don't bother reading them if you're not doing **OCR**.*

These pages describe what the OCR Sociology exam papers have been like for the past few years. We can't predict exactly what new exam papers will be like though — there may be a few changes. So it's important that when you take the exams, you **read the instructions and questions really carefully**. Don't assume they'll always follow the same pattern.

You'll have a *1 Hour Exam* on the *"Power and Control"* unit

1) There are **6 topics** included in this paper: **Crime and Deviance**, **Education**, **Health**, **Popular Culture**, **Social Policy and Welfare**, and **Protest and Social Movements**. You only have to answer a question about **one** of them.

2) There are usually **12 essay questions** — two on each topic. Choose **one question** on a topic you've studied.

3) The questions tend to follow the **same pattern**. They usually start with the words "**Outline and assess…**" followed by a **sociological idea** (a view, explanation or theory). For example: "*Outline and assess the idea that crime and deviance are the results of labelling.*"

4) The essay is worth up to 60 marks — including marks for **knowledge and understanding**, **interpretation and analysis**, and **evaluation**. Make sure your essay includes all three skills.

You may do an exam on *"Applied Sociological Research Skills"*

1) This unit **can also be taken as coursework**, so you might not be doing this exam. If you're not sure, **check with your teacher** — don't prepare for an exam you're not going to sit...

2) This is a **stimulus response** paper. There will usually be **two items** (usually extracts or scenarios) about **sociological research**, which you won't have seen before, and you have to answer questions related to these items. There are often questions which ask you to describe how **you** would approach doing a piece of **sociological research**.

3) You have **90 minutes** for this paper, and the maximum marks total **60**. You have to answer **all the questions**.

You'll have an exam on *"Social Inequality and Difference"*

This is the **Synoptic Paper**, which means you need to use your knowledge from the **whole course, including your AS work**.

The exam is **90 minutes** long. There are **two questions** — you **choose one**. This is the usual format of the questions:

1) **Parts (a) and (b)** are based on items (sources) and are worth **6 marks** each.

2) **Part (c)** is a methods question, worth **12 marks**. You have to identify and explain two advantages, disadvantages, problems or reasons for a particular method, or issues relating to the operationalisation (see p.145) of key concepts.

3) **Part (d)** asks you to use your **wider sociological knowledge** and outline evidence either for or against a particular viewpoint. This question's worth **22 marks**.

4) **Part (e)** asks you to outline and assess sociological explanations and/or theories. It's very important to **evaluate** the theories. Make sure that you spend enough time on this question — it's worth **a whopping 44 marks**.

You Get Marks For...

AO just means 'Assessment Objective'

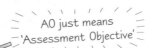

You Get Marks for *AO1 — Knowledge and Understanding* and *AO2 — Identification, Analysis, Interpretation and Evaluation*

1) In the A2 exam, more of the marks are for AO2 skills than they were at AS level. However much knowledge you display, if you don't **analyse and evaluate** it you'll miss out on most of the marks.

2) Remember — the A2 is not just studying new and different topics from AS but studying topics in more **depth**. Examiners want to see:
   - More evidence of **critical evaluation** and **interpretation**.
   - More reflective, **critical understanding** of sociological **theory** and **method**.

Oh... and don't forget **the basics**. You get marks for the **quality of your writing** on the long answer questions.

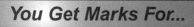

- Write as **neatly** as you can.
- Use good **grammar** and **punctuation**.
- Check your **spelling** — especially of words to do with sociology.
- Make sure you **answer the question**.

Do Well in Your OCR Exam

Here's a Short Essay Answer

(c) Identify and explain one advantage and one disadvantage of using informal interviews to find out about women's attitudes towards mothers who work outside the home. (12 marks)

Only describe one advantage and one disadvantage — that's all the question wants.

An advantage of using informal interviews is that the women would probably feel more comfortable and relaxed talking to the researcher in an informal setting, and this would make them more likely to talk honestly and in depth. In order for the data to be valid it is important that the interviewees should feel able to talk openly, and not be tempted to lie or withhold information from the interviewer. It is easier to build up trust between interviewer and interviewee in a relaxed, informal atmosphere. Oakley (1981) said that women respond well to a friendly interview style. This suggests that an informal interview would be more likely to provide good results in this case than a structured, formal interview.

Refer back to the wording of the question.

Mention studies if they're relevant.

A disadvantage of using informal interviews in this case is that the data couldn't be used to make valid, general conclusions about British women's attitudes to working mothers. The technique is time-consuming and only a small sample of women are likely to be interviewed. Also, the data from informal interviews is qualitative, which makes it harder to compare data and spot patterns (which is necessary in order to reach general conclusions). Quantitative research techniques, like multiple-choice questionnaires, would be better if a researcher wanted to be able to make general conclusions because it would be easier to have a large sample size and to compare the data from different respondents.

You don't need an introduction and conclusion for short questions.

Here's a Longer Sample Essay

(e) Outline and assess sociological explanations of ethnic inequalities in the UK. (44 marks)

There are a number of different sociological explanations of ethnic inequalities in the UK. Some explanations hold society responsible for ethnic inequalities; others blame the individual.

Include an introduction for long essay answers.

Many Functionalists believe that some level of ethnic inequality helps society to function smoothly. For example, Patterson (1967) and Banton (1983) argue that members of ethnic minorities are often more willing to take low status jobs and this is useful to society. This view could be criticised for ignoring the negative effect of inequality on members of ethnic minorities; it places the smooth running of society as a higher priority than the rights and well-being of people from ethnic minorities.

It's good if you can remember the dates of some of the studies.

New Right thinkers, like Peter Saunders, suggest that ethnic minorities have developed cultural attitudes that keep them in an underclass position. They argue that Western society is a meritocracy and that there is equality of opportunity. They say that if members of ethnic minorities worked hard and had the right attitude, they could achieve social and financial equality with the white majority. New Right theories can be criticised for ignoring factors such as racism and discrimination which might affect the opportunities available to members of ethnic minorities in British society.

Evaluate the theories as well as describing them.

Marxists disagree with the Functionalist and New Right views. They believe that inequality is a feature of capitalism, and that ethnic minorities face inequalities because they are often working class. There are different Marxist views within this general position. Westergaard and Resler (1976) believed that there was a unitary working class. They argued that capitalism exploits people of all ethnicities, including white people — and that ethnicity has little effect on experience of class oppression.

Refer to specific studies.

Marxists Castles and Kosack offer a different explanation. According to their "divided working class" approach, ethnic minorities tend to get lower status working class jobs than white people. Castles and Kosack believe that ethnic minorities are used by the capitalist class as a reserve army of cheap labour.

Another Marxist theory, suggested by Phizaklea and Miles suggests that the working class has been divided into fractions depending on their skill-level, gender and ethnicity. The capitalist system does this to create conflict between the fractions so they do not realise that they are being oppressed.

These Marxist approaches are fairly outdated and do not relate clearly to the contemporary UK. For instance, certain ethnic minority groups have become very successful in the labour market, e.g. people of African-Asian background. There are also now laws to prevent employers from discriminating against ethnic minorities, such as The Race Relations Act. This evidence suggests that the capitalist system is not seeking to exploit ethnic minorities. However, there is still some evidence of racial discrimination in the workplace. For example, in 1995 unemployment rates for white men were 8%, compared to 21% for Afro-Caribbean men.

Give evidence to back up points.

Weberians agree that the lower social classes include the largest proportion of ethnic minority people, and support the idea that ethnic minorities may form an 'underclass'. Rex and Tomlinson (1979) point out that ethnic minorities are more likely to be located in the secondary labour market, which means they have less secure and unskilled work. They receive poor wages and do not have good promotion prospects. Weberians say that this is often because of racism and discrimination, which mean members of ethnic minorities are treated as having low status.

There are many sociological explanations of the position of ethnic minorities in the UK. Marxists blame capitalism whereas New Right sociologists blame the individuals themselves. Functionalists see a positive side to ethnic inequalities, while Weberians blame racism and discrimination. The research and theories tend to focus on the disadvantaged and oppressed members of ethnic minorities. Andrew Pilkington (1993) is critical of this and points out that there are many members of ethnic minorities who are successful in British society, and that some ethnic minorities are more successful in British society than others. I would agree with Pilkington that many theoretical approaches have tended to lump ethnic minorities together in a simplified way. However, racism and ethnic inequalities do still exist in the contemporary UK, and this means sociologists will have to continue trying to explain why.

The conclusion is a good place to say your opinion.

Glossary

bourgeoisie Marxist term for the capitalist ruling class. They own the means of production (e.g. factories, equipment, raw materials).

capitalism An economic system based on private ownership of the means of production, distribution and exchange of commodities. In the capitalist system, labour itself becomes a commodity which employers buy for wages. Capitalism is associated with free trade and individual enterprise. It started in Europe and the US and has spread to become the dominant economic philosophy in most countries.

civil disobedience Protest action that breaks laws.

class A way of stratifying society, on the basis of people's social and economic status. Class is hierarchical — some classes are more privileged than others. The "class system" is criticised by Marxists.

classical liberalism The view that the market should be free, with minimum state intervention, and that individuals should take responsibility for themselves.

coding Numbered codes for each answer of a question on a multiple choice questionnaire. Coding makes it easy to turn the results into graphs and analyse them.

Communism A system of government which is theoretically based on a classless society and where private ownership has been abolished. It is influenced by the ideas of Marx and Engels. During the Cold War, there was conflict between capitalist Western countries and Communist countries like the USSR and China. With the end of the Cold War and the break up of the USSR, many formerly Communist countries have moved towards adopting capitalism. To some extent, this has discredited Communism as a viable political philosophy.

conformity Adherence to the norms and values of society. The opposite of deviance.

consensus Fundamental agreement within a society about that society's basic values. Functionalist theory suggests that, as a result of socialisation, the people in a society all share the same norms and values and this contributes to consensus.

correlation A measure of how closely two variables are related.

cultural capital The cultural skills and knowledge which children learn from their parents. Bourdieu claimed that upper and middle class children are more likely to have cultural capital than working class children and that this puts them at an advantage educationally.

cultural deprivation theory This theory claims that educational achievement and health vary according to social class because some classes lack the cultural values and knowledge which promote a healthy lifestyle and educational achievement.

culture The "way of life" of a society or group. Culture is made up of things such as language, customs, knowledge, norms and values. It is passed on by socialisation.

dependency theory A development theory which blames underdevelopment on colonialism.

desacrilisation Religious and spiritual beliefs ceasing to have a place in society.

deviance Something that goes against society's norms and values. Deviant behaviour is behaviour that society doesn't approve of.

discourse Any kind of discussion or communication (either written or spoken) about a subject. Foucault said that discourse was the rules and framework for how a topic can be discussed.

ethnocentric Centred around the values and interests of one particular ethnic group.

ethnography Research which studies the culture and way of life of a community. It is usually done by observation, and may also use interviews and case studies. Ethnography looks at social relationships, organisations, customs and practices. It is an Interactionist approach to sociological study and so produces qualitative data.

false consciousness Marxism says that workers are in a state of false consciousness about their place in society. They have learnt values and beliefs that support the interests of the ruling class (through their education, the media and religion), and this prevents them from realising how unfair capitalist society is.

false needs Things people think they need but which don't really satisfy them. Marxists say these false needs have been created by a capitalist culture which encourages consumerism.

falsification Trying to prove a hypothesis wrong.

feminism A broad movement which believes that social organisations and culture have been dominated by men to the exclusion of women. Feminists claim that this has devalued and disadvantaged women into a marginalised status. There are many varieties of feminism, e.g. liberal feminism, Marxist feminism, radical feminism and black feminism.

Fordism A type of industrial production based on scientific management, first used by car manufacturer Henry Ford. It uses a moving assembly line, with workers performing small, specialised tasks. This produces standardised parts for mass-produced products.

free market an economic system that lets supply and demand control prices, wages etc. rather than the government.

Functionalism An important sociological perspective about how society works, founded by Durkheim. Functionalists believe that society is made up of a number of institutions, each of which has a useful function and helps society to run smoothly, e.g. the family, the education system, religion. These institutions work in harmony because they have agreed norms and values, and this is essential for society to survive. Functionalists say that individuals internalise these norms and values (socialisation). Another term for Functionalism is "Consensus Structuralism". So now you know.

gender Sociologists say that gender (femininity and masculinity) is a social construction. Being male or female is the biological sex you're born with, while masculinity and femininity are identities you're socialised into.

globalisation The breaking down of traditional national boundaries as globally people become more interconnected. This happens due to factors such as the growth of multinational companies, improvements in communications and technology, increased migration of people between societies, and the global marketing of cultural products.

Hawthorne Effect When participants are aware they are taking part in an experiment, it often affects their behaviour. This is known as the Hawthorne Effect.

hegemony The domination of one group of people over others, or of one set of ideas and values over others. Law, religion, media, art science and literature may all be used to make the dominant group or values legitimate and to discredit the alternatives.

hidden curriculum The social norms and values that are taught at school, but not as part of the regular curriculum, e.g. conformity and respect for authority.

hierarchy A system which ranks people according to status. Any system where you have a boss in charge of people is a hierarchy.

hypothetico-deductive model Research favoured by positivist sociologists which is similar to the approach used in natural sciences. It involves using an experiment to test a hypothesis and then using the results to confirm, modify or reject the hypothesis.

iatrogenesis Illness caused by modern health care.

identity An individual's sense of self. This can be influenced by social factors such as class, gender, religion and ethnicity.

ideological state apparatus Institutions like the media, schools, Church and family which can spread the ideology of the state.

ideology A set of ideas and beliefs about the way things should be — often politically motivated.

individualist welfare Welfare system with selective, means-tested benefits.

infrastructure In Marxist theory, the infrastructure is the economic base of society (e.g. labour and manufacturing).

institutional racism When the policies, attitudes and actions of an institution discriminate against ethnic minorities — sometimes unintentionally.

institutions of society Things like the family, the Church, the education system, the health care system.

Interactionism A sociological approach which focuses on the actions and thoughts of individuals. Society is viewed as the product of interaction between individuals. "Interactionism", "Interpretivism" and "Social Action theory" are pretty much the same thing — so don't get confused if you see these other terms being used.

Glossary

labelling theory This theory says that the labels given to someone affect their behaviour, e.g. someone who is labelled a criminal is more likely to commit criminal acts. Labels also affect how other people treat someone, e.g. teachers might treat a child labelled a "troublemaker" more strictly.

LEDC Less Economically Developed Country.

Left Realism Sociological viewpoint which developed from Marxism. The approach focuses on working within the capitalist framework and aims to direct social policy to help the poor.

Marxism A theory and political ideology based on the views of Karl Marx (1818-1883). Marxists are opposed to capitalism, which they believe is based on the exploitation of the working class (proletariat) by the owning class (bourgeoisie). Original Marxist ideas have been developed and adapted by **neo-Marxists**. Some states have been run politically along Marxist lines, e.g. Cuba under Castro.

mass media Ways of communicating with large numbers of people, e.g. newspapers, TV, magazines, radio, Internet.

master status a quality in an individual that comes to dominate the way that they are treated or viewed, to the extent that all their other qualities are disregarded. This quality then takes on the status of a label. E.g. if someone with mental health problems is given the often negative label "mentally ill", and then finds that all their other qualities are then ignored, the label "mentally ill" has master status.

MEDC More Economically Developed Country.

media text Any piece of media — e.g. a book, a TV programme, an advert.

meritocracy A system where the best (most talented and hard-working) people rise to the top.

metanarrative A over-arching, all-encompassing story which gives meaning to history and events.

modernism View of society that tries to come up with big theories to explain all of society (metanarratives). Modernists try to investigate society scientifically.

moral panic A fear of a moral crisis in society. The mass media have a big role in starting moral panics in modern society.

neo-Marxism In the 20th century, some of Marx's followers revised and adapted his ideas to make them more relevant to modern society. Neo-Marxists often stress the importance of culture in sustaining capitalism, e.g. through the hegemony of capitalist ideas. Neo-Marxists include Gramsci, Althusser and Stuart Hall.

norm A social rule about what is correct and appropriate behaviour within a particular culture, e.g. queuing in a shop.

operationalisation Defining a concept and deciding how to measure it.

patriarchy A society where men are dominant. Feminists often describe male-dominated societies and institutions as "patriarchal".

peer groups People of the same or similar social status and age, e.g. a group of teenagers.

Physical Quality of Life Index (PQLI) A development index that measures infant mortality, literacy and life expectancy.

pluralism The belief that society is diverse and reflects the needs and views of everyone via democracy and the free market.

positivism A theoretical point of view which concentrates on social facts, scientific method and quantitative data (facts and figures). The positivist view is that human behaviour is determined by external social factors, and so is outside the control of the individuals in society.

post-Fordism Theory that work now tends to be more flexible and less repetitive than it was at the height of Fordism. It involves computer technology, multi-skilled workers, a less strict hierarchy, new organisation of workers and products made for quality rather than quantity.

postmodernism Theory which says there is no one objective truth or reality that everyone experiences. Postmodernism rejects the ideas of modernism, such as positivism and metanarratives.

postmodernity The world after the modern age — with flexible working, individual responsibility and people constructing their own identity.

poststructuralism The idea that there are no fixed meanings, and that people are controlled by language and signs.

qualitative methods of research Methods like unstructured interviews and participant observation that give results which tell a story about individuals' lives.

quantitative methods of research Methods like surveys and structured interviews that give results you can easily put into a graph or table.

reflexive sociology Research that accepts that the researcher's opinions have an effect on results, and takes this into account.

reliability Data is reliable if other sociologists using the same methods on the same group collect the same data. Quantitative data is usually the most reliable.

representative democracy Rule by the people, via voting in elections for representatives (e.g. MPs).

sanctions Rewards and punishments that reinforce social norms.

secularisation When religion loses its influence in society.

semiotic analysis Looking for hidden meanings in the structure of a text, image or object.

social construct An idea or belief that's created in society, and doesn't come from a scientific fact.

social democrats People who think the state should redistribute wealth, and that there should be a strong Welfare State paid for out of taxes. Social democrats believe in social equality.

social policy Government decisions which affect society, e.g. raising taxes, changing the benefits system, privatisation.

socialisation Passing on cultural values and norms from one generation to the next, so that they become internalised, i.e. part of everyone's way of thinking.

stereotype A generalisation about a social group — often inaccurate and insulting.

stratification The way society is divided up into layers or classes.

stratified sample A sample with the same proportions of gender, class, age etc. as the population you're studying.

subculture A group who share values and norms which are different from the mainstream culture.

superstructure In Marxist theory, the superstructure is the institutions in a society which aren't economic (such as legal, political, cultural and religious institutions) and the beliefs and values which these institutions propagate. It has a role in maintaining and sustaining the economic infrastructure.

symbolic communities Communities connected to each other through leisure or culture.

symbolic consumption Buying things that define who you are, e.g. a particular brand of clothing.

third way politics A political viewpoint that combines elements of right wing self-sufficiency and left wing social democracy.

triangulation Combining different research methods and data to get the best results.

underclass A social group at the bottom of the social hierarchy. New Right sociologists think they're lazy and dependent on welfare. Left wing sociologists think they're disadvantaged by the welfare system.

validity Data is valid if it gives an accurate picture of what's being measured.

value free research Research that isn't biased, and isn't influenced by the researcher's beliefs.

values A general belief in a society about what is important or what is right and wrong, e.g. freedom of speech is a value of Western society.

victim survey Survey asking if respondents have been victims of crime.

vocational education Education that provides the skills needed for a particular job.

Weber (1864-1920) Influential, early sociologist. Weber argued that the better a person's market situation, the better their life-chances, wealth and status would be. He also suggested that, as societies developed, secularisation would follow as people came to believe more in science. Weberians are followers of Weber's work and ideas.

welfare pluralism Mixture of state, private, voluntary and informal welfare provision.

World Systems theory Development theory which looks at the world as a single economic system where some countries have a lot of power and others don't have power.

References

These are details of studies which are discussed in the Revision Guide.

Abbott, P. and Wallace, C. (1990) *An Introduction to Sociology: Feminist Perspectives* (London: Routledge)

Abraham, J. (1995) *Divide and School: Gender and Class Dynamics in Comprehensive Education* (London: Falmer Press)

Acheson Report (1998) *Independent Inquiry into Inequalities in Health,* Chairman Sir Donald Acheson (London: Stationery Office)

Adamson, P. (1974) (*New Internationalist* May)

Adamson, P. (1986) 'The Rich, the Poor, the Pregnant' (*New Internationalist* Issue 270)

Adorno, T.W. and Horkheimer, M. (1973, first published 1944) *Dialectic of Enlightenment* (London: Allen Lane)

Akers, R.L. (1967) 'Problems in the sociology of deviance: Social definitions and behavior' (*Social Forces* 46)

Alcock, P. (1997, 2nd edition) *Understanding Poverty* (Basingstoke: Macmillan)

Althusser, L. (1969) *Lenin and Philosophy and Other Essays* (New York: Monthly Review Press)

Ang, I. (1985) *Watching Dallas* (London: Methuen)

Annandale, E. and Hunt, K. (1990) 'Masculinity, femininity and sex: an exploration of their relative contribution to explaining gender differences in health' (*Sociology of Health and Illness* 12)

Arber, S., Dale, A. and Gilbert, N. (1986) 'The limitations of existing social class of women' in A. Jacoby (ed.) *The measurement of Social Class* (Guilford: Social Research Association)

Arnold, M. (1993) *Culture and Anarchy* (Cambridge: Cambridge University Press)

Ashley, D. (1997) *History without a Subject* (Boulder: Westview Press)

Atkinson, J. (1986) *Changing Work Patterns: How Companies Achieve Flexibility to Meet New Needs* (London: NEDO)

Atkinson, J. M. (1978) *Discovering Suicide* (London: Macmillan)

Baechler, J. (1979) *Suicides* (Oxford: Blackwell)

Ball, S.J. (1981) *Beachside Comprehensive: A Case Study of Secondary Schooling* (Cambridge: CUP)

Banton (1983) *Racism and Ethnic Competition* (Cambridge: Cambridge University Press)

Barker, E. (1984) *The Making of a Moonie* (Oxford: Blackwell)

Barnes, C. (1992) *Disabling Imagery and the Media* (Derby: The British Council of Organizations of Disabled People)

Barrett, M. (1988) *Women's Oppression Today: Problems in Marxist Feminist Analysis* (London: Verso)

Baudrillard, J. (1981) *For a Critique of the Political Economy of the Sign* (St Louis: Telos Press)

Baudrillard, J. (1983) *Simulations* (New York: Semiotext)

Baudrillard, J. (1988) *The Ecstasy of Communication* (New York: Semiotext)

Bauman, Z. (1990) *Thinking Sociologically* (Oxford: Blackwell)

de Beauvoir, S. (1953) *The Second Sex* (London: Jonathan Cape)

Becker, H. S. (1963) *Outsiders: Studies in the Sociology of Deviance* (New York: The Free Press)

Becker, H.S. (1970) *Sociological Work* (New Brunswick: Transaction)

Becker, H.S. (1971) 'Social Class Variations in the Teacher Pupil Relationship' in Cosin, B.R. et al. *School and Society* (London: Routledge & Kegan Paul)

Bell, D. (1973) *The Coming of Post-Industrial Society* (New York: Basic Books)

Bellah, R. (1967) 'Civil Religion in America' (*Daedalus* 96 1-21)

Benyon, J. (1987) 'Turmoil in Cities' in Benyon, J. and Solomos, J. (eds.) *The Roots of Urban Unrest* (Oxford: Pergamon Press)

Benyon, J. (1987) 'British Urban Unrest in the 1980s' in Benyon, J. and Solomos, J. (eds.) *The Roots of Urban Unrest* (Oxford: Pergamon Press)

Berger, P. and Luckman, T. (1971) *The social construction of reality — a treatise on the sociology of knowledge* (Harmondsworth: Penguin)

Bernstein, B. (1970) 'Elaborated and Restricted Codes: Their Social Origins and Social Consequences' in Danziger, K. (ed.) *Readings in Child Socialisation* (Oxford: Pergamon)

Berthoud, R. (1997) 'Income and Standards of living' in Modood et al. *Ethnic Minorities in Britain: Diversity and Disadvantage* (London: PSI)

Beynon, H. (1992) 'The end of the Industrial Worker' in Abercrombie, N. and Warde, A. (eds.) *Social Change in Contemporary Britain* (Cambridge: Polity Press)

Blumler J.G. and Katz, E. (1974) *The uses of mass communications: Current perspectives on gratifications research* (Beverly Hills: Sage)

Bonger, W.A. (1916) *Criminality and economic conditions* (Boston: Little, Brown)

Bordua, D. (1962) 'Some comments on theories of group delinquency' (*Sociological Inquiry* 32)

Boserup, E. (1965) *The Conditions of Agricultural Growth* (Chicago: Aldine)

Bourdieu, P. (1967) 'Systems of education and systems of thought' (*International Social Science Journal* 19)

Bourdieu, P. (1974) 'The school as a conservative force, scholastic and cultural inequalities' in Eggleston (ed.) *Contemporary Research in the Sociology of Education* (London: Methuen)

Bourdieu, P. (1984) *Distinction: A Social Critique of the Judgement of Taste* (Cambridge, Massachusetts: Harvard University Press)

Bourdieu, P. (1986) 'The Forms of Capital' in Richardson, J. (ed.) *Handbook of Theory and Research for the Sociology of Education* (New York: Greenwood Press)

Bourdieu, P. and Wacquant, L.J.D. (1992) *An Invitation to Reflexive Sociology* (Cambridge: Polity Press)

Bowlby, J. (1946) *Forty-Four Juvenile Thieves* (London: Bailliere, Tindall and Cox)

Bowles, S. and Gintis, H. (1976) *Schooling in Capitalist America* (London: Routledge & Kegan Paul)

Box, S. (1981) *Deviance, Reality and Society* (London: Holt, Rinehart and Winston)

Bradshaw, J.R., Mitchell, D. and Morgan, J. (1987) 'Evaluating adequacy: the potential of budget standards' (*Journal of Social Policy* 16)

Braverman, H. (1974) *Labour and Monopoly Capitalism* (New York: Monthly Review Press)

Brown, P. and Lauder, H. (1997) 'Education, Globalization, and Economic Development' in Halsey, A.H., Lauder, H., Brown, P. and Wells, A.S. (eds.) *Education, Culture, Economy, Society* (Oxford: Oxford University Press)

Bruce, S. (1995) *Religion in Modern Britain* (Oxford: OUP)

Bruce, S. (2002) *God is Dead: Secularization in the West* (Oxford: Blackwell)

Busfield, J. (1983) 'Gender, Mental Illness and Psychiatry' in Ungerson, C. and Evans, M. (eds.) *Sexual Divisions, Patterns and Processes* (London: Tavistock)

Busfield, J. (2001) *Rethinking the Sociology of Mental Health* (Oxford: Blackwell)

Butler, D. and Kavanagh, D. (1985) *The British General Election of 1983* (London: MacMillan)

Butler, J. (1990) *Gender Trouble* (Place: Routledge)

Callinicos, A. (2003) *An Anti-Capitalist Manifesto* (Cambridge: Polity Press)

Campbell, A. (1981) *Delinquent Girls* (Oxford: Blackwell)

Carnap, R. (1936) 'Testability and Meaning' (*Philosophy of Science* 3)

Carnap, R. (1966) *The Philosophy of Science* (New York: Basic Books)

Carnell, B. (2000) 'Paul Ehrlich' (www.overpopulation.com)

Cartwright and O'Brien (1976) 'Social Class Variations in Health Care and in the Nature of General Practitioner Consultations' in Stacey, M. (ed.) *The Sociology of the NHS* (Keele: University of Keele)

Castles, S. and Kosack, G. (1973) *Immigrant Workers and Class Structure in Western Europe* (Oxford: Oxford University Press)

References

Chambliss, W.J. (1978) *On the Take: From Petty Crooks to Presidents* (Bloomington, Indiana: Indiana University Press)

Chambliss, W.J. and Mankoff, M. (1976) *Whose Law? What Order?* (New York: Wiley & Sons)

Chubb, J. and Moe, T. (1988) 'Politics, Markets, and the Organization of Schools' (*American Political Science Review* 82 December)

Cicourel, A.V. (1968) *The Social Organisation of Juvenile Justice* (New York: John Wiley)

Cloward, R. and Ohlin, L. (1960) *Delinquency and Opportunity: A Theory of Delinquent Gangs.* (Glencoe, Illinois: Free Press)

Coard, B. (1971) *How the West Indian Child is Made Educationally Subnormal in the British School System* (London: New Beacon Books)

Coates, K. and Silburn, R. (1970) *Poverty: The Forgotten Englishman* (Harmondsworth: Penguin)

Cohen, A. F. S. (1955) *Delinquent Boys* (Glencoe, Illinois: The Free Press)

Cohen, A. K. (1966) *Deviance and Control* (Englewood Cliffs, New Jersey: Prentice-Hall)

Cohen, A.P. (1985) *The Symbolic Construction of Community* (London: Routledge)

Cohen, P. (1984) 'Against the new vocationalism' in Bates, I., Clarke, J., Cohen, P., Finn, D., Moore,R. and Willis, P. (eds.) *Schooling for the Dole: the new Vocationalism* (London: Macmillan)

Cohen, R. and Rai, S. (2000) *Global Social Movements*, (eds.) (London: Althone Press)

Cohen, S. (ed.) (1971) *Images of Deviance* (London: Penguin)

Cohen, S. (1972) *Folk Devils and Moral Panics* (London: Paladin)

Connell, R. W. (1987) *Gender and Power: Society, the Person and Sexual Politics* (Cambridge: Polity in association with Blackwell)

Crewe, I. (1983) 'The disturbing truth behind Labour's rout' (*The Guardian*, 13 June)

Crewe, I. (1985) 'Can Labour rise again?' (*Social Studies Review* Sept.)

Crewe, I. (1987) 'A new class of politics' (*The Guardian*, 16 June)

Crook, S., Pakulski, J., and Waters, M. (1992) *Postmodernisation: Changes in Advanced Society* (London: Sage)

Culley, L. and Dyson, S. (2001) *Ethnicity and Nursing Practice* (Basingstoke: Palgrave)

Dahl, R.A. (1961) *Who Governs?* (New Haven: Yale University Press)

Dahrendorf, R. (1959) *Class and Class Conflict in an Industrial Society* (London: Routledge & Kegan Paul)

Dahrendorf, R. (1987) "The Erosion of Citizenship and its consequences for us all" (*New Statesman* 12 June)

Dale, A., Gilbert, G.N. and Arber, S. (1985) 'Integrating Women into Class Theory' (*Sociology*, 19)

Davie, G. (1994) *Religion in Britain since 1945. Believing without Belonging* (Oxford: Blackwell).

Davie, G. (2000) *Religion in Modern Europe. A Memory Mutates* (Oxford: OUP)

Davis, K. and Moore, W.E. (1945) 'Some Principles of Stratification' (*American Sociological Review* 10)

Dean, H. and Taylor-Gooby, P. P. (1992) *Dependency Culture: The Explosion of a Myth* (Hemel Hempstead: Harvester Wheatsheaf)

Department of Health and Social Security *Inequalities in health: report of a research working group* (Black Report) (London: DHSS)

Devine, F. (1992) *Affluent Workers Revisited* (Edinburgh: Edinburgh University Press)

Dewey, J. (1953) *Democracy and Education: An Introduction to the Philosophy of Education* (New York: Macmillan)

Dixon, A., Le Grand, J., Henderson, J., Murray, R. and Poteliakhoff, E. (2003) *Is the NHS equitable? A review of the evidence, LSE Health and Social Care Discussion Paper 11*, (London: LSE)

Douglas, J.D. (1967) *The Social Meanings of Suicide* (Princeton, New Jersey: Princeton University Press)

Douglas, J.W.B (1964) *The Home and School* (London: MacGibbon and Kee)

Downes, D. and Rock, P. (1988) *Understanding Deviance: a guide to the sociology of crime and rule-breaking* 2nd edition (Oxford: Oxford University Press)

Doyal, L. (2001) 'Sex, gender, and health: the need for a new approach' (*BMJ* 323)

Doyal, L. and Pennell, I. (1979) *The Political Economy of Health* (London: Pluto Press)

Driver, G. and Ballard, R. (1981) 'Contemporary Performance in Multiracial Schools: South Asian Pupils at 16+' in James, A. and Jeffcoate, R. (eds.) *The School in the Multicultural Society* (London: Harper and Row)

DuCille, A. (1996) 'Toy Theory: Black Barbie and the Deep Play of Difference' *Skin Trade* (Cambridge, Massachusetts: Harvard University Press)

Durkheim, E. (1897 translated 1951) *Suicide: A Study in Sociology* (London: Routledge)

Durkheim, E. (1925 reprinted 1961) *Moral Education* (Glencoe: The Free Press)

Dworkin, A. (1981) *Pornography: Men possessing Women* (London: The Women's Press)

Edgell, S. (1993) *Class* (London: Routledge)

Ehrlich, P. R. (1968) *The Population Bomb* (New York: Ballantine Books)

Eisenstadt, S.N. (1967) 'The Protestant Ethic Thesis' (*Diogenes* 59)

Entwistle, J. (2000) *The Fashioned Body: Fashion, Dress and Modern Social Theory* (Cambridge: Polity Press)

Eysenck, H. (1964) *Crime and Personality* (London: Routledge & Kegan Paul)

Eysenck, H. (1971) *Race, Intelligence and Education* (London: Temple Smith)

Featherstone, M. (1991) *Consumer Culture and Postmodernism* (London: Sage)

Ferguson (1983) *Forever Feminine: Women's Magazines and the Cult of Femininity* (London: Heinemann)

Ferri, E. and Smith, K. (1996) *Parenting in the 90s* (London: Family Policy Centre)

Feyerabend, P. (1975) *Against Method* (London: Verso)

Field, F. (1989) *Losing Out: The Emergence of Britain's Underclass* (Oxford: Blackwell)

Field, F. (1996) *Stakeholder Welfare* (Institute of Economic Affairs)

Fielding, N. (1981) *The National Front* (London: Routledge & Kegan Paul)

Finn, D. (1987) *Training without Jobs* (London: Macmillan)

Firestone, S. (1971) *The Dialectic of Sex* (London: Cape)

Fletcher G. and Allen J. (2003) 'Perceptions of and Concern about Crime' Chapter 8 in Simmons and Dodd (eds.) *Crime in England and Wales 2002/2003* (London: Home Office)

Foucault, M. (1971) *L'Ordre du Discours* (Paris: Editions Flammarion)

Foucault, M. (1972) *The Archaeology of Knowledge* (London: Tavistock)

Frank, A.G. (1967) *Capitalism and Underdevelopment in Latin America* (New York: Monthly Review Press)

Frank, A.G. (1971) *Sociology of Development and Underdevelopment of Sociology* (London: PlutoPress)

Fraser, N. (1989) *Unruly Practices: Power, Discourse and Gender in Contemporary Social Theory* (Cambridge: Polity)

Fraser, N. (1995) 'Politics, Culture and the Public Sphere: towards a Postmodern Conception' in Nicholson and Seidman (eds.) *Social Postmodernism: beyond identity politics* (Cambridge: CUP)

Frazer, E. (1987) 'Teenage Girls Reading Jackie' (*Media Culture and Society* vol.9)

Friedan, B. (1963) *The Feminine Mystique* (New York: Norton)

Friedman, M. (1962) *Capitalism and Freedom* (Chicago: Chicago University Press)

Frith, S. (1981) *Sound Effects: Youth, Leisure, and the Politics of Rock'n'Roll* (New York: Pantheon Books)

Frith, S. and McRobbie, A. (1990, first published 1978) 'Rock and Sexuality' in *On Record: Rock, Pop, and the Written Word* Frith, S. and Goodwin, A. (New York: Pantheon Books)

References

Fröbel, F., Heinrichs, J. and Kreye, O. (1980) *The New International Division of Labour* (Cambridge: CUP)

Fulcher, J. and Scott, J. (1999) *Sociology* (Oxford: OUP)

Fuller, M. (1980) 'Black Girls in a London Comprehensive School' in Deem, R. (ed.) *Schooling for Women's Work* (London: Routledge & Kegan Paul)

Gerth, H. and Mills, C. (eds.) (1948) *From Max Weber, Essays in Sociology* (London: Routledge & Kegan Paul)

Gauntlett, D. (2002) *Media, Gender and Identity: An Introduction* (London: Routledge & Kegan Paul)

George, V. and Page, R. (eds.) *Thinkers on Modern Welfare* (London: Hutchinson)

Ghaill, M. Mac an (1992) 'Coming of age in 1980s England: reconceptualising black students' schooling experience' in Gill, D., Mayor, B. and Blair, M. (eds.) *Racism and Education: Structures and Strategies* (London: Sage)

Ghaill, M. Mac an (1994) *The Making of Men: Masculinities, Sexualities and Schooling* (Milton Keynes: Open University Press)

Gibbs, J. and Martin, W.T. (1964) *Status Integration and Suicide* (Eugene, Oregon: University of Oregon Press)

Giddens, A. (1973) *The Class Structure of the Advanced Societies* (London: Hutchinson)

Giddens, A. (1984) *The Constitutions of Society* (Cambridge: Polity Press)

Giddens, A. (1987) *Social Theory and Modern Sociology* (Cambridge: Polity Press)

Giddens, A. (1990) *The Consequences of Modernity* (Cambridge: Polity Press)

Giddens, A. (1991) *Modernity and Self-Identity: Self and Society in the Late Modern Age* (Cambridge: Polity Press)

Giddens, A. (1998) *The Third Way — the Renewal of Social Democracy* (Cambridge: Polity Press)

Giddens, A. (2001) *Sociology* 4th edition (Cambridge: Polity Press)

Gillborn, D. (1990) *Racism, Ethnicity and Education* (London: Routledge)

Gillborn, D. and Mirza, H.S. (2000) *Educational Inequality, Mapping Race, Class and Gender* (London: Ofsted)

Gilroy, P. (1987) 'The Myth of Black Criminality' in Scraton, P. (ed.) *Law, Order and the Authoritarian State* (Milton Keynes: Open University Press)

Glass, D. V. and Hall, J. R. (1954) 'Social mobility in Great Britain: a study of inter-generation changes in status' in Glass (ed.) *Social Mobility in Britain* (London: Routledge & Kegan Paul)

Glendinning, C. and Millar, J. (1994) *Women and Poverty in Britain: The 1990s* (Hemel Hempstead: Harvester Wheatsheaf)

Glock, C.Y. and Bellah, R.N. (eds.) (1976) *The New Religious Consciousness* (Berkeley, CA: University of California Press)

Glock, C.Y. and Stark, R. (1965) *Religion and Society in Tension* (Chicago: Rand McNally)

Goffman, E. (1968) *Asylums* (Harmondsworth: Penguin)

Goldthorpe, J.H. (1980) *Social Mobility and Class Structure in Modern Britain* (Oxford: Clarendon Press)

Goldthorpe, J.H., Lockwood, D., Bechhofer, F., and Platt, J. (1968) *The Affluent Worker in the Class Structure* (Cambridge: CUP)

Goldthorpe and Payne (1986) 'On the Class Mobility of Women' (*Sociology* vol. 20)

Goldthorpe and Payne (1986) 'Trends in intergenerational mobility in England and Wales 1979-1983' (*Sociology* vol. 20)

Gordon (1976) 'Class and the economics of crime' in Chambliss, W.J. and Mankoff, M. (1976) *Whose Law? What Order?* (New York: Wiley & Sons)

Gough, I. (1979) *The Political Economy of the Welfare State* (London: Macmillan)

Gouldner, A. (1973) *For Sociology: Renewal and Critique in Sociology Today* (New York: Basic Books)

Graham, H. (1984) *Women, Health and the Family* (Brighton: Wheatsheaf Books)

Gramsci, G. (1971) *Selections from the Prison Notebooks* (London: Lawrence and Wishart)

Grant, W. and Marsh, D. (1977) *The Confederation of British Industry* (London: Hodder & Stoughton)

Griffiths R. (1988) *Community Care: Agenda for Action* (Griffiths Report) (London: HMSO)

Habermas, J. (1987) *The Theory of Communicative Action*, vol.2 (Boston: Beacon Press)

Hakim, C. (1996) *Key Issues in Women's Work* (London: Athlone Press)

Halbwachs, M. (1930) *Les Causes du Suicide* (Paris: Alcan)

Halevy, E. (1927) *A History of the English People in 1815* (London: Unwin)

Hall, S. (1992) 'The Question of Cultural Identity' in Hall et al. (eds.) *Modernity and its Futures* (Cambridge: Polity Press)

Hall, S. (1995) 'Negotiating Caribbean Identities' (*New Left Review*, 209)

Hall, S., Critcher, C., Jefferson, T., Clarke, J. and Roberts, B. (1978) *Policing the Crisis* (London: Macmillan)

Hallsworth, S. (1994) 'Understanding New Social Movements' (*Sociology Review*, Vol. 4 no. 1)

Halsey, A. H., Heath, A. F., and Ridge, J. M. (1980) *Origins and Destinations* (Oxford: Clarendon)

Hargreaves, D., Hester, S. and Mellor, F. (1975) *Deviance in Classrooms* (London: Routledge & Kegan Paul)

Harrison (1990) *Inside the Third World: The Anatomy of Poverty* 2nd edition (Harmondsworth: Penguin)

Hart, N. (1985) *The Sociology of Health and Medicine* (Ormskirk: Causeway Press)

Hayek, F. von (1944) *The Road to Serfdom* (Chicago: University of Chicago Press)

Hayter, T. (1971) *Aid as Imperialism* (Harmondsworth: Penguin)

Hayter, T. (1981) *The Creation of World Poverty* (London: Pluto Press)

Hayter, T. (1989) *Exploited Earth: Britain's Aid and the Environment* (London: Earthscan)

Heath, A. F. (1981) *Social Mobility* (Glasgow: Fontana)

Hebdige, D. (1979) *Subculture: The Meaning of Style* (London: Routledge)

Heelas, P. (1996) *The New Age Movement* (Oxford: Blackwell)

Heidensohn, F. (1986) *Women and Crime* (London: Macmillan)

Hempel, C. (1966) *Philosophy of Natural Science* (Englewood Cliffs, New Jersey: Prentice Hall)

Herberg, W. (1956) *Protestant – Catholic – Jew* (New York: Doubleday)

Hewitt, C.J. (1974) 'Elites and the distribution of power in British society' in Stanworth, P. and Giddens, A. (eds.) *Elites and Power in British Society* (Cambridge: CUP)

hooks, b. (1981) *Ain't I A Woman: Black Women and Feminism* (Boston: South End Press)

Hoselitz, B.F. (1964) *Sociological Aspects of Economic Growth* (Glencoe: The Free Press)

Hughes, G. (1991) 'Taking Crime Seriously? A critical analysis of New Left realism' (*Sociology Review* vol. 1 no. 2)

Humphreys, L. (1970) *The Tearoom Trade: Impersonal Sex in Public Places* (Chicago: Aldine)

Hutton, W. (1995) *The State we're in: Why Britain is in Crisis and how to Overcome it* (London: Vintage)

Hutton, W. (1997) 'Spend to save welfare and to make work' (*The Observer* 21st September)

Hyman, H. H. (1967) 'The Value Systems of Different Classes' in Bendix, R. and Lipset, S.M. (eds.) *Class, Status and Power* (London: Routledge & Kegan Paul)

Illich, I.D. (1971) *Deschooling Society* (Harmondsworth: Penguin)

Illich, I.D. (1975) *Medical Nemesis* (London: Calder and Boyars)

Jackson, P.W. (1968) *Life in Classrooms* (New York: Holt, Rinehart & Row)

Jacques, M. and Hall, S. (1997) 'Cultural Revolution' (*New Statesman* vol. 10, Dec 5th)

Jenkins, R. (1996) *Social Identity* (London: Routledge)

Johal (1998) 'Brimful of Brasia' (*Sociology Review,* 8)

Jones, S. (1998) *Criminology* (London: Butterworth)

Jordan, B. (1989) 'Universal Welfare Provision Creates a Dependent Population: The Case Against' (*Social Studies Review* Nov.)

References

Keddie, N. (1973) 'Classroom Knowledge' in Keddie, N. (ed.) *Tinker, Tailor — The Myth of Cultural Deprivation* (Harmondsworth: Penguin)

Kellner, P. and Wilby, P. (1980) 'The 1: 2: 4 rule of class in Britain' (*Sunday Times* 13th January)

Kelly, A. (1987) *Science for Girls* (Milton Keynes: Open University Press)

Kerr, C., Dunlop, J., Harbison, F. and Mayers, C. (1962) *Industrialism and Industrial Man* (London: Heinemann)

King, A. (1997) *The Lads: Masculinity and the New Consumption of Football* (London: Sage)

Kinsey, R., Lea, J. and Young, J. (1986) *Losing the Fight Against Crime* (Oxford: Blackwell)

Klein, N. (2001) *No Logo* (London: Harper Collins)

Kuhn, T.S. (1962) *The Structure of Scientific Revolutions* (Chicago: University of Chicago Press)

Labov, W. (1973) 'The logic of non-standard English' in Keddie, N. (ed.) *Tinker, Tailor – The Myth of Cultural Deprivation* (Harmondsworth: Penguin)

Le Grand, J. (1982) *The Strategy of Equality: Redistribution and the Social Services* (London: Allen and Unwin)

Le Grand, J. (1987) 'The middle-class use of the British Social Services' in Goodin, R. and Le Grand, J. *Not Only the Poor: the Middle Classes and the Welfare State* (London: Allen & Unwin)

Lea, J. and Young, J. (1984) *What Is To Be Done About Law and Order?* (Harmondsworth: Penguin)

Lea, J. and Young, J. (2002) 'Relative Deprivation' in *Criminological Perspectives* 2nd edition, McLaughlin, Muncie and Hughes (eds.) (London: Sage)

Leavis, F.R. (1930) *Mass Civilization and Minority Culture* (Cambridge: The Minority Press)

Lemert, E. (1951) *Social Pathology* (New York: McGraw Hill)

Lewis, O. (1959) *Five Families* (New York: Basic Books)

Lewis, O. (1961) *The Children of Sanchez* (New York: Random House)

Lewis, O. (1966) *La Vida* (New York: Random House)

Lombroso, C. (1876) *L'Uomo Delinquente* (Milan: Hoepli)

Lovering (1994) 'Employers, the sex-typing of jobs, and economic restructuring' in Scott, A.M. (ed.) *Gender Segregation and Social Change* (Oxford: Oxford University Press)

Luckmann, T. (1967) *The Invisible Religion* (New York: Macmillan)

Lukes, S. (1974) *Power: a Radical View* (London: Macmillan)

Lupton, T. and Wilson, C.S (1973) 'The Social Background and connections of top decision makers' in Urry and Wakeford (eds.) *Power in Britain, sociological readings* (London: Heinemann)

Lyotard, J.F. (1984) *The Postmodern Condition* (Manchester: Manchester University Press)

Mack, J. and Lansley, S. (1985) *Poor Britain* (London: Allen & Unwin)

Mack, J. and Lansley, S. (1992) *Breadline Britain 1990s: The Findings of the Television Series* (London: London Weekend Television)

MacNeil, C. (1990) 'The National Curriculum: a Black perspective' in Moon, B. (ed.) *New Curriculum — National Curriculum* (London: Hodder & Stoughton)

MacPherson of Cluny, Sir William (1999) *The Stephen Lawrence Inquiry: Report on an Inquiry by Sir William MacPherson of Cluny* (London: The Stationery Office)

Maduro, O. (1982) *Religion and Social Conflicts* (Maryknoll, New York: Orbis Books)

Maguire, M. (1997) 'Crime Statistics, Patterns and Trends: Changing Perceptions and their Implications' in Maguire, M., Morgan, R. and Reiner, R. (eds.) *Oxford Handbook of Criminology* (Oxford: Clarendon Press)

Malinowski, B. (1954) *Magic, Science, Religion and Other Essays* (New York: Anchor Books)

Malthus, T. (1798) *An Essay on the Principle of Population* (London)

Marcuse, H. (1964) *One Dimensional Man* (London: Routledge & Kegan Paul)

Marcuse, H. (1969) *An Essay on Liberation* (Boston: Beacon Press)

Marsh, D. and Locksley, G. (1983) 'Labour: the Dominant Force in British Politics?' in D. March (ed.) (1983) *Pressure Politics: interest groups in Britain* (London: Junction Books)

Marsh, I. (1986) *Sociology In Focus: Crime* (London: Longman)

Marshall, G., Newby, H., Rose, D. and Vogler, C. (1988) *Social Class in Modern Britain* (London: Hutchinson)

Marshall, G. and Swift, A. (1993) 'Social Class and Social Justice' (*British Journal of Sociology*, June)

Marshall, G. and Swift, A. (1996) 'Merit and Mobility: a reply to Peter Saunders' (*Sociology* vol. 30, no. 2)

Marsland, D. (1989) 'Universal Welfare Provision Creates a Dependent Population: The Case For' (*Social Studies Review* Nov.)

Marx, K. (1976, first published 1867) *Capital* (Harmondsworth: Penguin)

Marx, K. and Engels, F. (1985 first published 1848) *The Communist Manifesto* (Harmondsworth: Penguin)

Matthews, R. (1992) 'Replacing Broken Windows: Crime, Incivilities and Urban Change' in Young, J. and Matthews, R. (eds.) *Rethinking Criminology: the Realist Debate* (London: Sage)

Matza, D. (1964) *Delinquency and Drift* (New York: Wiley)

Mayo, E. (1933) *The Human Problems of an Industrial Civilization* (New York: MacMillan)

McKeown, T. (1976) *The Role of Medicine: Dream, Mirage or Nemesis* (London: Nuffield Provincial Hospitals Trust)

McRobbie, A. (1978) *Jackie: an Ideology of Adolescent Femininity* (Birmingham: CCCS)

McRobbie, A. (1999), *In the Culture Society: Art, Fashion and Popular Music* (London: Routledge)

McWhorter, J. (2003) 'How Hip-Hop Holds Blacks Back' (*City Journal* Summer)

McWhorter, J. (2004) *Doing Our Own Thing: The Degradation of Language and Music and Why We Should, Like, Care* (London: Heinemann)

Meehan, D. (1983) *Ladies of the Evening* (New York: Scarecrow Press)

Melluci (1989) *Nomads of the Present* (London: Hutchinson Radius)

Melton, G. (1993) 'Another Look at New Religions' (*The Annals of the American Academy of Political and Social Science* vol. 527)

Merton, R.K. (1968) *Social Theory and Social Structure* (New York: Free Press)

Mies, M. (1986) *Patriarchy and Accumulation on a World Scale: Women in the International Division of Labour* (London: Zed Press)

Milgram, S. (1974) *Obedience to Authority; An Experimental View* (New York: Harper & Row)

Miliband, R. (1969) *The State in Capitalist Society* (London: Weidenfeld and Nicolson)

Miller, W.B. (1958) 'Lower class culture as a generating milieu of gang delinquency' (*Journal of Social Issues* 14)

Miller, W.B. (1962) 'The impact of a "total community" delinquency control project' (*Social Problems* 10)

Miller, W.B. (1962) 'Lower Class Culture as a Generating Milieu of Gang Delinquency' in Wolfgang, M.E. et al. (eds.) *The Sociology of Crime and Delinquency* (New York: John Wiley and Sons)

Mills, C. W. (1956) *The Power Elite* (New York: Oxford University Press)

Mirza, H.S. (1992) *Young, Female and Black* (London: Routledge)

Mitsos, E. and Browne, K. (1998) 'Gender Differences in Education: The Underachievement of Boys' (*Sociology Review* vol. 8 no. 1)

Mitter, S. (1995) in Mitter and Rowbotham (eds.) *Women Encounter Technology: Changing Patterns of Employment in the Third World* (London: Routledge)

Modleski, T. (1982) *Loving with a Vengeance: Mass Produced Fantasies for Women* (Camden, CT: Archon Books)

Modood (1994) *Changing Ethnic Minorities* (London: PSI)

Modood, T. et al. (1997) *Fourth National Survey of Ethnic Minorities* (Policy Studies Institute)

References

Moir, A. and Jessel, D. (1995) *A Mind to Crime: The Controversial Link between the Mind and Criminal Behaviour* (London: Michael Joseph)

Morley (1980) *The Nationwide Audience* (London: BFI)

Mosca, G. (1939) *The Ruling Class* (New York: McGraw-Hill)

Mulvey, L. (1975) 'Visual Pleasure and Narrative Cinema' (*Screen* vol. 16, no. 3 autumn)

Murray, C. (1984) *Losing Ground* (New York: Basic Books)

Murray, C. (1989) 'Underclass' (*Sunday Times Magazine* 26 Nov.)

Murray, C. (1990) *The British Underclass* (London: Institute of Economic Affairs, Health and Welfare Unit)

Murray, C. (1993) 'The Coming White Underclass' (*Wall Street Journal*, Oct. 29)

Murray, C. (1994) *Underclass: The Crisis Deepens* (London: IEA)

Murray, C. (1997) *Does Prison Work?* (London: Institute of Economic Affairs)

Navarro, V. (1976) *Medicine Under Capitalism* (New York: Neale Watson)

Niebuhr, H.R. (1929) *The Social Sources of Denominationalism* (New York: Holt)

Oakley, A. (1981) *Subject Women* (London: Fontana Press)

Oakley, A. (1981) 'Interviewing Women: a Contradiction in Terms' in Roberts, H. (ed.) *Doing Feminist Research* (London: Routledge & Kegan Paul)

Oakley, A. (1984) *The Captured Womb: A History of the Medical Care of Pregnant Women* (Oxford: Blackwell)

Oppenheim, C. and Harker, L. (1996, 3rd edition) *Poverty: The Facts* (London: Child Poverty Action Group)

Pakulski, J. and Waters, M. (1996) *The Death of Class* (London: Sage)

Pantazis, C. and Gordon, D. (1999) 'Is Crime and Fear of Crime More Likely to be Experienced by the 'Poor'?' in Dorling, D. and Simpson, S. (eds) *Statistics in Society* (London: Arnold)

Pareto, V. (1916) A *Treatise on General Sociology* (New York: Dover)

Parker, G. (1985) *With Due Care and Attention: A Review of Research on Informal Care* (London: Family Policy Studies Centre)

Parmenter, K., Waller, J. and Wardle, J. (2000) 'Demographic Variation in Nutrition Knowledge in England' (*Health Education Research* vol. 15)

Parsons, T. (1937) *The Structure of Social Action* (New York: McGraw-Hill)

Parsons, T. (1951) *The Social System* (New York: The Free Press)

Parsons, T. (1959) 'The school class as a social system: Some of its functions in American society' (*Harvard Educational Review* 29)

Parsons, T. (1974) 'Religion in Postindustrial America' (*Social Research 41:2, p.193-225*)

Patrick, J. (1973) *A Glasgow Gang Observed* (London: Eyre Methuen)

Patterson (1967) *Dark Strangers* (Harmondsworth: Penguin)

Pearce, F. (1976) *Crimes of the Powerful* (London: Pluto Press)

Phizaklea, A. and Miles, R. (1980) *Labour and Racism* (London: Routledge)

Piachaud, D. (1981) 'Peter Townsend and the Holy Grail' (*New Society*, 10 Sept.)

Piachaud, D. (1987) 'Problems in the Definition and Measurement of Poverty' (*Journal of Social Policy* 16, no. 2)

Pilkington, A. (1993) 'Race and ethnicity' in Haralambos (ed.) *Developments in Sociology* vol. 9 (Ormskirk: Causeway Press)

Pilkington, A. (1997) 'Ethnicity and Education' in Haralambos, M. (ed.) *Developments in Sociology* (Ormskirk: Causeway Press)

Piore, M.J. (1986) 'Perspectives on Labour Market Flexibility' (*Industrial Relations*, Vol. 45 no. 2)

Plummer, K. (1979) 'Misunderstanding Labelling Perspectives' in D. Downes and P. Rock (eds.) *Deviant Interpretations* (Martin Robertson, London)

Plummer, K. (1995) 'Telling sexual stories: power, change and social worlds' (London: Routledge)

Pollert, A. (1988) 'Dismantling Flexibility' (*Capital and Class* vol. 34)

Popper, K. (1945) *The Open Society and its enemies* (London: Routledge)

Popper, K. (1959) *The Logic of Scientific Discovery* (London: Hutchinson)

Popper, K. (1963) *Conjectures and Refutations: The Growth of Scientific Knowledge* (London: Routledge)

Poulantzas, N. (1969) 'The Problem of the Capitalist State' (*New Left Review 58*)

Poulantzas, N. (1976) 'The Capitalist State: a Reply to Miliband and Laclau' (*New Left Review* Jan-Feb)

Redclift, M. (1987) *Sustainable Development: Exploring the Contradictions* (London: Methuen)

Redfield, R. (1947) 'The Folk Society' (*American Journal of Sociology* 1947, vol. 52)

Reiter, H. (1989) 'Party Decline in the West: A Skeptic's View' (*Journal of Theoretical Politics*, July 1989)

Rex, J. and Moore, R. (1967) *Race, Conflict and Community: A Study of Sparkbrook* (Oxford: OUP)

Rex, J. and Tomlinson, S. (1979) *Colonial Immigrants in a British City* (London: Routledge & Kegan Paul)

Rist, R. (1970) 'Student Social Class and Teacher Expectations: the Self-Fulfilling Prophecy in Ghetto Education' (*Harvard Educational Review* vol. 40)

Ritzer, G. (1993) *The McDonaldization of Society* (California: Pine Forge Press)

Roberts, K. (1999) *Leisure in Contemporary Society* (Wallingford: CABI Publishing)

Roberts, K., Cook, F.G., Clark, S.C and Semeonoff, E. (1977) *The Fragmentary Class Structure* (London: Heinemann)

Rojek, C. (1995) *Decentring Leisure: Rethinking Leisure Theory* (London: Sage)

Rostow, W.W. (1971) *The Stages of Economic Growth: A Non-Communist Manifesto* (Cambridge: CUP)

Rowntree, S. (1901) *Poverty: A Study of Town Life* (London: Macmillan)

Rowntree, S. (1941) *Poverty and Progress* (London: Longman)

Rowntree, S. (1951) *Poverty and the Welfare State* (London: Longman)

Runciman, W.G. (1990) 'How many Classes are there in Contemporary British Society?' (*Sociology* vol. 24)

Rutherford, J. (1988) 'Who's That Man' in Chapman, R., Rutherford, J. (eds.) *Male Order: Unwrapping Masculinity* (London: Lawrence and Wishart)

Saeed (1999) 'New ethnic and national questions in Scotland: post-British identities among Glasgow Pakistani teenagers' (*Ethnic and Racial Studies,* 22)

Sarlvik, B. and Crewe, I. (1983) *Decade of Dealignment* (Cambridge: CUP)

Saunders, P. (1990) *Social Class and Stratification* (London: Routledge)

Saunders, P. (1990) *A Nation of Home Owners* (London: Unwin Hyman)

Saunders, P. (1996) *Unequal but Fair? A Study of Class Barriers in Britain* (London: IEA)

Savage, M., Barlow, J., Dickens, P. and Fielding, T. (1992) *Property, Bureaucracy and Culture: Middle-class Formation in Contemporary Britain* (London: Routledge)

Savage, M. and Egerton, M. (1997) 'Social Mobility, Individual Ability and the Inheritance of Class Inequality' (*Sociology* vol. 31, no. 4)

Rt. Hon. The Lord Scarman (1981) *The Brixton Disorders, April 10-12, 1981: Inquiry Report. Chrm. Lord Scarman (Command Paper)* (London: The Stationery Office Books)

Scheff, T.J. (1966) *Being Mentally Ill* (Chicago: Aldine)

Schumpter, J. (1976, first published 1942) *Capitalism, Socialism and Democracy* (London: Allen and Unwin)

Schwartz, A.J. (1975) 'A Further Look at the Culture of Poverty: Ten Caracas Barrios' (*Sociology and Social Research* vol. 59, no. 4)

Scott, J. (1982) *The Upper Classes: Property and Privilege in Britain* (London: Macmillan)

Scott, J. (1991) *Who Rules Britain* (Cambridge: Polity Press)

References

Seiter, E., Borchers, H., Kreutzner, G., and Warth, E. M. (1989) (eds.) *Remote Control: Television, Audiences & Cultural Power* (London: Routledge)

Sharpe, S. (1994) *Just like a Girl: How Girls Learn to be Women* 2nd edition (London: Penguin)

Simmel, G. and Wolff, K.H. (1950) *The Sociology of Georg Simmel* (Glencoe, Illinois: Free Press)

Sklair, L. (1995) *Sociology of the Global System* (Hemel Hempstead: Prentice Hall)

Sklair, L. (2000) 'The Transnational Capitalist Class and the Discourse of Globalization' (*Cambridge Review of International Affairs* vol. 14, no. 1)

Smith, J. (1989) *Misogynies* (London: Faber)

Snider, L. (1993) *Bad Business: Corporate Crime in Canada* (Toronto: Nelson)

Snider, L. (1993) 'Theory and Politics in the Control of Corporate Crime', in Pearce, F. and Woodiwiss, M. (eds.) *Global Crime Connections: Dynamics and Control* (London: Macmillan)

Spender, D. (1983) *Invisible Women: Schooling and Scandal* (London: Women's Press)

Stanworth, M. (1983) *Gender and Schooling: A Study of Sexual Divisions in the Classroom* (London: Hutchinson)

Stanworth, P. and Giddens, A. (1974) 'An Economic Elite: A Demographic Profile of Company Chairmen' in Stanworth and Giddens (eds.) *Elites and Power in British Society* (Cambridge: Cambridge University Press)

Sugarman, B. (1970) 'Social Class, Values and Behaviour in Schools' in Craft, M. (ed.) *Family, Class and Education* (London: Longman)

Swann Report (1985) *Education for All* (London: HMSO)

Szasz, T. (1971) *The Manufacture of Madness* (London: Routledge & Kegan Paul)

Taylor, I. Walton, P. and Young, J. (1973) *The New Criminology* (London: Routledge & Kegan Paul)

Taylor, L. (1984) *In the Underworld* (London: Unwin)

Taylor-Gooby, P. (1985) *Public Opinion, Ideology and the State of Welfare* (London, Routledge)

Townsend, P. (1970) *The Concept of Poverty* (London: Heinemann)

Townsend, P. (1979) *Poverty in the United Kingdom* (Harmondsworth: Penguin)

Townsend, P., Corrigan, P. and Kowarzik, U. (1987) 'Deprivation' (*Journal of Social Policy* 16)

Toynbee, P. (2003) *Hard Work: Life in Low Pay Britain* (London: Bloomsbury)

Troeltsch, E. (1931 and 1956, originally 1912) *The Social Teachings of the Christian Churches* (New York: Macmillan)

Tuchman, G. (1978) 'Introduction: The Symbolic Annihilation of Women by the Mass Media' in Tuchman, G., Daniels, A.K. & Benét, J. *Hearth and Home: Images of Women in the Mass Media* (New York: Oxford University Press)

Tudor Hart, J. (1971) 'The Inverse Care Law' (*The Lancet* Saturday 27th Feb.)

Tumin, M. (1953) 'Some Principles of Stratification: A Conceptual Analysis' (*American Sociological Review* 18)

Tumin, M. (1967) 'Some Principles of Stratification: A Critical Analysis' in Bendix, R. and Lipset, S.M. (eds.) *Social Stratification: The Forms and Functions of Social Inequality* (Englewood Cliffs, NJ: Prentice Hall)

Walby, S. (1990) *Theorising Patriarchy* (Oxford: Blackwell)

Walker, A. (1990) 'Blaming the Victims' in Murray *The Emerging British Underclass* (London: IEA)

Walker, C. and Walker, A. (1994) 'Poverty and the Poor' in Haralambos (ed.) *Developments in Sociology* Vol. 10

Wallerstein, I. (1974) *The Modern World-System, Vol. I: Capitalist Agriculture and the Origins of the European World-Economy in the Sixteenth Century* (New York/London: Academic Press)

Wallerstein, I. (1980) *The Modern World-System, Vol. II: Mercantilism and the Consolidation of the European World-Economy, 1600-1750* (New York: Academic Press)

Wallerstein, I. (1989) *The Modern World-System, Vol. III: The Second Great Expansion of the Capitalist World-Economy, 1730-1840s* (San Diego: Academic Press)

Wallis, R. (1977) *The Road to Total Freedom: A Sociological Analysis of Scientology* (New York: Columbia University Press)

Wallis, R. (1984) *The Elementary Forms of the New Religious Life* (London: Routledge & Kegan Paul)

Walsh, M. (2001) *Research Made Real: A Guide for Students* (Cheltenham: Nelson Thornes)

Weber, M. (1958) *The Protestant Work Ethic and the Spirit of Capitalism* (New York: Scribner's Sons)

Weber, M: *See also under Gerth and Mills (1948)*

Wedderburn, D. (1974) *Poverty, Inequality and Class Structure* (Cambridge: CUP)

Weiner, G., Arnot, M. and David, M. (1997) 'Is the Future female?; Female Success, Male Disadvantage and Changing Gender Patterns in Education', in Halsey, A.H., Lauder, H., Brown, P. and Wells, A.S. (eds.) *Education, Culture, Economy, Society* (Oxford: Oxford University Press)

Westergaard, J. (1995) *Who Gets What? The Hardening of Class Inequality in the Late Twentieth Century* (Cambridge, Polity Press)

Westergaard, J. and Resler, H. (1976) *Class in a Capitalist Society* (Harmondsworth: Penguin)

Whittle, S. (2000) *The Transgender Debate: The Crisis Surrounding Gender Identities* (Reading: South Street Press)

Whyte (1955) *Street Corner Society* (Chicago: University of Chicago)

Willis, P. (1977) *Learning to Labour: How Working Class Kids Get Working Class Jobs* (London: Saxon House)

Willis, P. (1990) *Common Culture* (Buckingham: Open University Press)

Wilson, B. (1966) *Religion in a Secular Society* (London: C.A. Watts)

Wilson, B. (1970) *Religious Sects* (London: Weidenfeld & Nicolson)

Wilson, B. (1976) *Contemporary Transformations of Religion* (London: Oxford University Press)

Wilson, J. Q. (1975) *Thinking about Crime* (New York: Basic Books)

Wilson, J. Q. and Hernstein, R. (1985) *Crime and Human Nature* (New York: Simon and Schuster)

Wilson, J. Q. and Kelling, G. (1982) 'Broken Windows' (*Atlantic Monthly,* March)

Wolf, N. (1991) *The Beauty Myth* (London: Vintage)

Wood, S. (1989) *The Transformation of Work* (London: Unwin Hyman)

Woods, P. (1983) *Sociology and the School: An Interactionist Viewpoint* (London: Routledge & Kegan Paul)

Wright, C. (1992) 'Early Education: Multiracial Primary School Classrooms' in Gill, Mayor and Blair (eds.) *Racism and Education* (London: Sage)

Wright, E. O. (1978) *Class, Crisis and the State* (London: New Left Books)

Wright, E. O. (1985) *Classes* (London: Verso)

Wright, E. O. (1989) 'The comparative project on class structure and class consciousness: An overview' (*Acta Sociologica* Spring 32)

Wright, E. O. (1990) *The Debate on Classes* (London: Verso)

Wright, E. O. (1997) *Class Counts: Comparative Studies in Class Analysis* (Cambridge: Cambridge University Press)

Young, J. (1971) *The Drugtakers* (London: Paladin)

Young, J. (1988) 'Risk of Crime and Fear of Crime: A realist critique of survey-based assumptions' in Maguire, M. and Pointing, J. (eds.) *Victims of Crime: A new deal?* (Milton Keynes: Open University Press)

Zweig (1961) *The Worker in an Affluent Society: Family Life and Industry* (London: Heinemann)

Every effort has been made to ensure these references are as accurate and comprehensive as possible. For those studies where it has been difficult to obtain full details, we would be grateful for information. Please contact the publisher if you notice any inaccuracies or omissions, and we will gladly update the book at the next reprint. Thank you.

Index

Index

Index

Index